THE POLITICAL ECONOMY OF CHINA–LATIN AMERICA RELATIONS IN THE NEW MILLENNIUM

In this book, China–Latin America relations experts Margaret Myers and Carol Wise examine the political and economic forces that have underpinned Chinese engagement in the region, as well as the ways in which these forces have shaped economic sectors and policy-making in Latin America. The contributors begin with a review of developments in cross-Pacific statecraft, including the role of private, state-level, sub-national, and extra-regional actors that have influenced China–Latin America engagement in recent years. Part II of the book examines the variety of Latin American development trajectories born of China's growing global presence. Contributors analyze the effects of Chinese engagement on specific economic sectors, clusters (the LAC emerging economies), and sub-regions (Central America, the Southern Cone of South America, and the Andean region). Individual case studies draw out these themes.

This volume is a welcome addition to the growing body of literature on China–Latin America relations. It illuminates the complex interplay between economics and politics that has characterized China's relations with the region as a second decade of enhanced economic engagement draws to a close. This volume is an indispensable read for students, scholars, and policy-makers wishing to gain new insights into the political economy of China–Latin America relations.

Margaret Myers is Director of the China and Latin America program at the Inter-American Dialogue in Washington, DC.

Carol Wise is Associate Professor of International Relations at the University of Southern California. She specializes in international political economy and development, with an emphasis on Latin America.

Myers and Wise bring together some of the best minds in the business—including their own—to give us a brilliant update on the growing China–Latin American nexus. This must-read volume smartly punctures lazy myths and common hyperbole, and loads the reader with reams of essential facts and insightful analyses, to better grasp the complexities of the cross-Pacific ties that will define the 21st century.

Richard E. Feinberg, UC San Diego, most recently author of
Open for Business: Building the Cuban Economy (Brookings
Institution Press, 2016)

After an enlightening introduction this book is a comprehensive, up-to-date account of the growing complexities in economic and political relations between China and Latin America during this—still new—21st century. This well-documented volume, which explores new patterns of dependency and other competing themes, should be included in every discussion and analysis regarding this complicated relationship.

Romer Cornejo, El Colegio de México

This excellent collection avoids the pitfall of trying to identify a single China–Latin America relationship and instead searches for difference—different actors, different interests and different outcomes. The result is a book that provides a comprehensive overview of both the opportunities and challenges that have emerged from Chinese interactions with the region.

Shaun Breslin, University of Warwick

This timely volume with its range of perspectives comes at a welcome time as the international economic, political and security environment and the China–LAC relationship grows more complex. Myers and Wise have pulled together a stellar group of experts who provide new data and fresh perspectives on key topics. This should be required reading for students of Latin America as well as for policymakers interested in better understanding China's outward economic strategy.

Barbara Kotschwar, Adjunct Professor, Georgetown University
School of Foreign Service

From the perspective of their diverse backgrounds and expertise, the authors in Wise and Myers' volume offer a unique, multi-faceted examination of the transformational political, economic, social and security issues that have emerged in the 21st Century between China and Latin America as a whole as well as its major sub-regions.

Robert Devlin, Johns Hopkins School of Advanced International Studies
(SAIS)

THE POLITICAL ECONOMY OF CHINA–LATIN AMERICA RELATIONS IN THE NEW MILLENNIUM

Brave New World

Edited by Margaret Myers and Carol Wise

Routledge
Taylor & Francis Group

NEW YORK AND LONDON

First published 2017
by Routledge
711 Third Avenue, New York, NY 10017

and by Routledge
2 Park Square, Milton Park, Abingdon, Oxon, OX14 4RN

Routledge is an imprint of the Taylor & Francis Group, an informa business

Library of Congress Cataloging in Publication Data
Names: Myers, Margaret, 1980- editor. | Wise, Carol, editor.
Title: The political economy of China-Latin American relations in the new
    millennium : brave new world / edited by Margaret Myers and Carol
    Wise.
Description: New York, NY : Routledge, 2016. | Includes bibliographical
    references and index.
Identifiers: LCCN 2016010108| ISBN 9781138666184 (hbk) |
    ISBN 9781138666191 (pbk)
Subjects: LCSH: China—Foreign economic relations—Latin America. |
    Latin America—Foreign economic relations—China. | China—
    Economic policy. | Latin America—Economic policy.
Classification: LCC HF1604.Z4 L29635 2016 | DDC 337.5108—dc23
LC record available at https://lccn.loc.gov/2016010108

ISBN: 978-1-138-66618-4 (hbk)
ISBN: 978-1-138-66619-1 (pbk)
ISBN: 978-1-315-61948-4 (ebk)

Typeset in Bembo Std
by Swales & Willis Ltd, Exeter, Devon, UK

CONTENTS

ACKNOWLEDGMENTS

This project was made possible by generous funding from the Center for International Studies and The School of International Relations at the University of Southern California (USC). The Inter-American Dialogue in Washington, DC also provided financial support, through grants from Open Society Foundations and the Henry Luce Foundation. We are indebted to the Routledge editorial and production team for their steady guidance of the manuscript from the submission and review stage all the way up to the publication of the book. At Routledge, we want to especially thank Natalja Mortensen and Lillian Rand. We are also grateful to Helen Moss, Wenjia Wang, and Susan Ye for their editorial assistance. The manuscript benefitted greatly from the comments of four anonymous reviewers, as well as feedback the authors have received during presentations of these papers at various conferences and workshops. The political economy of China-Latin America relations is a dynamic and fast-moving topic, one we have sought to capture through inter-disciplinary analysis of the substantive issues that have stemmed from it. While far from comprehensive, it is our hope that these chapters can enjoy a healthy shelf life.

Margaret Myers
Washington, DC

Carol Wise
Los Angeles, CA

July 2016

INTRODUCTION

The Political Economy of China–Latin America Relations in the 21st Century

Carol Wise and Margaret Myers

On January 27, 2016 the *Financial Times* ran the following headline: "Beijing Warns Soros against Declaring 'War on the Renminbi.'" George Soros, the billionaire investor best known for "breaking the British pound in 1992," had just announced on Bloomberg TV that, among other things, he was betting against the Asian currencies in 2016.[1] The issuing of this remarkable salvo by Chinese leaders reflects the country's exponential leap to the very top of the international political economy over the past thirty years. From its entry into the World Trade Organization (WTO) in 2001, its surpassing of Japan to become the world's second largest economy, its first-place ranking amongst the emerging economies (EEs) as a destination for foreign direct investment (FDI), its emergence as the top exporter to world markets, and the designation of reserve-currency status for the Chinese yuan at the International Monetary Fund,[2] China has jumped over formidable economic hurdles more quickly than any other developing country—ever. Thus far, the 21st century has mainly been the Chinese century.

Our focus in this book is on China's rise in the new millennium, told from the standpoint of its rapidly growing ties with countries in the Latin American and Caribbean (LAC) region since 2001. Here, China has also been breaking all kinds of records. For example, China has surpassed the U.S. as a top destination for South American exports, and its policy banks have become the largest public lenders to LAC governments.[3] China, moreover, has launched bilateral free trade agreements (FTAs) with Chile (2006), Peru (2010), and Costa Rica (2011).[4] In that these three FTAs are WTO-plus,[5] they defy the pessimism of some with regard to China's true commitment to uphold international norms.[6] Rather, as with its entire reform effort, China is moving at its own pace. As commonplace as it has become to cite these dazzling achievements with regard to China–LAC relations, keep in mind that trends such as these were absolutely unthinkable two decades ago. The ascendance of China in the global economy, as well as in the LAC region, is largely a story about transforming the unimaginable into a concrete reality.

And yet, at least from the standpoint of China–LAC relations, we are still operating mainly at the level of stylized facts.[7] The first set of facts refers to the quick escalation of trade and investment flows from China to the LAC region since 2002. As Figure I.1 depicts, China–LAC trade only started to register significant gains around 2002; similarly, as can be seen in Tables I.1 and I.2, Chinese FDI (stocks and flows) in LAC was negligible until it too began to pick up in 2003. When these data are disaggregated a second set of stylized facts emerges: the magnitude and nature of China's growing trade and investment ties differ considerably across countries and sub-regions within Latin America. From 2003 to 2013 four of the South American countries (Argentina, Brazil, Chile, and Peru) that appear in Figure I.1 have enjoyed a commodity boom on a par with that which was underway at the turn of the last century (see Table I.3). Partly owing to buoyant Chinese demand for copper, iron ore, oil, and soybeans, all of which are abundant to varying degrees in these countries, prices on these commodities reached historical highs after 2003. As a result, all four countries have benefited from very favorable terms of trade and solid growth (see Figure I.2) for more than a decade and all have built up sizeable foreign exchange reserves.

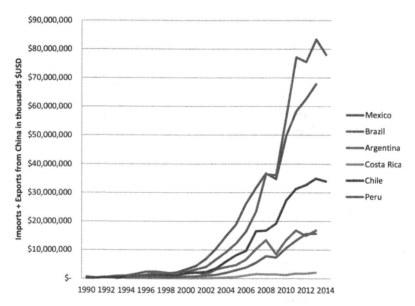

FIGURE I.1 Total Trade between China and Selected LAC Countries, 1990–2014

Source: UN Comtrade, http://comtrade.un.org/.

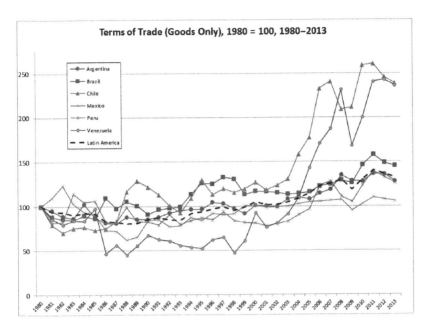

FIGURE I.2 Total Trade between China and Selected LAC Countries, 1998–2014

Source: ECLAC—CEPALSTAT, renormalized to 1980.

TABLE I.1 China's Outward FDI Stocks to LAC Countries and Two Regions, 2003–2014

Year	Latin America	Argentina	Brazil	British Virgin Islands	Cayman Islands	Chile	Mexico	Peru
2003	4,619.32	1.05	52.19	532.64	3,690.68	0.75	97.18	126.18
2004	8,268.37	19.27	79.22	1,089.38	6,659.91	1.48	125.29	125.82
2005	11,469.61	4.22	81.39	1,983.58	8,935.59	3.71	141.86	129.22
2006	19,694.37	11.34	130.41	4,750.40	14,209.19	10.84	128.61	130.40
2007	24,700.91	157.19	189.55	6,626.54	16,810.68	56.80	151.44	137.11
2008	32,240.15	173.36	217.05	10,477.33	20,327.45	58.09	173.08	194.34
2009	30,595.48	169.05	360.89	15,060.69	13,577.07	66.02	173.90	284.54
2010	43,875.64	218.99	923.65	23,242.76	17,256.27	109.58	152.87	654.49
2011	55,171.75	405.25	1,071.79	29,261.41	21,692.32	97.94	263.88	802.24
2012	68,211.63	897.19	1,449.51	30,850.95	30,072.00	126.28	368.48	752.87
2013	86,095.93	1,658.20	1,733.58	33,902.98	42,324.06	179.04	409.87	867.78
2014	106,111.13	1,791.52	2,832.89	49,320.41	44,236.72	195.83	541.21	907.98

Source: Author's calculation based on Comprehensive Economic, Industry and Corporate Data (CEIC), http://www.ceicdata.com/.

Note: In millions of US$.

TABLE I.2 China's Outward FDI Flows to LAC Countries and Two Regions, 2003–2014

Year	Latin America	Argentina	Brazil	British Virgin Islands	Cayman Islands	Chile	Mexico	Peru
2003	1,038.15	1.00	6.67	209.68	806.61	0.20	0.03	0.12
2004	1,762.72	1.12	6.43	385.52	1,286.13	0.55	27.10	0.22
2005	6,466.16	0.35	15.09	1,226.08	5,162.75	1.80	3.55	0.55
2006	8,468.74	6.22	10.09	538.11	7,832.72	6.58	−3.69	5.40
2007	4,902.41	136.69	51.13	1,876.14	2,601.59	3.83	17.16	6.71
2008	3,677.25	10.82	22.38	2,104.33	1,524.01	0.93	5.63	24.55
2009	7,327.90	−22.82	116.27	1,612.05	5,366.30	7.78	0.82	58.49
2010	10,538.27	27.23	487.46	6,119.76	3,496.13	33.71	26.73	139.0
2011	11,935.82	185.15	126.40	6,208.33	4,936.46	13.99	41.54	214.25
2012	6,169.74	743.25	194.10	2,239.28	827.43	26.22	100.42	−49.37
2013	14,358.95	221.41	310.93	3,221.56	9,253.40	11.79	49.73	114.60
2014	10,547.39	269.92	730.00	4,570.43	4,191.72	16.29	140.57	45.07

Source: Author's calculation based on Comprehensive Economic, Industry and Corporate Data (CEIC), http://www.ceicdata.com/.

Note: In millions of US$.

For Mexico and the Central American bloc, the opposite pattern has held owing to an absence of surplus commodities of the kind that China has voraciously bought up from the South American countries. This second group of countries has been on the defensive, with little to offset the flood of Chinese manufactured imports into this sub-region. Interestingly, despite these two distinct scenarios within Central and South America, a final set of stylized facts stems from the asymmetries between China and all countries in the LAC region. After registering average annual growth rates of 9–10 percent for some three decades, the Chinese economy towers over those of its LAC counterparts. For the commodity exporters, this has resurrected development debates from the 1960s concerning "unequal exchange," the "resource curse," and the heightened "dependency" of these countries on selling commodities to the Chinese market. For Mexico and the Central American countries—with the exception of Costa Rica—China's flood of manufactured exports into these markets has invoked reactions and attitudes akin to those of the 1950s, when most of the region embraced protectionism. Where relevant, we refer to these "retro" development themes throughout the volume.

The publication of this volume coincides with the winding down of the China boom and a precipitous fall in commodity prices, especially for crude oil. According to Beijing, China's slowing of growth to around 6–7 percent annually has been partly intentional, as policy makers there seek to shift away from a heavy reliance on exports and big investment projects at home, and more

TABLE I.3 Commodity Price Data for Selected Products, 2000–2015 (annual prices in US$)

Year	Crude oil, average ($/bbl)	Soybean oil ($/mt)	Soybeans ($/mt)	Fishmeal ($/mt)	Beef ($/kg)	Iron ore, cfr spot ($/dmtu)	Copper ($/mt)
2000	28,23	338,08	211,83	413,00	1,93	28,79	1.813,47
2001	24,35	354,00	195,83	486,67	2,13	30,03	1.578,29
2002	24,93	454,25	212,67	605,92	2,10	29,31	1.559,48
2003	28,90	553,92	264,00	610,71	1,98	31,95	1.779,14
2004	37,73	616,00	306,50	648,58	2,51	37,90	2.865,88
2005	53,39	544,92	274,69	730,96	2,62	65,00	3.678,88
2006	64,29	598,56	268,65	1.166,33	2,55	69,33	6.722,13
2007	71,12	881,43	384,05	1.177,25	2,60	122,99	7.118,23
2008	96,99	1.258,25	522,83	1.133,08	3,14	155,99	6.955,88
2009	61,76	848,69	436,92	1.230,25	2,64	79,98	5.149,74
2010	79,04	1.004,60	449,80	1.687,50	3,35	145,86	7.534,78
2011	104,01	1.299,33	540,67	1.537,42	4,04	167,75	8.828,19
2012	105,01	1.226,25	591,42	1.558,33	4,14	128,50	7.962,35
2013	104,08	1.056,67	538,42	1.747,17	4,07	135,36	7.332,10
2014	96,24	909,27	491,77	1.708,85	4,95	96,94	6.863,40
2015	42,70	738,00	369,00	1.540,00	3,90	47,00	4.800,00

Source: World Bank Commodity Market | (Pink Sheet), Dec. 2015. http://www.worldbank.org/en/research/commodity-markets.

Note: $ = US dollar; bbl = barrel; mt = metric ton; dmtu = dry metric ton unit; kg = kilogram.

toward services and domestic consumption. The pass-through for the LAC region as a whole has been a simultaneous slowing of growth to 1–2 percent on average since 2013.[8] Hindsight shows the extent to which LAC growth has been harnessed more tightly to the Chinese economy in the 2000s. For example, recent research conducted by IDB economist Ambrogio Cesa-Bianchi and his colleagues found that China's positive effect on LAC GDP growth has increased three times since 1990.[9] First, China's trade demand and capital supply enabled the LAC region to swiftly rebound from the 2008–2009 global financial crisis.[10] Argentina, Brazil, Chile, and Peru, for perhaps the first time ever, were able to engage in counter-cyclical policies when the global financial crisis (GFC) struck and to recover by 2010.[11]

Second, however, since 2013 we have seen how China's slowing of growth also constitutes a negative GDP shock of similar magnitude. The data on LAC GDP growth in Figure I.2 reflect a pattern of bust (2001–2002), boom (2003–2013 with a short dip during the global financial crisis), and back to near-bust by 2014. This fifteen-year cycle is the main departure point for this edited volume. Our purpose here is to delve into the more compelling development stories that have come to life during this period. Thus, rather than exploring the potentially transformative effects of China–LAC relations through a series of country case studies, we approach our subject thematically. Our first theme, in Part I, concerns cross-Pacific statecraft, while the second theme, in Part II, offers critical analyses of select development trajectories as these relate to China's growing presence in different clusters (the LAC emerging economies) and sub-regions (Central America, the Southern Cone of South America, and the Andean region). At the end of each part we do offer one individual case study, on Peru and Brazil respectively.

Cross-Pacific Statecraft: Aid and Capital Flows from China to Latin America

In Part I we dispense with other strands of common wisdom, for example the notion that China's entry into the LAC region is bellicose in nature,[12] or that the China–LAC relationship is a passing fancy that will fade along with the commodity boom itself.[13] We also steer away from normative positions regarding the rise of China in Latin America and simply stick with the here and now. Thus we assume that China is now a fixed feature of the LAC economic landscape and that China's intentions are developmental in nature—nothing more, nothing less—and not an affront to U.S. sovereignty in the Western Hemisphere.[14] Having said this, we begin with two chapters by seasoned scholars of China and Latin America: Chapter 1 by Benjamin Creutzfeldt, who writes on Chinese foreign policy toward the LAC region; and Chapter 2 by R. Evan Ellis, who offers insights on the two-way exchange between China and the U.S. vis-à-vis Latin America.

In his gripping biography of Deng Xiaoping, the prominent China scholar Ezra Vogel drives home the extent to which navigating the inner chambers of the Chinese party/state is like walking on a bed of nails.[15] In their respective chapters, both Creutzfeldt and Ellis similarly puncture the myth of the Chinese state as a well-coordinated and monolithic actor. Rather, the goals and policies of the Chinese central government are often at odds with "on-the-ground" realities in the enactment of China's activities in Latin America—be it aid, trade, loans, or FDI. Creutzfeldt thus calls for the "dual conceptualization" of China's interactions, distinguishing between strategies articulated by Beijing politicians and diplomatic representatives versus the more market-driven motivations of Chinese enterprises. Ellis follows with an assessment of U.S. views and influence on the China–Latin America relationship, cautioning that there will always be wary naysayers on China in the U.S. Both Creutzfeldt and Ellis elucidate the crucial role of diplomacy and advocate the need for a more pro-active approach toward China on the part of politicians and policy makers in the LAC region.

The chapters by Kevin P. Gallagher and Amos Irwin and by Barbara Stallings explore China's primary motivations for the provision of loans and aid respectively to certain LAC countries. In Chapter 3, Gallagher and Irwin examine the interests and activity of China's major policy banks, finding that China Development Bank and China Eximbank tend to operate according to commercial logic rather than in support of a political agenda. The emphasis of both banks on large loan sizes and market-based interest rates, along with a focus on industry and infrastructure, has much in common with the private sovereign bond market. The authors acknowledge that China's loans to LAC might also support the Chinese government's use of soft power and natural resource-related objectives, but they argue that these goals are secondary to the banks' commercial motivations. In Chapter 4, Stallings, however, interprets Chinese aid to LAC as a largely political tool intended to improve China's image in LAC and to secure access to the region's natural resources. Chinese aid, according to Stallings, also helps diminish Taiwan's political influence in the region and seeks to bolster Beijing's longstanding "One-China" policy.

In Chapter 5, Guo Jie and Margaret Myers draw a link between China's food security interests and agricultural investment in Latin America. They find that China has largely abandoned land purchase in Latin America in pursuit of greater vertical integration in global food supply chains. Chinese companies must nonetheless compete with multinational firms that have established a presence in LAC over the course of decades. They are further limited in certain cases by negative public reaction to proposed investments. In LAC agriculture and other sectors, Chinese deals are often a starting point for regional discourse on resource sovereignty.

In the mining sector in Peru, Cynthia Sanborn and Victoria Chonn Ching (Chapter 6) find considerable variation in approach by Chinese extractive firms, but also indicate that the Chinese firm Shougang has perpetuated the negative stereotype of a Chinese company that lowers standards to feed the home market's demand for ores. A learning process is nonetheless evident among Chinese companies and the institutions tasked with guiding them. After a series of explosive incidents, Chinese policy makers and regulators are increasingly aware of the importance of upholding high standards in overseas investment. They have instituted safeguards of their own that often match or surpass those of their hosts.

Development Trends since the Turn of the Millennium

We begin Part II of this volume with analysis of the China–Latin America trade outlook, the fundamentals of which have changed very little in the past decade and a half. The relationship is still very much characterized by extraordinary growth and asymmetry, wherein Latin America exports large quantities of primary commodities and imports China's increasingly higher value-added manufactures. This dynamic has prompted concern in LAC that this period of heightened economic engagement with China is a throw-back to earlier times, when most Latin American countries were highly dependent on world markets for the sale of their primary exports.[16] Also known as the resource curse, as originally coined by Max Corden and Peter Neary, this more specifically refers to the way that new natural resource discoveries or favorable price changes in one commodity can adversely affect other sectors of the economy, namely manufacturing.[17]

In Chapter 7, Carol Wise argues that concerns about the region's reliance on primary commodities fail to account for the considerable institution-building and economic modernization that have taken place since the 1950s and 1960s—the respective heydays of structuralist and dependency critiques.[18] The author suggests that the structural conditions that now prevail within most of these economies are markedly different, as evidenced by their ability to survive and rebound quickly from the 2008–2009 GFC. Although the GFC was a financial shock of even greater proportions than the 1929 meltdown that triggered the Great Depression of the 1930s, LAC banks (with the exception of those in Venezuela) were little exposed to the toxic assets that pushed the U.S. and European banking systems to the brink in 2008–2009. The GFC hit LAC on the trade side, as demand in developed-country markets collapsed, but LAC's recovery was also trade-led, and had much to do with the enormous fiscal stimulus that both China and the U.S. promptly infused into their respective economies. In a distinct break with the past, not a single LAC country was forced to turn to the International Monetary Fund (IMF) for assistance when the GFC hit. In earlier times, an event as jarring as the GFC would have triggered another "lost decade" in the region, but not so this time around.

Mariano Turzi elaborates on Wise's analysis in Chapter 8, with a study of China's soy imports from South America, which increased from almost nothing in 1995 to over 58 million tons in 2012. As China's growing population consumes more meat, and therefore demands more soy-based animal feed, grain producers in Brazil, Argentina, Uruguay, and Paraguay are poised to take on a new and strategic role in the world economy.

In Chapter 9, Rolando Avendaño and Jeff Dayton-Johnson find that, in stark contrast to dynamics in the Southern Cone, Central America has yet to experience much of any effect from China's growing presence. Unlike Mexican exports, which face stiff competition with Chinese exports in domestic and third markets, there is minimal trade competition between Central America and China. Central American economies remain largely oriented toward the U.S. market, limiting their ability to expand commercial ties with Asia. The authors suggest that the region's lackluster trade relations with China are also likely attributable to diplomatic considerations. With the exception of Costa Rica, the Central American nations still largely recognize Taiwan (the Republic of China) over mainland China (the People's Republic of China) as China's rightful government. By switching its allegiance to mainland China in 2007, Costa Rica was the recipient of highly generous side payments from China. So far, its neighbors have not followed suit.

The authors in Part II also observe the role of sub-national actors, interests, and institutions in shaping development trends in LAC. Anti-China coalitions continue to promote protectionist policymaking in countries such as Brazil, Argentina, and Mexico, for example. In Chapter 11, Dawn Powell remarks on Brazil's economic policy towards China in light of the major influx of Chinese imports and investment into Brazil in the 2000s. Powell describes the significance of domestic actors in the Brazilian political debate surrounding the "entrada chinesa," and their success in pressuring the government to adopt protectionist policies. In Chapter 8, Mariano Turzi similarly remarks on the complex interactions between the state and agricultural producers in the Southern Cone, finding considerable variation on a country-by-country basis.

In Chapter 10, Adam Chimienti and Benjamin Creutzfeldt analyze the role of civil society in shaping Chinese engagement in the Andean region of South America, as well as China's own commitment to national and well-established international rules around resource extraction in the sub-region. The authors judge that the purported principles of China's aid, trade, and investment with the developing world are indeed sincere and offer an opportunity to the leaders of these countries to set in motion processes and structures that address the social and environmental ills associated with recent increases in extractive activity. As Cynthia Sanborn and Victoria Chonn Ching indicate in Chapter 6, however, the downturn in global prices that began in 2012, and China's drive to increase mineral production in Peru have at times been at odds with domestic efforts at effective social and environmental regulation. In fact, the emergence of disputes between companies and communities over land and water rights, revenues, and environmental contamination have posed potential challenges and delays for all firms, including Chinese investors new to Peru.

Constructing a Brave New World

It is important to note that China's seemingly overnight presence in Latin America is just a small part of its assertive global outreach. In 2013, for example, total trade (exports and imports) between China and Latin America amounted to nearly US$278 billion,[19] whereas total U.S.–LAC trade was about US$880 billion that same year.[20] Similarly, as of year-end 2012, total U.S. FDI in LAC stood at roughly US$870 billion,[21] versus less than US$80 billion in total FDI inflows from China to LAC at year-end 2013.[22] China has now displaced the U.S. as the top trade partner for Brazil, Chile, and Peru, but in the bigger scheme of things Latin America still represents just a small slice of China's "going out" strategy.

China's economic relations with Latin America will continue to generate considerable concern in the region, especially regarding asymmetric trade and export homogenization. The challenges are readily apparent, as discussed in Part II of this volume. The fundamentals of the trade relationship have changed very little in more than a decade, despite calls in LAC and China for diversification.

And protectionist policies implemented by countries such as Brazil, Argentina, and Mexico in response to Chinese economic competition have arguably weakened the competitiveness of Brazilian and Argentine firms in global markets. At the same time, the relationship is growing exceedingly complex as a wider variety of domestic, regional, and extra-regional factors influences outcomes in bilateral and firm-level dealings. This has resulted in wide variations in outcomes for Chinese firms and other entities in LAC, making characterization of the China–LAC economic relationship a difficult and complex task.

Despite what could be characterized as a relatively grim outlook for future China–LAC economic relations, however, the chapters in this book offer some positive news. In Chapter 10, Chimienti and Creutzfeldt see a good-faith Chinese government commitment to aid, trade, and investment as a form of cooperation with the developing world. In Chapter 6, Sanborn and Chonn Ching report measurable improvement in terms of adherence to local and other standards among Chinese firms operating in Peru's mining sector. And, in Chapter 5, Guo and Myers suggest that China is no longer interested in purchasing large tracts of land in LAC for the cultivation of crops, but is instead investing across the value chain in Latin America, largely following Japan's approach to overseas resource investment.

Wise argues, moreover, that fears of a resource curse and the bursting of a decade-long commodity price bubble are simply not supported by the data. Currently some 40 percent of LAC exports are higher value-added manufactured goods. Thus, the usual crash of the manufacturing sector during a commodity price boom has yet to occur. Producers in the manufacturing sector in Argentina, Brazil, and Mexico may be concerned about stiff competition from China, but others in these same countries will admit that the purchase of cheaper Chinese intermediate inputs has enabled them to realize some productivity gains.[23] Powell (Chapter 11) supports this notion in her assessment of China's effects on Brazilian manufacturing. Moreover, and despite recent news of commodity price plunges in the financial media,[24] Table I.3 shows that any drop in prices since 2012 still leaves commodities like copper, crude oil, soybeans, iron ore, and fishmeal priced at two to three times the amount that these same goods sold for in 2000.

Nevertheless, it would be difficult to ignore the implications of LAC's sluggish growth since 2013. Lower commodity prices since 2012–2013 are certainly part of this story, as is the slowing of Chinese growth as policy makers there seek to reorient demand away from the external sector and toward services and domestic consumption. Back in 2009, Izquierdo and Talvi cautioned that the high growth rates which made the consolidation of macroeconomic reforms possible—averaging 6 percent regionally from 2003 to 2007 versus a 3 percent historical average rate of growth for Latin America—were driven disproportionately by Chinese demand.[25] The good news is that, because of macroeconomic restructuring and a commendable level of institutional reform,[26] some of the LAC countries can survive indefinitely on resource demand from China, India, and other emerging economies on the move. The bad news is that the advances made thus far have been a necessary condition for the recent surge in high growth, but these are still not sufficient for maintaining it. As Wise argues in Chapter 7, the current growth impasse cries out for yet another round of reforms—which focus on the micro-economic realm (regulatory quality, rule of law, control of corruption) and more assertively tackle the barriers to higher growth. With China moving forward assertively with its own strategy of microeconomic restructuring, the countries discussed in this volume would do well to follow suit.

Notes

1 Gabriel Wildau, "Beijing Warns Soros against Declaring 'War on the Renminbi,'" *Financial Times*, January 27, 2016.
2 Andrew Mayeda, "IMF Approves Reserve-Currency Status for China's Yuan," *BloombergBusiness*, November 30, 2015, http://www.bloomberg.com/news/articles/2015-11-30/imf-backs-yuan-in-reserve-currency-club-after-rejection-in-2010 (accessed January 30, 2016). The yuan and the renminbi are used interchangeably when referring to China's currency.
3 Rebecca Ray and Kevin Gallagher, "China–Latin America Economic Bulletin 2015 Edition," Working Group on Development and Environment in the Americas, Global Economic Governance Initiative, Discussion Paper 2015-9, Boston University, September 2015, p. 1.
4 See Carol Wise, "Playing Both Sides of the Pacific: Latin America's Free Trade Agreements with China," *Pacific Affairs*, vol. 89, no. 1 (2016), pp. 75–101.
5 With 161 members, 117 of which are developing countries, the WTO was created from the General Agreement on Tariffs and Trade in 1995 and tasked, among other things, with expanding the coverage of international trade agreements to include the protection of intellectual property rights (IPRs) and trade-related services and investment flows. Not all member countries have signed on to these newer trade agenda items; hence the term "WTO-plus" refers to those trade agreements which do cover these "new" agenda items or go even deeper, for example with new rules to govern e-commerce and digital trade. See https://www.wto.org/english/thewto_e/whatis_e/wto_dg_stat_e.htm (accessed October 26, 2015).
6 Mary Anastasia O'Grady, "The Middle Kingdom and Latin America," *Wall Street Journal*, September 3, 2004, p. 11.
7 Some departures from this mode are: R. Evan Ellis, *China in Latin America: The Whats and Wherefores* (Boulder, CO: Lynne Rienner, 2009); Adrian H. Hearn and José Luis León-Manríquez, eds., *China Engages Latin America: Tracing the Trajectory* (Boulder, CO: Lynne Rienner, 2011); Kevin P. Gallagher and Roberto Porzecanski, *The Dragon in the Room: China and the Future of Latin American Industrialization* (Stanford, CA: Stanford University Press, 2011); and Kevin Gallagher, *The China Triangle: Latin America's China Boom and the Fate of the Washington Consensus* (New York: Oxford University Press, 2016).
8 Alejandro Werner, "(Yet) Another Year of Subpar Growth: Latin America and the Caribbean in 2015," *iMF Direct*, January 21, 2015, http://blog-imfdirect.imf.org/2015/01/21/yet-another-year-of-subpar-growth-latin-america-and-the-caribbean-in-2015/ (accessed February 7, 2015).
9 Ambrogio Cesa-Bianchi, M. Hashem Pesaran, Alessandro Rebucci, and Tengteng Xu, "China's Emergence in the World Economy and Business Cycles in Latin America," *Economía*, vol. 12, no. 2 (2012), p. 32.

10 Carol Wise, Leslie Armijo, and Saori Katada, eds., *Unexpected Outcomes: How Emerging Economies Survived the 2008–09 Global Financial Crisis* (Washington, DC: Brookings Institution Press, 2015).

11 Manuel Pastor and Carol Wise, "Good-bye Financial Crash, Hello Financial Eclecticism: Latin American Responses to the 2008–09 Global Financial Crisis," *Journal of International Money and Finance*, vol. 52 (April 2015), pp. 200–217.

12 This, for example, is the position of some in the U.S. Congress. See Chairman Dan Burton, "Opening Statement," Hearing on China's Influence in the Western Hemisphere, Subcommittee on the Western Hemisphere, Committee on International Relations, U.S. House of Representatives, April 6, 2005.

13 Authors' interview with Political Science Professor Pan Wei, Director of the Center for Chinese and Global Affairs, Peking University, Lima, Peru, June 4, 2009.

14 Mary Anastasia O'Grady, "The Middle Kingdom in Latin America," *Wall Street Journal*, September 3, 2004.

15 Ezra Vogel, *Deng Xiaoping and the Transformation of China* (Cambridge, MA: Belknap Press, 2013).

16 Juan Carlos Gachúz, "Chile's Economic and Political Relationship with China," *Journal of Current Chinese Affairs*, no. 1 (2012), pp. 150–151; Rubén Gonzalez-Vicente, "The Political Economy of Sino-Peruvian Relations: A New Dependency?" *Journal of Current Chinese Affairs*, vol. 41, no. 1 (2012), pp. 98–131.

17 Max Corden and Peter Neary, "Booming Sector and De-industrialization in a Small Open Economy," *Economic Journal*, vol. 92 (1982), pp. 825–848. Also see the review essay by Victor Menaldo, "The New Political Economy of Natural Resources in Latin America," *Latin American Politics and Society*, no. 2 (2015), pp. 163–173.

18 This structuralist critique was formally articulated by Raúl Prebisch, *The Economic Development of Latin America and Its Principal Problems* (New York: United Nations Department of Social Affairs, 1950); the dependency school is perhaps most concisely analyzed by Fernando Henrique Cardoso and Faletto Enzo, *Dependency and Development in Latin America* (Los Angeles: University of California Press, 1979).

19 ECLAC, *First Forum of China and the Community of Latin American and Caribbean States (CELAC): Exploring Opportunities for Cooperation on Trade and Investment*, LC/L.3941, January 2015, p. 23, http://repositorio.cepal.org/bitstream/handle/11362/37578/S1421103_en.pdf;jsessionid=6E359708AE26F4EE754EDDCF585FAAC3?sequence=1.

20 Michael Fumento, "As the U.S. Sleeps, China Conquers Latin America," *Forbes*, October 14, 2014, http://www.forbes.com/sites/realspin/2014/10/15/as-the-u-s-sleeps-china-conquers-latin-america/.

21 James K. Jackson, "U.S. Direct Investment Abroad: Trends and Current Issues," Congressional Research Service, p. 3, https://www.fas.org/sgp/crs/misc/RS21118.pdf (accessed April 22, 2015).

22 Alicia Bárcena and Osvaldo Rosales, *The People's Republic of China and Latin America and the Caribbean: Towards a Strategic Relationship*, May 2010, p. 21, http://repositorio.cepal.org/bitstream/handle/11362/2957/S2010203_en.pdf?sequence=1.

23 Rhys Jenkins and Alexandre de Freitas Barbosa, "Fear of Manufacturing? China and the Future of Industry in Brazil and Latin America," *China Quarterly*, vol. 209 (2012), pp. 59–81.

24 See, for example, Lucy Hornby and Neil Hume, "Iron Ore Tumbles to Post-Crisis Era Low," *Financial Times*, March 27, 2015, http://www.ft.com/intl/cms/s/0/132ba452-d465-11e4-9bfe-00144feab7de.html#axzz3WxX8AOhw (accessed April 10, 2015).

25 Alejandro Izquierdo and Ernesto Talvi, *Policy Trade-offs for Unprecedented Times: Confronting the Global Crisis in Latin America and the Caribbean*, p. 5, http://www.bstu.org/Policy_trade_offs_pubB-635.pdf.

26 Pastor and Wise, "Good-bye Financial Crash, Hello Financial Eclecticism."

PART I

Cross-Pacific Statecraft

Aid and Capital Flows from China to Latin America

1

ONE ACTOR, MANY AGENTS

China's Latin America Policy in Theory and Practice

Benjamin Creutzfeldt

Introduction

The relationship between the People's Republic of China and Latin America has grown rapidly since then-president Jiang Zemin's tour of the continent in 2001, both in quantifiable terms and in the perceptions of politicians, business leaders, and foreign observers. At the end of 2008 Beijing published its first policy paper on Latin America and the Caribbean, a canvas of intentions that set out broad terms for bilateral cooperation, invariably described as a "win–win situation." The Chinese leadership has made numerous overtures to the governments of the region in the past few years, one of the most noteworthy being the speech by Premier Wen Jiabao at the UN's Economic Commission for Latin America and the Caribbean on June 26, 2012.[1] Wen's address, "Trusted Friends Forever," raised the character of the China–Latin America connection to something akin to poetic destiny. He outlined four specific proposals for furthering cooperation: political links, economic development, food security, and human and scientific exchange. These proposals were backed up with loans, funding, and financial targets.

The current government of Xi Jinping has continued the pattern with annual visits to the region, further incentives for cooperation, and the setting of targets for trade and investment. In the course of 2014, the most emblematic institution of the ever-closer ties between China and Latin America came into being, in the form of the China–CELAC Forum. This was modeled on the Forum of China–Africa Cooperation (FOCAC) that was created formally in 2000 during a summit in Beijing. China's interest in and support for the China–CELAC Forum has been emphatic since President Xi sent a congratulatory message to the CELAC summit in Caracas in January 2014. Xi also presided over a ministerial meeting for the official inauguration of the Forum in Brazil in July of that year, and hosted the inaugural ministerial summit in Beijing in January of 2015.[2]

This chapter considers aspects of agency theory and economic statecraft in China's relations with Latin America, looking at Beijing's overall foreign policy approach, its evolving relationship with the Latin American region, the interests underlying this relationship, and the challenges it faces. I discuss three broad issues: the core characteristics of China's foreign policy; China's view of Latin America's place within the grand scheme of things; and the role of state-owned enterprises (SOEs), small and medium-sized firms (SMEs), and other agents within those strategies and challenges. I then offer a possible explanation for the inconsistencies within the Chinese approach, and conclude with some observations on the prospects for China's foreign policy toward Latin America.

Various difficulties arise when trying to analyze this evolving relationship. Despite it being fairly contiguous in geopolitical and historical terms, the region of Latin America and the Caribbean shows deep divisions linguistically and in terms of its sociocultural and political identities.[3] Yet it would be just as misleading to consider China as a unitary actor: while Beijing promotes and reinforces the view of its principled, centrally guided approach, it has also been boosting outward global activity by its state-owned and private companies, through its Going Out strategy (走出去战略), occasioning a growing diversity of types of engagement.[4] As a consequence, China's unifying rhetoric, as exemplified by Premier Wen's speech, is echoed by a deafening din of splintered voices.

China's Foreign Policy

As China's footprint in every region of the world and every sphere of human endeavor grows, so does the debate as to what its true impact will be in the course of the twenty-first century. Opinions range from boisterous predictions that it will reach "superpower status" and "rule the world" within a generation[5] to more level-headed analyses that it will be a "partial power" at best.[6] China is, unquestionably, a major protagonist on the global stage and one that is increasingly shaping ideas and institutions the world over. As it matures into this role, its identity and actions are shaped by its own history and aspirations: its history as a humiliated power after the middle of the nineteenth century (百年国耻), the concurrent fear of losing control over its sovereign territory, and a deeply felt urge to regain influence. It could be said that China's core concerns are with social stability, national sovereignty, and steady consumption. These are inextricably linked with economic growth and reliable access to raw material supplies, energy, and food. What then do these core issues mean for Chinese foreign policy in Latin America?

They mean, essentially, that China's foreign policy strategies since 1978 are part and parcel of the country's modernization drive, and its principal target is the creation of an international environment conducive to this priority. The

Twelfth and Thirteenth Five-Year Plans describe a gradual transformation of the country's development model, with the combined goals of accelerating urbanization and domestic consumption, and creating sustainable industrial and investment structures. Going further, the State Council published the Energy Development Five-Year Plan,[7] where specific reference is made to the increasing volatility in global energy markets (全球能源市场波动风险加剧), a high-risk factor that directly affects the rest of the national economy. The preamble explains that "energy is the material basis for the progress of human civilization and an indispensable basic condition for the development of modern society. It remains a major strategic issue for China as the country moves towards its goals of modernization and common prosperity for its people."[8] Along this line, the priorities presented in these documents make clear that China's domestic concerns and requirements trump all foreign policy objectives. This can be seen in the fact that neither China's new foreign minister, Wang Yi, nor his predecessor, Yang Jiechi, are members of the Politburo. This reality leads some analysts to describe China's foreign policy as "highly deficient" and even to question whether China actually has a foreign policy.[9]

Given these caveats, China does in fact have very clearly written foreign policy principles. The Five Principles of Peaceful Coexistence (和平共处五项原则) were developed by the Chinese Communist Party in the 1940s as a basis for relations with the United States and articulated by Mao Zedong prior to the foundation of the People's Republic in 1949.[10] These included: mutual respect for territorial integrity and sovereignty; non-aggression; non-interference in others' internal affairs; equality and mutual benefit; and peaceful coexistence. Though to Western ears these principles may sound like platitudes or somewhat outdated propaganda, they continue to define Chinese foreign policy today.[11] The *objectives* are less succinctly set in stone, but in July 2009 then-president Hu Jintao explained that China's diplomacy "must safeguard the interests of sovereignty, security, and development."[12] This is officially defined as meaning (first) domestic political stability; (second) sovereign security, territorial integrity, and national unification; and (third) China's sustainable economic and social development.[13] This can be usefully transcribed by applying Evan S. Medeiros's summary as "fostering economic development, reassurance, countering constraints, diversifying access to natural resources, and reducing Taiwan's international space."[14]

These principles and objectives are tempered, then, by domestic necessities, and they must be considered in order to understand China's approach to the rest of the world. The country and its single-party leadership are challenged internally by environmental degradation, systemic corruption, and growing social inequality and externally by regional tensions and disputes. Sustained growth within what Jiang Zemin in 2002 declared a "period of strategic opportunity" (战略机遇期) is dependent upon social stability, continued scientific and industrial development, internal consumption combined with rising exports, the effective management of inflation and exchange rates, and a steady supply of raw materials for production and consumption. This has been reiterated by the Chinese leadership on multiple occasions, and Latin America has come to play a growing role in China's drive to diversify its markets and its sources of supply.

China's Relations with Latin America

China's interest in Latin America has grown at a quick pace since the turn of the century, and these rapidly expanding relations have found expression in numerous forms, beginning with high-level leadership diplomacy in 2001. This was evident, for example, when President Jiang Zemin visited Chile, Argentina, Brazil, Chile, Cuba, Uruguay, and Venezuela in April 2001, and made a separate visit to Mexico in 2002. This was followed by Hu Jintao's trips to Brazil, Argentina, and Chile in 2004 and Costa Rica, Cuba, and Peru in 2008, bringing in his wake a large entourage of Chinese officials and business people. These visits were part of China's growing engagement with all regions of the world, driven by the strategic analysis underlying the Tenth Five-Year Plan (2001–05) which suggested, among other things, that Chinese national oil companies should expand their activities in three strategic geographical areas, one of these being Latin America. The region has been an increasingly dynamic trading partner for China; in 2013 Latin America sold a total of US$112 billion to China (equivalent to 2 percent of regional GDP) and imported back from China US$142 billion in goods.[15] While a large part of this consisted of minerals, fossil fuels, and agricultural goods, China overtook the US in 2013 as the top destination for South America's exports consisting mainly of these goods.

In November 2008 China published its "Policy Paper on Latin America and the Caribbean" (as it had done previously for the European Union in 2003 and for Africa in 2006).[16] Reiterating its commitment to the Five Principles of Peaceful Coexistence, the Paper describes Latin America and the Caribbean as "an important part of the developing world and a major force in the international arena." The Chinese government "aims to further clarify the goals of China's policy in this region, outline the guiding principles for future cooperation between the two sides in various fields and sustain the sound, steady and all-round growth of China's relations with Latin America and the Caribbean." It states four broad goals which are to be promoted by means of policies and ties in the following fields: political, economic, cultural-social, and what it calls "peace, security and judicial affairs." The broad goals are: the promotion of mutual respect, trust, and "understanding and support on issues involving each other's core interests and major concerns"; the deepening of economic cooperation for the benefit of both sides, with China and Latin American nations each leveraging their respective strengths; and the expansion of cultural links with the aim of promoting the "development and progress of human civilization, and the insistence on the One-China principle as the political basis for cooperative relations."[17]

Under the heading of cultural diplomacy and academic exchange, China has established 33 Confucius Institutes across the region.[18] Zheng Bingwen et al. highlight China's recognition of the importance of scientific and human exchanges in real terms, with the goal of promoting soft power and counterbalancing the "negative opinions with regards to China's 'neo-colonialism' and the 'China Threat Theory.'"[19] The People's Republic has a considerable number of Latin America experts in universities and institutes in Beijing and Shanghai, many of whom publish in the respected Chinese-language *Journal of Latin American Studies* (拉丁美洲研究). There is no comparable journal, institute, or organization of Chinese studies in Latin America, although the *Red Académica de América Latina y el Caribe sobre China* is an important effort in this direction.[20] It is evident that there is a substantial lack of preparation and a fragmented response in Latin America to China's ever-growing footprint in the region.[21] While the Chinese government seeks bilateral agreements and increasing involvement in regional organizations, the countries remain relatively unprepared and largely unaware of what their neighbors are doing with regard to China. Having said that, there are new initiatives, in particular the Pacific Alliance created in April 2011, which constitute promising attempts to redress this tendency by coordinating political and trade initiatives, but measurable results have yet to be seen.[22] While China highlights the common cultural roots of the nations of Latin America, politicians and business people in the region tend to emphasize their differences, formulating vague ideas of national exceptionalism.[23] The questions that arise are: To what extent is the Chinese government in fact aware of this disconnect between its approach to Latin America and the local realities? To what extent is China conscious of the difficulties it faces in Latin America? What, if anything, is China doing to address this situation?

Following the diplomatic overtures initiated by China, Latin America has awakened to the new possibilities of Chinese partnership. Investment, bilateral exchanges, and agreements continue apace. Although there is significant variance from country to country, and from one economic sector to another, the importance of China as a major trading, investment, and lending partner helped Latin America sustain its growth even after the 2008–09 global financial crisis. Nonetheless, the response from Latin American leaders was hesitant and spotty after Hu's visit in 2004, was cautious and inconsistent after the Policy Paper in 2008, and continues into the present to be largely unplanned and incoherent across the region. According to Osvaldo Rosales of the UN's Economic Commission for Latin America and the Caribbean (CEPAL),[24] just three countries—Brazil, Chile, and Mexico—responded formally to the Policy Paper within a year of its publication. The divergence across the region can be seen in terms of trade volume and balance, as CEPAL statistics readily show, and equally in the numbers of state visits in either direction since 2001: Chile and Brazil top the list of countries in the region receiving state visits from China, while Brazil, Chile, and Venezuela are those whose leaders have most often travelled to China.[25] Of the 33 countries in the region, 21 have established diplomatic relations with the PRC, and only 6 of those have bilateral chambers of commerce.[26]

Even within the context of the multifaceted and evolving aspects of mutual engagement, it is clear that China's interest in the region is defined by its economic priorities. China's trade policy toward Latin America is designed to support sustained domestic economic development, as are Chinese investments and lending to the region. The single-minded objective here is that of investment and the diversification of resource suppliers, geared toward reducing China's disproportionate reliance on single states and their sometimes fickle governments. A key element of this approach is China's increased attempts at multilateralism, as reflected in the China–CELAC Forum hosted by Beijing in January 2015. The PRC is also a member of the Asia Pacific Economic Cooperation Forum (APEC), which also includes the Latin American countries of Chile, Mexico, Panama, and Peru. China also became a shareholder in the Caribbean Development Bank in 1998 and the Inter-American Development Bank (IDB) in 2009. It enjoys observer status in the Latin American Integration Association (ALADI), the Latin American Parliament, CEPAL, the Pacific Alliance (Chile, Colombia, Costa Rica, Mexico, and Peru), and the Organization of American States (OAS). It is also in permanent dialogue with regional economic organizations such as the Southern Cone Common Market (MERCOSUR), the Community of Andean Nations (CAN), and the Caribbean Community (CARICOM).[27] The Chinese government has initiated bilateral dialogue forums, such as the China–Latin America business summit (since 2007, under the auspices of the China Council for the Promotion of International Trade, CCPIT) and the China–Latin America Think Tank Forum (since 2010, sponsored by the Institute of Foreign Affairs, CPIFA).

On a country level, the analysis and listing of activities are not always straightforward. While it is easy to detect the thrust of Chinese government loans and corporate investment being directed at mining and hydrocarbons, the figures themselves vary widely depending on the source and definitions used. Colombia is a case in point: the country's national bank, the Banco de la República, puts Chinese investment in the country between 2000 and 2012 at US$43.5 million, by defining China's foreign direct investment only as direct transfers of funds originating in the PRC. In contrast, the Beijing office of Procolombia (formerly Proexport), the Colombian government entity in charge of promoting exports, tourism, and inward investment, speaks of a figure closer to US$2 billion.[28] This figure more closely reflects the real interests of China's SOEs in the country, as these allow for the acquisitions of assets previously owned by other multinational corporations.[29] These figures are likely to climb further, provided Colombia is able to respond adequately to declarations of interest encountered in China.[30]

The Basis of China's Latin America Policy

In order to assess China's approach to Latin America and the Caribbean it is helpful to explore Chinese sources. These can be divided into three groups: official statements and government declarations, scholarly publications, and the online press. In terms of official statements, I focus on those referring to the region as a whole, essentially China's 2008 Policy Paper on Latin America and the Caribbean and Wen's CEPAL speech mentioned above, as well as CCP studies and relevant statements made by officials. In terms of scholarly publications, there are the many general schools of international relations with sites and publications, and considerably fewer concentrating on Latin America, so that I limit myself here to the Institute of Latin American Studies (ILAS) at the Chinese Academy of Social Sciences (CASS) in Beijing. The last group, the online press and internet resources, is the richest and most diverse, but also quite complex to evaluate.[31] However, Allen Carlson and Hong Duan discuss the value and pitfalls of using the internet in the study of Chinese foreign relations and come to the conclusion that it is an increasingly useful tool, although "so far scholars have failed to fully realize its potential."[32]

Official Statements

It is sometimes difficult for Westerners, trained to be skeptical about political clichés, to take Chinese official pronouncements at face value. Hu Jintao's concept of "Harmonious World" (和谐世界)[33] is often considered vague and impractical; Wen's notion of "lasting friendship and common development" can understandably ring hollow to Western ears; and Xi Jinping's "Chinese Dream" is yet to be fully imbued with meaning. Nonetheless, it is important that these slogans be taken seriously, at least in the first instance, if we want to attempt to understand the Chinese approach to Latin America. At an international level, they are designed to mitigate the widely held international views of China as an aggressive expansionist power. Simultaneously, they play an important role in domestic ideology, as Jing Men has discussed, in mobilizing and unifying the country: "Chinese foreign policy is made to maintain its national interest."[34] A useful way to conceptualize the Chinese world view, which has its roots in the *Tianxia* vision, is in four concentric rings: the first ring corresponds to the territory administered (or claimed) by Beijing; the second ring represents the 17 terrestrial and maritime borders; the third ring describes the conjoined geopolitical regions of Asia; and finally there is the fourth ring, the world beyond. This, in turn, may be further subdivided, and it is fair to assert that Latin America is not a priority concern, except where related issues (such as energy supply or food security) render it central to China's foreign policy.

A second key to understanding China's view of Latin America is its emphasis on regional coherence and diversity within unity. This was best illustrated by a scene from the opening ceremony of the 2008 Olympic Games, when children representing the 56 nationalities of the PRC marched under the national flag. The Chinese government prioritizes national unity in its own cultural and national context, and regional integration and cooperation at an international level. Statements and articles reflecting official opinion underscore this perspective. In the words of Wen Jiabao, "we firmly believe that a growing Latin America and the Caribbean serves the interest of world peace and development."[35] In a similar vein, Sun Hongbo explains that "China expects steady and sound development of the Community of Latin American and Caribbean States, and hopes it can become a major platform for China–Latin American regional dialogue and cooperation in the future."[36] The region as a coherent platform neatly reflects the Chinese hope for unity and conflict-free international cooperation.

Scholarly Publications

The ILAS's *Journal of Latin American Studies* (*JLAS*) has become the prime reference on the relationship between Latin America and the PRC since its founding in 1979. A simple analysis of the 182 articles published in *JLAS* between 2010 and 2012 reveals that 63 percent explore regional issues versus 37 percent that discuss individual countries, among which Mexico and Brazil dominate, largely because of economic considerations. In terms of subject matter, only 19 articles are concerned explicitly with US influence in the Latin American region, half of these as part of historical discussions rather than matters of current affairs. It is only a small sampling, but it nonetheless permits the observation that the Chinese academic interest in Latin America, while informed in detail, is more interested in the whole rather than the sum of its parts.

An academic event in China confirms this notion. In November 2010, the Chinese government convened the first China–Latin America and the Caribbean Think Tank Forum in Beijing. Orchestrated by the Chinese People's Institute of Foreign Affairs and the CAF Development Bank of Latin America, most participants were either former diplomats or university researchers earmarked by the political affairs sections of China's embassies in the Latin American region. The aim was to identify themes of common concern in a "South–South" dialogue. Interestingly, what was missing was a Portuguese interpreter for the Brazilian participants. The image conveyed was that China views Latin America and the Caribbean as a coherent region—whether the region agrees or not—and Brazil as a power apart. The second Forum was held in July 2013 and showed significant advancements, defining nine program points around three themes—the new challenges facing commercial cooperation between China and the region, the prospects for humanistic exchange, and the deepening of bilateral cooperation. Biennial repeats of this forum are planned for the future.[37]

Mass Media

Although censorship persists in China, in particular through self-censorship imposed on all media and directed through guidelines issued by the CCP's Central Propaganda Department (aptly dubbed the "Ministry of Truth" by *China Digital Times*[38]), there is a fair variety of reporting. This is thanks to magazines such as *Caijing* (财经) and *Caixin* (财新), comparable to the London-based *Economist*, which are constantly pushing the boundaries of what is permissible within the People's Republic. In China, *People's Net* (人民网) is the most visible and is run by the *People's Daily* (人民日报), the official newspaper of the CCP. *Xinhua Net* (新华网) tends to cover much of the same ground, and multiple others feed off these information networks. *Global Times* (环球时报) is a more populist affiliate of *Xinhua/People's Net*. All these news outlets, in their original Chinese versions, coincide in catering to a Chinese public and at the same time reflecting to a large degree the official priorities and tendencies. Using Chinese search terms in the full-text online versions I have analyzed several thousand news items pertaining to Latin America and the Caribbean and its constituent countries, over the four-year period between October 2009 and October 2013. By searching a basic set of categories, I found just under 30,000 mentions of the umbrella term for "Latin America" within news items reporting on the region, compared to over 700,000 references to individual countries, led by Brazil (250,000) and Mexico (140,000) in number and proportion. Similar tendencies and distributions are observed across all four news sites reviewed.

There is a marked contrast between the more country-specific approach in the news media and the regional "broad brush" approach in government rhetoric. In spite of what would appear therefore to be relatively differentiated and country-specific reporting, the policy approach of the Beijing government and its resource-seeking enterprises is still much broader. As the Colombian news magazine *Semana* put it, the Pacific Alliance presents China with a paradox: while it offers an opportunity to improve relations with the five member countries, it also makes evident the tensions in the Latin American region—perhaps most tangible being the conspicuous omission of Ecuador from this pact. Since it began strengthening its relations with Latin America, China has been eager to channel discussions and negotiations through a single institution, just as it has done successfully with Africa since 2000.[39] When the vice president of one of China's largest SOEs visited Colombia in late 2012 and was told by local business people that Colombia was different in every respect from Venezuela and its other neighbors, he responded impatiently: "it's still Latin America [但还是拉美]."[40] This sentiment reflects the view China and its representatives hold of the region. We may tentatively conclude that there is a growing but slow-moving awareness in China of a certain incoherence between the government's strategic approach to Latin America and the widely diverging local realities in that region.

One Actor, Many Agents

In light of the thickening network of state visits, multilateral exchanges, and rapidly growing trade and investment flows, it is tempting to put a big bracket around these multi-layered activities and subsume them all under official declarations and government-led plans. A summary analysis of the growing and increasingly diverse presence of Chinese products and companies in the hemisphere lends itself quite naturally to generalizing—and even to far-reaching assumptions: "Chinese companies and China's diplomatic apparatus have become increasingly immersed in the business, social and political conditions [in Latin American countries]— and in some cases are even shaping those conditions to suit their interests."[41] It is important therefore to distinguish between the country China (the actor) and the companies on the ground in Latin America (the agents).

In this approach, I paraphrase the principal–agent theory as espoused by William Norris: "principals have one set of goals and objectives but they must rely on agents to act on behalf of the principals to realize these goals."[42] Norris goes on to outline four factors that determine and help evaluate this relationship: the intrinsic compatibility of goals, the market structure, the bureaucratic capacity, and the unity of the principal. It can be easily seen that, in the case of China, there is high intrinsic compatibility of goals. First, there are national priorities for energy, mineral, and food supplies, which coincide with the core activities of the major Chinese SOEs active in the Latin American region. There are coherence and interdependence in the market structure, in which the strategically important industry players have similar targets and methods, although they compete with each other beyond the state's directives. There is a strong unity of the principal, a one-party government with a large power base and extensive control of SOEs and private companies, through the party hierarchy and the broad membership base. And there is a fairly high degree of bureaucratic capacity, through the ability to influence and monitor, if not fully control, the agents' activities. Given such a high degree of multi-layer overlap between the actor and the agents, one might indeed be led to see the trade and investment strategies of Chinese companies as a centrally coordinated strategy, in the sense of economic statecraft, or "the use of economic resources by political leaders to exert influence in pursuit of foreign policy objectives."[43]

However, while it is true that China's global expansion was initiated by Deng Xiaoping's call for Reform and Opening-Up (改革开放) at the historic Third Plenary Session of the 11th Central Committee in late 1978, and that Chinese corporate and entrepreneurial worldwide activities were further stoked in the 1990s through the Going-Out policy (走出去) and the call to Go Global (走向世界), this does not paint the entire picture. Many analysts focus on national interests and the political interactions that underpin them as the driving force in China's stance toward Latin America. The media tend to have the same take on this matter, but for enterprises, whether state-owned or not, trade and investment are often only loosely linked to government policy. As Gastón Fornés and Alan Butt Philip have noted, "Chinese MNEs investing in Latin America do so for largely instrumental commercial reasons, and not at the behest of the Chinese government."[44] What is more, there is now "some evidence that Chinese [corporate] interests are also acquiring strategic assets for market-seeking purposes."[45] Erica Downs makes a similar observation in her study of overseas investments by Chinese SOEs and government support, noting that each of the entities involved in international deals "has their own interests to pursue [and] coordination [between the various agents] is not synonymous with top-down decision making."[46] She emphasizes that, "although many media reports [on multibillion-dollar oil-secured lines of credit] portrayed them as the quest of a monolithic China to secure oil and gas supplies, the reality is that these transactions involved multiple actors and a complex mix of motivations."

Combined with the fact that there is often a lack of direct engagement with local communities in Latin America by Chinese investors, situations regularly arise that run counter to the PRC's mottoes and intentions. As a result, there have been occasions in many parts of Latin America when corporate interests clash with the image that China seeks to project in the region. One such instance is the multiple problems Emerald Energy has encountered in Colombia since its acquisition by Sinochem, ranging from local protests to becoming victims of kidnapping, resulting in complaints and accusations brought before ministries and the press.

It does appear that Beijing is jittery about negative public relations, and in particular about its economic priorities being misconstrued as more ambitious geopolitical designs. For instance, in 2012 the International Court of Justice (ICJ) at The Hague ruled in favor of Nicaragua, and against Colombia, to redefine maritime frontiers in the Caribbean. Within a few days, Colombia's former foreign secretary, Noemí Sanín, publicly questioned the impartiality of the judges at The Hague, in particular that of the Chinese judge Xue Hanqin, in light of supposed Chinese national and business interests in a Nicaraguan proposal for a new interoceanic canal which would benefit from the ICJ ruling.[47] In other words, suspicions were aroused over a possible "dirty game" China may be playing as it gains a greater presence within international institutions. This type of assertion, however misguided and diplomatically untenable it may be, found fertile ground in a Latin American public largely ignorant about China and East Asia.[48] The Chinese embassy in Bogotá was quick to respond through various media outlets, pointing to a memorandum published by the PRC's Ministry of Commerce that denied and discouraged any Chinese company from involvement in the Nicaragua Canal project.[49]

Similar perceptions have led to anti-Chinese demonstrations in cities in Mexico. Adrian Hearn describes the often violent reactions within communities in the north of the country toward the growing presence of Chinese businesses.[50] Other countries in the region, such as Ecuador and Peru, have similarly seen negative reactions to the activities of foreign corporations—among them some Chinese—in the extractive sector. The number of popular protests and resistance by the productive sectors to the presence of China and its products is on the rise, whether it is the textile producers in Peru,[51] shoemakers in Colombia,[52] or protesters criticizing foreign petrol exploitation in Brazil. An anti-Chinese polemic is evident in the media and in public opinion, be this for tangible or existential reasons regarding prices and qualities, or in order to find a scapegoat for the problems arising from social disparity and the inefficiency of public policies, or simply out of ignorance and the lack of adequate familiarity with East Asia.

David Shambaugh discusses the strong centralized foreign policy decision-making hierarchy inside the Chinese government, though he concedes that there are strong spheres that influence the decisions made on the inside, which include intelligence organs, corporations, and civil society.[53] He quotes the president of the Shanghai Institute of International Studies as saying: "We used to have a monolithic singular voice and system, but after 1996 our foreign policy discourse has become more diversified . . . and there has been a proliferation of actors."[54] This became all the more so in the follow-up to the Third Plenary Session of the 18th Central Committee in late 2013. The underlying message of the Plenum's statement was a challenge to Chinese SOEs in that the government wants to make them more efficient and profit-focused. In this sense, Beijing has come to recognize that there are limits to its ability to direct even SOEs to engage in activities it considers in the country's prime interests, and is betting on market factors (including financing by China's policy banks and investment funds) to help keep the overseas activities of its many agents on a manageable path.

Conclusions

The image of China as a unitary actor in Latin America, or the notion that this region itself is uniform in its response to China, is simply mistaken. Moreover, persistent debates about China's entry into the Western Hemisphere continue to overlook the diversity of the many agents who have become involved in the region. Viewing the interactions and dynamics on different parallel planes may help resolve apparent contradictions, and distinguish clearly between strategies centrally proclaimed by Beijing's politicians and its diplomatic representatives, and the market-driven patterns of trade and investment. As to whether Beijing is aware of the discrepancies, Premier Li Keqiang's address to employees of SOEs in Peru in May 2015 is evidence that the Beijing leadership recognizes the need to appeal as much to its "agents" and expatriate citizens as to the governments with which it seeks to maintain a constructive dialogue. A close reading of China's evolving Latin America policy suggests both a selective multilateral approach of the Chinese government and an umbrella strategy based on venues like the

China–CELAC Forum. The following chapters highlight some of the emerging variations in an increasingly multi-layered relationship.

Notes

1 Wen Jiabao, "Trusted Friends Forever" (speech made at the Economic Commission for Latin America and the Caribbean of the United Nations, Santiago de Chile, 2012).
2 China, "Beijing Declaration of the First China–CELAC Forum ministerial meeting" (Beijing, 2015), www.chinacelacforum.org/eng/zywj_3/t1230938.ht (accessed June 12, 2016).
3 See for instance Manuel Castells, *Globalización, identidad y estado en América Latina, temas de desarrollo humano sustentable* (Berkeley, CA: UNDP, 1999); Alfredo Jiménez Barros, "Desarrollo, cultura e identidad en América Latina," *Eccos Revista Científica*, vol. 3, no. 1 (2001), pp. 57–74.
4 Chris Alden and Christopher R. Hughes, "Harmony and Discord in China's Africa Strategy: Some Predictions for Foreign Policy," *China Quarterly*, no. 199 (2009), pp. 563–84.
5 The most prominent example is in Martin Jacques, *When China Rules the World: The Rise of the Middle Kingdom and the End of the Western World* (London: Allen Lane, 2009). However, not all books with similarly emotive titles reach the same conclusion. See David Scott, *"The Chinese Century"? The Challenge to Global Order* (Basingstoke, UK: Palgrave Macmillan, 2008); or Peter Nolan, *Is China Buying the World?* (Cambridge, UK: Polity, 2012).
6 David Shambaugh, *China Goes Global: The Partial Power* (New York: Oxford University Press, 2013).
7 "State Council Publishes Full Text of Energy Development Twelve-year Plan" [国务院发布能源发展"十二五"规划全文], *Chinese Economy Net*, January 2013, http://www.ce.cn/cysc/ny/zcjd/201301/24/t20130124_21325226.shtml (accessed May 6, 2016).
8 "Full Text: China's Energy Policy 2012," *Xinhua*, October 24, 2012, quoted in *Global Times*, http://www.globaltimes.cn/content/740169.shtml (accessed November 24, 2014).
9 Wang Zheng, "Does China Have a Foreign Policy?" *Wilson Weekly*, 2013, http://www.wilsoncenter.org/article/does-china-have-foreign-policy (accessed May 8, 2016).
10 Sophie Richardson, *China, Cambodia, and the Five Principles of Peaceful Coexistence* (New York, NY: Columbia University Press, 2010).
11 Several authors underscore this point, such as Yan Xuetong, *Analysis of China's National Interests* [中国国家利益分析] (Tianjin: Tianjin Renmin Chubanshe, 1997). For a more recent discussion, see Song Xiaoping, "Elementos fundamentales del marco teórico de la política exterior de China," in Benjamin Creutzfeldt, ed., *China en América Latina: reflexiones sobre las relaciones transpacíficas* (Bogotá: Universidad Externado, 2012), p. 96.
12 Wang Jisi, "China's Search for a Grand Strategy: A Rising Great Power Finds Its Way," *Foreign Affairs*, (March/April 2011), www.foreignaffairs.com/articles/china/2011-02-20/chinas-search-grand-strategy (accessed June 17, 2016).
13 Dai Bingguo, "Adhering to the Path of Peaceful Development [坚持走和平发展道路]," *China News Net*, http://www.chinanews.com/gn/2010/12-07/2704984.shtml.
14 Evan S. Medeiros, *China's International Behavior: Activism, Opportunism, and Diversification* (Santa Monica, CA: Rand, 2009), p. 45.
15 Rebecca Ray and Kevin Gallagher, "China–Latin America Economic Bulletin 2015 Edition," Working Group on Development and Environment in the Americas, Global Economic Governance Initiative, Discussion Paper 2015-9, Boston University, September 2015.
16 "China's Policy Paper on Latin America and the Caribbean," http://www.gov.cn/english/official/2008-11/05/content_1140347.htm (accessed May 26, 2015).

17 For more detailed reflections on the 2008 Policy Paper, see the chapters by Riordan Roett and Sebastian Castañeda in Benjamin Creutzfeldt, ed., *China en América Latina: reflexiones sobre las relaciones transpacíficas* (Bogotá: Universidad Externado, 2012).

18 *Confucius Institute Online*, http://www.chinesecio.com/m/cio_wci (accessed November 24, 2014). This compares to 45 in Africa, only a little more than in South Korea (18), and considerably less than in the United States (86). These figures do not include "Confucius Classrooms."

19 Zheng Bingwen, Sun Hongbo, and Yue Yunxia, "Sesenta años de relaciones entre China y América Latina: retrospectivas y reflexiones," in Benjamin Creutzfeldt, ed., *China en América Latina*.

20 An initiative by Enrique Dussel Peters at the UNAM in Mexico City, http://www.redalc-china.org/index.html (accessed May 6, 2016).

21 This point is also made forcefully by David Shambaugh in his foreword to Adrian H. Hearn and José Luis León-Manríquez, ed., *China Engages Latin America: Tracing the Trajectory* (Boulder, CO: Lynne Rienner, 2011), p. xii.

22 See http://alianzapacifico.net/. The invitation was issued by then Peruvian president Alan García to his counterparts in Colombia, Chile, and Mexico to form an alliance for economic and agroindustrial integration and the advancement of free trade with a clear orientation toward Asia. Costa Rica became the fifth full member in 2013. It is worth noting that García, two times leader of the Latin American nation with the largest number of ethnic Chinese, describes the Alliance as part of the necessary response to China's growing role; see Alan García, *Confucio y la globalización: comprender China y crecer con ella* (Lima: Titanium Editores, 2013), p. 175ff.

23 For instance, during a conference at the Colombian Foreign Ministry in 2009, a Chilean representative recommended expanding regional cooperation in order to make more ample use of the FTA with China, to which the then-foreign minister Bermúdez responded, "We Colombians are not very good at cooperating."

24 Personal communication by author, March 2012.

25 The list most recently compiled by CEPAL is incomplete in that it omits some vice presidential visits, such as that of Xi Jinping in 2009, and does not account for head-of-state encounters at multilateral occasions such as BRICS. It nonetheless shows clear tendencies.

26 As a matter of fact, both Argentina and Colombia list *two* bilateral chambers of commerce each, but the PRC only recognizes one from each country. Peru presents a case apart, as its long history of immigration from China, as well as Chinese investment activities since the early 1990s, has led to the formation of numerous interest groups, such as the Herederos del Dragón (descendants of Chinese immigrants) and the Association of Chinese Businesses in Peru (秘鲁中资企业协会), in addition to the bilateral chamber of commerce. The low presence of independent commercial offices from Latin America in China is an impediment to market entry to China, though many business people avail themselves of other facilities, in particular from Spain, and entities from the Pacific Alliance members are set to coordinate efforts towards a stronger physical presence in China.

27 For a longer list and a discussion on China's multi-layered involvement in Latin America, see Ana Soliz Landivar and Sören Scholvin, "China in Lateinamerika: Chancen und Grenzen seines zunehmenden Einflusses," *GIGA Focus*, 6 (2011).

28 The Colombian government's figure is akin to that cited in the Heritage Foundation's database; see Heritage Foundation, "China Global Investment Tracker," http://www.heritage.org/research/projects/china-global-investment-tracker-interactive-map (accessed November 29, 2014).

29 María Camila Moreno provides a detailed list of Chinese investments in Colombia in "La política exterior de la República Popular China y su repercusión en las inversiones

en Colombia y América Latina," in Edgar Vieira, ed., *La transformación de China y su impacto para Colombia* (Bogotá: CESA, 2013), pp. 251–68.

30 Such an expression of interest is evident for instance in the article "Colombia: An Ideal Destination for Chinese Investments" [哥伦比亚: 中国企业投资的理想之地], *Hexun.com*, November 9, 2012, http://news.hexun.com/2012-11-09/147798009. html (accessed November 29, 2014).

31 Chinese is now the second most widely used language on the world-wide web, with over 500 million users, likely to overtake English within a few years. The use of online translation tools is tempting but distorts contents beyond recognition, and way beyond usefulness.

32 Allen Carlson and Hong Duan, "Internet Resources and the Study of Chinese Foreign Relations: Can Cyberspace Shed New Light on China's Approach to the World?" in Allen Carlson, Mary E. Gallagher, Kenneth Lieberthal, and Melanie Manion, eds., *Contemporary Chinese Politics: New Sources, Methods, and Field Strategies* (Cambridge, UK: Cambridge University Press, 2010), p. 106.

33 Hu Jintao introduced this concept at the 60th anniversary summit of the United Nations in September 2005, associating it with the goal of lasting peace and common prosperity (持久和平 , 共同繁荣).

34 Jing Men, "Changing Ideology in China and Its Impact on Chinese Foreign Policy," in Guo Sujian and Hua Shiping, eds., *New Dimensions of Chinese Foreign Policy* (Lanham, MD: Rowman & Littlefield, 2007), p. 34.

35 Wen, "Trusted Friends Forever."

36 Sun Hongbo, "Latin America Integration," *Xinhua*, December 5, 2011, http://news.xin huanet.com/english2010/indepth/2011-12/05/c_131288689.htm (accessed November 29, 2014).

37 Private communication from a participant at the second Forum. The author was present at the first Forum.

38 See http://chinadigitaltimes.net/china/ministry-of-truth/.

39 "La Mirada china," *Semana Special Issue "Rumbo Pacífico,"* December 2013, p. 26, http://www.semana.com/especiales/Semana__Rumbo_Pacfico/#/26/ (accessed May 6, 2016).

40 Zhang Xisheng, vice president of CRCC, during a meeting in Bogotá on July 27, 2012.

41 Evan Ellis, "Learning the Ropes," *Americas Quarterly*, vol. 6, no. 4 (Fall 2012), p. 28.

42 William Norris, "Thinking Clearly about China's Economic Statecraft," *Précis Feature* (MIT Center for International Studies, Boston, MA, Spring 2009); see in particular footnote 4 on p. 9 for the background literature on principal–agent theory.

43 James Reilly, "China's Economic Statecraft: Turning Wealth into Power," *Analysis* (Lowy Institute for International Policy, Sydney, NSW, November 2013).

44 Gastón Fornés and Alan Butt Philip, *The China–Latin America Axis: Emerging Markets and the Future of Globalisation* (London: Palgrave Macmillan, 2012), p. 75.

45 Ibid., p. 74.

46 Erica Downs, *Inside China, Inc: China Development Bank's Cross-Border Energy Deals* (Washington, DC: Brookings Institution, 2011), p. 58ff.

47 See "Noemí Sanín alerta de negocios de China y Nicaragua tras fallo CIJ," *LA F.m.*, May 8, 2013, http://www.lafm.com.co/noticias/noemi-sanin-alerta-de-nego-cios-137211 (accessed November 29, 2014). It should be noted, however, that the Colombian government subsequently distanced itself from the insinuations of the former foreign secretary. And yet Sanín, not to be dissuaded, has written a book to drive home her claim; see Noemí Sanín and Miguel Ceballos Arevalo, *La llegada del dragón: ¿falló la haya?* (Bogotá: Panamericana, December 2013).

48 Enrique Dussel Peters makes reference to this tendency in his interview with *China Files*; see "China: reto de élites políticas y económicas de América Latina," *China Files*,

June 20, 2011, http://china-files.com/es/link/10592/china-reto-de-elites-politicas-y-economicas-de-america-latina (accessed November 29, 2014).

49 Ministry of Commerce, "Warning on Risks in the Nicaraguan Canal Project" (关于尼加拉瓜运河建设项目的风险提示), November 15, 2012, http://hzs.mofcom.gov.cn/article/xxfb/201211/20121108435662.shtml (accessed November 29, 2014).

50 See Adrian H. Hearn, "Harnessing the Dragon: Overseas Chinese Entrepreneurs in Mexico and Cuba," in Julia C. Strauss and Ariel C. Armony, eds., *From the Great Wall to the New World: China and Latin America in the 21st Century* (Cambridge, UK: Cambridge University Press, 2011), pp. 111–33.

51 "China pide a Perú aplicar procedimientos correctos en el caso 'Gamarra,'" *America Economia*, September 8, 2013, http://www.americaeconomia.com/negocios-industrias/china-pide-peru-aplicar-procedimientos-correctos-en-el-caso-gamarra (accessed November 29, 2014).

52 "Marcha de empresarios del calzado llegó a la Plaza de Bolívar," *El Tiempo*, June 6, 2013, http://www.eltiempo.com/colombia/bogota/ARTICULO-WEB-NEW_NOTA_INTERIOR-12850002.html (accessed November 29, 2014).

53 Shambaugh, *China Goes Global*, p. 61ff. and elsewhere.

54 Ibid., p. 70.

2

COOPERATION AND MISTRUST BETWEEN CHINA AND THE U.S. IN LATIN AMERICA

R. Evan Ellis[1]

Because of the strong ties that the United States has with Latin America and the Caribbean, the U.S. has long been sensitive about the involvement of extra-hemispheric powers in the region.[2] In recent decades, China's expanding economic and political relationships with the region put that sensitivity to the test. U.S. Secretary of State John Kerry announced before the Organization of American States in November 2013 that the Obama administration was breaking from the U.S. historical legacy, embodied in the 1823 Monroe Doctrine, of resisting activities in the region by countries from outside the hemisphere.[3] Yet the scale and rate of growth of China's economic relationship over the past decade have captured the attention of leaders in the U.S., as well as in Latin America. From 2001, when the PRC was accepted into the World Trade Organization, through 2013, PRC bilateral trade with Latin America and the Caribbean grew 20-fold, from $15 billion in 2001 to $288.9 billion in 2013.[4] Between 2005 and 2013, leading Chinese banks provided an estimated $119 billion in credit to the region, of which three-quarters went to Argentina and the anti-U.S. regimes of the Bolivarian Alliance for the Americas (ALBA).[5] Although prior to 2010 cumulative Chinese investment in the region was less than $7 billion, approximately $10 billion of Chinese investment arrived in the region per year after that date.[6]

In addition, the concentration of China's loans and infrastructure projects in countries politically opposed to the U.S., and its selection of the Community of Latin American and Caribbean States (CELAC), which excludes the U.S. and Canada, as the principal multilateral forum for building its relationship with the region, has arguably raised concerns among U.S. decision makers.

This chapter explores China's engagement in Latin America and how the "rise of China" in the Western Hemisphere has affected U.S.–China relations.

Although written by a U.S. scholar, it attempts to represent a portion of the Chinese perspective as well, based on the author's research and interactions with his Chinese counterparts. The growing China–Latin America dynamic has brought about new areas of potential conflict and of possible collaboration. Areas of potential conflict include strategic calculations, issues related to governance in the region, and commercial competition with respect to products, resources, and bids for public contracts. Opportunities for cooperation discussed in this chapter include collaboration on trans-Pacific organized crime, medical and other humanitarian activities in the region, oversight of multinational corporate practices, and coordination and technical agreements on issues of trade triangulation.

China–Latin America Relations: U.S. Considerations

U.S. officials have long recognized that China's economic engagement with Latin America can make positive contributions to the development of the region.[7] Expanded revenues from primary product exports may contribute to economic growth, including resources for governments to build infrastructure and improve services in the realm of healthcare, education, and security. Investments from Chinese companies could also help to expand the number of jobs in the region, while purchases of intermediate goods from China have helped to make some manufacturing activities more competitive in countries like Brazil and Mexico. In select areas, financing from Chinese institutions may enable the implementation of important projects in key sectors, such as hydropower, wind and solar energy,[8] and new transportation infrastructure. Chinese officials describe their involvement in Latin America as beneficial not only to the region itself but also to the U.S. China has also publicly recognized U.S. official support of Sino-Latin American relations. Indeed, in 2012, officials from China's Ministry of Foreign Affairs acknowledged that the U.S. has repeatedly stressed that China–Latin America relations are conducive to the stability and development of Latin America.[9]

Both Republican and Democratic administrations within the U.S. have acknowledged the sovereign right of the Latin American countries to conduct relations with whatever nations they choose.[10] However, as noted previously, the advances of China into Latin America make many leaders in Washington profoundly uncomfortable. These concerns may be divided into three areas: (1) the impact of that engagement on the region itself; (2) the impact on U.S. policy goals in the region; and (3) the long-term Chinese agenda which underpins such engagement.

On the economic front, the U.S. recognizes the benefit to Latin America of exporting goods to China, but is concerned that the prevailing pattern of selling raw materials to China and purchasing Chinese manufactured goods in return may not be conducive to the long-term economic development of the region.[11] Such concerns have become more acute with the deceleration of Chinese economic growth, which has fallen from an annual average rate near 10 percent during the preceding three decades to a projection of around 6.3 percent for 2016 and 2017.[12] Such slowing growth has contributed to the decline in global commodity prices, decreasing the perceived benefit of those nations most closely involved in selling commodities to China. Indeed, China's official news agency, *Xinhua*, reported that declining commodity prices will mean that Latin America's exports to the PRC in 2015 are 14 percent less than during the previous year.[13]

Chinese resistance to importing higher value-added products from Latin America appears to be a consistent pattern across industries. For example, as indicated by Mariano Turzi in Chapter 8 in this volume, nations such as Argentina have objected to China's preference to import soybeans rather than soy oil or higher value-added products. Moreover, some Brazilian industrialists have claimed that China is contributing to the de-industrialization of that country, mainly owing to competition in third country markets. However, as Carol Wise points out in Chapter 7 in this volume, Brazil currently exports just 20 percent of its manufactured goods, implying that there is room for considerable expansion to address this concern.

Another challenge for the region is the dislocation of producers competing with Chinese products and services in domestic and third country markets such as the United States. Although Chinese firms are increasingly making important investments in the telecommunications, electricity transmission, manufacturing, and tourism sectors in Latin America, the focus of China's biggest loans to and investments in the region to date has been on the petroleum and mining sectors. Infrastructure projects which facilitate the extraction of these products or enhanced Chinese access to the region's markets have also dominated.[14]

Although the relationship of U.S. and European countries with Latin America during much of the twentieth century also concentrated on purchasing the region's commodities and exporting higher value-added manufactured goods in return, those relationships have become more diversified over time, and the value added of products exported today from Latin America and the Caribbean to the U.S. and Europe is generally higher than that of products exported from the region to the PRC. Moreover, U.S. and European companies have become important investors not only in Latin American primary product sectors but also in services, higher value-added manufacturing, and technology-intensive industries.

The U.S. is also concerned about the political and security-related consequences of Chinese economic engagement in the region. Chinese investments and bids for Latin American infrastructure projects involve negotiations with Latin American government officials in which hundreds of millions of dollars are at stake, expanding opportunities for corruption. The Chinese government and Chinese companies, like their U.S. counterparts, have formal rules against corrupt practices, although they aren't always effectively enforced.

Expanding Chinese engagement with the region is also generating unintended consequences in other areas that governments in the region are poorly equipped to face. These include the expansion of criminal activities between Asia and Latin America, facilitated by the growth of black market commerce in contraband goods, human trafficking, drugs and related chemicals, arms trafficking, and money laundering.[15] In September 2015, for example, three Colombians were indicted for laundering an estimated $5 billion through banks and other institutions in the PRC.[16] Other major incidents include a Chinese ship detained in Cartagena, Colombia, for attempting to smuggle explosive black powder to Cuba,[17] the sale to Chinese companies of metals illegally mined in Madre de Dios, Peru and Michoacán, Mexico, among others,[18] and ties between Mexico's Sinaloa Cartel and Chinese triads for obtaining precursor chemicals for the production of synthetic drugs.[19]

As China's presence in Latin America grows, the U.S. has also indicated that it expects the PRC to uphold environmental standards, security procedures, and other norms. The U.S. argues, for example, that Chinese companies should be required to fulfill social corporate responsibilities which go the extra mile in promoting such norms in the region. Similarly, some have openly worried that Chinese engagement with Latin America could taint the democratic process in the region.[20] In essence, the U.S. desires that China be a constructive partner overall in the Western Hemisphere.

Because Chinese activities in Latin America do not present a clear and compelling danger, the U.S. has not acted on its discomfort. For the U.S., the net impact of Chinese engagement with the region depends largely on how such engagement is conducted, and how the region itself manages the opportunities and risks afforded by that engagement.

China's Considerations

The dominant U.S. position in Latin America has long been a consideration for China in its relations with this region. Some Chinese perceive that, during the Cold War, the U.S. sought to impede China's ability to establish diplomatic relations with Latin American and Caribbean countries as an extension of its global "Containment Policy."[21] Indeed, such concerns had some substance insofar as China's post-1949 communist government believed that its support of national liberation movements in Latin America would help to combat "imperialism" in the periphery.[22]

With the exception of Cuba, it wasn't until the 1970s and the establishment of formal U.S.–China relations that the first wave of Latin American countries developed diplomatic ties with mainland China. The thaw in U.S.–China relations was arguably a key factor for enabling the PRC to engage diplomatically with Latin America. Other factors, such as the emergence of a bloc of newly independent "post-Colonial" governments in regions such as Africa, and the diversification of the foreign policy of LAC countries, also contributed to China's progress in gaining diplomatic recognition in Latin America.

Since the launching of market-oriented reforms in China in 1978, the progressive integration of China into the global economy increasingly brought Chinese goods to every part of the world. As Chinese firms have established a presence across the globe, seeking to expand China's position in global markets and move up the value-added chain in an array of goods and services markets in Latin America and the Caribbean, China's government has looked with some concern to the U.S. reaction, given U.S. sensitivity historically to the activities of extra-hemispheric actors in the region. Chinese officials have sought to reassure the U.S. that such engagement is primarily commercial in character, and hope that such reassurances, coupled with the primarily economic nature of Chinese activities in the region, will prevent the U.S. from reacting in a manner similar to its resistance to the expansion of ties by the Soviet Union in the region during the Cold War.

Whatever the U.S. perception of Chinese activities in Latin America, China clearly understands that the U.S. retains considerable influence over the course of China–Latin America relations. Chinese scholar Su Zhenxing ranked the U.S. presence in Latin America as one of the top five factors influencing the success of China's own relationship with the region, with the others being China's national strength, its geographic distance from the region, the question of Taiwan, and cultural differences which impair mutual understanding and trust between the PRC and the nations of the region.[23] Yet China does not see U.S. influence in the region merely as a factor that prevents the nations of the region from working more closely with China, but also as a factor that drives Chinese self-restraint, since China desires to maintain a healthy bilateral relationship with the U.S. and worries that U.S. perceptions of its activities in Latin America could damage the China–U.S. relationship.

This "U.S. factor" was arguably part of the impetus for establishing the U.S.–China strategic sub-dialogue on Latin America in 2006. The dialogue was launched on the U.S. side by then U.S. Deputy Assistant Secretary of State for the Western Hemisphere Tom Shannon, and has been continued, with some delays, by both of his successors to date, Arturo Valenzuela and Roberta Jacobson.

The dialogue seeks to avoid misunderstanding and build political trust between the U.S. and China as the latter expands its engagement with the Western Hemisphere. By means of the sub-dialogue, and through other mechanisms, the U.S. and China explore possible areas of cooperation in the region. At the same time, however, some scholars in China worry that the consultation mechanism could damage China's relations with Latin America and the Caribbean, by giving the appearance in Latin America that China is negotiating with the U.S. about the future of the Latin American and Caribbean region.

Sources of Mistrust between the U.S. and China in Latin America

As suggested in the previous section, developments in China's relationship with Latin America affects, and is affected by, the U.S.–China bilateral relationship. Despite the official policy of the Obama administration in the U.S. to not apply the Monroe Doctrine in Latin America, despite China's caution in engaging with the region, and despite U.S.–China bilateral coordinating mechanisms such as the U.S.–China Strategic and Economic Dialogue, China and the U.S. remain wary of and unable to effectively gauge each other's intentions in economic or political affairs, either in Latin America or in other parts of the globe. This difficulty, in part, is rooted in the starkly differing value systems, political traditions, and ways of doing business in the two countries.[24] Chinese officials tend to discount American discourse around democratic governance, whereas U.S. policymakers rarely take at face value China's assertions that its agenda in many emerging market countries is mainly economic in nature and that the political multiplier effects are certain to be "win–win" in nature.

China's growing role in the global economy has only intensified strategic mistrust between the two powers. Party leaders in Beijing have accused the U.S. of protecting politically sensitive industries and of leveraging the dollar's strength to its advantage. U.S. officials, for their part, have complained that China's renminbi is significantly undervalued and thus advantages Chinese exporters at the expense of American companies.[25] Tension between China and the U.S. has also been heightened by a number of diplomatic standoffs—including the erroneous 1999 American bombing of the Chinese embassy in Belgrade, China's support for North Korea and U.S. support of Taiwan, and the U.S. "pivot to Asia," with tensions mounting in late 2015 with the conduct by the U.S. of "freedom of navigation" patrols by its ships and aircraft within close proximity to new "artificial islands" that China is creating, replete with airbases, in the South China Sea. The relationship globally also continues to be complicated by what some in the U.S. see as credible evidence of sustained cyber-attacks by Chinese organizations against U.S. government and corporate targets, and increased reports of Chinese industrial espionage against U.S. companies.

Over the long term, such issues feed into the fundamental underlying question within both China and the U.S. of whether China's emergence as a global power, and an increasingly important partner for Latin America, will lead to hostile geopolitical competition with the U.S., or even to a major armed conflict. International relations theorists from Thucydides to the twentieth-century writer A.F.K. Organski have argued that the rise of one power in the world order to a position that rivals or supplants that of an existing one is a condition that is most likely to foster conflict.[26] More recently, U.S. political scientist John Mearsheimer has echoed this claim.[27] While the actual level that these tensions could reach is still unclear, there are a number of specific issues arising from Chinese engagement in Latin America that could generate new frictions between the two sides.

The Chinese, for example, perceive that the U.S. government closely monitors military collaboration between China and the countries of Latin America,[28] and that U.S. officials would be particularly concerned if China were to establish military alliances or seek access to military bases in the region. China, however, argues that its military presence in the Western Hemisphere has, to date, focused on training, education, and exercises that do not appear to threaten any third party. In this spirit, the spokesman for the Ministry of Defense of China has stressed that China adheres firmly to the principles of maintaining peace and stability in the region and the world, and has not directed its activities against third parties, nor used them to threaten any other country.[29] China maintains that it has assured the U.S. and the countries of Latin America that it will continue to actively carry out military exchanges with them, including dialogues on defense matters and other forms of cooperation, in accordance with these principles. In its 2008 White Paper on Latin America and the Caribbean, China openly indicated its interest in engaging with the nations of the region in the defense and security arena.[30] In its May 2015 National Defense Strategy White Paper, the PRC reaffirmed its interest in maintaining active defense and security relationships with military institutions not only in Latin America but throughout the world as a fundamental part of its national defense strategy.[31]

China contrasts its own level of military activities with those of the U.S., which maintains a significant force in China's own backyard, and has used these footholds in the past to influence the outcome of affairs that China regards as internal. Similarly, while Chinese companies have sold arms to Latin American countries that have been antagonistic toward the U.S., including Venezuela, Ecuador, and Bolivia,[32] Beijing argues that such sales have been insignificant in comparison with arms sales to the LAC region by U.S. companies, or for that matter the supply of advanced arms to Taiwan. Similarly, although China periodically deploys military forces to Latin America—including contributing forces to MINUSTAH, the U.N. peacekeeping force in Haiti, for eight years,[33] the sending of its hospital ship *Peace Ark* to the region in both 2011 and 2015,[34] and the realization of combat exercises with Chile,[35] Argentina, and Brazil[36] in November 2013—the PRC views such a presence as modest in comparison to U.S. forces stationed in the Pacific, and by contrast to U.S. defense treaties with multiple nations in Asia. As noted previously, the PRC also views its absence of formal military alliances in Latin America as evidence of its peaceful intent in the hemisphere. Indeed, from a Chinese perspective, because its engagement with Latin America has been so explicitly commercial and its declared intentions peaceful, U.S. concerns are interpreted by some in the PRC as part of a U.S. desire to contain China by blocking its access to certain actors in the region.

However Chinese military engagement is interpreted, it is likely to remain a topic of discussion between China and the U.S. as Latin American governments continue to expand arms purchases and military ties as part of their broader relationship with the PRC. This is especially the case when self-proclaimed anti-U.S. regimes, such as Venezuela, indicate a desire to explicitly enlist China as an ally in their campaigns against "imperialism" in the region,[37] even though China has sought to avoid the interpretation of its friendship with and economic assistance to such regimes as support for their anti-U.S. or anti-Western policies.

Beyond the military relationship itself, the expansion of Chinese commercial activities in the region, and in particular within strategically important sectors such as telecommunications and space, raises concerns within the U.S.[38]

A Reduction in U.S. Influence?

The "re-emergence" of China as a major global power has coincided with a perceived erosion of the position of the U.S.[39] During the past century, the U.S. effectively used both its military predominance in the hemisphere and its position as Latin America's principal market and source of capital in order to advance its policy agenda in the region, including adherence by countries of the region to U.S. preferences regarding human rights, democratic institutions, economic policies, and cooperation with the U.S. on a range of international issues. The rise of China as an alternative source of trade, investment, and finance for the nations of Latin America and the Caribbean has provided both anti-U.S. governments and other nations with alternatives to the U.S. for loans, investments, and markets, indirectly weakening U.S. leverage for advancing its policy goals.

As the Chinese government has supported the efforts of its companies to invest in, expand trade with, and engage in business activities across Latin America and the Caribbean, its public policy of "non-interference in the internal affairs of sovereign nations,"[40] has caused it to avoid officially conditioning its loans, investments, and other activities on the style of government or financial management of its partners. However, China's expanding trade and investment position in the region has, to a degree, sought to leverage its position to secure favorable treatment for its companies and personnel. In short, the availability of China as an alternate economic partner has arguably undermined the ability of the U.S. to advance its policy agenda in the region by economically underwriting a group of anti-U.S. states which partly or wholly reject Western banks, Western companies, and the conditions explicitly or implicitly associated with obtaining their resources, while giving the rest of the region expanded options for following the proscriptions of the U.S. when it serves their interests to do so, knowing that China may be waiting in the wings to offer other options.

As of late 2015, China had established three major loan funds in the region: the $10 billion China–LAC Industrial Cooperation Investment Fund, backed by China Development Bank, the People's Bank of China, and the PRC Foreign Exchange Control Board;[41] a $20 billion Special Loan Program for China–LAC Infrastructure Projects, operated by China Development Bank; and a separate $5 billion China–LAC Cooperation Fund, with coordinated components from China Export–Import Bank and the Inter-American Development Bank.[42] On top of this China announced a $3 billion China–Caribbean cooperation fund and directed funding at the country-specific level. China has also pursued such funding vehicles on a country-specific level. Jamaica, for example, is negotiating its second major fund for infrastructure projects with China,[43] and Costa Rica announced in November 2015 that it was seeking US$1 billion in financing from the PRC for infrastructure projects. Such financing is not negative per se, but the conditions pursued by the PRC, such as the use of Chinese contractors, to some degree undercut the standards of transparent, open competition for public works projects traditionally adhered to by Western institutions.

Despite these new funds, to date Chinese loans to the region have largely been concentrated in the countries of ALBA and Argentina. Such loans, in combination with Chinese investment, commodity purchases, and even arms and technology sales, have allowed the countries in question to stay afloat despite their embrace of policies that many in the U.S. regard as contrary to good governance and sustainable long-term development.[44] In the case of the ALBA countries, the ability to turn to Chinese funding has arguably bolstered the confidence of these governments to take actions against the interests of Western investors, institutions, and banks. Ecuador, for instance, despite having defaulted in December 2008 on interest payments on part of its US$10 billion foreign debt,[45] was able to secure almost US$11 billion in loans from China between 2009 and 2014, in addition to commitments in 2015 for an additional US$5.3 billion to help the government cope with financial difficulties caused by the steep fall in international oil prices.[46]

In a similar fashion, the Venezuelan administration of the late Hugo Chavez was able to secure over US$53 billion in loans from multiple Chinese banks between 2005 and 2013.[47] Indeed, during 2015, as the successor team led by Venezuelan President Nicolas Maduro weathered a deepening economic and political crisis that prompted widespread speculation over a possible default by the regime on its existing international debt obligations, the PRC committed US$5 billion of additional funds to help the government weather the crisis during the run-up to the December 6 midterm Congressional election, seen by many as a critical milestone for the regime's survival.[48] Yet even this massive infusion of capital failed to staunch the gains of the political opposition at the polls.

In Argentina, China offered over US$10 billion in loans to upgrade the nation's railroads at a time in which the country remained shut out of financial markets because of its 2001 debt default.[49] In 2015, China extended the country a $11 billion line of credit, and then reportedly expanded that credit by an additional $2 billion when it became apparent that Argentina had spent the money previously loaned, during the run-up to the October 2015 national elections.[50] In Bolivia, although Chinese investment to date has been modest, in October 2015 Vice President Alvaro Garcia Linera secured a commitment from China for a new $7 billion line of credit for a series of new energy and infrastructure projects.[51]

From the perspective of some in the U.S., the loans, investments, and export revenues provided to anti-U.S. administrations have contributed to their survival, and indirectly enabled nationalizations, reckless populism, and other activities which conflict with U.S. interests and the U.S. agenda in the region. In response to such criticisms, the Chinese government contends that it seeks commercial engagement with all countries of the region, and that it would actually contradict its neutrality towards the region if it did business only with those countries whose policies were aligned strictly with those endorsed by the U.S. Indeed, an argument can be made that the marked concentration of Chinese loans in anti-U.S. governments is, at least in part, a product of their willingness to agree to Chinese terms, which often include the use of Chinese contractors and labor. Yet, even without establishing "nefarious" Chinese intent, the net negative impact on the U.S. agenda and governability in the region remains the same.

Economic Competition

In terms of economic, trade, and investment relationships, China is a commercial competitor with the U.S. and its economic interests in Latin America. Although the Obama administration adopted a benign diplomatic posture and espoused the development of those elements of Sino-Latin American economic cooperation which are in line with the economic interests of the U.S., many in the U.S. are indeed concerned about the expansion of China's economic activity in Latin America. This is especially so in sectors such as construction and telecommunications where expanding competition between U.S. and PRC-based firms may generate tensions. As Chinese firms leverage access to financing from PRC policy banks and assistance from the Chinese government, allegations may arise from U.S. firms and other bidders that the award of a contract to a Chinese firm reflects undue influence by the Chinese government over that of the Latin American or Caribbean nation awarding the contract.

In addition to issues of commercial competition, some Chinese investments in the Americas are viewed as strategically sensitive. In January 1997, the government of Panama awarded concessions to the Hong Kong-based firm Hutchison Whampoa for the operation of port facilities on both sides of the Panama Canal, sparking public debate in the U.S. about the national security risk of a strategic waterway potentially falling under the control of the "Red Chinese."[52] More recently, the initiative by Chinese businessman Wang Jing to build a US$50 billion canal across Nicaragua has drawn significant attention, with speculation that the Chinese government has strategic interests in the project and gave tacit approval for it to go forward, even if neither the government nor its major banks have embraced the project.[53]

Beyond specific projects, in November 2004 Chinese President Hu Jintao's tour of Latin America, in which he talked of reaching US$100 billion in trade and commercial projects in the region within ten years, provoked hearings in both the U.S. House of Representatives and the U.S. Senate on what the PRC was "doing" in Latin America.[54] His successor's two high-profile trips to the region, including the anticipation of US$250 billion of Chinese investment in Latin America during the coming decade,[55] and China's choice to engage in the region through CELAC, an organization which explicitly excludes the U.S. and Canada,[56] arguably helped to prompt similar hearings in the U.S. House of Representatives in September 2015.[57]

Within the U.S., a deep mistrust arguably exists toward China. Americans are skeptical about the friendly intentions of the Chinese government, believing that what the Chinese will say or ultimately do in matters of business or politics depends on what they perceive their interests are at that moment. There is also U.S. skepticism as to whether China's assertion of its peaceful intentions in Latin America is just a guise to placate the U.S., particularly since China's further development depends heavily on access to U.S technology and markets. Correspondingly, as China grows more economically powerful, some wonder whether it will become more assertive with respect to the protection of its interests in Latin America, just as it has now adopted a much stronger stance with regard to territorial disputes in the South China Sea.

Potential Areas for China–U.S. Cooperation in Latin America

Although there are many potential sources of tension and misunderstanding between the U.S. and China in Latin America, there are also numerous areas where the two can cooperate. The following section offers several examples.

Sustained Strategic Dialogue

In order to construct a positive U.S.–China relationship in Latin America that manages potential conflicts and identifies new specific areas where cooperation and collaboration are possible, the U.S. and China should maintain an ongoing high-level dialogue on issues that arise from their overlapping activities and interests in the region. Such an institutionalized interaction was begun in 2006 in the form of the Latin America chapter of the U.S.–China Strategic and Economic Dialogue, and should continue, as it has, on a regular basis. In addition to a senior-level meeting which may only occur once a year, such dialogues should include ongoing interactions in the form of working groups, which would meet at least once a month to identify and seek to resolve issues, elevating those which are particularly pressing to the higher-level group. As a qualification, however, the focus of such meetings should not be U.S.–China collaboration in order to "manage" issues that concern both vis-à-vis Latin America.[58] Rather, the goal should be to identify ways for the U.S. and China to work more effectively in collaboration with the nations of the region.

Collaboration on Trans-Pacific Organized Crime

Latin American governments are ill equipped to effectively respond to the explosion of trans-Pacific organized crime that has accompanied the expansion of commerce between the two regions. Be it human trafficking, drugs, contraband goods, or money laundering, police and security forces in the region generally lack the capabilities in Mandarin and other Chinese dialects to question suspects and conduct investigations within Chinese communities. In addition, few organizations in the region have working-level technical contacts with counterpart organizations in China to follow leads in the course of their investigations. Chinese officials may not only have the data needed by Latin American law enforcement authorities, but also be able to provide linguistic support and even agents who could penetrate Chinese criminal networks operating in Latin American communities.

Conversely, Latin American law enforcement can provide needed information, language support, and agents to support Chinese authorities in investigating contraband networks, arms purchases, and similar transactions. As with Chinese and Latin American authorities, U.S. law enforcement entities have information relevant for combating these networks, which more often than not touch upon the U.S. They are also interested parties in the information that their Chinese and Latin American counterparts have gathered in these cases and may similarly be able to provide language and personnel support. In addition, U.S. authorities already have some experience working with Chinese law enforcement and may be able to use that experience to facilitate expanded cooperation with Latin American authorities. Interest in closer security collaboration might eventually come from Chinese companies operating on the ground in Latin America—particularly those involved in petroleum, mining, and construction operations in remote areas where criminal or insurgent groups are present.

Multinational Medical and Humanitarian Missions

The U.S. and China are currently conducting parallel but separate humanitarian exercises in the region. The November 2010 PRC–Peru bilateral medical exercise Angel de Paz[59] paralleled, on a smaller scale, humanitarian exercises by the U.S. Southern Command such as Beyond the Horizon (BTH) and New Horizons (NH), and Medical Readiness Training Exercises (MEDRETEs). Similarly, the December 2011 deployment of the Chinese hospital ship *Peace Ark* to the Caribbean,[60] and its December 2015 return, including stops in Mexico, Peru, Grenada, and Barbados,[61] paralleled the deployment of the USNS *Comfort* from April to September 2011 to Colombia, Costa Rica, Ecuador, El Salvador, Guatemala, Haiti, Jamaica, Nicaragua, and Peru, as part of Operation Continuing Promise.[62] While the value for both China and the U.S. of assisting Latin American nations through such activities is to build goodwill with their Latin American partners, there are other potential benefits for conducting such activities multilaterally. This includes expanding the amount of assistance provided, building confidence between U.S. and Chinese officials with regard to each other's activities in the region, and helping to reduce suspicion that either country is seeking to advance a strictly unilateral agenda through such aid.

Multinational Corporate Practices Oversight Board

Another source of tension growing out of China's expanding commercial relationship with LAC is the perception that Chinese corporations are not "competing fairly" with U.S. and other Western companies in their pursuit of contracts for infrastructure and other commercial activities. The Chinese, conversely, would argue that they are being victimized by unfair prejudices, often promulgated by powerful interests with a privileged position in the markets that the Chinese are entering. These interests, they would argue, are employing such prejudices against the Chinese to keep them out of the market. Moreover, such perceptions contribute to bitterness and mistrust on both sides when the losing party in a bid suggests to sympathetic government officials that the result was due not to the competitor's superior (or less expensive) product but rather to unfair competition.

In order to build confidence on all sides, the U.S., China, Latin American governments, and other interested parties could work together to create an oversight board that would review major public contracts and commercial deals, as well as provide a set of agreed-upon standards and best practices. Such a board would not have legal authority to decide cases, but rather would influence decision-making based on the technical competence of its members, access to data,[63] and a reputation for objectivity in the representation of all interested parties. If successful on matters of contracting, the activities of an oversight board might be expanded to examine environmental and labor practices, and even disputes between specific companies, local communities, and interest groups.

Such activities would arguably help Chinese companies advance their legitimate business activities in the region. On the one hand, the act of investigating cases and publishing reports, within the limits of protecting the proprietary information of all interested parties, would increase the perceived transparency of Chinese corporate activities in the region and help to separate legitimate concerns from unfounded rumors and biases. On the other hand, publication of the findings of such a board would enable other Chinese companies entering the region to learn from both the mistakes and the best practices of their co-nationals in areas ranging from public contracting to dealing with labor unions, communities, and interested societal groups.

Coordination and Technical Agreements Governing Triangulation

In many Latin American countries close to the U.S., Chinese businesses, in conjunction with local partners, are increasingly considering and constructing supply chains that use a given country as a platform for assembling goods from Chinese components, which are then sold to the U.S. market. Such an approach, in principle, achieves production cost savings by performing the majority of the work in China, and then final assembly operations in countries with free trade agreements (FTAs) with the U.S., including the North American Free Trade Agreement (NAFTA), the U.S.–Central American–Dominican Republic FTA (CAFTA-DR), and the U.S.–Colombia FTA.

Rules-of-origin clauses in these FTAs dictate that a certain percentage of production be realized by the LAC country prior to exporting these goods to the U.S. While such requirements appear straightforward, enforcing them requires the ability to assess the reasonableness of claims regarding the pricing of intermediate goods, as well as other complex accounting issues collectively known as "triangulation."

Although Chinese customs officials may understand their own country's accounting practices, they generally do not maintain visibility over products once shipped out of the country. Conversely, U.S. and Latin American customs officials do not always have adequate information on the value of components shipped from China versus the value realized during the assembly of the good in Latin America. Establishing joint U.S.–Chinese–Latin American "customs teams" could help to more effectively assess the reasonableness of the assigned valuation of goods at each point in the production chain. Doing so would increase confidence in the U.S. that FTAs with Latin America are not merely being used as a pass-through for the import of Chinese goods. It would also likely force Chinese companies to move the operations of more of their subcontractors to Latin America to legitimately meet rules-of-origin requirements, creating more value-added manufacturing jobs in Latin America. In the process, this could stimulate the integration of Chinese and Latin American production chains and expand overall sales of goods manufactured with Chinese components, helping to grow the businesses and international presence of mid-level Chinese producers and their Latin American counterparts.

Conclusions

The potential for the U.S. and China to collaborate with respect to their activities in Latin America depends on the ability of each to overcome longstanding strategic mistrust. In advocating stronger collaboration, it is important to recognize that the obstacles go deeper than mere perceptions and sentiments. To be effective, the kinds of collaboration described in this chapter require that the U.S., China, and their respective partners in Latin America and the Caribbean acknowledge that the net benefits of cooperation will more than compensate for the costs. To the extent that the U.S. acknowledges that a significant Chinese presence in the region over the long run is inevitable, the strategic benefit of such collaboration is to ensure that China participates in such a way as to be transparent and to strengthen institutions and good governance in the region to the benefit of all parties. For China as well, cooperating with the U.S. in Latin America requires a determination that the long-term benefits of such cooperation will outweigh the strategic costs.

To some degree for the Chinese, such cooperation implies accepting standards for corporate behavior which they did not invent and which may put them at a disadvantage next to those who already have the contracts and institutional relationships in the region. The benefit of cooperating with the U.S. is an expanding corporate presence and promotion of the local acceptance of Chinese firms as respected players in the region. Despite an abundance of possibilities for tension and misunderstanding between the U.S. and China, the cost of the U.S. and China struggling against each other as global enemies creates a solemn imperative for both sides to engage in mutual accommodation.[64] Latin America is one obvious place to do so.

Notes

1 Sun Hongbo of the Chinese Academy of Social Sciences provided information and insights for the section on "China's Considerations" in this chapter. However, responsibility for the characterization of those insights rests with the author.

2 For example, the Countering Iran in the Western Hemisphere Act of 2012 embodied the spirit of the Monroe Doctrine by declaring that "Congress finds ... the US has vital political, economic and security interests in the Western Hemisphere," House Resolution 3783, 112th Congress of the United States of America, 2nd Session, January 3, 2012.

3 John Kerry, "Remarks on U.S. Policy in the Western Hemisphere," U.S. Department of State, November 18, 2013, http://www.state.gov/secretary/remarks/2013/11/217680. htm.

4 International Monetary Fund, *Direction of Trade Statistics*, June 2014, p. 33.

5 Interamerican Dialogue, "China–Latin America Finance Database," http://thedialogue. org/map_list (accessed September 17, 2015).

6 CEPAL, "Chinese Foreign Direct Investment in Latin America and the Caribbean," November 2013, p. 11.

7 In a November 2009 speech at the Center for Hemispheric Defense Studies in Washington, DC, Dr. Frank Mora stated that China's deepening engagement in the hemisphere could play a productive role in ameliorating challenges which affect the region. Similarly, in a statement before the U.S. Senate Foreign Relations Committee, the then Principal Deputy Assistant Secretary of State for Western Hemisphere Affairs, Charles Shapiro, argued that China's engagement with Latin America could lead to increased cooperation with both the U.S. and nations of the region, for example on matters such as terrorism, transnational crime, and counter-narcotics. See Senate Foreign Relations Committee hearing on Challenge or Opportunity: China's Role in Latin America, September 20, 2005.

8 For a discussion of the impact of China on the renewable energy sector in Latin America, see R. Evan Ellis, "Are Big Chinese Energy Investments in Latin America a Concern?" *Manzella Report*, November 23, 2013, http://www.manzellareport.com.

9 "Foreign Ministry Official: China–Latin America Relations Benefit Latin American Stability and Development" [外交部官员: 中拉关系加强有利拉美稳定和发展], *Chinanews.com*, January 17, 2012, http://www.chinanews.com/gj/2012/01-17/3611197. shtml.

10 In May 2009, for example, addressing Chinese and Iranian engagement with Latin America, then Secretary of State Hillary Clinton declared, "We have no problem with any country, such as China, engaging in economic activities, business, and commerce with any country anywhere." "Hillary Clinton Warns Latin America Off Close Iran Ties," *BBC News*, December 11, 2009, http://news.bbc.co.uk/2/hi/8409081.stm.

11 See former Assistant Secretary of State Arturo Valenzuela, "Remarks to Town Hall at George Washington University," November 3, 2010, http://www.state.gov/p/wha/rls/rm/2010/151039.htm.

12 Toh Han Shih, "IMF Trims Forecast for China's GDP Growth, Raises Outlook for US," *South China Morning Post*, January 20, 2015, http://www.scmp.com/business/economy/article/1682780/imf-trims-forecast-chinas-gdp-growth-2015-and-2016-raises-united.

13 "Exports from Latin America, Caribbean to Contract 14 percent in 2015," *Xinhua*, October 21, 2015, http://news.xinhuanet.com/english/2015-10/21/c_134735366. htm.

14 For a detailed sector-by-sector analysis of where Chinese investments in the region have occurred, and associated challenges, see R. Evan Ellis, *China on the Ground in Latin America: Challenges for the Chinese and Impacts on the Region* (New York: Palgrave Macmillan, 2014).

15 For a discussion of emerging criminal linkages between China and Latin America and the Caribbean, see R. Evan Ellis, *The Strategic Dimension of China's Engagement with Latin America* (Washington, DC: Center for Hemispheric Defense Studies, October 2013), http://chds.dodlive.mil/files/2013/12/pub-PP-ellis.pdf, pp. 117–34.

16 Joseph Ax and Nate Raymond, "UPDATE 2: U.S. Charges Three in Multibillion-dollar Drug Money Laundering Scheme," *Reuters*, September 10, 2015, http://www.reuters.com/article/2015/09/10/usa-crime-drugtrafficking-idUSL1N11G1XV2015 0910#ZrR6WzWblmJZJtgo.99.

17 "China dice que carguero detenido en Cartagena llevaba material militar 'ordinario,'" *El País*, March 4, 2015, http://www.elpais.com.co/elpais/colombia/noticias/china-dice-carguero-detenido-cartagena-llevaba-material-militar-ordinario.

18 See, for example, Laurence Culliver, "How Chinese Companies Sustain Organized Crime in Mexico," *Vice News*, June 25, 2014, https://news.vice.com/article/how-chinese-mining-companies-sustain-organized-crime-in-mexico.

19 See, for example, Bryan Harris, "Hong Kong Triads Supply Meth Ingredients to Mexican Drug Cartels," *South China Morning Post*, January 12, 2014, http://www.scmp.com/news/hong-kong/article/1403433/hong-kong-triads-supply-meth-ingredients-mexican-drug-cartels.

20 Zhu Hongbo, "Recent Developments in China–Latin America Relations and the United States' Latin America Policy" [近期中拉关系的发展与美国的拉美政策], *Journal of Latin American Studies*, vol. 4 (2006), pp. 60–65.

21 Huang Zhiliang, "Documenting China–Latin America Diplomatic Ties" [中拉建交纪实], Shanghai Dictionary Publishing House, 2 (2007).

22 In their analyses, scholars such as Immanuel Wallerstein have traditionally divided the world into the nations of the developed "Core," such as the U.S. and Europe, and nations of the "periphery," including the lesser developed states of Latin America, Asia, and Africa.

23 Su Zhenxing, "How to Face the Future of China–Latin America Relations" [中拉关系如何面向未来], *Journal of Latin American Studies*, 2 (2009), p. 18.

24 Kenneth Lieberthal and Wang Jisi, *Addressing US–China Strategic Distrust*, John L. Thornton China Center Monograph Series, no. 4 (Washington, DC: Brookings Institution, 2012).

25 Although the International Monetary Fund (IMF) declared that the renminbi was no longer undervalued in mid-2015 (see "China's Currency Is 'No Longer Undervalued,' says IMF," *Financial Times*, May 26, 2015, p. 1), this changed with the unexpected devaluation of the renminbi in August 2015. Moving forward, China's currency can again be declared "undervalued" or superficially cheap vis-à-vis the euro and U.S. dollar.

26 See A.F.K. Organski, *World Politics* (New York: Alfred Knopf, 1968). For an application of power transition theory to the contemporary U.S.–China relationship, see Zhiqun Zhu, *US–China Relations in the 21st Century: Power Transitions and Peace* (New York: Routledge, 2006).

27 John Mearsheimer, *The Tragedy of Great Power Politics* (New York: W.W. Norton, 2001).

28 Based on multiple off-the-record conversations with Chinese scholars.

29 "Defense Officials and Military Contacts in Latin America Do Not Threaten Other Countries" [国防部官员与拉美军事交往不威胁其他国家], *Xinhua*, November 16, 2008, http://news.xinhuanet.com/newscenter/2008-11/16/content_10366058_1.htm.

30 Government of the People's Republic of China, "China's Policy Paper on Latin America and the Caribbean (Full Text)," November 2008, http://in.china-embassy.org/eng/zgbd/t521025.htm.

31 State Council Information Office of the People's Republic of China, "China's Military Strategy," May 26, 2015, http://eng.mod.gov.cn/Database/WhitePapers/index.htm.

32 See, for example, R. Evan Ellis, "Should U.S. Be Worried about Chinese Arms Sales in the Region?" *Latin America Goes Global*, May 11, 2015, http://latinamericagoesglobal.org/2015/05/should-u-s-be-worried-about-chinese-arms-sales-in-the-region/.

33 Colum Lynch, "In Surprise Move, China Withdraws Riot Police from Haiti," *Foreign Policy*, March 25, 2010, http://foreignpolicy.com/2010/03/25/in-surprise-move-china-withdraws-riot-police-from-haiti/.

34 "China's Naval Hospital Ship Calls at U.S. Port," *Xinhua*, November 4, 2015, http://news.xinhuanet.com/english/2015-11/04/c_134781091.htm.

35 "PLAN's Taskforce Conducts Maritime Joint Exercise with Chilean Navy," Ministry of Defense of the People's Republic of China Official Website, October 12, 2013, http://eng.mod.gov.cn/TopNews/2013-10/12/content_4470459.htm. See also "Armadas de China y Chile realizaron ejercicios navales," *Noticias FFAA Chile*, October 16, 2013, http://noticiasffaachile.blogspot.com/2013/10/armadas-de-china-y-chile-realizaron.html.

36 "PLAN Taskforce Conducts Joint Maritime Exercise with Brazilian Navy," Ministry of Defense of the People's Republic of China Official Website, October 28, 2013, http://eng.mod.gov.cn/DefenseNews/2013-10/28/content_4472787.htm.

37 "Pekín se desmarca de vínculo ideológicos con Venezuela a la llegada de Chávez," *El Universal*, September 23, 2008, http://www.eluniversal.com/2008/09/23/pol_ava_pekin-se-desmarca-de_23A2007487.

38 See, for example, Ellis, *Strategic Dimension of China's Engagement with Latin America*, pp. 51–84.

39 See, for example, Thomas L. Friedman and Michael Mandelbaum, *That Used to Be Us: How America Fell Behind in the World It Invented and How We Can Come Back* (New York: Picador, 2011); Vassilis K. Fouskas and Bulent Gokay, *The Fall of the US Empire: Global Fault-Lines and the Shifting Imperial Order* (London, Pluto Press: 2012); and Mark Urban, "Is the US an Empire in Decline?" *BBC*, September 20, 2012, http://www.bbc.co.uk/news/world-us-canada-19667754.

40 See Ministry of Foreign Affairs of the People's Republic of China, "China's Initiation of the Five Principles of Peaceful Co-existence," http://www.fmP.R.C..gov.cn/mfa_eng/ziliao_665539/3602_665543/3604_665547/t18053.shtml (accessed September 16, 2015).

41 "China Launches Fund for LatAm Industrial Cooperation," *China.org*, September 1, 2015, http://www.china.org.cn/china/Off_the_Wire/2015-09/01/content_3647 3985.htm.

42 "Introduction of the China–LAC Cooperation Fund," China–CELAC Forum Official Website, June 2, 2015, http://www.chinacelacforum.org/eng/ltdt_1/t1269475.htm.

43 See, for example, Balford Henry, "CHEC Negotiations Are On," *Jamaica Observer*, October 11, 2015, http://www.jamaicaobserver.com/business/CHEC-negotiations-are-on-_19232980.

44 For a detailed discussion of the impact of Chinese funding for ALBA on the political dynamics of the region, see R. Evan Ellis, "Chinese Engagement with the ALBA Countries: A Relationship of Mutual Convenience?" in Bruce M. Bagley and Magdalena Defort, eds., *Decline of the U.S. Hegemony? A Challenge of ALBA and a New Latin American Integration of the Twenty-first Century* (Lanham, MD: Lexington Books, 2015), pp. 345–68.

45 Simon Romero, "President: Ecuador Orders Debt Default," *New York Times*, December 13, 2008, http://www.nytimes.com/2008/12/13/world/americas/13briefs-PRESIDENTORD_BRF.html?_r=0.

46 "China da $5.296 millones en crédito para proyectos," *El Universo*, January 7, 2015, http://www.eluniverso.com/noticias/2015/01/07/nota/4404361/creditos-chinos-30-anos.

47 "Pdvsa y China invertirán $40 mil millones en la Faja," *El Universal*, December 3, 2010, http://www.eluniversal.com/2010/12/03/eco_art_pdvsa-y-china-invert_2125958.

48 Chinese and Venezuelan experts consulted for this study confirmed that there was only one $5 billion loan, announced multiple times, and not two separate loans. Moreover, the loan would be principally used to repay other obligations incurred by Chinese companies operating in the country, with very little disbursement of new funds. See "Venezuela recibirá al cierre de 2015 préstamo por $5.000 millones de China," *El Universal*, September 25, 2015, http://www.eluniversal.com/economia/150925/venezuela-recibira-al-cierre-de-2015-prestamo-por-5000-millones-de-chi.

49 "Argentina y China firmarán millonarios acuerdos, pese a disputa por la soja," *America Economia*, July 6, 2010, http://www.americaeconomia.com/economia-mercados/comercio/argentina-y-china-firmaran-acuerdos-comerciales-pese-disputa-por-soja.

50 Javier Blanco, "Para evitar que caigan las reservas, le pidieron más crédito a China," *La Nacion*, September 28, 2015, http://www.lanacion.com.ar/1831745-para-evitar-que-caigan-las-reservas-le-pidieron-mas-credito-a-china.

51 "Bolivia Says China to Lend $7 Billion for Energy, Transport Infrastructure," *Reuters*, October 19, 2015, http://www.reuters.com/article/2015/10/19/us-bolivia-china-loans-idUSKCN0SD2A420151019#hKdxuqCGkzsGSAo0.99.

52 See, for example, Howard LaFranchi, "Panama Canal's Security Worries," *Christian Science Monitor*, December 14, 1999, http://www.csmonitor.com/1999/1214/p6s2.html.

53 See, for example, R. Evan Ellis, "The Nicaragua Canal: Commercial and Strategic Interests Disguised as a Megaproject," *Latin Trade Business Intelligence*, December 3, 2014, http://latintrade.com/the-nicaragua-canal-commercial-and-strategic-interests-disguised-as-a-megaproject/.

54 These include a hearing in April 2005 by the House Subcommittee on the Western Hemisphere, and by the Senate Foreign Relations Committee in September of the same year. See *China's Foreign Policy and 'Soft Power' in South America, Asia, and Africa* (Washington, DC: Congressional Research Service, 2008), http://fas. org/irp/congress/2008_rpt/crs-china.pdf. See also R. Evan Ellis, "The US, Latin America and China: A 'Triangular Relationship'?" Working Paper, Inter-American Dialogue, 2012, http://www.thedialogue.org/PublicationFiles/IAD8661_China_Triangular0424v2e-may.pdf.

55 Steven Kaplan, "Why China Is Investing $250 billion in Latin America," *Washington Post*, February 4, 2015, https://www.washingtonpost.com/blogs/monkey-cage/wp/2015/02/04/why-china-is-investing-250-billion-in-latin-america/.

56 "1st China–CELAC Ministerial Forum: Big Deal or Missed Opportunity?" *Dialogo Chino*, January 9, 2015, http://dialogochino.net/1st-china-celac-ministerial-forum-big-deal-or-missed-opportunity/.

57 See, for example, R. Evan Ellis, "China's Activities in the Americas," Testimony to the joint hearing of the Subcommittee on the Western Hemisphere and the Subcommittee on Asia and the Pacific, U.S. House of Representatives Foreign Affairs Committee, September 10, 2015, http://docs.house.gov/meetings/FA/FA07/20150910/103931/HHRG-114-FA07-Wstate-EllisE-20150910.pdf.

58 For a discussion of how such an approach is poorly received in Latin America, see Ellis, "The US, Latin America and China."

59 "Operación Conjunta China–Perú de Rescate Medico Humanitario 'Ángel de la Paz'," *Maquina de Combate*, November 24, 2010.

60 As examples of press coverage of the visit, see "Ja Welcomes Chinese Medical Ship," *Jamaica Observer*, October 30, 2011, http://www.jamaicaobserver.com/news/Ja-welcomes-Chinese-medical-ship_10045788.

61 "China's Naval Hospital Ship Calls at U.S. Port," *Xinhua*, November 4, 2015, http://news.xinhuanet.com/english/2015-11/04/c_134781091.htm.

62 Terri Moon Cronk, "USNS Comfort Completes Humanitarian Mission," U.S. Department of Defense, *DOD News*, September 2, 2011, http://www.defense.gov/news/newsarticle.aspx?id=65236.

63 Such access could be bolstered by a multilateral treaty in which each signatory agreed to allow representatives of the committee access to its personnel and documents under specified conditions in the course of reviewing a case.

64 See Burn Loeffke, *China: Our Enemy? A General's Story* (Seattle, WA: Pacific Institute Publishing, 2012), p. 85.

3

CHINA'S ECONOMIC STATECRAFT IN LATIN AMERICA

Evidence from China's Policy Banks

Kevin P. Gallagher and Amos Irwin[1]

Introduction: China's Economic Statecraft in Context

China's global reach is increasingly being felt across the world. Nearly every country now enjoys growing amounts of trade with China. For many, China is now a source of foreign investment as well. The China Investment Corporation, China's sovereign wealth fund, is a growing presence in global equity markets. As Barbara Stallings argues in chapter 4 of this volume, China's state ministries coordinate to provide growing amounts of foreign aid across the world.[2] The People's Bank of China is engaged in creating numerous currency swaps worldwide. And, finally, China's policy banks are providing increasing amounts of finance to sovereign governments.

Scholars both inside and outside of China are attempting to understand the motivations behind China's rapid economic expansion. Drawing on the work of Baldwin, recent authors have classified the manner in which China exerts economic power on a global scale into three categories.[3] First, there is a growing concern that the goal of China's economic activity is to project soft power. Here, China is willing to operate at an economic loss in order to bolster political diplomacy and gain strategic alliances for noneconomic ends.[4] Indeed, this is the driving concern among those who analyze Venezuelan–Chinese economic relations. The second categorization is referred to as extractive diplomacy. Here, China is motivated to invest in natural resources, with little consideration of short-term profit, in order to lock up natural resources for its growing and diversifying economy. For example, scholars have debated whether China is engaging in loans-for-oil mainly in order to secure oil supplies.[5] Finally, the developmental state view holds that China acts as a neo-developmental state that guides state and private sector investments to make a commercial profit.

We examine Chinese policy bank finance against the backdrop of these over-lapping viewpoints. In doing so, we provide the first comprehensive estimates of Chinese finance to sovereign governments in Latin America. We then organize and compare the activities of Chinese policy banks with those of their counterparts in Latin America—international financial institutions (IFIs) and private markets. If China were motivated solely by projecting soft power, we would expect Chinese policy banks to be subsidizing credit to nations that converge with China's geopolitical policy objectives. If China were motivated by the need to lock up natural resources we would see the majority of finance go toward natural resource sectors and that such finance would also be subsidized as a loss to the Chinese policy banks. If China were primarily motivated by the commercial objectives of a modern developmental state, we would expect that China's finance would be offered at market rates regardless of politics or the share of natural resource extraction in loan portfolios.

We find that Chinese finance in Latin America is now larger than finance from the World Bank, Inter-American Development Bank (IDB), and United States Export–Import Bank on an annual basis. Moreover, we find that the bulk of Chinese finance goes toward natural resources and natural resource-linked infrastructure projects. However, such investments do not track political alignments and are largely offered at market rates. Where Chinese rates are measurably more favorable than IFIs or private markets, it is due to China's commodity-backed risk instruments and the way the Chinese structure financing between sovereign governments and Chinese state-owned enterprises (SOEs). Therefore, we conclude that Chinese finance in Latin America is motivated by the goals of a developmental state. In the process, China is indeed securing a great deal of natural resources, but without taking a great loss. China is also projecting soft power by focusing on infrastructure and industrialization versus the development paradigms projected by the World Bank and the IDB.

Chinese Lenders in Latin America

China's central government owns both of China's leading financiers to Latin America, the China Development Bank (CDB) and the China Export–Import Bank (China Ex-Im). During 1994 reforms of the financial sector, the Chinese government created CDB and China Ex-Im as "policy banks," whose loans would explicitly support the government's policy objectives.[6] Prior to 1994, policy lending had been the responsibility of the "Big Four" Chinese banks (Bank of China, China Construction Bank, Agricultural Bank of China, and ICBC), so the new policy banks were designed to free the Big Four to act as commercial banks. In separating policy from commercial lending, the government sought to reduce bank managers' moral hazard. If managers could blame all their losses on policy loans, they had an incentive to direct their commercial loans toward high-risk, high-return projects.[7] The creation of separate policy banks would hold the commercial banks accountable for rational, market-based lending.

CDB and China Ex-Im follow slightly different mandates, which both revolve around strengthening Chinese industry. CDB mainly supports China's macroeconomic policies—laid out in the Five-Year Plans—focusing on eight areas of development: electric power, road construction, railway, petroleum and petrochemical, coal, postal and telecommunications, agriculture and related industries, and public infrastructure.[8] An estimated 73.7 percent of CDB's total new loans went to these sectors.[9] In contrast, the China Ex-Im Bank's mandate is to: "facilitate the export and import of Chinese mechanical and electronic products, complete sets of equipment and new- and high-tech products, assist Chinese companies with comparative advantages in their offshore project contracting and outbound investment, and promote international economic cooperation and trade."[10] It achieves these objectives through the use of export credits, loans to overseas construction and investment projects, and concessional loans.

Although the government designed the reforms to divorce policy and commercial lending, Chinese banks continue to mix these two lending categories. Steinfeld points out that the government still forces the nominally commercial banks to bail out state-owned enterprises.[11] At the same time, the policy banks have become quite commercial. Former CDB head Chen Yuan married the bank's policy objectives with sound commercial loans so that CDB has high profits and a balance sheet that is even healthier than those of China's big commercial banks.[12] China Ex-Im Bank also lends much of its capital at or near commercial rates and boasts a low share of nonperforming loans.[13] Ex-Premier Wen Jiabao announced in 2007 that the policy banks eventually would be converted into commercial banks, but the process stalled following the 2008–09 global financial crisis.[14]

The Chinese government's Going Global policy has brought this amalgamation of commercial and policy lending to the international stage. In 1998, then President Jiang Zemin championed the internationalization of Chinese investment and lending. He argued that "Regions like Africa, the Middle East, Central Asia, and South America with large developing countries [have] very big markets and abundant resources; we should take advantage of the opportunity to get in."[15] As Downs points out, CDB is the main bank supporting this strategy with loans to Chinese and foreign companies overseas.[16] Bräutigam adds that "the Eximbank has been at the center of China's strategy of 'going global.'"[17] Over the last five years, both banks have reached new heights in international lending.

There is no easy way to measure Chinese bank loans to Latin America. Unlike the World Bank and the IDB, Chinese banks do not regularly publish detailed figures regarding their loan activities. We follow the lead of scholars such as Bräutigam,[18] who examine government, bank, and press reports in both

China and borrowing countries in order to compile a list of loans and their characteristics. This method is highly imperfect. Although we have gone to great lengths to ensure reliability by confirming reports in both China and Latin America and the Caribbean (LAC), our estimate should not be taken as a precise figure. On the one hand, we may have underestimated Chinese finance in Latin America, because we do not examine many loans under US$50 million. On the other hand, we may have overestimated the total in the event that the most recent loans are partially or entirely cancelled or if a line of credit is not fully committed.

We consulted a wide variety of publicly accessible sources to gather details on each loan. We found loan agreements published by the Venezuelan and Bolivian governments in their Official Gazettes. Brazil's state-owned oil company, Petrobras, is a publicly traded corporation; we uncovered the interest rate on CDB's loan-for-oil deals with Petrobras by examining the company's filings with the US Securities and Exchange Commission (SEC). We also discovered Chinese loans in the Jamaican and Venezuelan government's annual filings with the SEC. We classified loans as commercial or concessional based on reports from Chinese embassies in the borrowing countries. We found details on Brazilian and Ecuadorian loans-for-oil in local newspaper interviews with the countries' finance ministers. We only include one detail that is not publicly accessible online—the interest rate on the 2008 China Ex-Im Bank loan to the Chinalco company in Peru, which we learned in interviews with company officials in Lima. We supplemented and double-checked all sources with newspaper articles or governments both in the borrowing countries and in China. We omit loans that have not been confirmed by reliable sources on both sides of the Pacific.

Acquiring World Bank and IDB loan information to compare with the Chinese loans was more difficult than we had anticipated. The Western and international financial institutions publish lists of loans in their annual reports, and the World Bank even publishes individual loan contracts—but it withholds key details. The World Bank considers the interest rates on outstanding loans to be proprietary information and refused to provide it officially for this study. For interest rates, which are the most important indicator of the fairness of a loan, we had to approach these otherwise transparent institutions in the same way as their Chinese counterparts. We acquired World Bank, IDB, and Andean Development Corporation (CAF) interest rate information by combing through SEC filings by the borrowing countries, as well as a confidential interview we conducted with a World Bank staff member.

Since 2009, CDB and China Ex-Im have overtaken the World Bank and IDB in finance to Latin America governments (Table 3.1). Prior to 2007, China's annual financing to Latin American governments and state firms, for instance, had never exceeded US$1 billion, but in 2007 it jumped to US$4.8 billion. In 2009, it more than tripled to US$15.7 billion, in line with the totals from the

TABLE 3.1 Comparison of Chinese and IFI Bank Loans to Latin America

	Total loans							
	2005	2006	2007	2008	2009	2010	2011	Total
China	0.3	0	4.8	0.4	15.7	35.6	7.9	64.7
World Bank	5.2	5.9	4.6	4.7	14	13.9	9.6	57.9
IDB	7.1	6.4	7.7	11.2	15.5	12.5	10.9	71.3
US Ex-Im	0	0.1	0	0	1.1	1	2.7	5

Note: In US$ billions. Chinese loan data includes only those loans distributed to LAC governments or state-owned enterprises.

World Bank and IDB. In 2010, finance doubled to US$35 billion, more than the World Bank and IDB combined. Since 2005, about 80 percent of this financing has come from CDB and 10 percent from China Ex-Im.[19] Approximately two-thirds of funding was given as loans, about 25 percent as credit lines, often to individual Chinese companies, and the remainder as framework agreements.

Neither Soft Power nor Extractive Diplomacy

If China was engaged solely in projecting soft power or motivated by resource security, it would be financing Latin American governments at a loss in exchange for political favors or natural resources. This section of the chapter shows that Chinese finance is indeed different from finance from the IFIs in the sense that it does indeed track the natural resource and infrastructure sectors. However, this finance does not appear to be politically motivated and is offered at market rates.

Chinese lending differs from IFI and export credit agency (ECA) loans in many of its characteristics, starting with size. Chinese banks offer much larger loans than the IFIs. Chinese banks lent 92 percent of their funds as packages of US$1 billion or greater, compared to 20 percent for the World Bank, 11 percent for IDB, and 8 percent for the US Ex-Im Bank. In addition, Chinese lending differs with regard to its higher interest rates. Rather than trying to undercut IFIs or export–import banks by offering low interest rates, as some have argued, Chinese banks generally charge higher rates. And, contrary to popular belief, Chinese banks charge commercial rates on their largest loans. Still, some small loans, most categorized as foreign aid, do carry concessional or subsidized interest rates.

CDB offers mostly commercial interest rates that exceed the World Bank, IDB, and CAF rates[20] (Table 3.2). As one example, in 2010 CDB offered Argentina a US$10 billion loan at 600 basis points above LIBOR. The same year, CAF's rates on loans to Argentina ranged from 155 to 235 basis points above LIBOR. The World Bank's International Bank for Reconstruction and

TABLE 3.2 CDB and World Bank Loan Interest Rates

Year	Lender	Borrowing country	Borrower	Spread (basis points above LIBOR)	Amount ($m)	Payment period	Purchase requirements	Loan-for-oil
2010	CDB	Argentina	Government	600	10,000	19	Yes	No
2009	CDB	Mexico	América Móvil	>100	1,000	10	Yes	No
2009	CDB	Brazil	Petrobras	280	10,000	10	Yes	Oil
2010	CDB	Venezuela	PDVSA and BANDES	50–285	20,000	10	Yes	Oil
2000	World Bank	Brazil	Electrobras	30–55	43.4	15	No	No
2007	World Bank	Chile	Government	5	34.8	10	No	No
2010	World Bank	Argentina	Government	85	30	25	No	No

Sources: Chinese, Inter-American Dialogue Database; World Bank, Interview, World Bank lending department official, 2011.

Development (IBRD) charged Argentina a spread of roughly 85 basis points.[21] The Chinese interest rate is hundreds of basis points larger than both CAF and IBRD rates. In 2009, CDB gave Brazil a US$10 billion loan at 280 basis points over LIBOR. The IBRD gave Brazil a US$43.4 million loan in 2000 at a variable spread of 30 to 55 basis points. Although we were unable to confirm IDB interest rates on specific loans, the general rates posted on both IDB and IBRD web pages are well below the Chinese rates.[22] CDB charges much higher interest rates than these IFIs, despite the prevailing conventional wisdom to the contrary.

China Ex-Im Bank subsidizes its smaller loans on the grounds that they constitute development aid for low-income countries, although these loans constitute only a fraction of total Chinese lending. The subsidized rates on small loans are somewhat lower than those of the US Ex-Im Bank (Table 3.3). China Ex-Im Bank's lowest-interest loans were its 2 percent loans to Jamaica in 2007 and Bolivia in 2009. In order to offer these loans, China Ex-Im Bank receives subsidies directly from the Ministry of Finance.[23] China budgets these subsidies as official development aid, although OECD countries prohibit mixing export credits with development aid. To compare China and US Ex-Im interest rates on loans to different countries, we use the OECD's country risk premiums to compensate for the fact that some countries are riskier than others.[24] While the US Ex-Im Bank charged 1.5 percent to 2.5 percent above the OECD risk premium, China Ex-Im Bank's interest rates on small loans ranged from 0.31 percent below the premium to 0.69 percent above it. From the US Ex-Im Bank's perspective, these rates undercut US Ex-Im rates and make Chinese deals more competitive. From China Ex-Im's perspective, it is blending export promotion with development aid to offer lower-cost options to countries in need. In any case, these loans constitute only 1.2 percent of total Chinese lending to the region.

The bulk of China Ex-Im's funding, like that of CDB, comes at higher interest rates. Eighty-two percent of China Ex-Im funding to Latin American borrowers carried commercial interest rates well above those of US Ex-Im.[25] These commercial-rate loans include a US$2.4 billion loan for the Baha Mar resort in the Bahamas and two loans to finance dams in Ecuador totaling US$2.2 billion.[26] China Ex-Im Bank is not undercutting US Ex-Im on these loans; it charged 6.9 and 6.35 percent interest on the Ecuador loans, about 2 percent higher than US Ex-Im rates even adjusting for Ecuador's high risk premium.[27]

Chinese banks also differ from IFIs by directing the majority of their loans to industry and infrastructure. Chinese banks channel 87 percent of their loans into the energy, mining, infrastructure, transportation, and housing (EMITH) sectors (Table 3.4). Only 29 percent of IDB loans and 34 percent of World Bank loans go to the EMITH sectors. Instead, the IDB and World Bank direct more than a third of their loans toward the health, social, and environment sectors, which receive no Chinese investment.

TABLE 3.3 China and US Ex–Im Bank Loan Interest Rates

Year	Lender	Borrowing country	Borrower	Interest rate	Rate minus OECD risk premium	Amount ($m)	Payment period	Purpose
2007	China Ex-Im	Jamaica	Government	2	−0.31	45	20	Convention center
2009	China Ex-Im	Bolivia	YPFB	2	−0.31	60	20	Oil and gas
2010	China Ex-Im	Ecuador	Government	6.9	4.39	1,682.70	15	Dam
2010	China Ex-Im	Ecuador	Government	6.35	4.39	571	15	Dam
2010	China Ex-Im	Jamaica	Government	3	0.69	340	5	Roads
2009	US Ex-Im	Mexico	Pemex	3.81	2.04	600	10	Oil
2009	US Ex-Im	Mexico	Electrica del Valle de Mexico	4.3	2.53	81	4	Wind energy
2009	US Ex-Im	Brazil	MRS Logistica	3.3	1.53	87		Trains
2010	US Ex-Im	Domincan Republic	Pueblo Viejo Dominicana	4.02	1.8	375		Vehicles
2010	US Ex-Im	Honduras	Energia Eolica de Honduras	4.42	2.11	159	18	Wind energy

Sources: Chinese, Inter-American Dialogue Database; US, US Ex-Im Annual Reports.

TABLE 3.4 Bank Loans to Latin America by Sector, 2005–11

	Total ($m)	World Bank ($m)	IDB ($m)	Chinese ($m)
Health	8,135	5,993	2,142	0
Education	3,157	1,775	1,382	0
Water, environment	6,794	2,222	4,573	0
Public administration	8,762	4,798	3,964	0
Finance, trade	5,849	2,169	2,030	1,650
Housing, infrastructure	51,900	4,490	5,551	41,858
Energy, mining	9,824	1,967	2,713	5,144
Other	6,809	96	1,263	5,450
Total	101,228	23,510	23,616	54,102

Sources: Chinese, Inter-American Dialogue Database (including Chinese loans to LAC private companies); World Bank and IDB, respective Annual Reports.

Note: World Bank and IDB data from 2010–11 only.

Chinese banks also provided financing to a significantly different set of countries than the IFIs and Western banks. From 2005 to 2011, Chinese banks dedicated 60 percent of their lending to Venezuela and Ecuador. This is an enormous share considering that these countries make up only 8 percent of the LAC region's population and 7 percent of its GDP. Over the same period, Venezuela and Ecuador received 9 percent of IDB loans and less than 1 percent of World Bank loans (Table 3.5). IFIs and Western banks instead dominate lending to Mexico, Colombia, and Peru.

From 2005 to 2011, only Brazil and Argentina had received significant shares of finance from both Chinese and Western sources. In both cases, the vast majority of the Chinese funds came from a single loan. In the case of Brazil, 85 percent

TABLE 3.5 Recipients of World Bank, IDB, and Chinese Lending, 2005–11

	Total ($m)	World Bank ($m)	IDB ($m)	China ($m)
Venezuela	46,148	0	6,148	40,000
Brazil	42,068	15,200	14,747	12,121
Argentina	30,532	8,209	10,923	11,400
Mexico	29,705	15,395	13,309	1,000
Colombia	13,030	6,293	6,662	75
Ecuador	10,766	487	3,025	7,254
Peru	8,968	3,450	3,318	2,200
Guatemala	3,246	1,485	1,761	0
El Salvador	3,227	1,206	2,021	0
Panama	3,205	757	2,448	0
Other	25,044	5,373	14,290	5,381
Total	215,940	57,856	78,652	79,431

Sources: World Bank and IDB, respective Annual Reports; Chinese, Inter-American Dialogue Database (including loans to private enterprises in LAC).

of the lending came from a US$10 billion loan issued in 2009 to fund an ambitious offshore oil project using Chinese inputs. In Argentina, US$10 billion came in the form of a single loan to buy Chinese trains.

The country difference is especially stark for large loans. Among the World Bank, IDB, and US Ex-Im Bank loans of US$1 billion or greater, 93 percent went to the Latin American economic powerhouses with good credit ratings— Brazil and Mexico. Chinese banks, on the other hand, gave 64 percent of their large loans to high-risk Ecuador and Venezuela, which received no large loans from the IFIs or US Ex-Im.

Chinese banks differ from the IFIs in a number of other ways. Unlike the IFIs, they do not seek to reform their borrowers by making the loans conditional on internal policy changes. Instead, like ECAs, Chinese banks almost always tie their loans to the purchase of Chinese goods. We found conditions in most arrangements requiring the borrower to purchase Chinese construction, oil, telecommunications, satellite, and train equipment. Some set aside only a small portion of tied funds, like CDB's US$1 billion loan-for-oil to Ecuador in 2010, which mandated 20 percent Chinese purchases. At the other extreme, China Ex-Im Bank gives 100 percent export credits, such as a US$1.7 billion loan to pay a Chinese company to build the Coca-Codo Sinclair hydroelectric dam in Ecuador in 2010. When Venezuela committed to spend the majority of its US$20 billion loan in 2010 on Chinese goods and services, CDB denominated half in Chinese yuan.[28] This is the largest Chinese-currency loan to date, but China Ex-Im has also issued yuan-denominated lines of credit to Jamaica and Bolivia for equipment and construction.[29]

Chinese banks have also begun cooperating with state-owned oil companies to arrange loan packages known as "loans-for-oil." Loans-for-oil deals with Latin America have reached US$53 billion in only five years, more than two-thirds of China's total commitments to the region (Table 3.6). Venezuela has negotiated five such loans since 2007, totaling US$36 billion. Brazil signed one for US$10 billion in commitments in 2009. Ecuador signed a US$1 billion loan-for-oil deal in 2009 and a second in 2010. In 2011, it added two more worth a total of US$3 billion.

A loan-for-oil deal generally combines a loan agreement and an oil-sale agreement that involves two countries' state-owned banks and oil companies. The money flows in a triangular pattern. First, CDB grants a billion-dollar loan to an oil-exporting government like that of Ecuador. Ecuador's state oil company, Petroecuador, signs a contract to ship hundreds of thousands of barrels of oil to China every day for the life of the loan. Chinese oil companies then buy the oil at market prices and deposit their payments into Petroecuador's CDB bank account. CDB withdraws the interest payments directly from Petroecuador's account.

We conclude that loans from Chinese banks and IFIs do not overlap significantly in Latin America because each gives different-size loans at varying interest rates to diverse sectors in different countries. Chinese loans are larger,

TABLE 3.6 Chinese Loans-For-Oil in Latin America, 2007–2012

Year	Borrowing country	Borrower	Lender	Amount ($m)	Purpose
2007	Venezuela	BANDES and PDVSA	CDB	4,000	Funding infrastructure, other projects
2008	Venezuela	BANDES and PDVSA	CDB	4,000	Infrastructure, including satellite
2009	Brazil	Petrobras	CDB	10,000	Pre-salt oil technology
2009	Ecuador	Petroecuador	PetroChina	1,000	Advance payment for Petroecuador oil
2010	Ecuador	Petroecuador	CDB	1,000	80% discretionary, 20% oil-related
2010	Venezuela	BANDES and PDVSA	CDB	20,000	Funding infrastructure
2011	Ecuador	Petroecuador	CDB	2,000	70% discretionary, 30% oil-related
2011	Ecuador	Petroecuador	PetroChina	1,000	Advance payment for Petroecuador oil
2011	Venezuela	PDVSA	CDB	4,000	Infrastructure
2012	Ecuador	Government	CDB	2,000	Budget deficit
2012	Venezuela	BANDES and PDVSA	CDB	4,000	Joint infrastructure financing fund
Total				53,000	

Source: Inter-American Dialogue Database.

carry higher interest rates, fall in the EMITH sectors, and are concentrated in Ecuador and Venezuela. The IFIs give smaller loans, with lower interest rates, to a wider range of sectors including health, environment, and public administration, and direct far more funding to pro-US governments like Mexico and Colombia. Both Chinese banks and IFIs give substantial loans to Brazil and Argentina.

Comparison with the Private Market

Chinese lending has more in common with the traditional source of large, market-rate infrastructure funding for Latin America, which comes mainly from the private banks and the sovereign bond market. Latin American governments have traditionally relied on sovereign bond emissions and loans from Western commercial banks for large infrastructure and industry loans. Unlike the IFIs, these lenders prefer infrastructure and industry loans in order to guarantee their profits. The banks and bond lenders do not subsidize interest rates, so that borrowing governments pay a high premium for their high-risk home markets.

We used two sets of financial data to assess the private market rate that should be compared to the Chinese interest rates. First, we looked at Bloomberg data on coupon rates for sovereign debt emissions by the borrowing governments. If the governments had not issued sovereign bonds in approximately the same year with similar maturity, we found coupon rates for sovereign debt emissions by other governments with the same debt rating. Second, we consulted the sovereign debt interest rate according to JP Morgan's Emerging Markets Bond Index Plus (EMBI+). The EMBI+ spread represents the interest rate spread above US Treasuries of a government's previously issued dollar-denominated sovereign debt and Brady bonds as traded on the secondary market.

Our comparison found that Chinese interest rates are closer to market rates than IFI rates, though measurably lower. For example, Ecuador is paying 6.9 percent and 6.35 percent interest on two 2010 dam loans from China Ex-Im. CDB is charging Ecuador 7.25 percent for the first loan-for-oil, 6 percent for the second, and 6.9 percent for the third. There is no easy private market equivalent, since Ecuador has not issued sovereign bonds since 2005, when its ten-year bonds paid 9.375 percent. The average coupon rate for governments with B− Bloomberg Composite Ratings for 7- to 23-year maturity in 2009 to 2011 was 7.8 percent.[30] The EMBI+ spread on Ecuador's 2005 bonds in the secondary market in 2010 to 2011 ranged from 7.5 percent to 10 percent.[31] The Chinese rates are thus similar but lower.

In Argentina's case, the Chinese rates also appear similar but lower. Argentina paid 600 basis points above LIBOR on a 2010 CDB loan, which today adds up to roughly 6.5 percent. The same year, Argentina offered sovereign debt with similar maturity at rates ranging from 7.82 percent to 8.75 percent. As with Ecuador, the average coupon rate for governments with B− Bloomberg

Composite Ratings for 7- to 23-year maturity in 2009 to 2011 was 7.8 percent.[32] JP Morgan's EMBI+ spread for Argentina in 2009 to 2011 ranged from 8 to 10 percent.[33] Thus the Chinese rate clearly falls below the private market rates.

Brazil's state-owned oil company, Petrobras, also received China's financing at lower rates than it can access on the private market. Its US$10 billion loan from CDB in 2009 carried an interest rate of 2.8 percent over LIBOR, or roughly 3 to 4 percent. Also in 2009, Petrobras issued corporate bonds worth US$1.5 billion and US$2.5 billion at 6.875 and 5.75 percent, respectively.[34] Again, Chinese banks charge less than the private market.

In Venezuela's case, the Chinese banks charged rates well below those of the private market. CDB gave the US$20 billion loan at a floating rate of 50 to 285 basis points over LIBOR, or roughly between 1 percent and 4 percent. Meanwhile, Venezuela has issued sovereign debt at rates more than twice as high—between 7.75 percent and 12.75 percent from 2009 to 2012.[35] Its EMBI+ spread for the same period ranged from 10 to 12 percent.[36] Compared to the cases of Ecuador and Argentina, this interest rate differential is surprisingly large.

This difference stems from the Chinese banks' use of equipment purchase requirements and oil supply contracts. The purchase requirements allow Chinese banks to reduce their exposure to default risk and offer lower interest rates. China's 2010 "loan" of US$10 billion to Argentina is a credit line for state-owned Chinese railway companies. Even if Argentina defaults on the loan, the Chinese government doesn't lose everything—the railway companies have still made billions of dollars' worth of sales. As a result, CDB can charge Argentina a lower rate on its loan than private lenders, which have no affiliated railway companies.[37]

The loans-for-oil arrangement allows China to make loans to otherwise non-creditworthy borrowers by reducing the risk of borrower default. As CDB founder Chen Yuan has stated, "backing loans with oil shipments effectively keeps risks to a minimum level."[38] CDB can siphon interest directly out of the oil payment, ensuring that, if the country wants to export oil to China, it will have to pay back the loan. Lower default risk means lower risk premiums and reduced interest rates. Looking at the low interest rates on Venezuela and Ecuador's loans-for-oil, it does appear that CDB has reduced its risk considerably through the loan-for-oil arrangements.

Some have suggested that China's oil contracts are exploiting the Latin American borrowers, but there is no evidence for this assertion. In fact, financing terms in loans-for-oil agreements seem better for the South American countries. Ecuador is the only country to reveal details on its loans-for-oil. Ecuadorian oil analyst Fernando Villavicencio argued that the terms, which include crude oil differentials and deal premiums, "represent million-dollar losses for the Ecuadorian state."[39] However, the prices that Ecuador published are in line with its recent prices for commercial deals.[40] All reports on Venezuela and Brazil's loans-for-oil indicate that they are also based on market prices.[41]

The rates of Chinese banks may also be lower than private rates owing to the Chinese government's willingness to retaliate using other levers under its control. When foreign governments have threatened the Chinese government economically, the Chinese government has retaliated using entirely separate economic means. For example, when Argentina filed anti-dumping lawsuits against Chinese manufacturing products, China cut off imports of products like soy oil and beef. Argentina withdrew its anti-dumping cases and the imports resumed.[42] China is willing to retaliate across the economic spectrum using its wide array of government bodies and state-run enterprises. Thus, foreign governments are less likely to default on Chinese loans compared to those of a private bank with no outside means of retaliation.

Explaining the Borrowing Countries

These lower interest rates allow nations with little access to global capital markets to borrow when they cannot afford the interest rates charged by the private market. Argentina and Ecuador have had difficulty accessing global credit markets given that they defaulted on their sovereign debt in 2001 and 2008–09, respectively.[43] The Venezuelan government has also alienated private investors. As a result, the sovereign debt markets charge Argentina, Ecuador, and Venezuela roughly 8 to 12 percent more than US Treasuries (Table 3.7). These are four to six times higher than interest rate spreads for South American countries with similar-sized economies. For example, Colombia and Peru pay roughly 2 percent more than Treasuries.[44] Chinese

TABLE 3.7 Chinese Lending and Government Debt Ratings

Country	Percentage of Chinese lending	OECD risk rating	OECD premium	S&P rating	EMBI+ debt spread
Chile	0	2	162	A+	
Panama	0	3	177	BBB–	186
Mexico	0	3	177	BBB	188
Peru	0	3	177	BBB	218
Brazil	13	3	177	BBB	219
Costa Rica	0	3	177	BB	
Colombia	0	4	198	BBB–	195
Bolivia	1	6	231	B+	
Jamaica	1	6	231	B–	
Ecuador	12	7	251	B–	838
Argentina	14	7	251	B	935
Venezuela	56	7	251	B+	1220

Sources: Inter-American Dialogue Database; JP Morgan, "Index Group: EMBI+ (JP Morgan)"; OECD, "2011 ASU"; OECD, "Country Risk Classifications."

banks loaned disproportionately large amounts to these high-risk countries, compensating for the lack of sovereign debt lending.

Owing to China's risk-reducing arrangements, including equipment purchase requirements and loans-for-oil, Chinese banks have taken up lending to risky countries abandoned by conventional sovereign lenders. As energy economist Roger Tissot argues, "Chinese financing is often the 'lender of last resort.' It is not a cheap one, but due to the concern the international financial community has over Venezuela and Ecuador, and the large risk premiums they would charge, Chinese lending is an attractive option."[45] Indeed, China's surrogate sovereign lending has helped Ecuador heal after its default by covering its budget deficit. Only two years after the default, Ecuador had largely regained investor confidence. Government bonds are performing better than any others in Latin America. Ecuador's sovereign debt spreads dropped from crisis-time values of over 40 percent down to 6.2 percent in 2013.[46] Owing to the influx of Chinese funding, government investment has been able to drive record economic growth.[47] By taking the place of shell-shocked sovereign lenders, China has given Ecuador a second chance to rebuild investor confidence.

China's choice of borrowing countries may seem to support the soft power argument, but in fact it lends greater credence to the commercial argument. Since the mainstay of Chinese funding goes to the populist governments of Venezuela, Ecuador, and Argentina, it might seem that China's main motive is to build a South–South left-of-center alliance. However, these are also the countries that have scared off conventional private debt financiers, which now charge astronomical rates. Since Chinese banks face lower risks as a result of purchase requirements, loans-for-oil, and outside means of retaliation, these countries offer the greatest opportunities for profit. If China were seeking to curry favor among populist governments, it would spread the money out to Bolivia, Cuba, El Salvador, and others rather than showering Venezuela with more billion-dollar loans. Venezuela is eager to deepen its political alliance with China, although the latter has kept its distance from Venezuela's political rhetoric. Moreover, if China were looking to shore up its soft power, one would expect such finance to be greatly subsidized. Instead, as we have shown, the banks are lending at rates well above those of the IFIs and only slightly below those of the private market.

One might also suggest that China's choice of countries supports the resource-seeking hypothesis, but this also seems secondary to commercial profit. We do find some evidence that a large share of Chinese finance to Latin America targets the infrastructure and industrial sectors in countries richly endowed with natural resources. However, if the underlying goal were to lock up resources at the expense of short-term profits, China's policy banks would be offering concessional rates instead of charging the full cost of financing. China's infrastructure loans would also focus on extracting the resources, as with roads, power plants, or ports, rather than centering on housing and telecommunications.

It is important to acknowledge that a globalizing developmental state also exudes soft power, but in a different way. Rather than using Chinese finance to sway governments for geopolitical ends, the Chinese policy banks are implicitly exhibiting a different model of development and sovereign finance. Chinese finance is larger, set at longer terms, and channeled toward a difference set of sectors than loans made by Western financial entities. Moreover, Chinese loans have none of the controversial conditionalities inherent in Western finance. Finally, Chinese finance takes on more risk given the nature of commodity-backed financing and purchase relationships with Chinese firms. In the long run, if these financial arrangements succeed relative to the spotty record of Western-backed development banks,[48] the Chinese will be sending a message about larger development finance models. At this writing, however, it is simply too soon to tell.

Conclusion

In 2010, Chinese policy banks overtook the World Bank and the IDB in lending to Latin America. Chinese finance has much in common with the private sovereign debt market in terms of large loan size, high interest rates, and a focus on industry and infrastructure. The main difference is that Chinese banks offer slightly lower interest rates. The rates are not low enough to be considered concessional subsidies to support a political agenda. Instead, the rates may well reflect lower risk. China ties its loans to equipment purchase requirements and oil purchase contracts in order to reduce risk and offer finance to countries that otherwise cannot afford it. While it can be difficult to distinguish between the three types of economic statecraft outlined above, we find that the driving force behind China's economic statecraft is largely commercial in nature. We do acknowledge, however, that commercial-led motivations also implicitly project soft power and explicitly engage in extractive activity, although we see these motivations as secondary. We conclude that China's Going Global strategy is just that—a strategy by a neo-developmental state seeking to support national champions in gaining global market share in order to benefit the Chinese political economy.

Notes

1 A version of this chapter was previously published in *Pacific Affairs*, vol. 88, no. 1 (March 2015).
2 See Barbara Stallings, "Chinese Aid to Latin America: Trying to Win Friends and Influence People," Paper presented at a Workshop on China–Latin American Relations, University of Southern California, Los Angeles, August 5, 2013.
3 David Baldwin, *Economic Statecraft* (Princeton, NJ: Princeton University Press, 1985); Deborah Bräutigam and Tang Xiaoyang, "Economic Statecraft in China's New Overseas Special Economic Zones: Soft Power, Business, or Resource Security?" *International*

Affairs, vol. 88, no. 4 (2012), pp. 799–816; Shaun Breslin, "Understanding China's Regional Rise: Interpretations, Identities, and Implications," *International Affairs*, vol. 85, no. 4 (July 2010), pp. 817–35.

4 See for example Joshua Kurlantzick, *Charm Offensive: How China's Soft Power Is Transforming the World* (New Haven, CT: Yale University Press, 2007).

5 C.Z. Chao, "'Loans for Oil'—China's New Search for Overseas Oil Sources," *Economic Research Guide*, no. 13 (2010); EIU, "Brazil/China Economy: Deeper Inroads—Latin America," *Economist*, August 16, 2010; Wenran Jiang, *The Dragon Returns: Canada in China's Quest for Energy Security*, China Papers 19 (Toronto: Canadian International Council, 2010); Cynthia Arnson and Jeffrey Davidow, *China, Latin America, and the United States: The New Triangle* (Washington, DC: Woodrow Wilson International Center for Scholars, January 2011).

6 Deborah Bräutigam, *The Dragon's Gift: The Real Story of China in Africa* (Oxford, UK: Oxford University Press, 2009), p. 79.

7 Edward Steinfeld, *Forging Reform in China: The Fate of State-owned Industry* (Cambridge, UK: Cambridge University Press, 1998), p. 71.

8 China Development Bank, "80% of CDB's Loans Go to Eight Areas Including Electric Power, Roads and Railways—CDB Vigorously Supports Development of Real Economy," June 13, 2013, http://www.cdb.com.cn/english/NewsInfo.asp?NewsId=4590 (accessed May 20, 2015).

9 China Development Bank, "Strategic Focus," n.d., http://www.cdb.com.cn/english/Column.asp?ColumnId=86 (accessed November 18, 2014).

10 China Export–Import Bank, "The Export–Import Bank of China," n.d., http://english.eximbank.gov.cn/profile/intro.shtml (accessed October 10, 2013).

11 Steinfeld, *Forging Reform in China*, p. 70.

12 Erica Downs, *Inside China, Inc: China Development Bank's Cross-Border Energy Deals*, John L. Thornton China Center Monograph Series no. 3 (Washington, DC: Brookings Institution, March 2011), p. 11, http://www.brookings.edu/~/media/research/files/papers/2011/3/21%20china%20energy%20downs/0321_china_energy_downs.pdf (accessed November 18, 2014).

13 Bräutigam, *Dragon's Gift*, p. 114; Downs, *Inside China, Inc.*

14 Downs, *Inside China, Inc.*

15 Yuan Chen, "The Shape and Significance of Jiang Zemin's 'Going Abroad' Policy" (in Chinese), *Literature of the Chinese Communist Party*, no. 1 (2009), http://mall.cnki.net/magazine/article/DANG200901013.htm (accessed July 7, 2016).

16 Downs, *Inside China, Inc.*

17 Bräutigam, *Dragon's Gift*, p. 112.

18 Ibid.

19 For up-to-date statistics, see Boston University Global Economic Governance Initiative and Tufts University Global Development and Environment Institute, "China–Latin America Finance Database," http://thedialogue.org/map_list.

20 World Bank rates are not officially concessional, but it offers interest rates that are far lower than those available to these countries in the private market. As a result, the borrowers themselves recognize World Bank funding as concessional: South African National Treasury, "Description of the Republic of South Africa," Exhibit 99D to Form 18-K, U.S. Securities and Exchange Commission, 2007, http://www.sec.gov/Archives/edgar/data/932419/000095013607008246/file3.htm (accessed October 10, 2013).

21 World Bank Treasury, "IBRD Lending Rates and Loan Charges," 2010, http://treasury.worldbank.org/bdm/htm/ibrd.html (accessed December 20, 2011); Republic of Argentina, "Form 18-K: Annual Report," United States Securities and Exchange Commission, December 31, 2010, http://www.sec.gov/Archives/edgar/data/914021/000090342311000486/roa-18k_0928.htm (accessed February 17, 2013).

22 World Bank Treasury, "IBRD Lending Rates and Loan Charges"; IDB, "Current and Historic Loan Charges for Ordinary Capital Loans," IDB Finance website, 2013, http://idbdocs.iadb.org/wsdocs/getdocument.aspx?docnum=35769969 (accessed February 16, 2013).

23 AFP, "Bolivian Army Buys 6 Chinese H425 Helicopters," XAirforces Aviation Society website, December 22, 2011, http://www.xairforces.net/newsd.asp?news id=739&newst=1 (accessed January 10, 2012); Deborah Bräutigam, "Aid 'With Chinese Characteristics': Chinese Foreign Aid and Development Finance Meet the OECD-DAC Aid Regime," *Journal of International Development*, vol. 23, no. 5 (2011), p. 756.

24 OECD, "2011 ASU: Quarterly Update of MRS and Resulting MPR—Q4/2011," 2011, http://www.oecd.org/dataoecd/7/4/47652563.pdf (accessed December 20, 2011); OECD, "Country Risk Classifications of the Participants to the Arrangement on Officially Supported Export Credits," 2011, http://www.oecd.org/dataoecd/47/29/3782900.pdf (accessed December 20, 2011).

25 This figure excludes one joint loan from China Ex-Im and Bank of China for which we found no interest rate information.

26 Ministry of Foreign Affairs of the People's Republic of China, Interview with Ambassador to the Bahamas Hu Shan by *Xinhua* reporters (in Chinese), 2011, http://www.fmprc.gov.cn/chn/gxh/wzb/zwbd/dszlsjt/t833738.htm (accessed January 12, 2012).

27 Embassy of the People's Republic of China to the Republic of Ecuador, "Ecuadorian Embassy Holds Meeting to Explain Coca-Codo Sinclair Dam Project" (in Chinese), Embassy website, 2010, http://ec.china-embassy.org/chn/jmwl/t675731.htm (accessed January 12, 2012).

28 José de Córdoba, "China-Oil Deal Gives Chávez a Leg Up," *Wall Street Journal*, November 9, 2011, http://online.wsj.com/article/SB10001424052970203733504577026073045462.html (accessed December 20, 2011).

29 Urban Development Corporation, "Montego Bay Convention Centre," September 2009, http://www.udcja.com/Fact%20Sheet/Fact_sheet_ MontegoBayConCnt.pdf (accessed January 10, 2012); E. Morales, "Ley No 187: Ley de 22 de Noviembre de 2011," *Gaceta Oficial de Bolivia*, 2011, http://www.gacetaoficialdebolivia.gob.bo/edicions/view/315NEC (accessed January 10, 2012).

30 Search for sovereign bonds rated B− with maturity 7 to 23 years, 2009–11, via Bloomberg LP (accessed October 10, 2013).

31 JP Morgan, "Index Group: EMBI+ (JP Morgan)," *Financial Bonds Information*, 2011, http://www.cbonds.info/cis/eng/index/index_detail/group_id/1/ (accessed December 20, 2011).

32 Search for sovereign bonds rated B− with maturity 7 to 23 years, 2009–11, via Bloomberg LP (accessed October 10, 2013).

33 JP Morgan, "Index Group: EMBI+ (JP Morgan)."

34 Petrobras, "Notes to the Consolidated Financial Statements," *Annual and Transition Report, Form 20-F*, US Securities and Exchange Commission, May 20, 2010, F-48, http://sec.edgar-online.com/petrobras-petroleo-brasileiro-sa/20-f-annual-and-transition-report-foreign-private-issuer/2010/05/20/section46.aspx (accessed October 9, 2013).

35 Search for Venezuelan sovereign bonds, 2009–12, via Bloomberg LP (accessed October 10, 2013).

36 JP Morgan, "Index Group: EMBI+ (JP Morgan)."

37 Nathan Gill, "China Fuels Latin America's Biggest Debt Rally by Financing Ecuador Budget," *Bloomberg*, June 24, 2011, http://www.bloomberg.com/news/2011-06-24/china-lifts-latin-america-s-best-performing-debt-by-funding-ecuador-budget.html (accessed January 12, 2012).

38 Michael Forsythe and Henry Sanderson, "Financing China Costs Poised to Rise with CDB Losing Sovereign-Debt Status," *Bloomberg*, May 2, 2011, http://www.

bloomberg.com/news/2011-05-02/financing-china-costs-poised-to-rise-with-decision-on-cdb-debt.html (accessed January 12, 2012).

39 "Más petróleo va a China," *El Universo*, September 14, 2010, http://www.eluniverso.com/2010/09/14/1/1356/ya-exporta-mas-petroleo-atado-prestamo-china.html (accessed January, 12 2012).

40 "Negociaciones con Petrochina van a indagación fiscal," *El Universo*, December 16, 2010, accessed January 12, 2012, http://www.eluniverso.com/2010/12/16/1/1356/negociacio-nes-petrochina-van-indagacion-fiscal.html; "Ecuador Widens Orient Crude Differential by US$0.508/bbl for Dec," *Recent Business News*, December 21, 2010, http://ourbusinessnews.com/ecuador-widens-oriente-crude-differential-by-0-508bbl-for-dec (accessed January 12, 2012); "Petroecuador sells 9.36Mb of Napo, Oriente Crude," *Business News Americas*, April 7, 2008, http://www.bnamericas.com/news/oilandgas/Petroecuador_sells_9,36Mb_of_Napo,_Oriente_crude (accessed January 12, 2012).

41 Córdoba, "China-Oil Deal Gives Chávez a Leg Up"; Chao, "'Loans for Oil.'"

42 Rodrigo Orihuela, "Argentina Sets Levies and Ends Anti-Dumping Investigation on Chinese Goods," *Bloomberg*, July 22, 2010, http://www.bloomberg.com/news/2010-07-22/argentina-stops-china-anti-dumping-probes-after-failure-to-end-oil-spat.html (accessed December 20, 2011).

43 JP Morgan, "Index Group: EMBI+ (JP Morgan)."

44 Ibid.

45 Margaret Myers, Kirk Sherr, and Roger Tissot, "How Is China Changing Latin America's Energy Sector?" *Latin American Advisor*, Inter-American Dialogue, July 22, 2011, http://www.thedialogue.org/page.cfm?pageID=32&pubID=2710 (accessed January 12, 2012).

46 JP Morgan, "Index Group: EMBI+ (JP Morgan)."

47 Gill, "China Fuels Latin America's Biggest Debt Rally."

48 See William Easterly, *The White Man's Burden: Why the West's Efforts to Aid the Rest Have Done So Much Ill and So Little Good* (New York: Penguin Press, 2007).

4

CHINESE FOREIGN AID TO LATIN AMERICA

Trying to Win Friends and Influence People

Barbara Stallings

Introduction

China has become a major player among foreign aid donors, as it has in other economic arenas, but it is far more difficult to trace its aid activities because China considers aid data to be a state secret. Various ideas have been offered as to why systematic data are not available—lack of information on the part of the Chinese officials in charge of the aid program, not wanting to arouse domestic opposition to aid when poverty remains a serious issue in China itself, not wanting to stimulate competition among recipients to increase their aid allocations—but there are no definitive answers. The lack of information has led to wild exaggerations about the size and scope of China's foreign aid, including that to Latin America. One recent article in a respected publication, for example, spoke of Latin America receiving "hundreds of billions of dollars annually," although the author admitted that the amount "remains unconfirmed."[1]

Most of the research on China's foreign aid has focused on Africa, the region that receives the largest share of Chinese aid. Dozens of studies have examined the growing links between the two.[2] Chinese and African leaders frequently exchange visits, and China has established a triennial summit (the Forum on China–Africa Cooperation or FOCAC) to showcase its activities in the region. FOCAC is typically the occasion for China to pledge large amounts of assistance to Africa, such as President Xi Jinping's promise at the FOCAC VI in December 2013 of US$60 billion over the ensuing three years. Studies carried out in individual African countries show a mixed picture of Chinese aid. It provides a new source of money for some of the poorest countries in the world, enabling them to increase their growth rates and reduce poverty. At the same time, China obtains raw materials needed to keep its own factories running. Such a quid pro quo is part of what the Chinese call a "win–win" approach to foreign assistance. One of the main attractions to African leaders of China's way of doing business is that it eliminates—or at least reduces—the political and economic conditionality that typically accompanies aid from the West. This aspect has made Chinese aid very controversial among Western donors, who claim that it enables repressive governments to avoid mending their ways.[3]

This chapter aims to provide a more realistic analysis of China's aid to Latin America than is currently available. Despite the data limitations, some useful things can be said. The chapter draws on the only two official Chinese government reports on foreign aid, the so-called White Papers on Foreign Aid,[4] and supplements them with articles and press information on the topic and interviews carried out in Beijing in June 2010, June 2012, and May/June 2013. My argument is that Chinese aid to Latin America is mainly a political tool in three senses. First, it showcases the positive side of China's growing relations with the region, especially since Chinese aid is almost completely demand-driven. Second, it helps China advance its One-China policy in the context of its longstanding political battle against the diplomatic recognition of Taiwan. Since nearly half of the countries that maintain diplomatic relations with Taiwan are in Latin America and the Caribbean, the scope is large. Third, it may help to open doors for the large-scale natural resource projects in which China is mainly interested. Given these characteristics, Chinese foreign aid—in possible contrast to foreign direct investment (FDI) and commercial loans from China—poses no serious threat to the United States in Latin America.

The chapter is organized as follows. It begins with a sketch of the history of Chinese aid, which goes back to the early days of the People's Republic of China (PRC). In the case of Latin America, Cuba was the first recipient, beginning in the early 1960s. The chapter goes on to discuss the purposes—economic, political, cultural, and humanitarian—of Chinese aid today, and to provide data on the volume and types of aid flows worldwide. It then focuses on Latin America, with discussion of the volume and types of aid—specifically in the form of grants, interest-free loans, and concessional loans—and the countries involved. It also compares Chinese aid to Latin America with that of the United States and other donors. The chapter next looks at a set of case studies to identify the types of activities that are carried out with aid funds. The cases include Cuba, Bolivia, the English-speaking Caribbean islands, and Costa Rica. The chapter concludes with a summary of the analysis and a discussion of the advantages and disadvantages for Latin America of the Chinese style of foreign aid.

This chapter complements two others in the book. First, Chapter 3 (by Gallagher and Irwin) analyzes the large, commercial loans to selected Latin American countries provided by the China Development Bank (CBD) and China's Export–Import Bank (Eximbank). As the authors report, the large majority of these loans are provided on commercial terms and are frequently designed to fund natural resource projects. Moreover they go heavily to countries—Venezuela,

Ecuador, and Argentina—which do not receive foreign aid from China. In addition to the commercial loans from CBD and Eximbank, Gallagher and Irwin include in their data Eximbank's concessional loans, which are a major topic of this chapter, but they indicate that the latter are only a tiny fraction of the total.

The other complementary analysis is found in Chapter 9 (by Avendaño and Dayton-Johnson), which examines the role of China in six Central American countries with a strong emphasis on trade relations. The six are El Salvador, Costa Rica, Guatemala, Honduras, Nicaragua, and Panama. Of the six, only Costa Rica recognizes the PRC; the other five recognize Taiwan and thus are not eligible for foreign aid from China (with the exception of disaster aid). Costa Rica is explicitly discussed in this chapter, but the others are not, since China does not provide foreign aid to them.

Historical Background[5]

Over the six and a half decades since the Chinese Communist Party consolidated its victory on the mainland, China has been both a donor of foreign aid and a recipient. Following Kobayashi, we can divide the years since the founding of the PRC into three subperiods.[6] The first ran from the early 1950s to the beginning of the economic reforms in 1979. During these years, while China received aid from the Soviet Union, it was a net donor, with aid decisions taken mainly on the basis of politics and ideology. The second began with Deng Xiaoping's reform initiatives, which turned China toward a market economy. Despite the maintenance of a small aid program, China began to seek foreign aid as a way to finance the modernization of its economy, eventually becoming a net recipient. In the third subperiod, China's emergence as a major economy in the 1990s, other countries and multilateral institutions began to slow or withdraw their aid. At the same time, China began to increase its own aid outflows and to reform its approach to aid. No longer was ideology to be the main determinant of aid decisions; rather, China would use aid to help support its economic growth. As Chin points out, and as can be seen in Figure 4.1, China again became a net donor in 2005.[7]

In China's first period as a net donor, the main motivation was to help fellow socialist countries and to break China's isolation following the Chinese Communist Party victory in 1949. In an extraordinary effort for a country as poor as China in the 1950s and 1960s, the government allocated more than 3 percent of its total fiscal outlays and 1 percent of its GNP for foreign aid.[8] The first donations went to North Korea and North Vietnam, but after the Bandung Conference of African and Asian nations in 1955 China expanded its aid to nonsocialist developing countries. In this period, Premier Zhou Enlai laid out the basic principles of Chinese foreign aid, which remain central to this day. They focused on equality between donor and recipient, mutual benefit, and "no

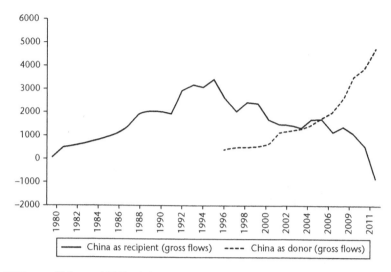

FIGURE 4.1   China as Aid Recipient and Donor, 1980–2011

Source: Stallings and Kim, *Political Economy of East Asian Foreign Aid*, chap. 4.

Note: In millions of US$.

strings attached." In reality, the Chinese rarely use the terms "aid," "donor," or "recipient," preferring instead to speak of "South–South cooperation."

As China began its economic reforms in the early 1980s, the focus shifted to domestic issues, and the aid bureaucracy was demoted in the governmental hierarchy. Nonetheless, a small aid program was maintained in line with China's self-identity as a leader of the developing world. More attention was paid to the efficiency of projects, however, and grants declined as a share of total aid. Meanwhile, aid flows into China grew rapidly. While the United States led the West's political rapprochement with China, Japan became its main economic benefactor. Japan provided half or more of China's bilateral aid from the early 1980s through the mid-2000s. Multilateral agencies were also significant donors, with the World Bank by far the largest of these. China's net aid inflows reached a peak in 1995, when the country received about US$3.4 billion from a combination of bilateral and multilateral donors. These large inflows, together with the shrinkage of its own aid program, meant that China was a net aid recipient in this period.

By the mid-1990s, China's economy was booming, and it set out to reestablish itself as a major aid power. The approach was quite different from that of the 1950s and 1960s. In line with the new market economy, foreign aid was to be carried out on a business-like basis. The Export–Import Bank was established in 1994 and began making concessional loans the following year.[9] These loans soon became one of the main channels for Chinese aid, together with the traditional grants and interest-free loans managed by the Ministry of Commerce (MOFCOM). An aid reform program began to focus on improving the institutions managing China's foreign aid. This was critical as the volume of aid increased substantially from the early 2000s, and greater coordination was necessary. Unlike other Asian countries, however, China has continued to be both a recipient and a donor, although it admits that it does not need the money. A partial explanation for this behavior is that China fears losing its identity as a developing country, which is essential to the way it deals with countries in Africa, Asia, and Latin America. As mentioned, the dominant rhetoric from the Chinese side is that it is engaging with the recipients of its aid and other resources as a partner rather than being involved in a donor–recipient relationship.

Goals and Characteristics of Chinese Aid in the 2000s

Goals

Economic aims have received most of the attention in the academic literature and especially in journalistic accounts of China's overall aid program today. In particular, the focus has been on the connection between Chinese aid and access to natural resources, especially oil but also minerals and agricultural commodities. The argument is that China provides money to help extract minerals and grow crops and to build the infrastructure required to export the raw materials back to China. Another economic aim is to help Chinese firms gain a foothold in other developing countries. Since Chinese companies carry out the big Chinese-financed projects abroad, they become familiar with countries, governments, and local businesses, placing them in a good position to win future contracts that are financed by other sources.

A second goal involves politics and diplomacy, the objectives of which have changed over time. Initially the main political aim was to help fellow socialist countries. Holdovers from this approach include important recipients in East Asia (North Korea, Vietnam, and Laos) and Latin America (Cuba). Today, however, China uses its resources to gain allies throughout the developing world to support causes it believes in. Important among these are support for China's right to manage its domestic affairs as it sees fit, especially its right to define human and minority rights as it chooses. Another major cause concerns the status of Taiwan as a province of China. In Africa and Latin America, this has led to attempts to persuade the remaining countries that recognize Taiwan to switch their allegiance to the PRC; aid and other resources have been used as inducements in this campaign. This so-called competitive checkbook diplomacy between the PRC and Taiwan was limited after a 2008 "truce" was declared between the two, although some aid continues to flow from each side, albeit in a more discreet way.

China's aid flows also have cultural aims, which support economic and political goals. China has run education and training programs for students from developing countries since the 1950s. Between 2010 and 2012, nearly 2,000 training sessions were held in developing countries or in China for officials and technical personnel. These involved nearly 50,000 individuals from developing countries.[10] The Chinese government hopes that these people will come to identify themselves with China and the Chinese way of doing things. In particular, there is interest in spreading the Chinese model of development to other countries. China also needs well-trained cadres to help run and maintain projects that are constructed in the developing world with Chinese funds. In addition to bringing students to China, the program of Confucius Institutes in many parts of the world, including Latin America, helps to spread the word about China and Chinese values.

Finally, China has humanitarian goals for its aid, although humanitarian objectives are a small share of total aid. Chinese medical teams attend patients in developing countries on an ongoing basis, especially in rural areas that do not have other access to medical care. In the 2010 to 2012 triennium, 55 Chinese medical teams provided services in 54 developing countries.[11] On a more occasional basis, when required, resources have been devoted to help developing countries deal with emergencies of various kinds, including natural disasters (earthquakes, hurricanes, floods, and so on), famines, and plagues. Such disasters are among the few instances where aid is provided in the form of cash and where countries that recognize Taiwan can be recipients.

Volume and Allocation

As indicated at the beginning of the chapter, there are no systematic data on Chinese foreign aid, as there are for donors that are members of the Development Assistance Committee (DAC) of the Organisation for Economic Co-operation and Development (OECD). DAC members are required to provide detailed data on an annual basis. In the absence of data, extremely varying estimates of the volume of Chinese aid have been made. One of the reasons for the variation concerns the definition of "aid." Some analysts consider any money that China provides to developing countries to be aid; in recent years, this approach has produced very large numbers.[12] DAC members, however, use a much more restrictive definition for what is called official development assistance (ODA). To be counted as ODA, according to DAC guidelines, aid must involve "flows of official financing administered with the promotion of the economic development and welfare of developing countries as the main objective, and which are concessional in character with a grant element of at least 25 percent (using a fixed 10 percent rate of discount)."[13]

My approach in this chapter is to get as near as possible to the ODA concept for Chinese aid flows—although this is clearly difficult owing to lack of information on the terms of concessional loans. My estimates, based on the methodology of Brautigam and Kitano[14] and confirmed by Chinese government officials,[15] indicate that current aid volume to all countries combined is around US$5 billion per year. These flows are made up of two main components: grants and interest-free loans, which are managed by MOFCOM, and concessional

TABLE 4.1 ODA-like Aid Flows from China, 1996–2013

Year	Official budget for external assistance ($m)	Eximbank concessional loans ($m)	Total gross aid ($m)
1996	387	23	410
1997	428	71	499
1998	449	66	515
1999	474	80	554
2000	554	91	645
2001	524	128	652
2002	555	145	700
2003	576	154	730
2004	667	185	852
2005	826	236	1,062
2006	922	409	1,331
2007	1,278	821	2,099
2008	1,567	725	2,292
2009	1,723	1,289	3,012
2010	1,745	1,771	3,516
2011	2,335	2,090	4,425
2012	2,764	2,845	5,609
2013	2,908	3,855	6,763

Source: Stallings and Kim, *Political Economy of East Asian Foreign Aid*, chap. 4.

loans, which are handled by the Eximbank. Debt relief and contributions to multilateral agencies are not included. These flows have increased very rapidly, as can be seen in Table 4.1, but the figures presented are on the modest end of the available estimates.

The only sectoral breakdown for Chinese resources is for overall flows; no regional or country data are available by sector. We start with the MOFCOM grants and interest-free loans. The government's White Papers report that these take the form of complete projects, goods and materials, technical cooperation, education and training programs, medical assistance, humanitarian aid, volunteer programs, and debt relief. According to the amount of money involved, the complete projects are most important, representing about 40 percent of the total. These are mainly infrastructure and production, but public facilities (civic buildings, sports and cultural facilities, water supply, and some social expenditure) are also significant.

With respect to the concessional loans, the first White Paper provides information on the allocation by sector between 1995 and 2009. There is no evidence that this breakdown varies substantially in the present period. As seen in Figure 4.2, the breakdown was as follows: economic infrastructure (61 percent), industry (16 percent), energy and resource development (9 percent), agriculture (4 percent), public facilities (3 percent), and others (7 percent). The sectoral composition of Chinese aid, then, is vastly different from that of most Western

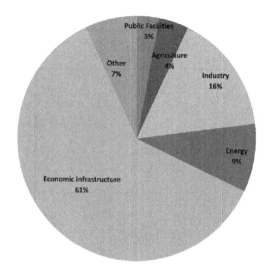

FIGURE 4.2 Sectoral Distribution of Concessional Loans, 1995–2009

Source: Chinese State Council, China's Foreign Aid (2011).

countries. The latter focus on small-scale social projects and stress the role of democracy, human rights, and governance, whereas China—like other Asian countries—provides large-scale infrastructure and production facilities, with stimulating growth being the dominant goal.[16]

Two further characteristics of Chinese aid need to be underscored. First, China and other Asian donors see aid as one part of a package of funds that promotes the development of recipient countries. Thus, Chinese aid is typically managed together with other financial flows, such as commercial loans and FDI. The Eximbank's participation in foreign aid institutionalizes this confusion, since its main function is to provide export credits on commercial terms. Concessional loans are only a small part of Eximbank's portfolio, and it refuses to disaggregate the various components. Thus, as both Brautigam and Mawdsley indicate, the boundaries between aid and other flows are quite porous.[17]

A second characteristic concerns the relationship between aid and firms (public or private) in China. Aid projects are generally carried out by Chinese companies, which use Chinese inputs and often employ Chinese workers. Indeed, the majority of aid funds never leave China, since they are disbursed to Chinese firms rather than developing country governments. Only those amounts that are used to buy local inputs and hire a small number of local workers are expended in the recipient country. It is argued that this enables projects to be carried out much more quickly than if monies flowed through recipient government channels. It is even argued that this is a way to avoid corruption on the recipient side, since Chinese firms handle the funds.[18] Any possible benefits aside, this is another way in which Chinese aid differs from DAC norms, which frown upon so-called "tied aid."

Chinese Aid to Latin America

History

In comparison with Asia and even Africa, relations between China and Latin America following the foundation of the PRC were much weaker.[19] The two main exceptions were Cuba and Chile. Cuba was the first Latin American country to establish diplomatic relations with the PRC, after the advent of the Castro regime in 1960. Recognition was rewarded by various types of Chinese aid—including food, weapons, and training programs—during the following decade. After a break due to Sino-Soviet disputes, China and Cuba have again become close allies, as will be discussed in more detail later in the chapter.[20]

Ten years later, soon after Salvador Allende was elected president on a socialist ticket, Chile became the first South American country to recognize China. Again Chinese aid followed, including food, a long-term loan, and cash assistance following a natural disaster. In January 1973, the hard-pressed Allende sent his foreign minister to Beijing to request further assistance. Premier Zhou Enlai agreed, but lectured Chile on its policies:

> China firmly supports the just struggle of the Chilean people, and would be willing to supply as much aid as we can. However, what you have implemented so far is more ambitious than what we did in the first decade after 1949. You seem not to rely on yourself, but on foreign aid. That is dangerous.[21]

In keeping with its policy of noninterference in the politics of recipient countries, China continued relations with Chile after the military government took power in 1973 as well as with its democratic successor.[22]

In the course of the 1970s and 1980s, following the US lead, all of the major Latin American countries established diplomatic relations with China, although a substantial number of smaller countries continued to recognize Taiwan. The relationship between aid and recognition has always been opaque; sometimes the two have gone together, and in other cases they have not. As we will discuss later, the competition between the PRC and Taiwan for the allegiance of Latin America has been an important issue in the history of China's foreign aid to the region.

As late as 2000, trade with Latin America represented only 2.8 percent of China's exports and 2.4 percent of its imports. For Latin America as a whole, the share of trade with China was even smaller, although it was larger for some individual South American countries. Indeed, the Asian country that was the most important economic partner for Latin America in the early postwar decades was not China, but Japan. The relationship between Japan and Latin America shrank considerably from the early 1990s, however, as a consequence of Japan's own economic problems.[23] In the last decade, trade links between China and Latin

America have burgeoned. Substantial amounts of FDI came later in the decade, together with commercial loans from the China Development Bank and the commercial window of the Export–Import Bank.[24] At the regional level, China has observer status at the Organization of American States (OAS) and joined the Inter-American Development Bank (IDB), which signed a partnership agreement with China's Eximbank in 2009 to finance various projects in the region.

Volume and Allocation

How does Chinese aid fit into this picture? Aid amounts are small in comparison to commercial loans, and the distribution across countries is quite different. My argument is that aid flows are predominately a political tool involving both carrot and stick. With respect to the former, small amounts of aid allocated by recipient request are a way to win friends and pursue China's soft power strategy in the region.[25] With respect to the latter, China discourages those that still recognize Taiwan by withholding aid. About half of those countries are in the Latin America and Caribbean region. In addition, aid may help grease the political wheels for acceptance of the large projects financed by FDI and commercial loans, although there appears to be little overlap between aid recipients and recipients of support for large investment projects.

According to China's State Council, Latin America and the Caribbean accounted for 12.7 percent of total Chinese foreign aid in 2009 but only 8.4 percent in 2010 to 2012. This is compared to 51.8 percent for Africa and 30.5 percent for Asia in the more recent period (see Figure 4.3). Even the 8.4 percent share for Latin America in 2010 to 2012 was surprisingly large, exceeding the region's share of China's trade (6.5 percent) and FDI (5.9 percent) for the same years.[26] Multiplying this share by the estimated amount of total Chinese foreign aid in 2013 indicates that the absolute volume of China's foreign aid to Latin America and the Caribbean was about US$560 million.

Table 4.2 puts this figure into perspective by comparing it to the main DAC donors. The table shows that China ranks fifth in gross disbursements of ODA to Latin America, behind the United States, Germany, France, and Norway. By this estimate, China represented about 7 percent of Latin America's ODA flows in 2013, while the United States accounted for 23 percent, more than three times China's share. Thus, concern about the large amounts of Chinese resources going to the region does not derive from foreign aid per se as opposed to FDI and commercial loans from Chinese institutions. In terms of foreign aid, the United States remains the top donor.[27]

With respect to individual recipients of Chinese foreign aid in Latin America and the Caribbean, we know that this includes 19 countries.[28] This number excludes the 12 countries that recognize Taiwan: Belize, Dominican Republic, El Salvador, Guatemala, Haiti, Honduras, Nicaragua, Panama, Paraguay, St. Kitts and Nevis, St. Lucia, and St. Vincent and the Grenadines. It also excludes

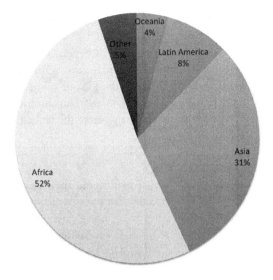

FIGURE 4.3 Geographical Distribution of Foreign Aid, 2010–12

Source: Chinese State Council, China's Foreign Aid (2014).

Argentina, Brazil, and Chile, since they are considered too advanced to receive aid.[29] Dividing the US$560 million by the 19 countries gives an average allocation of around US$30 million per country per year—a relatively small amount, though sufficient to fund a number of projects desired by political leaders in

TABLE 4.2 Bilateral ODA to Latin America and Caribbean by Donor Country, 2013

Country	Amount ($m)	Share (%)
United States	1,816	23.1
Germany	1,514	19.3
France	860	11.0
Norway	825	10.5
Canada	430	5.5
Japan	387	4.9
Spain	336	4.3
United Kingdom	259	3.3
Switzerland	205	2.6
Sweden	140	1.8
Other DAC	508	6.5
China	568	7.2
Total	7,848	100.0

Sources: OECD/DAC Statistics online (CRS—gross disbursements) for all except China; Table 4.1 for total Chinese aid and Figure 4.3 for estimated percentage to Latin America

the recipient countries. The demand-driven character of Chinese aid caters to the interests of political leaders. Moreover, the roster of Latin American and Caribbean recipients is consistent with China's general tendency to give some money to a large number of countries, which goes against DAC norms that oppose aid fragmentation. This reinforces the idea of aid as a political tool for buying friends rather than having a significant economic impact. Other types of resources, such as FDI and commercial loans, serve the latter aim.

Types of Aid

While no breakdown of aid to Latin America and the Caribbean by different modalities is available, we can reasonably assume that aid to the region reflects the more general patterns described in the Chinese government's White Papers on Foreign Aid. As explained earlier, these modalities are grants, interest-free loans, and concessional loans.

The White Papers state that China's grants are used to support small-scale social infrastructure (e.g., hospitals, schools, low-cost housing, and water supply projects), as well as human resource development, technical cooperation, and emergency humanitarian aid. An important item for Latin America is human resource training, and Chinese grants have supported this area. In connection with President Xi's visit to the region in 2014, for example, he promised 6,000 government scholarships for Latin Americans during the 2015 to 2019 period. In addition, China will invite 6,000 Latin American officials and technical staff for training courses together with 400 for master's programs in China.[30] In the last round, such scholarships provided free tuition and accommodation plus a monthly stipend of US$120–$230. Areas of study included Chinese language, medicine, international trade, and international relations.[31] The Technical Cooperation among Developing Countries (TCDC) program sponsors other training opportunities. Courses cover areas such as agricultural economics, computer science, solar energy, and medicine. Students needed only to cover the cost of travel to China.[32]

Chinese grant aid has also provided assistance to natural disaster victims in Latin American and Caribbean countries. The most prominent example was the 2010 Haitian earthquake. Even though Haiti does not have diplomatic relations with the PRC, China was among the first countries to send search and rescue teams. It also contributed medicines, tents, food, water, and other equipment for the equivalent of US$4.4 million. Additional funds were provided later.[33] Other examples have included emergency help for a dengue fever epidemic in Ecuador, a mudslide in Bolivia, a hurricane in Uruguay, an earthquake in Peru, and the H1N1 flu epidemic in Mexico.[34]

Interest-free loans are used mainly to construct public facilities. These typically have an amortization period of 20 years, with 10 years of grace. A number of Caribbean countries have received these loans for varied projects, including to construct a community center in Barbuda, a national stadium in the Bahamas, schools in Barbados, a stadium in Jamaica, and a national sports arena in Costa Rica. Government buildings financed by interest-free loans include the prime minister's residence in Trinidad and Tobago and the foreign ministry in Suriname.[35] Interest-free loans are the only type of aid for which debt relief is given. Only two Latin American countries have had loans renegotiated: Cuba and Guyana.[36]

Finally, the Eximbank's concessional loans are a relatively new aid instrument, dating from 1995. These loans carry interest rates of 2 to 3 percent, with a repayment period of 15 to 20 years and a grace period of 5 to 7 years. Funds for concessional loans are raised on the international capital markets. Since the rates charged to borrowers are below market rates, a subsidy is provided through MOFCOM's aid budget. The overall sectoral distribution of these loans was shown in Figure 4.2, which indicated a heavy focus on economic infrastructure. Latin American projects appear to be similar.

Lack of information on the terms of Eximbank loans makes it hard to identify particular examples. One recent study lists a number of low-interest rate projects that provide an illustration of their characteristics: construction of an electricity project in Potosí, Bolivia (2007); construction of a motorway to the Nassau (Bahamas) International Airport (2009); construction of natural gas production facilities and acquisition of conveyer equipment in Bolivia (2009); construction of a national university in the Dominican Republic (2009); and lines of credit for Ecuador and Trinidad and Tobago (2009).[37] Gallagher et al. report a number of Eximbank loans in the 2005 to 2011 period. Based on the amount of the loan, the characteristics of the borrower, and the type of project, we can assume that the following were likely to have been concessional loans: a convention center in Jamaica (US$45 million in 2007); home gas lines and drilling rigs for Bolivia's state oil company (US$60 million in 2007); airport construction in the Bahamas (US$58 million in 2010); infrastructure construction in Bolivia (US$68 million in 2010); shoreline reconstruction in Jamaica (US$58 million in 2010); and infrastructure construction in Bolivia (part of a medium-sized package for US$300 million that also included a helicopter purchase in 2011).[38]

Case Studies of Chinese Aid

To understand the process better, we examine four cases that illustrate different aspects of Chinese aid to Latin America and the Caribbean. The cases include Cuba (a long-time ally, governed by a communist party); Bolivia (a new, leftist partner); the English-speaking Caribbean islands (a group of nonaligned countries courted by China); and Costa Rica (the most prominent recent example of a Latin American country switching its allegiance from Taiwan to the PRC).

Cuba

In some senses, Cuba is the North Korea of the Western Hemisphere as far as relations with China are concerned. Although Cuba's flirtation with nuclear weapons ended many years ago, it is tied to China by ideological as well as communist party links; it receives a large amount of Chinese aid in relative terms; and it is frequently badgered by China to change its economic policies and follow the Chinese model. China's relations with Cuba are broad and continuous, not limited to one-off projects or particular sectors. They include support for industrial development, infrastructure, human capital formation, and mutually reinforcing strategic support at the international level. Recently oil has come into the picture.

Cuba's early recognition of China and its support in international fora have earned it the gratitude of several generations of Chinese leaders. President Hu described China–Cuba relations as those between "good comrades, good friends, and brothers."[39] Nonetheless there was a period when the two were distant, as Cuba sided with the Soviet Union in the Sino-Soviet disputes of the 1970s and 1980s. With the collapse of the Soviet Union in 1991, however, China and Cuba resumed their close relationship.

China is Cuba's second largest trading partner after Venezuela, and Cuba is China's second largest trade partner in the Central America/Caribbean area after Costa Rica. Both in the 1960s and since the early 1990s, Cuba has received fairly large amounts of aid from China, often announced in the context of reciprocal visits by top leaders. This aid has been in the form of grants and interest-free loans, since Cuba's economy is not strong enough to justify the deployment of Eximbank concessional loans. Moreover, Cuba is one of only two Latin American countries to have had its interest-free loans rescheduled by China; the most recent case took place in 2009.

Early aid packages included trade and financial components. Shortly after diplomatic recognition, Ernesto (Che) Guevara led a Cuban delegation to Beijing, where the two governments signed economic and technological agreements. China agreed to provide a US$60 million interest-free loan to Cuba, buy a million tons of sugar, and train 200 Cuban technicians. Cuba would buy Chinese rice and consumer goods. In 1963, after one of Cuba's frequent hurricanes, China provided US$28 million in humanitarian assistance. The two countries supported each other in diplomatic settings. China protested the US invasion at the Bay of Pigs and the events constituting the missile crisis, while Cuba has backed its ally's One-China policy.[40]

When relations resumed in the early 1990s, the Cuban economy was in dire straits because of the collapse of the Soviet Union, and the government hoped that China would come to its rescue.[41] In 1993, President Jiang Zemin visited Cuba and promised to help tide the country over the crisis.[42] Part of this help took the form of grants and loans for specific projects and humanitarian purposes.

More importantly, it came to involve support to develop Cuba's industrial and trade capacity. For example, China first provided Cuba with a large number of bicycles, and then helped Cuba to set up a bicycle factory. Similar policies were followed with a variety of products (e.g., washing machines, air conditioners, televisions, computer parts). Likewise, rather than shipping buses to Cuba, China sent parts and assembled them on the island, helping to train Cuban workers in the process. China also supported the reconstruction of Cuban ports with Chinese equipment.[43] When President Xi Jinping visited in 2014, in addition to offering US$115 million for port facilities, a pilot agricultural park was agreed upon, which included Chinese training for Cuban workers.[44]

In a set of complementary actions, China has directly supported the development of human capital in Cuba. President Hu's visits in 2004 and 2008 focused on this area. Aid included the delivery of thousands of computers for local universities. Hu also promised to send Chinese technicians to live in Cuba to supervise and train local workers involved in Chinese investment projects.[45] Support for language and cultural studies are considered a vital part of China–Cuban relations, and Cuban technicians are enrolled in relevant programs. In 2002, the University of Havana established a Center for Chinese Language Training.[46]

Chinese firms—the majority of which are government owned—have also been involved in relations with Cuba. As of 2011, Cuba had an investment stock of US$146 million from Chinese companies. The sectors included agriculture, tourism, telecommunications, and light industry.[47] A number of Chinese firms have set up offices in Cuba to promote the export of Cuban products (such as nickel, sugar, and various medical and biological products) to China. Cuba has recently opened the opportunity for foreign firms to invest in the petroleum sector, and Chinese firms are among the most active.[48]

Bolivia

While Cuba's relationship with China dates back to 1960, Bolivia's links began 45 years later when President-elect Evo Morales included Beijing in a whirlwind international tour in late 2005, preceding his inauguration. Morales was looking for help in developing his poverty-stricken country, and his ideological affinity with China made it seem a good fit for obtaining assistance. In meetings with President Hu and other high-level Chinese leaders, agreements were reached to promote Chinese investment in Bolivia (especially in energy, mining, and agriculture), expand trade relations, and increase foreign aid. Nonetheless, China has been cautious in its relationship with Bolivia, perhaps concerned about political instability in Bolivia itself.[49]

Since Bolivia is the poorest country in South America, it is an obvious candidate for Chinese grants and interest-free loans to finance social projects. Perhaps as an inaugural gift, in January 2006 China provided US$4 million for the construction of a new ministry of housing. Over the succeeding years, there have been many donations in kind of equipment (for the construction of a new highway between La Paz and Cochabamba), vehicles (motor cycles, tractors, ambulances), and consumer goods (televisions, computers). Credits for technical cooperation have also been provided.[50] At the same time, its untapped mineral wealth made Bolivia attractive to Chinese companies and the larger, commercial loans from the China Development Bank and the Eximbank. One important use of these loans is to improve Bolivia's deficient infrastructure, which makes it difficult to get natural resources to market. Bolivia received six loans from the Eximbank between 2009 and 2015.[51] Three were for infrastructure, one was for home gas lines and drilling rigs, and a fourth was for the purchase of a Chinese telecommunications satellite, and the last was the purchase of 2,000 Chinese buses. Together the six loans amounted to US$1.6 billion.

The largest Bolivian joint venture under discussion with China is the El Mutún mine, said to be the largest iron ore deposit in Latin America. Originally a joint venture with the Indian firm Jindal, the investment was ended when Jindal did not fulfill the terms of the contract. After years of speculation in the press that China would take over the project, a deal between Bolivia and the Chinese state firm Sinosteel was finally signed in March 2016. Currently Chinese engineers are doing preparatory work on the mine. Other projects of a commercial sort are also under discussion between Chinese firms and the Bolivian government, including several in the areas of transportation, utilities, and mining.[52] It may well be that the smaller projects, both grants and concessional loans, have helped to burnish China's image when it comes to competition over large natural resource projects.

Caribbean Islands

A somewhat surprising focus of Chinese interest is Cuba's small Caribbean neighbors. Of the 15 nations that are members of the Caribbean Community (CARICOM), only three—Haiti, Jamaica, and Trinidad and Tobago—have populations of more than a million people. Most are former European colonies with no traditional ties to China; moreover, all but Haiti have per capita incomes that exceed that of China itself. Nonetheless, the ten that recognize the PRC have extensive and growing relations that include foreign aid as an important component.

The explanation seems to derive from the political nature of China's foreign aid. On the one hand, the Caribbean is fertile ground in the battle against Taiwan. On the other hand, it is possible to gather the support of many nations with a relatively small amount of aid. This is made much easier since the economies of most of the islands are facing various difficulties, and the United States and Europe have cut their assistance substantially. China also has some economic interests in the area, but they are limited.

A prominent Jamaican economist and diplomat reports that China's move into the area dates from the early to mid-2000s and began with technical assistance programs. By 2005, Chinese aid to CARICOM countries amounted to US$87 million, with the largest recipients being Belize, Dominica, Guyana, Jamaica, and Suriname. The amounts then increased, with a spurt in 2007 in connection with the region's hosting of cricket's World Cup competition that year. As in other parts of the developing world, especially in Africa, China's aid has centered on highly visible infrastructure projects and public works.[53]

In several cases, Chinese funds were connected to the One-China policy and its encouragement of these countries to shift their diplomatic relations from Taiwan to the PRC. The most storied case in the Caribbean is the small island of Dominica (population 68,000). In 2004, Dominica switched its recognition to the PRC. In return, it received US$100 million in grants to carry out four projects: a sports stadium, a grammar school, the reconstruction of the road linking the two main cities, and the rehabilitation of the main hospital on the island.[54] St. Lucia constitutes a less successful case from the Chinese viewpoint. In 2007, after China had spent ten years building sports facilities and hospitals, St. Lucia reestablished relations with Taiwan.[55]

In addition to relations with individual Caribbean nations, China is a member of the Caribbean Development Bank and the Bank's Special Development Fund. Perhaps more importantly, the Chinese government has initiated the China–Caribbean Economic and Trade Cooperation Forum, similar to FOCAC in Africa, through which it meets with presidents, prime ministers, and other high officials of Caribbean countries every three years or so to pledge resources and discuss common interests. The first such meeting was held in Jamaica in 2005, the second in China in 2007, and the third (and most recent) in Trinidad and Tobago in 2011. At the Trinidad and Tobago meeting, Chinese Vice Premier Wang Qishan said that China would take six steps to deepen cooperation in the ensuing three years: provide US$1 billion in preferential loans; offer capacity-building courses for at least 2,500 Caribbean trainees; boost cooperation on environmental issues; enhance cultural and educational exchanges; promote trade and tourism, including Chinese tour groups going to the Caribbean; and increase cooperation on agriculture and fisheries.[56] A China–Caribbean Business Council has also been established.

Costa Rica

The best-known and the most important case in recent years of a Latin American country switching its allegiance from Taiwan to the PRC was Costa Rica in 2007. While the Costa Rican population is less than 5 million and it does not have oil or minerals, it is a country with other kinds of attractions. It is the wealthiest and most stable country in Central America and has considerable international prestige. This comes from its high literacy and education levels, its democratic political system, its lack of an army, its well-known ecological preservation policies and associated ecotourism, and its high-tech industries. Thus, wooing Costa Rica was perhaps the most important task in China's running battle with Taiwan, since Costa Rica could serve as a beacon for other countries thinking about switching allegiance.

As a result, Costa Rica was offered a gamut of rewards from China when it recognized the PRC. Foreign aid played a role in this process, although it was only one component. In terms of aid, China provided US$180 million of grants for projects of Costa Rica's choosing, becoming Costa Rica's largest source of foreign aid. It also agreed to purchase US$300 million of Costa Rican government bonds on very favorable terms: 12 years for repayment and an interest rate of 2 percent.[57] A much larger US$900 million loan to expand Costa Rica's oil refinery—with the idea that it would process oil from Venezuela and other exporters—aroused controversy that was only resolved in early 2015. A feasibility study is now being started for the refinery, which will produce green fuels as well as refine gasoline and diesel.[58] Recognition of the PRC was followed by a state visit by President Hu and the negotiation of a free trade agreement, China's third in Latin America. Relations continued to expand and, in 2013, newly installed President Xi Jinping visited Costa Rica, where he pledged US$400 million in loans to extend a road from central Costa Rica to the main seaport and US$100 million to replace public transportation vehicles.[59]

Conclusions

China's foreign aid constitutes one element—a small but important one—in that country's attempts to expand its relationships in Latin America and the Caribbean. Although it is much smaller than some previous analysts have suggested, China's foreign aid can serve useful purposes from that country's point of view. Grants, interest-free loans, and concessional loans together can help win friends among politicians and citizens alike. These resources help to show the friendly face of China to potential opponents before demands for natural resources and market privileges begin. The fact that Chinese aid is demand-driven means that recipient governments can ask for whatever they want, and the Chinese will normally go along.[60]

In addition, foreign aid can garner support for China in international fora concerning such issues as Taiwan's status, human rights, Tibet, and ethnic minorities. While recipients—especially in small Caribbean countries—are puzzled as to why China is devoting so much attention to them, it seems to be taken for granted that support for China goes along with the aid. For example, after the spate of loans during President Xi's 2013 visit to Costa Rica, the foreign minister said that it would "only be natural for China to ask us for support at the United Nations."[61]

Despite some fears that have been expressed, the increased interest that China has shown in Latin America does not pose a threat to the United States at this time.[62] This is especially the case with China's foreign aid. As we have seen, the United States provides three times the amount of aid to Latin America that China does: US$1.8 billion per year compared to only US$560 million in 2013. In addition, US diplomats and aid officials have extensive experience in the region, familiarity with the language and culture, and knowledge of Latin American ways of operating. China lacks all of these, as its own officials admit. Moreover, China is extremely reluctant to challenge the United States in its own sphere of influence, since its relations with the United States are far more important than its links with Latin America.[63] Beyond foreign aid, however, China has indeed surpassed the US in terms of its commercial loans to some Latin American countries, and it is closing the gap with stock of FDI.

Is the new Chinese interest in Latin America and the Caribbean good for those countries, and are there ways to improve the balance between China and the region? With respect to the first question, Chinese aid and other resources provide money when Western powers are unwilling or unable to offer as much aid as they have in the past. This is especially relevant for governments that have serious fiscal problems, such as many in the Caribbean. Moreover, from some governments' perspectives, Chinese aid is advantageous, since it comes without the usual political and/or economic conditionality of aid from Western donors and multilateral institutions.

At the same time, however, the focus on natural resources has caused substantial concern among many Latin American governments and businesses. Some analysts suggest that Latin American exporters are getting an unfair deal on the prices offered by the Chinese; Gallagher et al. counter this argument.[64] Prices aside, perhaps the most significant problem—and a very old one—is the volatility introduced by reliance on natural resource exports. This issue is coming to a head once again, as China's growth rate has slowed and its demand for oil, copper, iron ore, and other commodities has fallen off. In turn, the price for commodities has fallen. The combined result is slowing growth in Latin American countries that are important providers. For non-commodity exporters, especially Mexico, the trade relationship with China has never been very positive.

Regarding how to improve the relationship between China and Latin America, an initial step at the bilateral level would be for Latin American governments to request finance for projects that would improve their economies and strengthen their social safety nets, rather than ask for stadiums or new government buildings. Such an approach could well increase China's respect for the governments and increase their willingness to make additional contributions. Only Cuba has established an aid relationship with China that actually helps in the development process. Some of the policies that China has followed with respect to Cuba could provide innovative ideas for other countries in the region.

Moving beyond the bilateral level, an obvious approach to a better balance is to engage in joint negotiations over Chinese investment in the region and entry to the Chinese market for goods other than natural resources. In the Caribbean context, this idea has been put forward by a former diplomat who said that it was in the Caribbean's interest for all countries to recognize the PRC, since only then could they initiate joint discussions to improve the quality of their relationship:

> It is in the interest of the entire group of . . . CARICOM [countries] to settle a long-term and predictable aid, trade, and investment agreement with China along the lines of the Lomé and Cotonou treaties they had with the EU. But CARICOM will not be able, collectively, to negotiate such a treaty with China while five of its members remain tied to Taiwan.[65]

On a larger scale, the new Pacific Alliance—currently composed of Chile, Colombia, Mexico, and Peru—is another venue in which significant negotiations with China could take place. All are interested in expanding their links with Asia in general and China in particular. They represent a significant economic force: a third of Latin America's GDP and the majority of its exports. In this case, the countries are not generally recipients of foreign aid, but they might be interested in China's programs of technical assistance and training, which are supported by grant aid. More importantly, they could negotiate on trade and investment relations, which could help level the playing field for themselves as well as others in the region.

Notes

1 Martin Viero, "Chinese (Un)official Development Aid," *Americas Quarterly*, vol. 6, no. 1 (2012).

2 On China and Africa, see Ian Taylor, *China and Africa: Engagement and Compromise* (London: Routledge, 2006); Chris Alden, *China in Africa* (New York: Zed Books, 2007); Penny Davies, *China and the End of Poverty in Africa: Toward Mutual Benefit?* (Bromma, Sweden: Diakonia, 2007); Robert I. Rotberg, ed., *China into Africa: Trade, Aid, and Influence* (Washington, DC: Brookings Institution, 2008); Deborah Brautigam, *The Dragon's Gift: The Real Story of China in Africa* (New York: Oxford University Press, 2009); Ian Taylor, *China's New Role in Africa* (Boulder, CO: Lynne Rienner, 2009); Larry Hanauer and Lyle J. Morris, *Chinese Engagement in Africa: Drivers, Reactions, and Implications for US Policy* (Washington, DC: Rand Corporation, 2014).

3 On the controversies about Chinese aid, see Moises Naim, "Rogue Aid," *Foreign Policy* (March 2007); Ngaire Woods, "Whose Aid? Whose Influence? China, Emerging Donors, and the Silent Revolution in Development Assistance," *International Affairs*, vol. 84, no. 6 (2008), pp. 1205–21; Sebastian Paulo and Helmut Reisen, "Eastern Donors and Western Soft Law: Towards a DAC Donor Peer Review for China and India," *Development Policy Review*, vol. 28, no. 5 (2010), pp. 535–52.

4 Chinese State Council, *China's Foreign Aid* (Beijing: Information Office, State Council, 2011 and 2014).

5 Barbara Stallings and Eun Mee Kim, *The Political Economy of East Asian Foreign Aid* (New York: Palgrave MacMillan, forthcoming 2017), chap. 4.

6   Takaaki Kobayashi, *Evolution of China's Aid Policy*, Working Paper 27 (Tokyo: Japan Bank for International Cooperation (JBIC) Institute, 2008).

7   Gregory T. Chin, "China as a 'Net Donor': Tracking Dollars and Sense," *Cambridge Review of International Affairs*, vol. 25, no. 4 (2012), pp. 579–603.

8   Li Xiaoyun, "China's Foreign Aid to Africa," Paper presented at workshop on "Managing Foreign Aid Effectively: Lessons for China?" International Poverty Reduction Center of China, Beijing, March 27–28, 2008.

9   Concessional loans have lower-than-market interest rates and long amortization periods. These are in contrast to what we refer to as commercial loans, which are provided on market terms.

10   Chinese State Council, *China's Foreign Aid* (2014).

11   Ibid.

12   The best known is the study by New York University's Wagner School of Public Policy, which claimed that China provided US$25 billion annually by 2007; see Thomas Lum, Hannah Fischer, Julissa Gomez-Granger, and Anne Leland, *China's Foreign Aid Activities in Africa, Latin America, and Southeast Asia* (Washington, DC: Congressional Research Service, 2009). See also Charles Wolf, Jr., Xiao Wang, and Eric Warner, *China's Foreign Aid and Government-Sponsored Investment Activities: Scale, Content, Destinations, and Implications* (Washington, DC: Rand Corporation, 2013).

13   This definition is now in the process of being changed, partly owing to the very low interest rates available on the private capital markets.

14   Brautigam, *Dragon's Gift*, app. 6; Naohiro Kitano and Yukinori Harada, *Estimating China's Foreign Aid, 2001–2013*, Working Paper 78 (Tokyo: JICA Research Institute, 2014).

15   Interview by author, Beijing, June 2013.

16   Stallings and Kim, *Political Economy of East Asian Foreign Aid*, chaps. 1 and 4.

17   Brautigam, *Dragon's Gift*; Emma Mawdsley, *From Recipients to Donors: Emerging Powers and the Changing Development Landscape* (London: Zed Books, 2012).

18   Interviews by author, Beijing, June 2012 and May 2013.

19   There was a history of Chinese immigration much earlier; see Walton Look Lai and Chee-Beng Tan, eds., *The Chinese in Latin America* (Leiden, Netherlands: Koninklijke Brill, 2010). In addition, after the Communist victory in 1949, another wave of Chinese immigration took place, but obviously the latter did not help promote close relations between Latin America and the PRC.

20   Jiang Shixue, "China's Aid to Latin America" (unpublished), Chinese Academy of Social Science, 2010.

21   Ibid., p. 9.

22   China was the only socialist country that maintained relations with Chile's military government.

23   For a comparison of Japanese and Chinese economic relations with Latin America, see Barbara Stallings, "Does Asia Matter? The Political Economy of Latin America's International Relations," in Javier Santiso and Jeff Dayton-Johnson, eds., *The Oxford Handbook of Latin American Political Economy* (New York: Oxford University Press), pp. 210–32.

24   See these trends in Enrique Dussel Peters, *Chinese FDI in Latin America: Does Ownership Matter?*, Discussion Paper 33 (Medford, MA: Tufts University, Working Group on Development and Environment in the Americas, 2012); and Kevin Gallagher, Amos Irwin, and Katherine Koleski, *The New Banks in Town: Chinese Finance in Latin America* (Washington, DC: Inter-American Dialogue, 2012). An updating of the latter is found in Chapter 3 of this book.

25   R. Evan Ellis, "Chinese Soft Power in Latin America: A Case Study," *Joint Force Quarterly*, no. 60 (2011), pp. 85–90.

26   These data are from the International Monetary Fund, *Direction of Trade Statistics Yearbook, 2015* (Washington, DC: IMF, 2012) and the Chinese Ministry of Commerce,

2013 Statistical Bulletin of China's Outward Foreign Direct Investment (Beijing: China Statistics Press, 2012), respectively. The FDI calculation excludes Hong Kong, the Cayman Islands, and the British Virgin Islands. The latter two are well-known tax havens, while FDI to Hong Kong is frequently involved in "round-tripping." Note that Dussel Peters's analysis, based on proprietary data, suggests that Latin America is a larger recipient of FDI flows than do Chinese government statistics.

27 On US foreign aid, see Curt Tarnoff and Larry Nowels, *Foreign Aid: An Introductory Overview of US Programs and Policy* (Washington, DC: Congressional Research Service, 2005); Carol Lancaster, *Foreign Aid: Diplomacy, Development, Domestic Politics* (Chicago: University of Chicago Press, 2007), chap. 3; Carol Lancaster, *George Bush's Foreign Aid: Transformation or Chaos?* (Washington, DC: Center for Global Development, 2008); Robert K. Fleck and Christopher Kilby, "Changing Aid Regimes? US Foreign Aid from the Cold War to the War on Terrorism," *Journal of Development Economics*, no. 91 (2010), pp. 185–97. On US versus Chinese foreign aid, see Thomas Lum et al., *Comparing Global Influence: China's and US Diplomacy, Foreign Aid, Trade, and Investment in the Developing World* (Washington, DC: Congressional Research Service, 2008); and Wolf et al., *China's Foreign Aid and Government-Sponsored Investment Activities.*

28 Chinese State Council, *China's Foreign Aid* (2014).

29 Interviews by author, Beijing, June 2010 and May 2013.

30 Xinhua News Service, July 18, 2014, http://news.xinhuanet.com/english/china/2014-07/18/c_133493925.htm (accessed July 1, 2016).

31 *China Daily*, November 19, 2008, based on Ministry of Education statistics, http://www.chinadaily.com.cn/china/2008-11/19/content_7218053.htm (accessed July 1, 2016).

32 Hartmut Sangmeister, "China's Development Policy in Latin America and the Caribbean," *Digital Development Debates*, no. 3 (2011).

33 *China Daily*, January 22, 2010, www.chinadaily.com.cn/world/haitiearthquake/2010-01/17/content_9332575.htm (accessed July 7, 2016).

34 Jiang, "China's Aid to Latin America."

35 Sangmeister, "China's Development Policy."

36 Interviews by author, Beijing, May 2010 and June 2013.

37 Sangmeister, "China's Development Policy."

38 Gallagher et al., *New Banks in Town.* Some slightly different data are presented in the Inter-American Dialogue Database on Chinese Finance to Latin America (www.thedialogue.org).

39 Zuo Pin, "A Survey of the Relationship between Cuba and China: A Chinese Perspective," *Cuba in Transition*, vol. 20, Papers and Proceedings of the 20th Annual Meeting of the Association for the Study of the Cuban Economy, Miami, FL, July 29–31, 2010, p. 197.

40 Ibid.

41 Nash says that Cuba tried to use the Cuban Chinese population to attract PRC help. Thus they improved conditions for a part of the population that had been discriminated against for years. See Paul Nash, "How the Chinese Are Helping to Transform Cuba, Again," *Diplomatic Courier* (May/June 2013).

42 Jiang, "China's Aid to Latin America."

43 Adrian Hearn, "China, Global Governance and the Future of Cuba," *Journal of Current Chinese Affairs*, vol. 41, no. 1 (2012), pp. 155–79.

44 *China Daily*, July 23, 2014, http://chinadaily.com.cn/world/2014xibricssummit/2014-07/23/content_17907780.htm (accessed July 1, 2016).

45 Hearn, "China, Global Governance and the Future of Cuba."

46 Mao Xianglin, Carlos Alzugaray Treto, Liu Weiguang, and Adrian H. Hearn, "China and Cuba: Past Present, and Future," in Adrian H. Hearn and José Luis León-Manríquez, eds., *China Engages Latin America: Tracing the Trajectory* (Boulder, CO: Lynne Rienner, 2011), pp. 187–201.

47 Chinese Ministry of Commerce, *2013 Statistical Bulletin.*
48 Mao et al, "China and Cuba."
49 R. Evan Ellis, *China in Latin America: The Whats and Wherefores* (Boulder, CO: Lynne Rienner, 2009), chap. 5.
50 Ibid.
51 Inter-American Dialogue Database on Chinese Finance to Latin America (www.thedialogue.org)
52 R. Evan Ellis, *China on the Ground in Latin America: Challenges for the Chinese and Impacts on the Region* (New York: Palgrave Macmillan, 2014), chap. 3.
53 Richard Bernal, "The Growing Economic Presence of China in the Caribbean," Paper presented at the IMF/UWI conference on "The Caribbean Challenges after the Global Crisis," Barbados, January 27–28, 2010; and Richard Bernal, "China and Small-Island Developing States," *African East-Asian Affairs*, no. 1 (2012), pp. 3–30.
54 Sir Ronald Sanders, "China's Presence in Dominica," *Caribbean News Now*, April 28, 2011, http://www.caribbean360.com/index.php/opinion/389630.html#axzz1L32alt QI (accessed July 1, 2016).
55 Francisco Haro Navejas, "China's Relations with Central America and the Caribbean States: Reshaping the Region," in Adrian H. Hearn and José Luis León-Manríquez, eds., *China Engages Latin America: Tracing the Trajectory* (Boulder, CO: Lynne Rienner, 2011), pp. 203–20.
56 Chinese Ministry of Foreign Affairs, "Wang Qishan Pledges to Further Deepen China–Caribbean Cooperation," Press release, September 13, 2011, http://np.china-embassy.org/eng/zgwj/t858984.htm (accessed July 7, 2016). For recent U.S. analysis, see Caitlin Campbell, "China's Expanding and Evolving Engagement with the Caribbean," US–China Economic and Security Review Commission Staff Report, May 16, 2014.
57 Graham Bowley, "Cash Helped China Win Costa Rica's Recognition," *New York Times*, September 13, 2008; Kevin Casas-Zamora, "Notes on Costa Rica's Switch from Taipei to Beijing," Paper presented at National Defense University, Washington, DC, November 6, 2009.
58 Zach Dyer, "Biofuels Would Be Produced at Chinese Refinery in Limon, Says Costa Rican Oil Chief," *Tico Times*, January 10, 2015.
59 Isabella Cota, "China Lends Costa Rica $400 Million on Xi Visit," *Reuters*, June 3, 2013, http://www.reuters.com/assets/print?aid=USBRE95218820130603 (accessed July 1, 2016).
60 Interview by author, Hanoi, July 2013.
61 Cota, "China Lends Costa Rica $400 Million." Later, the minister changed his statement to say that no strings had been attached to the loan offers: "It's been our initiative, since we are friends, to offer our position in the region and help them start new friendships with other countries here."
62 See references and discussion in Barbara Stallings, "The US–China–Latin American Triangle: Implications for the Future," in Riordan Roett and Guadalupe Paz, eds., *China's Expansion into the Western Hemisphere: Implications for Latin America and the United States* (Washington, DC: Brookings Institution, 2008), pp. 239–60.
63 Interviews by author, Beijing, May/June 2013.
64 Gallagher et al., *New Banks in Town.*
65 Sir Ronald Sanders, "Settling the China Question: A Caribbean Challenge," *BBC*, May 5, 2008, http://www.bbc.co.uk/caribbean/news/story/2008/05/printable/080 502_sanders0505.shtml (accessed July 1, 2016).

5

CHINESE AGRICULTURAL INVESTMENT IN LATIN AMERICA

Less There Than Meets the Eye?

Guo Jie and Margaret Myers

Introduction

China's agricultural investment in Latin America and the Caribbean (LAC), whether by private or state-owned firms, is not well understood. This is principally the result of the limited availability of data on China's overseas agricultural foreign direct investment (FDI). China's National Bureau of Statistics makes its FDI data available to the public, but these figures are often outdated or reported only in aggregate (whether by region or industry).[1] Chinese data also naturally exclude deals made by international firms, although China is known to hold majority shares in multinational companies with investments in overseas agriculture.

Thus, the documentation of major agricultural investments relies to a considerable extent on media reports, which have tended to focus in recent years on Chinese "land grabbing" in LAC and other regions, or the state-led purchase or lease of large tracts of land for the cultivation of crops to be exported back to China. Thought to be motivated by China's increasingly dire food security outlook, Chinese land investments are also commonly referenced in academic writing and in reports published by non-governmental organizations and international financial institutions.

In general, media and other reports portray a land-deprived China, conducting large-scale, foreign land purchases to feed its growing population. Reporting of this sort was especially prevalent around 2008, in the midst of the world food crisis. At that time, China's Ministry of Agriculture was reportedly in the process of formulating a new policy on outward agricultural investment, including a possible strategy of overseas land purchase and leasing to guarantee domestic food supply.[2] Subsequent investments in farmland by Chinese firms alarmed the international community, even prompting changes in land-related legislation in certain countries. By 2011, *The Economist* had labeled China the world's largest land grabber, estimating that the Asian nation had bought or leased twice as much land as other presumed "grabbers."[3]

While many reports suggest that China is active in purchasing and leasing overseas land, the amount of land reportedly purchased or leased varies considerably depending on the source. In LAC alone, reports of total land "grabbed" vary by as much as 730,000 hectares in certain cases. There is also considerable disparity in reporting on individual deals. Some sources indicate, for example, that the Chinese firm Chongqing Grain Group purchased 200,000 hectares of land in Bahía, Brazil in 2008, whereas others suggest that the company leased only a few hundred hectares.

This chapter evaluates the widespread claim that China is a prominent "land grabber" by critically examining accounts of Chinese land investment in LAC. By way of in-country interviews and extensive media and academic analysis, we provide what we see as the most accurate account to date of investment in the region's agricultural land by Chinese firms. In contrast to much of the existing reporting, we find that Chinese land grabbing is a rare phenomenon in LAC. Our confirmed land deals are far more limited in number and scale than those generally reported in the media and other sources.

We begin the chapter with an overview of China's food security challenges, as identified in both Chinese and international literature and in Chinese policy documents. We continue with an analysis of China's evolving approach to overseas agricultural engagement, which increasingly discourages land purchases in favor of other forms of investment. This is followed by a review of the dozens of Chinese land grabs commonly referenced in the media and other sources as having taken place in LAC. We provide some context for these deals, including information on the firms involved, their motivations, and the extent to which they were directed in any way by the Chinese state, as is widely assumed in media reports.

Because land grabbing, as traditionally conceived, is intended to augment a given country's food supply, this chapter focuses specifically on land-related investment for the cultivation of crops or for other phases of food production. We do not examine land purchases in LAC that are associated with the extractive sector or forestry projects, for example, even though China has established a robust presence in these industries in recent years.

Feeding the Masses: China's Challenges

Agriculture and rural society feature prominently in China's centuries-long economic development. Land reform was a principal feature of the Chinese Communist Party's (CCP) reform effort under Mao Zedong, although many in the older generations still recall—and are arguably influenced by—their experiences during the period of extreme famine in the late 1950s and early 1960s, the result of ill-conceived government policies. Agricultural reform was also central to China's economic transformation under Deng Xiaoping in the post-1978 reform era. The household responsibility system, which enabled families to sell some crops on the free market, was adopted in 1981 and later extended to other sectors of the economy. More recently, President Hu Jintao and Premier Wen Jiabao sought to tackle China's "three rural issues" (三农问题), namely low agricultural mechanization, extreme rural–urban disparity, and low quality of life for China's farmers.

China's recent efforts to achieve domestic food security also have a strong historical basis. Chinese authorities established grain storage systems as far back as the Warring States Period (475–221 BC). Then as now, Chinese leaders drew linkages between food shortages, price shocks, and social stability. As a scholar at China's National Development and Reform Commission (NDRC), a government agency with broad administrative and planning authority, argued in 2008, in the midst of the global food crisis, "food prices were the main triggers for turmoil in the past, and with millions of poor laborers concentrated in our cities, [China] cannot underestimate the risk of violence."[4] Over the past decade, China's food policy has therefore sought to both ensure food supply and control food prices.

China nonetheless faces major obstacles to achieving food security. Land limitations are chief among them. According to 2011 statistics published by the Food and Agriculture Organization of the United Nations,[5] China accounts for nearly one-fifth of the world's population, but only has approximately 8–10 percent of the world's arable land.[6] What exists in the way of farmable land is also diminishing as a result of rapid urbanization,[7] natural disasters, and ecological restoration initiatives (e.g., China's Grain for Green program).

Pollution is further depleting China's already limited supply of arable land. More than 16.1 percent of Chinese agricultural land is contaminated, according to findings from a June 2014 Ministry of Land and Resources report on pollution.[8] A 2013 western media report paints an even bleaker picture, suggesting that upwards of 70 percent of China's farmland is polluted.[9] The United Nations Office of the High Commissioner for Human Rights found in 2012 that at least 37 percent of China's land was environmentally degraded, if not entirely contaminated.[10] Soil contamination is often the result of the overuse of fertilizer, as Chen Wenfu at the Chinese Academy of Engineering has noted. The organic content found in black soil in Jilin province, for instance, dropped from 8 percent in the 1950s to less than 2 percent today. Heilongjiang and Liaoning provinces are reportedly experiencing similar problems.[11]

Low agricultural productivity is yet another challenge as China seeks to achieve domestic food security. By the end of 2013, China's agricultural mechanization rate was only 61 percent,[12] much lower than that of the U.S., EU, or Japan (which are all around 90 percent). Chinese agriculture has come a long way over the past 30 years, although both productivity and safety standards are still far behind those of other countries. China is the world's second largest corn producer, but yields are well below those in the U.S. or Argentina.[13] Improving productivity will require mechanization, more sophisticated farming methods, the development of large cooperative farms, and reforms that incentivize migration to urban centers.[14]

As China contends with its supply-side challenges, domestic demand for a wide variety of agricultural goods is increasing. The Chinese population is consuming more food as income levels rise. Urban residents in particular are also consuming different types of food as new goods enter the market and as Chinese seek to provide their families with increasingly balanced diets. Demand for meat, fruit, milk, and eggs has grown across all income groups in recent decades. According to one estimate, the traditional per capita food consumption ration (grains: meat–fish: vegetables–fruit) shifted from an 8:1:1 pattern in 1980 to a 4:3:3 pattern in 2005.[15] As China National Cereals, Oils and Foodstuffs Corporation (COFCO) president Ning Gaoning indicated, Chinese are increasingly consuming "more meat than rice" and "more milk than tea."[16] Rapidly rising demand for meat—often referenced by the world's major feed grain exporters—is expected to continue through at least 2022, when China becomes the world's largest consumer of pork on a per capita basis.

Toward Agricultural Self-Sufficiency

China's leadership is well aware of the country's agricultural challenges and has implemented numerous policies in recent decades to improve domestic food security. As early as 1990, a grain storage system was introduced to regulate supply and demand and to enable China to respond effectively to fluctuations in the price of grain. Following China's accession to the World Trade Organization (WTO) in 2001, the country abolished the collection of agricultural taxes and developed a series of price supports and subsidies to increase grain production.[17]

In a 1996 white paper entitled "The Grain Issue in China" (中国的粮食问题), the Chinese government set an ambitious 95 percent self-sufficiency target for grains (which at that time included rice, wheat, corn, and soy).[18] Self-sufficiency goals were announced yet again in the country's National Long-term Security Plan, 2008–2020 (国家粮食安全中长期规划纲要),[19] at the height of the global food crisis. The crisis highlighted China's considerable dependence on other countries and multinational traders for the supply of certain foods (e.g., soybeans), and even for domestic production. Agriculture Minister Han Changfu noted in 2012 that China relies on seed imports to grow many of its vegetables and imports a large percentage of its agricultural processing machines.[20]

In 2014, China's Number One Document (一号文件), a central policy paper that generally focuses on rural reform and agricultural modernization, set new goals for agricultural self-sufficiency. These include: "absolute

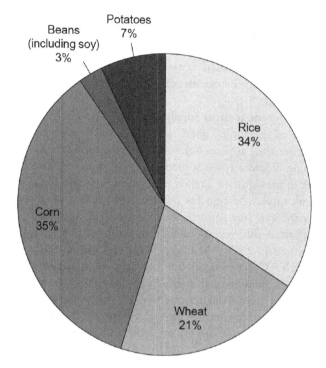

FIGURE 5.1 China's Main Grain Production, 2014

Sources: National Bureau of Statistics, *Bulletin on Grain Production in 2014*, http://www.stats.gov.cn/tjsj/zxfb/201412/t20141204_648275.html (accessed July 6, 2014).

security" （口粮绝对安全, interpreted as near 100 percent self-sufficiency)[21] in the production of rice and wheat, which are considered critical "food grains" (口粮); 95 percent self-sufficiency in the production of staple foods (e.g., rice, wheat, and corn, or 谷物); and 80 percent self-sufficiency in all grains (粮食), including soy.[22] The "all grains" target has been downgraded since the 1990s (from 95 percent to 80 percent), reflecting both rising domestic demand and production limitations (see Figure 5.1).

In support of these self-sufficiency targets, China has announced grain-specific "red lines." Of the 1.8 billion mu (or 120 million hectares) of land reserved for agricultural production, China will dedicate 1.65 billion mu specifically for the production of grain (rice, wheat, corn, and soy). Of that amount, 1.4 billion mu are reserved exclusively for rice, wheat, and corn (谷物) production. Under the new guidelines, China will also place more emphasis on food quality and greater priority on meat, vegetable, and fruit production, all of which require less land than grains and create more jobs.[23]

China is generally expected to achieve fairly high rates of self-sufficiency in major grains. Domestic food demand will continue to increase in the coming years. Demand for wheat and corn, in particular, should rise from around 470 million tons today to about 560 million tons by 2025.[24] But the agricultural production increases required to achieve the new targets—of about 2.5 percent per year over the next 13 years—are "eminently achievable," according to Hong Kong-based Gavekal Dragonomics.[25] Significant yield improvements can be made through better soil management, irrigation technologies, pest control, and other basic improvements in farm management.[26]

China's much higher target for rice, wheat, and corn (95 to near 100 percent self-sufficiency) is only achievable, however, so long as China prioritizes the domestic production of these three "staple" grains over other crops. In many cases, rice, wheat, and corn are being grown instead of soy, which has smaller yields than other grains. Chinese farmers planted an additional 1.4 million hectares of corn in 2012, about half of which came from replacing soybeans.[27] The prioritization (by both the government and individual farmers) of staple grains over soy, combined with skyrocketing demand for animal feed and cooking oil, has contributed to the boom in China's soy imports in recent years. In 2012, China imported over 80 percent of the soybeans necessary to satisfy domestic consumption.

This dynamic has driven much of China's agricultural engagement with Latin America over the past decade. Brazil and Argentina consistently feature among China's top sources of agricultural imports. Soybean and soymeal exports make up a considerable portion of both countries' exports to China—71 percent for Argentina (2013) and almost 41 percent for Brazil (2012), as indicated in Chapter 8 in this volume by Mariano Turzi.[28] If we consider the share of soybean exports to China as a percentage of total commodity exports from Brazil and Argentina—82.6 percent and 64.6 percent, respectively—China's share is even higher.

A web of tariffs and subsidies underpins China's self-sufficiency targets, including the decision to rely on imports of soy and some other commodities, for example some fruits, milk, and luxury food products that are not efficiently produced at home. China maintains high tariffs on all imports of corn, wheat, and rice above a yearly quota of 7.2 million tons, 9.6 million tons, and 5.3 million tons, respectively, which makes additional imports extremely expensive.[29] The maximum tariff on soybean imports, in contrast, dropped from 114 percent to 3 percent in 2002, contributing to a sharp increase in soy imports in the following years.[30]

Eyeing Foreign Agriculture

China's recent food security policy is consistent with its so-called "two markets, two resources" (两个市场 两种资源) strategy.[31] This concept was first described in 1982 by former CCP chairman and general secretary Hu Yaobang, and later adopted by President Jiang Zemin to encourage international trade in a variety of sectors. Though not clearly defined, "two markets, two resources" suggests reliance not only on China's domestic market but also on international markets for the provision of much-needed raw materials and agricultural resources.

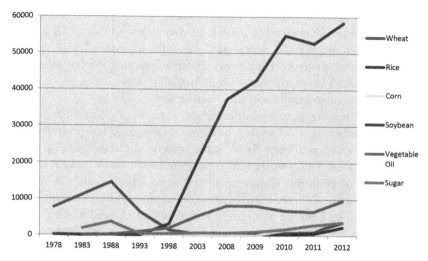

FIGURE 5.2   China's Agricultural Imports, 1978–2012

Sources: China Customs Statistics; China Statistical Yearbook.

Note: In thousands of tons.

As we have indicated, China's need to supplement internal production with foreign agricultural imports is urgent, especially in the case of soy. Driven by much lower trade tariffs and booming demand (see Figure 5.2), soybean imports are predicted to rise to around 83 million tons by 2024 (soy imports totaled 63.38 million tons in 2013 and 71.4 million tons in 2014).[32]

China's supply-related challenges, along with statements like Minister of Agriculture Han Changfu's announcement in 2010 that "[t]he time and conditions are ripe for the country's agricultural companies to 'go out'"[33] raised concerns in the 2000s about a possible Chinese government-driven quest for foreign land. At the time, countless media reports, journal articles, and databases (see GRAIN and International Institute for Sustainable Development) tracked China's land acquisitions across the globe. Concerns heightened in the midst of the 2008 food crisis when China's Ministry of Agriculture was rumored to have submitted a draft proposal to the State Council that specifically encouraged overseas land investments, although no such policy was ever publicly released.[34]

While there have indeed been some high-profile Chinese investments in foreign land in recent years (see the next section for examples in Latin America), China's current thinking on overseas agricultural investment would appear to support very different objectives. Increasingly, Chinese agricultural overseas foreign direct investment (OFDI) is focused not on overseas farming and related land purchases but on investment across the industry supply chain in an effort to control both supply and pricing. China's OFDI in farming therefore accounts for a very minor share of the country's total agricultural OFDI.

Land purchases are not viewed as necessarily supportive of China's current food security objectives. As Cheng Guoqiang, senior research fellow at the State Council Development Research Center noted, "merely cultivating foreign lands doesn't bring you pricing power."[35] Domestic backlash within foreign countries against China's initial attempts to purchase or lease their land has also limited China's focus on land grabbing in more recent overseas investment policy.[36] As Cheng suggested in a 2013 press report, land purchases have led some countries to view Chinese investors as "neo-colonialists."[37]

China's preference for other forms of overseas agricultural investment is also indicative of a growing interest, especially on the part of COFCO, China's top grain trader, in competing more effectively with agricultural multinationals, for example ADM, Bunge, Cargill, and Louis Dreyfus (ABCD). As COFCO president Patrick Yu indicated in a 2011 media interview, the ABCD companies now control almost the entire raw material base in North America and South America. He added that "the ABCD firms offer a good example for COFCO given their successful involvement throughout the industry supply chain," explaining that the ABCD are not involved in farming but instead procure crops from farmers and provide agricultural services and infrastructure.[38]

This thinking is also increasingly supported at the government level. In 2013, *Caijing* magazine published key findings from several reports on overseas agricultural investment produced by a Ministry of Agriculture research team. To boost China's food supply, the team recommended minimizing land purchases and focusing on agricultural logistics and processing when investing overseas,[39] presumably with the aim of increasing Chinese control over foreign production, processing, and logistics for commodities like soy that cannot be supplied domestically in sufficient quantities.[40] The team's other recommendations included improving access to foreign agricultural resources, selling surplus Chinese agricultural goods on the world market, effectively branding Chinese agricultural products for international sale, and improving China's agricultural competitiveness by adopting advanced technologies from abroad.[41]

China is actively supporting these food security objectives with earmarked loans and subsidies, and by facilitating public offerings in China and in overseas equity markets.[42] COFCO has been a major recipient of financing from the China Development Bank (CDB) and the Agricultural Bank of China, for example. The company's chairman, Ning Gaoning, expressed interest in 2012 in expanding overseas investments in South and North America, Australia, and Russia, with over US$10 billion in funding available for overseas mergers and acquisitions (M&A).[43] Established in 2011 by the Ministry of Commerce and Ministry of Finance, the Outward Economy and Technology Cooperation Special Fund is supportive of various forms of overseas agricultural investment, although among these is the purchase or lease of land for animal husbandry.[44] The NDRC has also evidently been drafting a strategic plan for agriculture "going out" since 2013, which is expected to introduce additional policy incentives for agricultural companies seeking to operate internationally.[45]

In the following section we examine the practical application of China's agricultural policy in Latin America. Here we find that Chinese activity in LAC has largely shifted in accordance with newly articulated overseas agricultural investment guidelines. Chinese agricultural firms are increasingly investing not in land for crop production but across the entire food supply chain. Some are doing so to support China's food security objectives, while others are more clearly driven by profit-based incentives.

Land Grabs in Latin America?

China's agriculture firms are relative newcomers in Latin America, as are Chinese firms in other sectors. Although China–Latin America engagement dates back to the Mao Zedong era, principally in the form of bilateral trade and Communist Party and other exchanges, China's economic engagement with the region has boomed in just the past two decades. Trade, rather than investment, has been the principal focus of China–Latin America agricultural engagement. As indicated in much of the literature on China and Latin America, China's imports of soy and to a lesser extent fruits and certain luxury food items (e.g., coffee and wine) feature prominently in bilateral trade.

China has taken incremental steps towards diversifying its agricultural trade with Latin America in recent years. China's recent approval of Argentine corn and fruit imports, for example, is indicative of China's interest in expanding agricultural partnerships.[46] Already an importer of large quantities of Argentine soy, China accepted its first shipment of genetically modified corn from Argentina in August 2013 by means of Bunge, one of the aforementioned ABCD firms.[47] China has also agreed to allow imports of Brazilian corn, providing a key market for surging production in that South American nation. Brazil is a principal exporter of soybeans to China, although the country is hoping to export more in the way of value-added agricultural goods. China's removal of its Brazilian beef ban, first announced during President Xi Jinping's visit to Brazil in July 2014, was therefore welcome news for Brazil.[48]

In contrast to the trade relationship, Chinese agricultural investment in Latin America is far more limited. China's presence is clearly growing in this sector, often in line with the strategies described in the previous section, although a thorough account of China's agricultural investment in Latin America is no easy task. China's agricultural firms have been present in the region in various forms for decades, but information on their investments is often bewildering. As we noted at the outset of this chapter, data on China's overseas agricultural investment are limited, in both China and Latin America. It is often the case, moreover, that Chinese deals are announced by the media or other sources, but then fall through. However, because their demise is seldom reported, these deals tend to live on in myth. They become "zombie deals," as China–Africa expert Deborah Brautigam calls them.

Even the many reports and databases focusing exclusively on China's land purchases or leases are subject to wide variation. GRAIN's land grab dataset reports that China has purchased or leased more than 1 million hectares of farmland in Latin America. However, a 2012 report by Irna Hofman and Peter Ho finds that China "grabbed" only about 300,000 hectares in the region.[49] Land Matrix, a land monitoring initiative, reports around 500,000 hectares, whereas the International Institute for Sustainable Development reports nearly 800,000 hectares purchased or leased by China.

We find that many of the deals reported in land grab studies and databases (and therefore accounting for their larger numbers) either have yet to materialize or have fallen through entirely, leading to these considerable disparities in reporting. In fact, after our extensive review of reported land grabs in Latin America, our numbers are far lower than any of those reported thus far. We can confirm just over 70,000 hectares of land that have either been purchased outright or leased by China for crop cultivation.

China's purchased or leased land in Latin America is not only far less impressive in scale than generally believed, but these deals are also not easily classifiable as land grabs. As conceived in much of the literature, "land grabbing" involves the state-led purchase of large tracts of land for the cultivation of crops and eventual export of the yields back to the "grabbing" country.[50] Although there are some deals conducted by state-owned or provincial firms, not all of these necessarily pertain to China's supply-related challenges. A review of confirmed Chinese land investment in Latin America (see Table 5.1) suggests the following.

1. China's Agricultural Investment in Latin America Is Only Occasionally Focused on Land Purchases or Leases

Despite the dozens of "land grabs" by Chinese firms in Latin America that have been documented in international media and other reports, we can confirm with confidence only ten examples of successful Chinese land investment in Latin America.[51] And, of our confirmed land purchases or leases (see Table 5.1), many are relatively small in scale. China's land-related investment in Venezuela, although it is difficult to confirm exact details, amounts to only about 3,500 hectares in total. The Pengxin Group, a private firm, was responsible for one of the largest agricultural land deals in the region—the development of a soybean processing zone in Santa Cruz, Bolivia. At 12,488 hectares, however, this is still a relatively small acquisition, especially in comparison with the hundreds of thousands of hectares typically referenced in land grab reporting. Even COFCO, China's largest grains trader, has purchased only 350 hectares of land in Latin America, in this case for the development of a vineyard in Chile.

Closer examination of these deals also reveals that not all are tied to crop production for the purpose of Chinese consumption. The first Chinese land grabs in Latin America took place in Cuba and Mexico in 1996 and 1998, respectively. Consistent with Brautigam and Tang's analysis of the evolution

TABLE 5.1 Confirmed Chinese Purchases or Leases of Latin American Land

Year	Country	Region(s)	Project	Land (ha)	Amount ($m)	Investor
1996	Cuba	Pinar del Río and Granma	Rice farming	5,000 in Pinar del Río and 3,259 in Granma	24	Suntime Group
1998	Mexico	Campeche	Rice and other cash crop cultivation	1,005	2.7	Suntime Group
2001	Venezuela	Guárico	Farming	2,000		Tongwei Group Co. Ltd.
2001	Venezuela	Barina	Farming	535		Guangxi Sisal Group Company Ltd.
2004	Venezuela	Lara and Falcón	Sisal demonstration project	450 in Lara and 200 in Falcón	3	Guangxi Sisal Group Company Ltd.
2007	Brazil	Rio Grande do Sul and Tocantins	Soybean farming	700 in Rio Grande do Sul and 16,100 in Tocantins	48.6	Zhejiang Fudi Agriculture Group and Agricultural Bureau of Heilongjiang Province
2010	Chile	O'Higgins	Winery	350	18	COFCO Wine and Spirits
2010	Bolivia	Santa Cruz	Soybean industrial zone	12,488	27.2	Pengxin Group Co.
2011	Jamaica	Clarendon, Westmoreland, and Saint Catherine	Sugarcane farming and factories	27,800	9	COMPLANT International Sugar Industry Co., Ltd.
2013	Chile	Araucanía, Maule, Coquimbo, Valparaíso, and Bío	Fruit farms	370		Joyvio Group

of Chinese overseas agricultural investment,[52] these early deals were actually a form of foreign assistance. They were specifically intended to improve local rice and other cash crop cultivation. In the case of Suntime's Mexico venture, the company eventually expanded into other businesses, including import–export, tourism, and real estate investment.[53]

Our numbers come in far lower than those in other reports, in part because we have excluded two major deals that are very often cited in the media and are generally listed in land grab databases on Latin America. These are: the purchase of 300,000 hectares in Argentina's Rio Negro province by Heilongjiang Beidahuang Nongken Group Co. in a joint venture with the Argentine firm Cresud;[54] and the Chongqing Grain Group's often reported purchase of 200,000 hectares of land in Bahía, Brazil for soybean farming and a soybean processing facility. Other unconfirmed, stalled, or rejected land deals are listed in Table 5.2.

Beidahuang's Rio Negro deal was the first example of large-scale Chinese agricultural investment in Argentina. The proposed US$1.5 billion transaction involved the 20-year lease of 300,000 hectares of land.[55] In November 2011, however, the Rio Negro superior court ruled that the project be suspended. There has been no public information on the status of the deal subsequent to a change in the provincial government in December 2011.[56] Chongqing Grain Group nonetheless indicated that it invested over 300 million renminbi in Argentina as of December 2013, presumably in undocumented land deals, other phases of agricultural production, or different economic sectors. As Dawn Powell explains in detail in Chapter 11 in this volume, the Bahía, Brazil deal was not cancelled, but has been in negotiation or stalled from the onset.[57] An agreement was eventually reached between Chongqing Grain Group and the Bahía government in 2011, but as of early 2015 work had yet to commence in any form.

2. The Chinese Firms Investing in Latin America's Agricultural Land Are Diverse

As indicated in our list of confirmed deals, the Chinese firms involved in land purchases or leasing in Latin America are quite different. The list includes both small firms and large ones. Some are private (Pengxin and Zhejiang Fudi, for example), whereas others are state-owned or affiliated with a specific province. These firms are also geographically dispersed, hailing from all corners of China.

The motivations of China's so-called "land grabbers" are also unique. Some companies, like Zhejiang Fudi, are self-motivated and profit-seeking. An *ifeng.com* article from 2009 provides a detailed description of the origins of Zhejiang Fudi's Brazil land purchase.[58] According to the *ifeng.com* account, the deal was initiated by village party secretary Zhu Zhangjin and 50 farmers from Huafeng village in the historically entrepreneurial Zhejiang province. Faced with land limitations at home—there are only 3,000 acres of arable land in Huafeng—the villagers explored the possibility of pooling their individual financial resources to buy Brazilian land for soy production. They had read in a Chinese newspaper

TABLE 5.2 Unconfirmed or Stalled Land Deals

Year	Country	Region(s)	Project	Land (ha)	Amount ($m)	Investor
2005	Brazil		Cotton and soybean farming	200,000		Shanghai Pengxin International Group Ltd.
2008	Brazil	Bahía	Soybean farming and industrial complex	200,000	2,470	Chongqing Grain Group
2010	Colombia	Orinoquía	Cereals	400,000		
2010	Brazil	Bahía and MAPITO (Maranhão, Piauí, and Tocantins)	Grain production and a bioenergy sector	200,000–250,000		Pallas International Consultants Group
2010	Bahamas	Abaco	Vegetable, fruit, and livestock production and processing plant	5,000		
2011	Argentina	Rio Negro	Soybeans, corn, and wheat farming	300,000	1,500	Heilongjiang Beidahuang Nongken Group Co.
2012	Argentina	Cordoba	Soybean and dairy farming	10,000	1,200	Chongqing Grain Group
2012	Argentina	Chaco	Soybean	130,000	420	Chongqing Grain Group
2013	Venezuela	Guarico, Barinas, Apure, Delta Amacuro, and Portuguesa	Corn, rice, and soybean production	60,000		Beidahuang

about Brazil's fertile land and long growing season. After establishing Zhejiang Fudi Agriculture Group, they purchased 16,800 hectares in Rio Grande do Sul and Tocantins for the production primarily of soy. Once harvested, the soy was shipped back to China, where it was processed into cooking oil and animal feed in a Shandong facility also owned by Zhejiang Fudi Agriculture Group.[59]

COFCO's 350 hectare land deal in Chile (see Table 5.1) was also a profit-making venture, although it additionally supports the expansion of China's domestic wine industry. The company's investment in Chile allows for the production of Great Wall wine in China's off-season. Both COFCO and the *China Daily* reported that the vineyard will have a wine production capacity of 14,000 tons per year and a yield of approximately 16 tons of wine per acre.[60] COFCO similarly purchased land in France and Australia for wine production. To address growing demand for wine among Chinese consumers, France's Chateau Lafite Rothschild is investing US$16 million in 25 hectares in Shandong province to produce premium red wine for the Chinese market. Moet Hennessy owns 30 hectares in southern Yunnan province, where it is making a top-end Chinese red wine for the domestic market.[61]

As China's largest grain trader, COFCO has interests in Latin America that extend beyond wine production. The company, according to chairman Ning Gaoning, is also engaged in logistics, processing, and trading ventures in order to secure the external food supply. COFCO is looking to acquire foreign firms to help secure supplies of commodities, including soybeans, wheat, and sugar, as demand for more and different types of foods increases in China and elsewhere in the world.[62] In March 2014, COFCO announced that it was buying a 51 percent stake in Dutch grains trader Nidera. Nidera's appeal, according to COFCO president Yu Xubo, is its "powerful procurement platform" in Brazil, Argentina, and Central Europe.[63] COFCO also purchased a 51 percent stake in the Noble Group Ltd. in April 2014. Reuters reported in May 2015 that China Investment Corporation, China's sovereign wealth fund, would set up a joint venture with COFCO (COFCO Investment Holdings) to control the latter's investments in both Nidera and Noble.[64]

The range of firms involved in overseas agricultural investment is even more striking when looking beyond land purchases or leases at a wider set of agricultural deals (see Table 5.3). Firms such as the Noble Group,[65] the Chongqing Grain Group, Sanhe, and China National Heavy Machinery Corporation have invested in factories, pressing plants, mills, and other agricultural infrastructure in Latin America. Even firms in non-agricultural industries like telecommunications are participating in the broader financialization of the commodity trade and agricultural production. As indicated in a 2013 McKinsey & Company report, many private Chinese entrepreneurs have identified the food chain as their next big thing. Investing outside rather than inside China is an opportunity to diversify assets geographically and to avoid the high prices associated with the domestic food industry.[66]

Of note when examining examples of Chinese land purchases and leases in Latin America is not only their diversity but that very few appear to be operating overseas based on explicit central government directives. Many are driven by

Chinese domestic demand and the promise of related profit, but it is difficult to make the case that these firms are actively sent abroad by the Chinese government for the overseas production of specific crops, as is often implied in the land grab narrative. Zhejiang Fudi's Brazil investment was purely entrepreneurial. The company has since sold its Brazil assets. Pengxin (acquired by Hong Kong Holdings Company)[67] operates internationally, having developed considerable expertise in animal husbandry. Media descriptions of Pengxin frequently mention the company's support of China's "going out" objectives, but Pengxin's decision to invest in Bolivia appears to have been its own.

Joyvio's investment in a Chilean fruit orchard (see Table 5.1) seemingly embodies both state and shareholder interests. The company is owned by Legend Holdings, which also houses the Chinese tech firm Lenovo. Legend Holdings has indicated an interest in diversifying into the food business, as it seeks to bring its high-profile and widely trusted brand into an industry burdened by safety scandals. As a result, the company reportedly invested more than 1 billion renminbi in Joyvio, which will cover the complete chain of production, from food processing to distribution and retailing.[68] Joyvio now sells its Chilean fruit to the Chinese market.

TABLE 5.3 Examples of Chinese Agricultural Investors in Latin America by Country

Country	Chinese investors
Brazil	CHINATEX (中纺集团)
	Beijing Triunion Cereals and Oils Co. Ltd. (联众博亚)
	Sanhe Huifu OFCO Fodder Protein Products Co., Ltd. (三河汇福)
	Wuxi Five-star Garden (无锡五星花园)
	Jiangsu Muyang Group Co., Ltd. (江苏牧羊)
	Zhejiang Fudi Agriculture Co., Ltd. (浙江福地)
	Weiteng Investment Co. (广州伟腾)
	Shandong Guanfeng Hi-tech Seed Co., Ltd. (山东冠丰)
	Chongqing Red Dragonfly Oil Co. Ltd. (红蜻蜓粮油)
Argentina	Beidahuang Nongken Group Co. (北大荒农垦)
	Sanhe Huifu OFCO Fodder Protein Products Co., Ltd. (三河汇福)
	Chongqing Red Dragonfly Oil Co. Ltd. (红蜻蜓粮油)
	BBCA Group (安徽丰原)
	Huishang Group (徽商集团)
Venezuela	Shenzhen China–Venezuela Agricultural Investment Co., Ltd. (中委农业投资)
	Guangxi Nongken Group (广西农垦)
	Yunan Defu Wood Products Co., Ltd. (云南德福)
Bolivia	Pengxin Group (上海鹏欣)
Chile	Qingdao MingYue Seaweed Group Co., Ltd. (青岛明月海藻)
Uruguay	Sichuan Demetre Biological Sci-tech Co., Ltd. (四川迪美特)
Peru	Sichuan Tingjiang New Material, Inc. (四川亭江新材料股份有限公司)
Cuba	Suntime Group (新天集团)
Mexico	Suntime Group (新天集团)

3. Chinese Firms Encounter Numerous Obstacles When Investing in Latin American Agriculture

Latin America is an attractive destination for Chinese agricultural firms, as it has been for many other international agricultural traders and investors. But China faces numerous challenges when attempting to invest not only in land but also in other elements of agricultural production in Latin America. In its pursuit of greater vertical integration in global food supply chains, the "two markets, two resources" strategy pits China's private and public firms against the likes of the powerful ABCDs, which have established a presence in international markets over the course of decades. In many cases, Chinese firms have been unable to compete effectively with these agricultural giants.

Chinese investors are further limited in certain cases by negative public reaction to proposed investments in LAC countries. Although China has purchased far less land in Latin America than have other countries, Chinese deals continue to be a primary focus of regional discourse on agricultural sovereignty. As Hofman and Ho note, "China's actions and moves around the world are often held under a 'global magnifying glass,'" and thus more likely to be noticed. Less known are the increasing numbers of agricultural investments taking place intra-regionally and by domestic groups within countries.[69]

Strong local reactions to Chinese agricultural investment are still fueled by a belief that China is trying to buy up land in large quantities across the world. Negative reactions to Chinese deals are also occasionally the result of successful lobbying on the part of domestic interest groups. Some of these groups have been negatively impacted by China's growing presence in the region. Others, though less clearly affected, stand to benefit by taking an anti-China policy stance. Dawn Powell elaborates on this point in Chapter 11 in this volume.

China-related backlash is thought to have inspired changes to land legislation in Brazil and Argentina. Although there is debate about the factors which contributed to Brazil's 2010 reinterpretation of its land law, Carlos Pereira and João Augusto de Castro Neves attribute the move to a belief in Brazil that land acquisitions, mainly by China's state-owned enterprises, could have a negative impact on security issues and land and commodity prices.[70] Reuters similarly reported that the land law's reinterpretation occurred because of concerns about "large purchases by sovereign wealth funds, particularly from the Middle East, and by Chinese buyers."[71] If passed, the reinterpreted land law restricts acquisition by foreign persons of land characterized as rural, closing a legal loophole that had permitted foreign interests to circumvent existing restrictions by creating a Brazilian-based company. As Powell explains, there have since been efforts to relax restrictions for the purchase of land by foreigners, with the possible exclusion of sovereign wealth funds.

On December 22, 2011 the Argentine lower house passed the Ley de Protección al Dominio Nacional sobre Propiedad, Posesión o Tenencia de Tierras Rurales in a similar effort to restrict foreign purchase of the country's land. Like the Brazilian reinterpretation, Argentina's new law was also attributed

TABLE 5.4 Diversity of Chinese Companies Investing in Agriculture

Food and agriculture		Other industries	
State-owned	Privately owned	State-owned	Privately owned
COFCO (central SOE; grain trade and production, food processing)	Shuanghui (former municipal SOE; pork)	China Investment Corp. (sovereign wealth fund)	Shanghai Zhongfu (property developer)
Chongqing Grain (provincial SOE; grain trade and production)	Yili Industrial (dairy)	Sinochem (central SOE; petrochemical group)	Shanghai Pengxin Group (mining, agriculture, property)
Bright Foods (provincial SOE; dairy)	Synutra (infant formula specialist)	Sinomach (central SOE; machinery and construction)	
Heilongjiang Beidahuang (provincial SOE; grain trade and production)			
COMPLANT (subsidiary of central SOE SDIC; sugar producer)			

to perceived Chinese land grabbing. *Territorio Digital* wrote in December 2011 that the legislation was adopted because of "the interests of large countries with food shortages, such as India and China, in buying land in Argentina."[72] *La Nación* wrote in August 2011 that the debate was taking place at a time when Rio Negro's "radical, *Kirchnerismo*-allied" governor, Miguel Saiz, was "about to sign an agreement with China for the exploitation of provincial land."[73] Whether motivated by genuine concern or by political objectives, the legislation seeks to prohibit foreign investment in Argentine land. Other Latin American nations have debated similar, albeit less stringent, legislation in recent years.

In addition to these challenges, Chinese firms have also had plenty of disagreements with local firms and governments over terms, land use rights, and other issues, resulting in stalled or terminated negotiations in certain cases. Even successful deals encounter difficulties. The 2010 lease from the Jamaican government of 27,854 hectares of land for the cultivation of sugarcane by the Chinese company COMPLANT is one such example. COMPLANT initially failed to deliver on its sugar production targets in Jamaica, in both raw sugar and milled cane. This was especially damaging to the company's reputation, considering that local workers are paid based on production numbers. There have also been some concerns in Jamaica about low levels of cooperation between COMPLANT and other local sugarcane farmers.[74]

Looking Ahead: New Trends in Chinese Overseas Agricultural Investment?

China's "land grabbing" activity in LAC is far less remarkable than generally believed. Overall, China's land deals in the region are few in number and small in scale. In addition, China's agricultural land purchases and leases in Latin America have only rarely been supportive of the country's food security objectives. Thus far, Chinese land deals in LAC are dominated by private ventures (as in the case of Zhejiang Fudi and Pengxin) or cases of Chinese overseas development assistance (e.g., Suntime's Mexico and Cuba deals). Nor is there clear evidence of considerable government support in recent years for overseas "land grabbing." In fact, the individuals and institutions responsible for China's overseas agricultural investment policy have at times actively discouraged overseas land purchases in favor of other forms of investment.

Whether motivated by profit, government directives, or a combination thereof, Chinese firms, like their multinational counterparts, are interested not just in buying land but also in investing across the production chain. As in other sectors, China—through special financing mechanisms and other incentives—is especially encouraging of overseas M&A, which provides its firms with access to a wider range of markets, industries, and technologies. Having received considerable support from CDB and the Agricultural Bank of China, COFCO alone aspires to invest more than US$10 billion in overseas M&As in the agricultural sector over the next five years.[75]

China is devising still other means by which to facilitate agricultural supply. The Chinese government's possible support for a Transoceanic railway—running from a still undetermined port on Peru's coast, through Bolivia, to the Santos port in Brazil—is closely aligned with China's food security objectives, for example. This deal is still very much in the planning phase, but feasibility studies have already been conducted for certain portions of the proposed railway. Like COFCO's recent deals, China's regional railway initiatives are indicative of a growing preference for investment in various phases of agricultural production, including transport logistics. The proposed Peru-Bolivia-Brazil passage would facilitate the export of soy and other raw materials to China while supporting Chinese construction firms and machinery exporters.

Numerous agricultural cooperation agreements have also been brokered in support of China's overseas interests. The first China–Latin America and the Caribbean Agricultural Ministers' Forum was held in Beijing in June 2013 and attended by 16 ministers and 9 vice ministers of agriculture from LAC. During the forum, China and 21 Latin American and Caribbean countries[76] signed the Beijing Declaration of China–Latin America and the Caribbean Agricultural Ministers, which states that China and Latin America will "jointly promote investments in agribusiness." The forum also created a US$50 million special fund to conduct agricultural cooperation projects, presumably with some support from private capital. China has in addition signed bilateral deals concerning agriculture, fishing, forestry-related, and other cooperation agreements with several Latin America and Caribbean countries. For example, a joint action plan between China and Brazil encourages two-way investment in agriculture with a focus on grain and food processing.

China's need to complement its internal production will mean high rates of agricultural demand and trade with major producers in Latin America far into the future. The country's growing interest in overseas agricultural investment also presents new, potentially attractive opportunities for partnership and agricultural development in the LAC region. The extent to which China's LAC investments and other agreements are successful will continue to depend on governmental, interest group, and popular reactions to China's presence in the countries where it seeks to invest. Whether these deals will truly benefit Latin American nations depends on national and local government consideration of environmental and other challenges associated with agricultural sector expansion. China is nonetheless seeking to establish itself as a trusted agricultural partner in the region, through diplomatic channels, development assistance, and increasingly varied agricultural investment.

Notes

1 See Sinosure's January 1, 2014 report on China's overseas agricultural investment for a regional break-down of OFDI data: http://www.sinosure.com.cn/sinosure/xwzx/rdzt/ckyj/ckdt/xyzt/ncpxy/163958.html (accessed July 6, 2016).

2 Duncan Freeman, Jonathan Holslag, and Steffi Weil, "China's Foreign Farming Policy: Can Land Provide Security?" *BICCS Asia Paper*, vol. 3, no. 9 (2008).

3 "When Others Are Grabbing Their Land," *Economist*, May 5, 2011, http://www.economist.com/node/18648855 (accessed July 6, 2016).

4 Freeman et al., "China's Foreign Farming Policy."

5 Food and Agriculture Organization of the United Nations (FAO), International Fund for Agricultural Development (IFAD), and World Food Programme (WFP), *The State of Food Insecurity Report, 2011* (Rome: FAO, IFAD, and WFP, 2011).

6 FAOSTAT Database, http://faostat.fao.org/site/291/default.aspx (accessed August 20, 2013). Chinese officials tend to claim that China has 10 percent of the world's arable land.

7 Organisation for Economic Co-operation and Development (OECD), "OECD/FAO Expect Slower Global Agricultural Production Growth," June 6, 2013, http://www.oecd.org/newsroom/oecd-fao-expect-slower-global-agricultural-production-growth.htm (accessed October 11, 2013).

8 Ministry of Environmental Protection of China, and Ministry of Land and Resources of China, "Nationwide Earth Pollution Bulletin" [全国土壤污染公报], April 17, 2014, http://www.mep.gov.cn/gkml/hbb/qt/201404/W020140417558995804588.pdf (accessed July 6, 2016).

9 Niu Shuping and David Stanway, "In China, Food Scares Put Mao's Self-Sufficiency Goal at Risk," *Reuters*, May 22, 2013, http://www.reuters.com/article/2013/05/22/us-china-pollution-rice-idUSBRE94L17J20130522 (accessed October 14, 2013).

10 United Nations Office of the High Commissioner for Human Rights (UNOHCHR), "Report of the Special Rapporteur on the Right to Food: Addendum—Mission to China," January 20, 2013, http://daccess-dds-ny.un.org/doc/UNDOC/GEN/G12/101/94/PDF/G1210194.pdf?OpenElement (accessed October 11, 2013). For the latest Chinese data on land degradation, see http://paper.people.com.cn/rmrb/html/2014-12/18/nw.D110000renmrb_20141218_2-03.htm (accessed July 6, 2016). For data on land quality, see the Ministry of Agriculture's December 2014 document: http://www.moa.gov.cn/govpublic/ZZYGLS/201412/t20141217_4297895.htm (accessed July 6, 2016).

11 "Overuse of Fertilizers Is Robbing Northeast Grain Heartland of Its Valuable Topsoil," *South China Morning Post*, December 9, 2014, http://www.scmp.com/news/china/article/1658606/over-use-fertilisers-may-threaten-chinas-rich-grain-growing-northern (accessed July 6, 2016).

12 "Representative Wang Jinfu: Higher Agricultural Mechanization Rate Is Essential for the Growth of Family Farming" [王金富代表: 培育家庭农场更需加快推进农业机械化], *Xinhua.net*, March 7, 2014, http://news.xinhuanet.com/politics/2014-03/07/c_119662082.htm. According to China's State Council Information Office, China has achieved a farming mechanization rate of over 75 percent for rice and corn, and nearly full mechanization of wheat production.

13 Bryan Lohmar, "Modernizing Agriculture: Planting the Seeds of Reform," *China Economic Quarterly*, September 2013.

14 Ibid.

15 Philip C.C. Huang, "China's New-Age Small Farms and Their Vertical Integration: Agribusiness or Co-ops?" *Modern China*, vol. 37, no. 107 (2011), http://mcx.sagepub.com/content/37/2/107.full.pdf (accessed October 12, 2013); Philip C.C. Huang and Peng Yusheng, "The Conjuncture of Three Historic Tendencies of Change and the Future of Small-Scale Chinese Farming," *Huang Zongzhi*, no. 4 (2007), pp. 74–88.

16 "China's Cofco Lays Out Global Agricultural Ambition," *Financial Times*, April 2015, http://www.ft.com/fastft/311202 (accessed July 6, 2016).

17 Guo Jie's Presentation at the Inter-American Dialogue's China and Latin America Agriculture Workshop, Washington, DC, November 20, 2013, http://www.thedialogue.org/china_and_latin_america_agriculture_workshop (accessed July 6, 2016).

18 State Council Information Office of China, "The Grain Issue in China" [中国的粮食问题], http://www.scio.gov.cn/zfbps/ndhf/1996/Document/307978/307978.htm (accessed April 8, 2015).

19 The plan also mandated improving the trading system for grain imports and exports, and strengthening inter-governmental relations with the world's major grain producers, to establish reliable agricultural cooperation in the long run. Chinese companies were encouraged to "go out" and secure grain imports.

20 "Major SOEs Map Out Agricultural 'Going Out'" [农业布局"走出去"三大央企圈定重点], February 11, 2012, http://www.eeo.com.cn/2012/0211/220696.shtml (accessed July 6, 2016).

21 "Chinese Agriculture Minister on Food Security: Ensure 100% Self-Sufficiency for Rice and Wheat" [农业部长谈粮食安全: 确保水稻小麦100%自给], December 26, 2013, http://finance.sina.com.cn/china/20131226/065617756550.shtml (accessed July 6, 2016).

22 CCP and the State Council, "Orders on Deepening Rural Reform and Promoting Agricultural Modernization" [关于全面深化农村改革加快推进农业现代化的若干意见], January 19, 2014, http://www.gov.cn/gongbao/content/2014/content_2574736.htm (accessed July 6, 2016).

23 "No. 1 Document Draws Three Lines for Food Security" [一号文件框定粮食安全战略自给率给出三项指标], December 21, 2013, http://www.eeo.com.cn/2013/1221/253870.shtml (accessed July 6, 2016).

24 Will Freeman, "Grain Imports: Feeding the Hungry Hordes," *GK Dragonomics*, March 2013.

25 Ibid.

26 Ibid.

27 China's 2012 Agricultural Production Statistics, Dim Sums, in reference to a December report from China's National Bureau of Statistics and the Bureau's Statistical Communique released in February 2012, http://dimsums.blogspot.com/2013/03/chinas-2012-agricultural-production.html (accessed July 6, 2016).

28 Also see Eduardo Daniel Oviedo, "Argentina Facing China: Modernization, Interests, and Economic Relations Model," *East Asia*, no. 30 (2013), pp. 7–34; and Daniel Cardoso, "China–Brazil: A Strategic Partnership in an Evolving World Order," *East Asia*, no. 30 (2013), pp. 35–51.

29 National Development and Reform Commission, "Conditions for Grain Import Tariff Quota Application and the Principles for Quota Allocation 2015" [2015年粮食进口关税配额申领条件和分配原则], December 10, 2014, http://www.sdpc.gov.cn/gzdt/201412/t20141212_651980.html (accessed July 6, 2016).

30 Freeman et al., "China's Foreign Farming Policy."

31 Cheng Guoqiang, "Thoughts on Implementing a Global Strategy for Agriculture" [程国强: 对实施全球农业战略的思考], *cpcnews.cn*, October 4, 2013, http://theory.people.com.cn/n/2013/1004/c40531-23104465.html (accessed July 6, 2016).

32 General Administration of Customs of China, "Import Statistics for Major Goods" [2014年12月全国进口重点商品量值表], http://www.customs.gov.cn/publish/portal0/tab49666/info729731.htm; Ministry of Agriculture of China, *China Agricultural Outlook Report (2015–2024)* (Beijing: China Agricultural Scientech, 2015).

33 From Minister Han Changfu's speech at a meeting with agricultural companies following the 2010 Central Rural Conference; see http://www.farmer.com.cn/news/jjsn/201012/t20101225_604623.htm (accessed July 6, 2016).

34 Teng Xiaomeng, "Policy Proposal to Buy and Rent Land Overseas to Grown Grain Submitted to the State Council" [海外买租地种粮政策建议方案上报国务院], *Sina.com*, May 8, 2008, http://finance.sina.com.cn/roll/20080508/01074842380.shtml (accessed April 8, 2015).

35 "Where Does Chinese Agriculture Go Out? Becoming Traders Rather than Farmers" [中国农业"走出去"出路在哪里？做"粮商"而不是做"农民"], *Ceweekly.cn*, December 23, 2013, http://www.ceweekly.cn/2013/1223/71657.shtml (accessed July 6, 2016).

36 Author interview, Beijing, April 2015.

37 "Where Does Chinese Agriculture Go Out?"

38 COFCO, "For Global Competition in Agricultural Products We Need a Powerhouse" [全球农产品竞争　我们需要强者], http://www.cofco.com/cn/about/3638.html (accessed April 10, 2015).

39 Jiao Jian, "China's Rice Bags Tied around Others' Waist: Soybeans and Three Main Staple Foods Depend on Imports" [中国米袋子系在别人腰间：大豆及三大主粮依赖进口], *ifeng Finance*, December 09, 2013, http://finance.ifeng.com/a/20131209/11235014_2.shtml (accessed July 6, 2016).

40 Irna Hofman and Peter Ho, "China's 'Developmental Outsourcing': A Critical Examination of Chinese Global 'Land Grabs' Discourse," *Journal of Peasant Studies*, vol. 39, no. 1 (March 2012), pp. 1–48; Frederick H. Gale, "China's Agricultural Policy and U.S. Access to China's Market," Testimony before the U.S.–China Economic and Security Review Commission, April 25, 2013.

41 Jiao, "China's Rice Bags Tied around Others' Waist."

42 Gale, "China's Agricultural Policy and U.S. Access to China's Market."

43 "COFCO Sows Seed of Further Overseas Growth," *China.org.cn*, November 15, 2012, http://www.china.org.cn/business/2012-11/15/content_27119559.htm.

44 Ministry of Commerce of the People's Republic of China, "Management Method for the Outward Economy and Technology Cooperation Special Fund," April 18, 2011, http://www.mofcom.gov.cn/article/b/bf/201104/20110407525027.shtml (accessed July 6, 2016).

45 Jiao, "China's Rice Bags Tied around Others' Waist."

46 Gale, "China's Agricultural Policy and U.S. Access to China's Market."

47 Hugh Bronstein, "Exclusive: China Oks Entry of First Big Cargo of Argentine Corn," *Reuters*, August 7, 2013, http://www.reuters.com/article/2013/08/07/us-argentina-china-corn-idUSBRE97515E20130807 (accessed July 6, 2016).

48 "China Approves Brazilian Corn Imports—Papers," *Reuters*, November 6, 2013, http://www.reuters.com/article/2013/11/06/brazil-corn-china-idUSL2N0IR0ND20131106 (accessed July 6, 2016).

49 Hofman and Ho, "China's 'Developmental Outsourcing.'"

50 For example, see ibid.

51 Our research is limited to land grabs for crop production. We do not include purchases of forest for timber production, for example.

52 Deborah Brautigam and Tang Xiaoyang, "China's Engagement in African Agriculture: 'Down to the Countryside,'" *China Quarterly*, no. 199 (2009), pp. 686–706.

53 "Suntime International Economic and Technological Cooperation (Group) Ltd." [新天国际经济技术合作（集团）有限公司], Xinjiang Production and Construction Corps, December 25, 2014, http://www.bingtuan.gov.cn/bt/jrbt/mqmp/512933.shtml (accessed July 6, 2016).

54 Shane Romig, "Hungry China Shops in Argentina," *Wall Street Journal*, June 20, 2011, http://www.wsj.com/articles/SB10001424052702303823104576391621352528138 (accessed July 6, 2016).

55 Rodrigo Orihuela, "China's Top Farmer to Invest in Argentina's Patagonian Winemaking, Corn," *Bloomberg*, June 9, 2011, http://www.bloomberg.com/news/articles/2011-06-08/beidahuang-will-invest-1-5-billion-on-patagonian-farms-that-it-won-t-own (accessed July 6, 2016).

56 "Sodero Nievas avala suspender la aplicación del convenio agroalimentario con China," *barilochense.com*, November 22, 2011, http://www.barilochense.com/notas/sodero-nievas-avala-suspender-la-aplicacion-del-convenio-agroalimentario-con-china-y-propone-que-soria-reencauce-el-proyecto?indice_clasificados=1&rubro_id=11&subrubro_id=28 (accessed July 6, 2016).

57 Author interview with China–Brazil Business Council, Rio de Janeiro, August 2013.

58 Hu Junhua, "Farmers in Zhejiang Organize Cooperatives to Purchase Land and Plant Soybeans in Brazil" [浙江农民组织合作社巴西买地种大豆], *ifeng Finance*, February 19, 2009, http://finance.ifeng.com/news/hgjj/20090219/387402.shtml (accessed July 6, 2016).

59 Ibid.

60 "COFCO Buys Chilean Vineyard for $18m," *China Daily*, September 21, 2010, http://www.chinadaily.com.cn/business/2010-09/21/content_11336062.htm (accessed July 6, 2016).

61 Zhou Siyu, "Moet Hennessy Toasts Launch of Yunnan Winery," *China Daily*, May 11, 2013, http://www.chinadaily.com.cn/bizchina/2013-05/11/content_16491986.htm (accessed July 6, 2016).

62 "Cofco Seeks Acquisitions to 'Balance' China's Food Demand," *Bloomberg Businessweek*, November 2, 2011, http://www.businessweek.com/news/2011-11-02/cofco-seeks-acquisitions-to-balance-china-s-food-demand.html (accessed July 6, 2016).

63 "China Buys Majority Stake in Nidera as Part of Its Investment in Food Assets," *MercoPress*, March 5, 2014, http://en.mercopress.com/2014/03/05/china-buys-majority-stake-in-nidera-as-part-of-its-investment-in-food-assets (accessed July 6, 2016).

64 "China's COFCO, CIC to Set Up JV to Run Agricultural Businesses," Reuters, May 12, 2015, http://www.reuters.com/article/2015/05/12/cic-cofco-jointventure-idUSB9N0XK05920150512 (accessed July 6, 2016).

65 COFCO just purchased a majority share in this company, and China's sovereign wealth fund, China Investment Corporation, is a 16 percent shareholder.

66 Gordon Orr, "What's in Store for China in 2013," McKinsey & Company, January 2013, http://www.mckinsey.com/insights/economic_studies/whats_in_store_for_china_in_2013 (accessed July 6, 2016).

67 Li Jing, "Peng Xin Has a Clear Prototype: Controlling Four Companies, the Head of the Company Is Low-key and Ambitious" [鹏欣系雏形清晰: 控股四家公司 掌门人低调有事业心], *ifeng Finance*, July 15, 2013, http://finance.ifeng.com/a/20130715/10165124_0.shtml (accessed July 6, 2016).

68 Celine Sun, "Legend Applies Its Tech Know-How to Fruit," *South China Morning Post*, November 18, 2013, http://www.scmp.com/business/companies/article/1358932/legend-applies-its-tech-know-how-fruit (accessed July 6, 2016).

69 Hofman and Ho, "China's 'Developmental Outsourcing.'"

70 Carlos Pereira and João Augusto de Castro Neves, "Brazil and China: South–South Partnership or North–South Competition?" *Foreign Policy at Brookings*, no. 26 (2011), http://www.brookings.edu/~/media/research/files/papers/2011/4/03%20brazil%20china%20pereira/03_brazil_china_pereira.pdf (accessed July 6, 2016).

71 Peter Murphy, "Brazil Mulls Leasing Farmland to Foreigners," *Reuters*, May 9, 2011, http://www.reuters.com/article/2011/05/09/us-brazil-land-idUSTRE74856K20110509.

72 "Oficializaron una nueva Ley de Tierras que rige en todo el país," *Territorio Digital*, http://www.territoriodigital.com/notaimpresa.aspx?c=4545896295323533 (accessed April 10, 2015).

73 "An Agreement between China and Rio Black Stirs Controversy," *La Nación*, http://www.lanacion.com.ar/1401319-un-acuerdo-entre-china-y-rio-negro-genera-polemica (accessed April 10, 2015).

74 China and Latin America Agriculture Workshop, Inter-American Dialogue, http://www.thedialogue.org/china_and_latin_america_agriculture_workshop (accessed July 6, 2016).

75 COFCO, the country's largest trader of grains and edible oils, said it will add investment worth more than $10 billion to fund overseas mergers and acquisitions in the next five years. See more at http://www.thecropsite.com/news/9570/cofco-to-expand-overseas-ma#sthash.uw9jDizO.ljxxNo9u.dpuf (accessed July 6, 2016).

76 Signatories include: Antigua and Barbuda, Argentina, Bahamas, Barbados, Bolivia, Brazil, Chile, China, Colombia, Costa Rica, Cuba, Dominica, Ecuador, Grenada, Guyana, Jamaica, Mexico, Peru, Suriname, Trinidad and Tobago, Uruguay, and Venezuela (Declaración de Beijing, 2013).

6

CHINESE–PERUVIAN RELATIONS IN THE MINING SECTOR

Learning Step by Step

Cynthia Sanborn and Victoria Chonn Ching[1]

Introduction

One of the most dramatic changes in Latin America in the 21st century has been the expanded role of China as a trade and investment partner for most of the region. Peru is one of the countries most engaged in and affected by expanding relations with China. Over the last ten years, the mineral and energy demands of a rapidly growing China offered exceptional opportunities for Peru in terms of attracting new investment and expanding markets for its traditional primary exports. In this period, copper, iron, gold, and other minerals accounted for 50 to 60 percent of total Peruvian exports, 25 percent of foreign direct investment, and 15 percent of tax revenues.[2] Although Western multinationals have provided the bulk of foreign direct investment (FDI) in minerals in Peru since the country's extractive industries were privatized in the early 1990s, China became the main destination for these minerals, and Chinese FDI in this sector is projected to account for about 36 percent of the total mining investment in the decade ahead.[3]

This expanded relationship with China helped Peru to become one of the region's economic success stories in the 21st century, achieving sustained positive growth from 2001 to 2014, and slashing poverty levels by more than half in the same period. However, this natural resource-led bonanza also revived longstanding concerns about the risks of excessive dependency on primary commodity exports, and the structural challenges to achieving a more diversified and productive economy.[4] As Chinese demand for minerals and oil has been higher than the world average, some argue that the nature of the China–Peru relationship further reinforces this pattern.[5]

Dependency on mineral exports, and on China, has also raised concerns in Peru about the human rights and environmental implications of this activity. For some, the advantages of attracting Chinese investment have been tempered by concerns over the ability of Chinese-owned firms to comply with global standards in such areas as revenue transparency, environmental, and labor policies.[6] The mining industry within China has had severe problems with safety and environmental regulations, and Chinese companies have not practiced the kind of transparency that many in Latin America have come to demand—nor have they been active participants to date to uphold better standards. However, some analysts also argue that the key issue is not whether a company is Chinese, or of any other nationality, but rather the willingness and capacity of host countries to regulate them adequately.[7]

Peruvian policy makers are aware of the risks of primary export dependency, as well as those posed by large-scale extractive activities, for local communities and the natural environment. To address the first challenge, Peru has aggressively pursued free trade agreements (FTAs) with China and at least 18 other countries, aimed at diversifying the country's trade and investment partners and markets. To address the second challenge, Peruvian policy makers have adopted measures to raise standards in the extractive industries, and to use the revenues that they generate to advance various development goals.[8] Peru joined the Extractive Industries Transparency Initiative (EITI) in 2007, and in 2011 became the first country in the Americas to be declared compliant within that framework. In 2008 Peru established a new Ministry of the Environment, which has vied with the Ministry of Energy and Mines (MINEM) to regulate the environmental impacts of the extractive industries. In 2011, Peru also became the first country in the region to establish domestic legislation to implement ILO Convention 169, which guarantees the right of indigenous and tribal peoples to prior consultation on major public policies that affect their lives, including the authorization of extractive activity.[9]

But, as global mineral prices have fluctuated and moved into a downturn since 2012, the drive to increase mineral production in Peru has often conflicted with efforts at effective environmental and social regulation. Government initiatives in this area have been hampered by institutional weaknesses, conflicts of interest, and strong resistance from investors. There have been numerous and often violent disputes between companies and communities over land and water rights, revenue distribution, and environmental contamination, including high-profile cases that have engaged national and transnational activists and the international media.[10] Such conflicts pose potential challenges and delays for all firms, including Chinese investors new to the country.

In this context, our research has focused on Chinese involvement in the Peruvian mining sector at both the macro level—with changing trade and investment patterns—and the micro level, examining the performance of Chinese firms operating on the ground.[11] In regard to the latter, we have focused on: whether Chinese investment in the Peruvian mining sector has social or environmental impacts that are significantly different from those of non-Chinese investments in those same sector; whether Chinese companies comply with Peruvian policies and regulations to a lesser or greater degree; and whether the Peruvian authorities apply the same standards to them. Through the use of case studies, we have examined how and to what extent Chinese companies have reacted differently than their industry peers to local communities and other stakeholders. This chapter briefly summarizes our findings at both levels, and draws conclusions about the nature of this relationship today and in the years ahead.

Peruvian–Chinese Trade and Investment: A Gradual Evolution

Relations between Peru and China date to the mid-19th century, and Peru's diplomatic relations with the People's Republic of China date to 1971.[12] However, direct Chinese investment in Peru only began in 1992, when the state-owned Shougang Group bought the state-owned iron ore company Empresa Minera de Hierro del Peru (Hierro Peru); another 15 years would pass before more significant Chinese investments arrived. In fact, the Peru–China relationship really took off after 2004, when Peru granted market economy status to China, and especially in 2007, when Chinese firms invested in several major mining projects.[13] In 2008 both countries established a "strategic partnership," leading to the negotiation of the Peru–China Free Trade Agreement in 2009. For Peru, this was a fundamental part of a broader strategy to diversify the country's economy through trade and investment, while for China it was part of the ongoing "Going Out" effort at globalization. By 2011, China had replaced the United States as Peru's main trading partner. That same year the Association of Chinese Enterprises was formed, with 43 members and support from the Chinese Embassy. By 2014 the Association had 61 members, and some 120 Chinese firms were legally registered to operate in Peru, in mining and energy, telecommunications, machinery, agriculture, construction, and commerce.[14]

Between 2013 and 2015 the diplomatic and trade relations between China and Peru further deepened. In 2013, leaders of the two nations celebrated their "comprehensive strategic partnership" by signing 11 bilateral accords aimed at optimizing trade and strengthening cooperation in agriculture, infrastructure, mining, and social programs. That same year, the first Chinese bank, Industrial and Commercial Bank of China (ICBC), was authorized to operate in Peru. The Chinese National Petroleum Company (CNPC) also purchased Peru's holdings of Petrobras, the Brazilian oil giant, giving control over some 40 percent of Peru's hydrocarbon production to Chinese companies. In December 2013, President Humala inaugurated the Toromocho copper project, operated by the Aluminum Corporation of China (Chinalco), which promised to increase total copper production by 20 percent. This was followed by the purchase of Las Bambas in 2014, another copper mega-project, by MMG, a company backed by China Minmetals. These two projects alone are expected to contribute at least a full point to Peruvian gross domestic product (GDP).[15] In Table 6.1 we show the entire portfolio of projects now in the pipeline or underway.

TABLE 6.1 Main Chinese Investments in Peru

Year	Investor	Partners	Project	Sector
1992	Shougang Corporation/Shougang Hierro Perú S.A.A.		Marcona	Mining
1993–94	China National Petroleum Corporation (CNPC)/Sapet		Lot VI/VII (Talara, Piura)	Energy, oil, and gas
2002	Tiens Group/Tianshi Perú S.A.C.			Manufacturing
2005	China National Petroleum Corporation (CNPC)/Sapet		Lot 111 (Madre de Dios)	Energy, oil, and gas
2007	Aluminum Corporation of China (Chinalco)/Minera Chinalco Perú S.A.		Toromocho	Mining
2007	Zijin Mining Group/Río Blanco Copper S.A.	Zijin (45%), Tongling Nonferrous (35%), Xiamen C&D (20%)	Rio Blanco	Mining
2007	Beijing Rich Gold/Jintong Mining		Llama TY01	Mining (exploration)
2008	China Minmetals Corporation–Jiangxi Copper Corporation/Lumina Copper S.A.C.	Minmetals (60%), Jiangxi Copper (40%)	Galeno	Mining
2008	Junefield Company Limited/Junefield Group		Cercana	Mining
2009	Shougang Corporation/Shougang Hierro Perú S.A.A.		Marcona Expansion	Mining

Year	Company	Ownership	Project	Sector
2009	Nanjinzhao Group/Jinzhao Mining Peru S.A.		Pampa del Pongo	Mining
2010	Bank of China	Bank of China, Interbank		Financial
2010	Industrial and Commercial Bank of China (ICBC)/ICBC Peru Bank		China Desk Perú	Financial
2011	Minera Shouxin Peru	Baiyin Nonferrous Group (51%), Shougang (49%)	Proyecto Explotación Relaves	Tailings
2012	China National Petroleum Corporation (CNPC)/Sapet	CNPC (45%) Pluspetrol Norte S.A. (55%)	Lot 1AB (Olaya, Loreto)	Energy, oil, and gas
2012	China National Petroleum Corporation (CNPC)/Sapet	CNPC (27%), Pluspetrol Norte S.A. (73%)	Lot 8 (Trompeteros, Yanayacu, Loreto)	Energy, oil, and gas
2013	China National Petroleum Corporation (CNPC)/PetroChina		Lot X (Talara), Lot 58 (Camisea)	Energy, oil, and gas
2013	China National Petroleum Corporation (CNPC)/PetroChina	CNPC (46.16%), Repsol (53.84%)	Lot 57 (Camisea)	Energy, oil, and gas
2013	Pacific Andes International Holdings Ltd./China Fishery Group			Fishery
2014	MMG Ltd.	MMG Ltd. (62.5%), Guoxin Investment Corporation (22.5%), CITIC Metal (15%)	Las Bambas	Mining

Source: Authors' elaboration based on information from various sources, including: American Heritage Foundation; ITC calculations based on UN Comtrade statistics; ProInversion; MINEM; Sanborn and Yong, "Peru's Economic Boom and the Asian Connection"; and Irwin and Gallagher, "Chinese Mining Investment in Latin America."

In 2015, Chinese Premier Li Keqiang visited Peru on a South American tour, and the two countries signed further bilateral cooperation agreements in existing and new areas of trade and investment, infrastructure construction, and Chinese assistance for improving local industrial capacity.[16] A highlight of the visit was the announcement that China, Brazil, and Peru would undertake feasibility studies on a proposed new Transoceanic Railway project, which would link Brazil's Atlantic coast to the Peruvian Pacific in order to facilitate the export of goods from Latin America to China. Fully aware of criticism within the region regarding the asymmetry of China–Peru trade relations, as most of what China imports from Latin America is raw materials, and most of what it sells back is manufactured goods, Li stressed the need for an "updated model" of cooperation: "both sides need to join hands in pursuing industrial modernization and a transformation of their economic growth models."[17]

Taking a step back, we ask whether China has helped or hindered Peru's effort to grow and diversify its economy. The record to date is decidedly mixed. On the upside, trade between Peru and China quadrupled after the FTA went into effect, from US$4 billion in 2010 to US$15.9 billion in 2014.[18] China accounted for 18 percent of Peru's total exports and roughly 3.5 percent of GDP by 2014.[19] Although Peru trades with most of the world, China became its main trading partner, the leading destination for its exports, and Peru's main supplier of capital goods. On the downside, as in the rest of Latin America, Peruvian exports to China have remained largely primary goods, with four products—copper, iron, lead, and fishmeal—constituting the lion's share of the total. This largely explains the country's positive overall trade balance through 2012. Furthermore, the relative share of these goods has changed since the 1990s, with mineral and oil products increasing from 13 percent of total exports to China in 1997 to 83 percent in 2014.[20] The concentration of copper exports, in particular, has risen considerably. The recent decline in Chinese demand for copper has thus contributed to a significant slowdown in Peru's growth.[21]

Meanwhile, from 2001 to 2014, Peru's imports from China grew fivefold relative to the size of the economy (from 0.69 percent to 4.4 percent of GDP),[22] outpacing overall exports, which roughly doubled as a share of Peru's GDP in the same period. Yet, although Chinese imports compete with local products in sectors such as footwear, textiles, and garments, where the trade balance remains negative, this has not exactly led to "de-industrialization," as Peru did not have a significant industrial base to begin with. Two other points are worth making here. First, the overall effect of an expanded market and better access to competitive intermediate goods appears to have outweighed the negative effects of Chinese imports on specific sectors,[23] and, second, Peruvian negotiators were successful in exempting China's access to these sectors in the context of the Peru–China FTA.[24]

With regard to nontraditional exports, the Peruvian Ministry of Trade reports that these doubled between 2010 and 2014, to more than US$473 million.[25] The

FTA has been important, allowing 83.5 percent of Peruvian exports to enter China with zero tariffs and providing some protection for Peruvian products most vulnerable to Chinese competition.[26] While nontraditional exports are still a tiny share (5 percent) of total exports to China in value, they have been on the rise. Within the first year of implementation of the Peru–China FTA, the number of Peruvian exporters to China grew by 30 percent, to about 500 companies, and Peru exported 140 new nontraditional products to China—particularly in the chemical, agricultural, and fishing sectors. Peru's agricultural exports to China have grown 8.7 times since the FTA went into effect. The real challenge for Peru is to nurture this trend and to take more pro-active measures to ensure that, as Chinese demand evolves, Peru will be prepared to provide it with higher value-added products.[27]

Direct investment from China in Peru has been slower to materialize. However, Peru ranks second only to Brazil as a destination for Chinese FDI in Latin America. In 2014 Peru captured nearly half of all *projected* Chinese investment in the region,[28] and total Chinese investment committed in Peru was estimated to be about US$18 billion.[29]

However, the majority of the capital invested by China is still concentrated in the country's three primary sectors—mining, fishing, and hydrocarbons—and most of it involves Chinese SOEs managed by the central or local governments. In spite of the expanding array of cooperation agreements and companies present, the actual stock of Chinese FDI on the ground in Peru remains relatively low. Although it is difficult to trace the total amount of FDI coming from China into Latin America owing to the use of tax havens in the Caribbean, the Peruvian authorities estimated this to be about US$1.8 billion in 2013 (48 percent in minerals, 40 percent in fisheries). As of June 2015, China remained only the 17th largest source of FDI in Peru by nationality.[30]

In the mining sector, nonetheless, China is the largest single investor in Peru today, and Chinese SOEs hold an estimated 36 percent of the total projected portfolio.[31] At least 14 Chinese firms, primarily state-owned but also some with private or mixed capital, have invested in mineral projects in Peru's Northern and Central Highlands, as well as in hydrocarbon development in the Amazon. A major attraction of Chinese FDI in this sector has been the size of projected investments, and the ability of Chinese firms to commit resources over the longer term. As seen in Table 6.1, the majority of Chinese investments are concentrated in copper and iron, and since 2007 they have involved new concessions purchased directly or through the takeover of junior firms. Most are still in the exploration stages, though Toromocho—one of the largest Chinese investments to date, at US$4.82 billion—began operations in December 2013.

Overall, while Chinese investors have shown increased interest in other sectors of the economy—including logistics and port operations, and transportation infrastructure—interviews with businesspeople and diplomats from both countries suggest that there are numerous obstacles for Chinese state-owned firms and individual entrepreneurs wishing to expand into these areas. Some of these are related to Peru's basic regulatory requirements for all investors, including such tasks as obtaining work visas, translating and officiating documents, and obtaining permits for various stages of operations. Tender processes for infrastructure investments tend to be complicated. There are also personal challenges for investors, such as long delays in obtaining visas for family members.

More specific obstacles to attracting investment from China stem from low compatibility between the Chinese and Peruvian tax and legal frameworks and financial systems. This mismatch is made worse by the lack of professionals on both sides with the appropriate language and cultural skills.[32] At a higher level, although Peruvian policy makers have been successful at negotiating FTAs and other state-to-state accords, Peru does not seem to have as clear a strategy for following up on these opportunities. The Peruvian state, moreover, does relatively little to finance or otherwise support private entrepreneurs in this process. Although nontraditional export promotion is a stated objective of the Peruvian authorities, it has not been given the kind of sustained attention and investment that are required in the current competitive environment. The neoliberal reforms of the 1990s left a legacy of aversion to state-guided industrial policies or direct export-sector promotional efforts. As a result, most business with Asia today is driven by private companies and individuals with little assistance from the government, which results in lost opportunities for better negotiations and better deals.

Once a tender offer is won, Chinese investors are also not used to negotiating and communicating with a large number of actors aside from the Peruvian central government. Yet, depending on the type of investment, this may require negotiations with popularly elected regional and municipal authorities, leaders of rural and indigenous communities, urban trade unions and neighborhood associations, activist nongovernmental organizations, and diverse media, along with local bankers and business competitors. Such a range of actors is normal in a volatile democracy like Peru's, and successful Western investors have learned over time how to navigate these potential hurdles. Chinese businesspeople and diplomats, however, are less experienced at multi-stakeholder relations and are less accustomed to the constant demands for accountability from non-state actors. Nonetheless, as our case studies of Chinese investment in the mining sector suggest, they are learning quickly.

Extractive Governance and Chinese Engagement

In recent years Peru has been something of a laboratory for extractive industry reforms. China has also undergone major efforts at industrial and environmental reform over the past decade, including new regulations and guidelines that seek to promote the compliance of its firms with global standards. As they go overseas, leaders of Chinese firms must learn to respond to the expectations of local governments and communities and to contribute to local development. However, many remain hesitant to open up to the media or to civil society groups, or to share what they consider to be sensitive information.[33] China's new guidelines are weak on enforcement mechanisms and often lack grievance procedures or other venues for conflict resolution. Hence, it is especially important that host countries such as Peru have such mechanisms in place.

In this section we examine three areas of extractive industry reform in Peru, focusing on how Chinese firms are engaged in or influenced by them, how their performance compares to that of others in this industry, and whether policy makers treat them any differently than firms from other countries. Interestingly, while all firms doing business in Peru should face the same regulations, such questions are rarely raised about the behavior of firms of other nationalities, whereas they have been the focus of recent research on the Chinese companies operating both sides of the Pacific.[34]

Revenue Transparency and Distribution

Since 2005, Peru has been a participating country in the Extractive Industries Transparency Initiative, a global initiative that involves meeting high common standards for reporting taxes and other payments made by companies to governments, in the mining and hydrocarbon industries. The idea is to prevent significant tax evasion or irregular payments and to demonstrate to citizens the real fiscal contributions made by these industries. As numerous experts have stressed, greater transparency on the part of companies and governments is a necessary step for making both more accountable to citizens, and ensuring that the revenues generated by the extractive industries are used to promote the longer-term development needs of the societies in which they operate.[35] Peru was the first country in the Americas to become compliant with EITI standards. Although the EITI is voluntary, the majority of leading producers and taxpayers in the mining and hydrocarbon sectors participate, including all of the International Council on Mining and Metals (ICMM) members operating in Peru.[36] The Chinese, however, were on the sidelines until 2014.

It is important to note that, because of the more recent nature of Chinese FDI, only two Chinese companies in these industries pay significant taxes in Peru: Shougang Hierro Peru and Sapet (CNPC). Neither of them participated in the first three EITI Peru reports, which covered taxes paid from 2004 to 2012. Yet, because other major multinational firms that are not yet paying significant income taxes chose to participate, the absence of Chinese companies in this report earned them a reputation for lack of transparency.

According to Chinese executives operating in Peru, the omission of their firms from EITI Peru was due to the lack of authorization from their headquarter companies in China. Starting in 2011, the Humala administration assigned permanent staff from MINEM to work with a tripartite EITI Commission, which involved representatives from industry and civil society, the idea being to encourage executives of non-participating companies to join.[37] In 2012 one Chinese-owned firm, Lumina Copper, began to participate, and in 2014 Shougang and Sapet followed suit, in what was the fourth EITI Peru report (covering tax payments for 2013).[38] Participation by Chinalco and China Minmetals (the majority owner of MMG, owner of the Las Bambas copper project in Apurimac) is still pending.

Regarding revenue distribution, since 2003 50 percent of all income taxes paid by mining firms to the central government have been redistributed to the regional, provincial, and municipal governments in which their extractive activity is located. This is called the "mining canon," and in some parts of the country it means that enormous new revenues are in the hands of mayors, regional presidents, and others who could invest in much-needed infrastructure and services for their communities.

As mentioned, in the mining sector the only major Chinese taxpayer is Shougang Hierro Peru, based in the district of Marcona, in the region of Ica. This is one of the most economically dynamic regions in Peru, with socioeconomic indicators above the national average, which is due to a combination of mining, commercial agriculture, fishing, and tourism. Within Ica, however, Marcona also has the best social and economic record, and Shougang is the largest taxpayer as well as employer. According to company officials, around 70 percent of the town's adult population works for the Chinese firm or depends on someone who does, while Peru's Ministry of the Economy reports that since 2006 over 40 percent of the monetary transfers that Marcona receives comes from the mining canon.[39] Company officials also claim that, as of late 2012, the firm has provided an estimated US$967 million in tax payments and other contributions, and that between 2004 and 2012 it contributed US$74.75 million.[40]

While tax revenues from the extractive industries expanded local government budgets in numerous regions of Peru, local authorities have in fact had considerable difficulty investing these revenues in ways that address basic needs and sustainable development goals. Given this situation, private firms have been motivated to intervene directly, through numerous social programs and community relations initiatives. A World Bank study identified some 40 foundations, NGOs, trusts, and social funds created by the mining industry in Peru in recent years.[41] Three of these endeavors are sponsored by Chinese-owned firms: Shougang, Chinalco, and MMG.

Given its longer time of operation, it is no surprise that Shougang leads the way among Chinese companies in local social investment. From 2007 to 2014, Shougang designated about US$21.5 million to local development needs in its area of operation, as part of the Programa Minero de Solidaridad con el Pueblo (PMSP), created by the Peruvian government in lieu of applying a windfall profits tax. Shougang's contribution is channeled through a nonprofit created by the company in 2007, Asociacion Civil del Hierro: Progreso y Desarrollo.

Because the amount committed under this program was related to overall profits, it is not fair to compare Shougang's net contribution with that of larger, copper-based companies in the sector, such as Antamina (US$693 million) and Yanacocha (US$202 million). However, in a 2011 ranking of company transparency in these mining companies with regard to the PMSP, Shougang's association ranked 32 out of 39 companies.[42] Other companies with similarly low transparency were Cerro Verde (a U.S.-owned firm), Xstrata Tintaya (owned by the Anglo-Swiss Glencore), and Minsur (Peruvian owned). While Shougang has not been entirely transparent about what it has spent, it is not the only firm in this position.

Unlike most other mining investors in Peru, Shougang and Chinalco also maintain literal "company towns" in their areas of influence. Shougang provides basic services and infrastructure for the town of Marcona, an arrangement inherited from the Peruvian state in the privatization process, while Chinalco had to relocate an entire town and build a new one, complete with housing and services, to make way for its mine. Both of these novel situations are discussed further below.

Labor Rules and Regulations

Critics of Chinese firms operating overseas often claim that they have less respect for state-authorized labor unions, or a greater tendency to violate workers' rights. In some countries they have also been criticized for bringing in large numbers of Chinese workers instead of hiring locally. In Peru, however, there are still few Chinese firms operating with significant labor forces, and no Chinese company employs a large number of Chinese nationals.

Shougang has the largest work force among Chinese firms in Peru, employing 4,200 people including 2,000 direct hires, just 20 to 40 of whom are Chinese.[43] Irwin and Gallagher examine government data from 1993 to 2006 and place this company in the middle, among industry peers, for compliance with labor standards.[44] These authors argue that the total pay and benefits received by Shougang workers are among the highest in the industry, including a larger-than-average number of workers on regular payroll and participating in profit-sharing. This is also the only mining firm in Peru that continues to provide housing for all of its employees, as well as basic services to the community in which they live.

At the same time, Shougang has had the highest number of strikes and days lost over union disputes over the years in Peru's mining sector. Our interviews with union leaders suggest that the main disagreements involve a dual salary scale which applies a less favorable regime to newer workers. Another point of contention is the company's failure to provide a safer working environment. Outdated machinery, apparently more common in Shougang than the industry average in the firm's early years, contributed to workplace accidents. For their part, company officials argue that they inherited a highly politicized union leadership that is unwilling to recognize major new investments the company has made in the mine and plant in recent years.[45]

Chinalco began operations in December 2013, and by April 2014 company sources claimed 1,247 direct hires, out of a total 2,500 that they expect to have in place when fully operational. Only six employees at that time were Chinese.[46] Initial observations and interviews with staff from rival firms suggested that as of mid-2014 Chinalco was paying wages above the market average.

Mining is a high-risk activity, but firms should take measures to reduce accidents and protect their workers. Since 2011 the Ministry of Energy and Mines has published annual fatal accident rates by firm, with totals of 42 to 52 per year. In these four years, Shougang had two fatalities, one in 2012 and the other in 2014. Chinalco had three, one in 2011 and two in 2013. In contrast, Buenaventura reported three to four fatalities per year, and Southern Peru Copper (part of Grupo Mexico) had two or three per year. The majority of fatal accidents involve older Peruvian firms.[47]

In general, there is high demand for skilled workers in the Peruvian mining industry, and it would be hard for any major company to systematically violate labor laws or pay low wages without losing its work force. However, there is a tendency among some firms to avoid granting union rights and full benefits by hiring tertiary workers. So far, this practice seems less prevalent among the Chinese companies in Peru.[48]

One of the most frequent demands by communities where mining operations take place in Peru is for local hiring. Companies are often pressured to hire workers from adjacent areas, and this is a key issue when negotiating exploration or construction permits. Some companies include explicit promises of local hiring in contracts or in published agreements with community leaders. In the mining industry overall, MINEM reported that in 2012 around 53 percent of employees were members of local communities, 46 percent from other regions, and just 0.26 percent foreigners.[49] While Peru does not demand a specific percentage of local hires in mining projects, companies are expected to promote local employment, and to report such efforts to the ministry.

Shougang officials claim that 70 percent of the population of the city of Marcona depends economically on the company.[50] This is an exceptional case, as Marcona has been a company town since the 1950s. Chinalco has not published local employment numbers, but has reported investing considerable sums in 2012 and 2013 in temporary hiring for construction and other tasks and is expected to give preference to locals in the longer-term hiring process. The lack of people with appropriate technical and physical qualifications makes this a challenge. Chinalco is investing in scholarships and training programs for local residents in order to increase their prospects for hiring.[51]

In 2010, Lumina Copper signed a Social Accord and a series of agreements with the adjacent community of La Encañada, Cajamarca, in which the company agreed to designate 90 percent of all non-skilled jobs to local residents.[52]

However, the project has been stalled since 2013. In the Las Bambas project in Apurimac, the new Chinese owner (MMG) agreed to honor a prior commitment to provide at least one job per family in the local community, as well as maintaining a social fund with 14 investment projects in place as of 2015.[53]

In sum, mining company officials in Peru agree that it is necessary to establish and maintain good relationships with local residents for the successful operation of their projects, and that local hiring plays a very important role here. Although most Chinese firms are in the early stages of exploration or operation, to date they appear to be making as much effort as others in this sector to meet these expectations.

Environmental Rules and Regulations

Since the mining industry was privatized in the early 1990s, authorities have struggled to establish a viable legal framework for regulating the environmental impact of this inherently polluting activity.[54] Primary responsibility for such regulation lies with the central government, and until 2008 it was the task of MINEM to review and approve the environmental impact assessments (EIAs) presented by investors. This meant that the same ministry acted as judge and jury, since it is also responsible for promoting new mining investment. In 2008, however, the Ministry of the Environment (MINAM) was created, with nationwide authority to manage environmental plans and oversee environmental regulatory compliance. Within the ministry, the Office of Environmental Assessment and Control (OEFA) is responsible for monitoring the environmental conduct of firms in the mining, energy, fishing, and industrial sectors, and for applying sanctions where appropriate. In late 2015 the government also announced the inauguration of a National Service of Environmental Certification for Sustainable Investments (SENACE), tasked with reviewing and approving EIAs for high-risk projects.[55]

For the most part, Chinese firms have complied with environmental regulations in Peru, and Chinese firms have had fewer environmental sanctions overall than firms from other countries. For example, data from two successive oversight agencies, OSINERGMIN and OEFA, which cover the period from 2007 to 2014 suggest that the amount paid by Shougang in fines for environmental infractions has been less than that for Doe Run, Volcan, or Buenaventura, but higher than that for Yanacocha or Antamina (see Table 6.2). In total, the firms that have had to pay the most for infractions are not Chinese, but of U.S. or Peruvian origin. More recent Chinese-owned projects are not comparable owing to their shorter time frame of operation; for example, the Rio Blanco project (majority-owned by Zijin) was sanctioned in the exploration stage.

One of the most interesting cases has been that of Toromocho. In March 2014, the OEFA ordered Chinalco to halt activities at this recently inaugurated mine after inspectors detected a runoff of acid wastewater into two nearby lakes.[56] Apparently, unusually high rainfall caused an overflow before adequate

TABLE 6.2 Environmental Fines on Mining Firms in Peru, 2007–14, by Regulatory Agency

	By agency (UIT)		Total: Real (2014) value		
	OSINERGMIN	OEFA	UITs	Soles (UIT = 3800)	USD (2.87 soles)
Doe Run	865	10,133	10,998	41,791,374	14,561,454
Volcan	1,287	5,746	7,033	26,723,880	9,311,456
Buenaventura	530	1,012	1,542	5,858,042	2,041,130
Shougang	213	1,004	1,217	4,626,234	1,611,928
Minera Yanacocha	268	381	649	2,467,036	859,594
Milpo	190	406	596	2,263,698	788,745
Antamina	14	359	373	1,419,110	494,463
Rio Blanco (Zijin)	100	0	100	380,000	132,404
Chinalco	0	71	71	270,256	94,166

Sources: Authors' elaboration based on data from: Gerencia de Fiscalización Minera; Organismo Supervisor de la Inversión en Energía y Minería—OSINERGMIN; Dirección de Fiscalización; Sanción y Aplicación de Incentivos; Organismo de Evaluación y Fiscalización Ambiental—OEFA; and Superintendencia Nacional de Aduanas y Administración Tributaria—SUNAT.

Note: UIT (*Unidad Impositiva Tributaria*) is a tax unit that serves as a benchmark to determine tax obligations and penalties under law. Its amount varies from year to year and is established by decree, according to macroeconomic calculations made by the Peruvian tax authority, SUNAT.

drainage was built. Given the expectations riding on this project, this was a dramatic move by MINAM and a blow to the company's public relations efforts. Yet the company's response was rapid, the structure was reinforced, and a few days later OEFA authorized Chinalco to resume operations.[57] As a result of this incident, the Association of Chinese Companies in Peru asked MINAM to organize informational meetings for all of its members to explain Peru's environmental regulations to newcomers.[58]

Case Studies in Peru: Learning Step by Step

Based on the comparative data and experiences we have analyzed in Peru, we conclude that there is no one "Chinese way" of doing business in Latin American mining. Diverse Chinese firms operate in this region, most of which are state-owned enterprises regulated by different levels of government in China, but some of which are also owned by private capitalists. Rather than generalize, it is important to analyze more closely each firm and project. Two of the most important cases that we have examined are Shougang (Marcona) and Chinalco (Toromocho).

Shougang: Not the Best Start

Marcona was the first Chinese-owned mine in South America, and is currently the largest iron ore operation in Peru. It involves a mine and smelter initially founded in the 1950s by the U.S.-based Marcona Mining Company, which was expropriated by Peru's military government in 1975 and turned into Empresa Minera de Hierro del Peru. In 1992 it was sold to the Shougang Group, a state-owned conglomerate in Beijing. At the time of the purchase, Hierro Peru was experiencing economic losses, an aging labor force, and a highly politicized union.

While Peruvian officials hoped that new foreign investment would modernize the firm and improve production, Shougang executives were looking to turn this firm into China's leading steel producer. Hence, China paid US$120 million for this operation, considerably more than Peru expected to receive at the time and a price analysts thought was far too high.[59] To sweeten this deal, half of the work force was fired by the Peruvian government, but apparently these laid-off workers were allowed to remain in company housing. Various sources indicate that when Shougang arrived it evicted them and brought in Chinese workers to take their place, leading to violent protests. As a result, the Chinese workers were quickly sent back home.[60]

Privatization in the 1990s had also come with the promise of improved conditions for workers, but Shougang's efforts on that score during its first decade of ownership were limited. The company's main priority was to revive production, so executives were not flexible with union negotiations, leading to frequent strikes. This backfired politically, as the Hierro Peru workers had allies in the labor movement, the media, and national politics. Even as things improved for the firm, labor relations remained difficult to manage. The company continued to have annual labor troubles through 2015.[61]

Today Shougang remains the sole iron producer in Peru and has become highly profitable. Yet it also is one of the most criticized foreign mining firms in the country. In addition to ongoing tensions with its union, Shougang was criticized for reneging on its original investment commitment and postponing plans to modernize the mine. The company had initially agreed to invest US$150 million in 1992–95, but problems in the parent company in China apparently made it impossible to comply during this period.[62] According to Shougang's general manager, their request to extend the time frame to meet this commitment was denied by the Peruvian government, even while others were approved, and instead they were fined for noncompliance.[63]

Shougang has also had conflicts with the surrounding community over the provision of water and electricity services. Before Shougang's arrival, Hierro Peru provided these services without charge to Marcona. Although this was not part of the privatization package, apparently local authorities were unwilling or unable to assume these responsibilities, and Shougang found itself continuing to provide them to Marcona. Today this is done through a contract with the municipality, though problems with access and distribution are often attributed to the firm.

For many Peruvians, and for the international media, Shougang represents the negative stereotype of a Chinese company that lowers standards to feed the demand for ores. But is this really the case? Objectively, Shougang has not performed significantly worse than its Peruvian or other foreign counterparts. From 1996 to 2006, Shougang apparently spent US$12.7 million to build a new tailings deposit, reduce dust and gases, and protect against oil spills.[64] In 2007, the company completed the construction of a wastewater treatment plant for the town, although according to Shougang officials it did not start operating until 2013 owing to the lack of trained personnel within Marcona city hall.[65]

It could be concluded, then, that Chinese firms do not have especially low standards, but rather that the Peruvian authorities have been weak in enforcing norms which apply to operating firms in this sector. Shougang also inherited a more difficult situation than most new investors. But this does not explain the persistent conflicts the firm has generated with its workers and neighbors, or its absence from multi-stakeholder fora such as the Grupo de Dialogo Minero, in which numerous other firms with conflicts engage in constructive dialogue with activists, media, and other groups. A more positive view of Shougang is further betrayed by the firm's reticence to invest more time and resources to improve community and public relations.

For some observers, these problems demonstrate broader cultural and political differences between Western companies and Chinese enterprises overseas, as the latter have less experience with free trade unions and local community relations.[66] Yet more recent cases suggest that Shougang's problems may have more to do with this specific company rather than its general Chinese origins. Indeed, the company has been facing an increasing number of challenges in an industry with increasingly fierce competition. It also appears to be trailing behind other more modern firms.

Shougang's relationship with the Peruvian state is also distinct from that of others. The company had a good relationship with the Fujimori administration (1990–2000), but that had soured by the late 1990s. Under the Toledo administration (2001–06), the Shougang deal was scrutinized as part of a series of congressional investigations on earlier privatization deals, and both company officials and the Peruvian government were suspected of corruption, although the charges were eventually dropped. Meanwhile, Chinese companies moving into Peru more recently have tried to learn from the mistakes of their predecessors, including not only Shougang but also Western-owned firms. A leading example is Chinalco.

Chinalco: Adhering to New Standards

The Aluminum Corporation of China is also an SOE, and as such is one of the world's largest aluminum producers. In 2007, Chinalco acquired the Canadian junior firm Peru Copper Inc., which included rights to the concession of the Toromocho project and a commitment to build an open-pit copper mine and processing plant in the Junín region of central Peru.[67]

To date, Chinalco has invested over US$3 billion in this project, making it one of the top 20 copper projects in the world.[68] It is projected to have an operating lifespan of 32 years and to increase Peruvian copper production by 20 percent.[69] The project is also expected to produce major income tax revenues in the medium term, and to create some 2,500 jobs directly and 7,500 indirectly over the project's lifespan. Located in a historic mining region, this project stands out for its promise to use state-of-the-art construction, to invest in an acid water treatment plant for the entire area of operation, and to undertake a complex process of relocation of the nearby town of Morococha, in order to make way for the mine.

Upon obtaining the rights to develop Tormocho, Chinalco executives explicitly aimed to establish this as a socially and environmentally responsible project that would comply with global standards. The first CEO of Minera Chinalco Peru, Gerald Wolfe, was previously head of Antamina, a company considered to be a global model for corporate social responsibility. The CEO of Minera Chinalco Peru at time of writing, Huang Shanfu, had retained a management team and work force that was primarily Peruvian. Chinalco also retained the community relations consultants originally hired by Peru Copper and worked with them to carry out the relocation of the town of Morococha. Furthermore, Chinalco established a consortium with two Peruvian firms to implement social infrastructure projects in the area under the Obras por Impuestos program.[70] These projects would include improved access to drinking water, sewage, and water treatment for the residents of the district of Yauli, in Junín.

Upholding these standards has not been easy, however. The biggest challenge faced by Chinalco to date has been the relocation process. As with Shougang, Chinalco inherited responsibility for what might be called a modern-day "company town." In this case, however, the company was expected to both move and rebuild a town of 5,000 residents from the bottom up. This process has not been without controversy, but the level and complexity of the relocation were unprecedented in Peruvian mining history. Objectively, the town of Morococha was a bleak site. A former mining camp, it was rundown and lacking in basic services, including a limited water supply, and the majority of residents were renters who lived in overcrowded and dilapidated buildings.[71] According to representatives from the community relations firm hired by Chinalco, the relocation was initially going to be funded by the Peruvian government, but once the Chinese state became the owner of the project it was decided that the company would assume this responsibility.[72]

Despite the promise of improved living conditions, residents of Morococha had mixed feelings about the move and considerable uncertainty about the outcome. By late 2013, however, the majority had agreed to relocate to a site just 6 kilometers away. For the minority who resisted, including the town's mayor, the main concern appeared to be the negotiation of a better deal with the company. At that point, the Peruvian government issued a declaration of emergency, with an evacuation order to be complied with by February 21, 2014.[73] The argument was that the area was unfit for occupation—a situation that has been in place for decades. Temporary tents were installed to house those who would not be considered beneficiaries of Chinalco in the new town, and electricity was interrupted in the old Morococha. This was viewed as the government's forceful attempt to vacate the remaining residents.[74] While Chinalco repeatedly emphasized that it would not use force in the relocation, the presence of a small group of holdouts has remained a challenge for the company.

Other challenges emerged around conditions in the new town and nearby communities. Nueva Morococha is a city created by a law approved by Congress in September 2013. Although located just 6 kilometers away, the new town is farther away from Peru's busy Central Highway, causing residents to complain of a decline in business for local entrepreneurs. In the environmental impact assessment for Toromocho, Chinalco mentioned that it would promote local employment, but no explicit agreements were made at the time of the move. Some residents of the new town received employment offers to work in the Toromocho mine, while others work in nearby mines or seek alternative forms of income generation. Furthermore, although all of the families relocated to Nueva Morococha were offered their own home, with running water, a modern sewage system, and property titles, the granting of such titles by local authorities has been delayed and the company remains the legal owner of the town.[75]

In sum, Toromocho has produced both benefits and challenges for Peru and for its Chinese owners. Without doubt it is one of the better examples of community relocation in Peru, as it has prioritized dialogue and consensus rather than the use of force, and has tried to provide better living conditions for those who moved.[76] Chinalco is also offering better wages and benefits than the industry average, and its financial backing appeared to be strong as of 2015. However, whether its operations will generate the income desired in a declining market, and fulfill the promise of meeting the highest social and environmental standards in the industry, remains to be seen.

Conclusions

The relationship with China is fundamental for Latin America today and in the years ahead. Despite its economic slowdown, China has pledged to invest some $250 billion in Latin America over the next decade. Governments, companies, and civil society organizations in the region will need to work hard to ensure that such investment not only generates profits and needed tax revenues but also raises local living standards and protects the environment for the generations to come.[77]

This has not necessarily been the case to date. Recent country case studies and aggregate analysis have found that Chinese trade and investment in Latin America in the 21st century have also been a driver of environmental degradation and social conflict.[78] This is because Latin American exports to China, as well as Chinese investment in the region, have been more concentrated in primary commodities—especially minerals and hydrocarbons—than Latin America's economic relations with the rest of the world. Such investments produce fewer direct jobs than manufactured or agricultural exports, use about twice as much water, and emit more net greenhouse gases compared to overall exports from the region. However, research in this region has also identified cases of good practice and fast learning in responding to these risks, by Chinese investors, Latin American governments, and civil society organizations, from which broader lessons can be drawn. This is the case in Peru.

Since the 1990s, all Peruvian administrations have emphasized the importance of free trade and private initiative to expand economic opportunities. They have also promoted the extractive industries as the main driver of growth, especially when rising demand from a growing China brought high prices for copper, iron, and other ores. To the extent that Chinese demand has been more concentrated in these sectors than demand from the rest of the world, the relationship with China has reinforced Peru's overall position—and vulnerability—as a primary exporter.

As we point out in this chapter, however, this does not represent a case of "de-industrialization," since Peru is and always has been a primary commodity exporter, blessed (or cursed) with a rich array of minerals, as well as historically abundant forests and fisheries. New investments from China have allowed Peru to develop large-scale mining projects with state-of-the art technology and important spinoffs in other sectors of the economy. Meanwhile, Peru's FTA with China aimed to open the door to greater diversification of Peruvian exports. Progress on this has been slow, as nontraditional exports to China remain just a fraction of the total, but they have expanded in recent years—and more so to China than to the rest of the world.

Recently, China and Peru have signed agreements to explore investment in infrastructure as well as the extractive industries. A Chinese firm recently won a bid to construct a major Amazonian waterway,[79] and China has declared its intention to invest in a huge Transoceanic Railway project that will link Brazil and Peru. Peru and China have also signed cooperation agreements in other sectors, including agriculture, science, and technology.

Ultimately, however, the diversity of goods and services that Peru can export to China (and to the rest of the world) depends on the policies of its national governments, the capacities of its private sector, and the combined efforts of the two to identify and respond to new markets and demands. China has made enormous efforts to invest in the study of Latin America in its schools and universities, and in promoting academic and cultural exchange with the region. Unfortunately, the same does not hold on the Peruvian side. Although China and Peru have deep historical ties that can facilitate contemporary relations, including a large Chinese immigrant population, successive Peruvian governments have invested little in expanding knowledge of China or improving the capacity of the business sector and other professionals to engage constructively with the Asian giant. Peruvian universities have only recently incorporated the study of China into their curricula.[80]

Meanwhile, if investments from China are to improve living standards in Peru for this generation and those to come, it is fundamental that the Peruvian authorities defend high standards and safeguards in these high-risk industries. Peru has become a regional leader in promoting revenue transparency, for example joining the Extractive Industries Transparency Initiative and working with Chinese investors so that they, too, will join this effort. As discussed here, some Chinese companies in Peru have also exceeded local standards and outperformed their peers. Peruvian civil society organizations have worked hard to hold governments and companies accountable. Non-governmental organizations (NGOs) have organized, demanded better safeguards and oversight mechanisms, and mounted global campaigns against the most symbolic cases to create awareness and to hold actors accountable. Indeed, in democratic contexts NGOs, academia, and other civil society actors have helped the government at all levels, as well as Chinese firms, to learn from experience and mitigate conflicts.

However, in the effort to retain declining investment, policy makers today face enormous pressure to roll back existing environmental and social protections and to reduce hard-won rights for local communities. Demands for deregulation will worsen as the Chinese economy slows down and countries like Peru find themselves with less bargaining power. Tensions are high in countries like Peru around the impact of extractive activity, and constructive community relations are fundamental to the success of such long-term investments. This involves investing in the protection of local environments as well as in decent jobs and local development opportunities.

Chinese policy makers and regulators are also increasingly aware of the importance of upholding high standards in their overseas investments, and have instituted safeguards of their own that match or surpass those of their local hosts. Yet they still lack enforcement power and sufficient transparency. As detailed in the GEGI report, such measures could be greatly enhanced by the use of formal reporting and grievance mechanisms, which would allow Latin American governments and civil society to assist in the difficult task of managing investment from abroad.[81]

As we have seen, in Peru today Chinese investors are taking on major community relations challenges, including responsibility for virtual "company towns" such as Marcona and Nueva Morococha. More recently, a third case emerged when MMG (owned by China Minmetals) took over the huge Las Bambas copper project from Glencore in 2014, a move which involved not only the relocation and maintenance of a small town in Apurimac, one of the poorest regions of the Peruvian Andes, but also the upholding of environmental and social commitments negotiated over years by the prior owners. When the Chinese owners tried to modify these investments in order to reduce costs in

2015, violent protests erupted, and they learned the hard way of the risks of underestimating the importance of good local communication and community relations.[82]

Based on our case studies in Peru's conflict-ridden mining sector, we have argued that there is no clear pattern of Chinese corporate conduct. While there are some characteristics that may distinguish Chinese firms operating in Peru from others—state ownership and support on the one hand and less experience with transparency, free press, and free trade unions on the other—on the ground they have also differed considerably. In some cases that we studied, neither the Chinese investors nor their country's diplomats conducted due diligence on the social conditions they would face, and the Peruvian authorities may not have been forthcoming about these conditions either. This was true of the investment made by Shougang in the early 1990s, but also in more recent cases, such as that of the Zijin Company and a copper project in the northern region of Piura.[83] Although the Chinese government had a strong interest in making these investments work, their overseers may have initially been too inexperienced, or too far away, to guide such efforts.

However, in the Peruvian case we also observe two important trends: increasing interest and efforts by the Chinese state to regulate the activities of its overseas firms, with new directives and guidelines; and fast learning by Chinese investors and their political allies. This includes learning from other firms in the industry, Western as well as Chinese, and hiring better managers and consultants to guide them through the various processes involved. There is also increased effort by both Chinese and Peruvian government authorities to help these firms develop major projects, which for the most part is not different from the support received by other investors in this industry.

Peru today hosts some of the most widely watched cases of Chinese mining investment in South America. In each case, Chinese SOEs have committed to maintaining state-of-the-art mining operations, and sustaining entire towns and communities in which living conditions are expected to improve. This has not been the case historically in Peru, and is apparently rare in China as well. For China, and for Peru, a lot is riding on the ability of both sides to show the world that they are serious about complying with global standards.

Notes

1 The authors wish to thank Veronica Hurtado of CIUP for research assistance on this chapter. This chapter is adapted from a broader text entitled "Chinese Investment in Peru's Mining Industry: Blessing or Curse?" by Cynthia Sanborn and Victoria Chonn Ching, Boston University GEGI Discussion Paper, 2015–18.

2 According to the Peruvian Central Bank, mining accounted for almost 25 percent of FDI in 2013. For more information, see "Foreign Direct Investment," *ProInversión*, http://www.investinperu.pe/modulos/JER/PlantillaStandard.aspx?are=1&prf=0&jer=6037&sec=17 (accessed June 27, 2016). In 2014, however, tax revenues from mining fell to 8 percent of total tax revenues. More information can be found in Peru National Office of Tax Administration (SUNAT), "Cuadro No. 31:

Ingresos tributarios recaudados por la SUNAT—tributos internos según actividad económica, 1998–2015 (millones de soles)," http://www.sunat.gob.pe/estadisticasestudios/busqueda_actividad_economica.html (accessed June 27, 2016).

3 "Empresas chinas controlan el 36% de la cartera de proyectos mineros en el Perú," *El Comercio*, August 28, 2015. More data about Peru's mining portfolio can be found in Ministerio de Energía y Minas (MINEM), *Annual Mining Report 2014*, http://www.minem.gob.pe/_publicacion.php?idSector=1&idPublicacion=501 (accessed June 27, 2016).

4 Cynthia Sanborn and Alexis Yong, "Peru's Economic Boom and the Asian Connection," in Cynthia J. Arnson and Jorge Heine, with Christine Zaino, eds., *Reaching across the Pacific: Latin America and Asia in the New Century* (Washington, DC: Woodrow Wilson International Center for Scholars, 2014), p. 62; John Authers, "Peru Rebirth Illustrates the China Effect," *Financial Times*, October 9, 2015.

5 Cynthia Sanborn and Victoria Chonn Ching, "Chinese Investment in Peru's Mining Industry: Blessing or Curse?" Discussion Paper 2015-8, Working Group on Development and Environment in the Americas from the Global Economic Governance Initiative at Boston University, 2015, p. 3; Agence France-Presse (Rio de Janeiro) and Associated Press (Santiago), "Chinese Premier Li Keqiang Returns from South America with a Caseful of Deals," *South China Morning Post*, May 26, 2015.

6 Barbara Kotschwar, Theodore Moran, and Julia Muir, "Do Chinese Mining Companies Exploit More?" *Americas Quarterly*, Fall 2011 (Impact Investing: Profit Meets Purpose), http://www.americasquarterly.org/do-chinese-mining-companies-exploit-more (accessed June 27, 2016); Thomas L. Friedman, "Red China or Green?" *New York Times*, June 30, 2006.

7 Amos Irwin and Kevin Gallagher, "Chinese Mining Investment in Latin America: A Comparative Perspective," *Journal of Environment and Development*, vol. 22, no. 2 (2013), pp. 207–34; Rubén Gonzalez Vicente, "The Political Economy of Sino-Peruvian Relations: A New Dependency?" *Journal of Current Chinese Affairs*, vol. 41, no. 1 (2012), pp. 97–131.

8 Javier Arellano-Yanguas, *¿Minería sin fronteras? Conflicto y desarrollo en regiones mineras del Perú* (Lima: IEP, 2011).

9 Cynthia Sanborn and Alvaro Paredes, "Consulta Previa: Perú," *Americas Quarterly*, Spring 2014.

10 See for example Jacqueline Fowks, "El conflicto minero en Cajamarca atenaza al Gobierno de Perú," *El País*, June 22, 2012; Jacqueline Fowks, "El conflicto minero se enroca en el Perú," *El País*, September 30, 2015.

11 Cynthia Sanborn and Victor Torres, *La economía china y las industrias extractivas: desafíos para el Perú* (Lima: Fondo Editorial de la Universidad del Pacífico y CooperAcción, 2009). This discusses the expansion of the Chinese economy in general and its investments in Latin America. In Sanborn and Yong, "Peru's Economic Boom and the Asian Connection," the authors aim to provide a better understanding of the complex and evolving relationship between Peru and its Asian trade partners, and the role they may have played in the country's development and growth processes. In Sanborn and Chonn Ching, "Chinese Investment in Peru's Mining Industry," the authors provide an analysis of Chinese mining investment in Peru through the analysis of three case studies.

12 Peru has the largest ethnic Chinese population in Latin America. In the mid-19th century, some 100,000 Chinese men came as indentured servants, to replace African slaves in the sugar plantations and guano fields and to work as servants and artisans. In subsequent decades Chinese nationals would arrive in different capacities. See Isabelle Lausent-Herrera, "The Chinatown in Peru and the Changing Peruvian Chinese Communities," *Journal of Chinese Overseas*, no. 7 (2011), pp. 69–113.

13 Sanborn and Torres, *La economía china*.

14 "Las inversiones chinas en Perú sumarán US$12 mil millones," *La República*, August 13, 2014.

15 Ministerio de Economía y Finanzas (MEF), "Marco Macroeconómico Multianual 2015–2017 Revisado," 2014, p. 3; "China–Peru Trade Exchange to Rise by 5% in 2016," *Andina*, December 8, 2015.

16 Yinan Zhao and Yunbi Zhang, "China, Peru to Diversify Trade Focus," *China Daily*, May 23, 2015; "China and Peru Agree to Study Transcontinental Rail Link," *Reuters*, May 23, 2015.

17 Shannon Tiezzi, "China Seeks 'Updated Model' for Latin America Cooperation," *Diplomat*, May 28, 2015.

18 A similar amount was estimated for 2015, while projected trade value in 2016 is 5 percent higher. See "China–Peru Trade Exchange to Rise by 5% in 2016."

19 Data from the International Trade Center—Trademap. See http://www.trademap. org/Bilateral_TS.aspx?nvpm=1|604||156||TOTAL|||2|1|1|2|2|1|1|1|1 (accessed June 27, 2016).

20 Sanborn and Yong, "Peru's Economic Boom and the Asian Connection," p. 71.

21 Authers, "Peru Rebirth Illustrates the China Effect."

22 Instituto Nacional de Estadística e Informática (INEI), "Volumen exportado a China creció 236.3%," July 23, 2014 (accessed June 27, 2016). Data from Trademap and the World Bank also seem to indicate that imports from China to Peru have experienced the larger increase in comparison to other trade partners. See Trademap, "List of Supplying Markets for a Product Imported by Peru. Product: TOTAL All products," http://www. trademap.org/Country_SelProductCountry_TS.aspx; and World Bank, "GDP at Market Prices (Current US$), http://data.worldbank.org/indicator/NY.GDP.MKTP.CD/coun-tries/PE?display=default (accessed June 27, 2016).

23 Carolina Cárdenas and Giuliano Gavilano, *El efecto de las importaciones provenien-tes de China en los salarios reales: una aproximación microeconómica para el caso peruano entre los Años 2007 y 2010*, Investigación Económica No. 2 (Lima: Departamento de Economía, Universidad del Pacífico, 2013).

24 Carol Wise, "Playing Both Sides of the Pacific: Latin America's Free Trade Agreements (FTAs) with China," *Pacific Affairs*, vol. 89, no. 1 (March 2016), pp. 75–100.

25 Ministerio de Comercio Exterior y Turismo (MINCETUR), *Reporte de Comercio Bilateral Perú–China* (Lima: MINCETUR, 2015), p. 6.

26 Fernando Gonzalez Vigil, "Relaciones de comercio e inversión del Perú con el Asia-Pacífico," in Instituto de Estudios Internacionales (IDEI) (ed.), *Veinte años de Política Exterior Peruana (1991–2011)* (Lima: PUCP, 2012), pp. 209–41; Cámara de Comercio Perú-China (CAPECHI), "Resumen Ejecutivo—Tratado de Libre Comercio entre Perú y China," p. 2.

27 "China, Peru Face Challenges, Opportunities in Trade," *Xinhua*, April 18, 2015.

28 See for instance "Perú es el Segundo país receptor de inversions chinas en Latinoamérica," *Andina*, November 23, 2015.

29 In September 2014, the Peru–China Chamber of Commerce estimated total pro-jected Chinese investment in Peru as US$9.3 billion for the prior 12 months. See "Perú concentró el 50% de inversion china el ultimo año," *RPP*, September 3, 2014; "Chinese Investment Important Drive for Peru's Economy," *Xinhua*, October 22, 2015. However, in May 2015 government sources claimed total Chinese investment in 2014 was US$18 billion. See "China, Peru Face Challenges, Opportunities in Trade."

30 See ProInversión, http://www.proinversion.gob.pe/modulos/jer/PlantillaPopUp.aspx? ARE=0&PFL=0&JER=5975 (accessed June 27, 2016).

31 Javier Prialé, "Empresas chinas controlan el 36% de la cartera de proyectos mineros en el Perú," *Gestion*, August 28, 2015. See also MINEM, *Annual Mining Report 2014*.

32 While China has promoted Latin American studies and Spanish language training programs nationwide, Peru has few professionals with basic knowledge of China and its languages, and only a few universities that have relations with China. See for instance Patricia Castro Obando, "La onda académica en China" [The academic wave in China], *El Comercio*, December 28, 2015.

33 Global Witness and Syntao, "Transparency Matters: Disclosure of Payments to Governments by Chinese Extractive Companies," January 2013, http://www.global witness.org/transparencymatters (accessed June 27, 2016); and Sanborn and Torres, *La economía china*.

34 Guo Jie, "Too Big to Fail? China's Economic Presence in Latin America," *Zhongguo Guoji Zhanlüe Pinglun, 2014* [China international strategy review, 2014] (Beijing: Shijie Zhishi Chubanshe, July 2014), pp. 160–77; Gonzalez Vicente, "Political Economy of Sino-Peruvian Relations"; Irwin and Gallagher, "Chinese Mining Investment in Latin America"; and Sanborn and Torres, *La economía china* highlight the analysis of Chinese companies operating in Peru.

35 Terry Lynn Karl, "Ensuring Fairness: The Case for a Transparent Fiscal Social Contract," Working paper, Initiative for Policy Dialogue, September 2006.

36 Peru 2013 EITI Report, https://eiti.org/report/peru/2013 (accessed June 27, 2016).

37 Cynthia Sanborn was a member of the Peruvian EITI Commission from 2007 to 2014. See http://eitiperu.minem.gob.pe/.

38 Peru 2013 EITI Report.

39 MEF, "Consultas de Transferencias a Gobiernos Nacional, Regionales y Locales: Año 2004 a la fecha," 2016, https://mef.gob.pe/index.php?option=com_content&view=article&id=457&Itemid=100957&lang=es (accessed June 27, 2016).

40 Interview with Kong Aimin, Lima, May 19, 2014. See also Shougang Hierro Peru S.A.A., *Memoria 2013 Shougang Hierro Peru* (Peru: Shougang Hierro Peru S.A.A., 2013). The material provided by the company is not available for public distribution.

41 World Bank, "Mining Foundations, Trust and Funds: A Sourcebook," June 2010, http://siteresources.worldbank.org/EXTOGMC/Resources/Sourcebook_Full_ Report.pdf (accessed June 27, 2016).

42 "No se cumplió con presentar informes del aporte minero," *El Comercio* (printed edition), September 5, 2011. For the report in Spanish by Grupo Propuesta Ciudadana, see Epifano Baca and Gustavo Avila, "Ranking de Transparencia de las Empresas Mineras," http://www.resourcegovernance.org/sites/default/files/Ranking%20de%20Transparencia%20SPANISH.pdf (accessed June 27, 2016).

43 Interview with Kong Aimin, Lima, May 19, 2014.

44 Irwin and Gallagher, "Chinese Mining Investment in Latin America."

45 Interview with Kong Aimin, Lima, May 19, 2014.

46 Personal communication via electronic correspondence with Alvaro Barrenechea, Gerente de Asuntos Corporativos, Minera Chinalco Peru S.A., April 2, April 23, and June 2, 2014.

47 For more details about mining accidents in Peru, see MINEM, "Estadística de accidentes mortales en el sector minero" [Statistics of mortal accidents in the mining sector], http://www.minem.gob.pe/_detalle.php?idSector=1&idTitular=170&idMenu=sub151&idCateg=170 (accessed June 27, 2016).

48 Irwin and Gallagher, "Chinese Mining Investment in Latin America."

49 "Empleo en Minería" [Mining employment], in MINEM, *Annual Mining Report 2013*, http://www.minem.gob.pe/minem/archivos/file/Mineria/PUBLICACIONES/ANUARIOS/2013/05EMPLEO.pdf (accessed June 27, 2016).

50 Interview with Kong Aimin, Lima, May 19, 2014.

51 See for instance Press Center from Minera Chinalco Peru, "Se entregaron becas para talleres en CETEMIN."

52 MINEM, "Informe Trimestral Octubre–Diciembre 2010," 2010, p. 49, http://www.minem.gob.pe/minem/archivos/Informe%20Trimestral%20Octubre%20-%20Diciembre%202010%20_2web_(2).pdf (accessed June 27, 2016).

53 Edson Eaerle, "MMG: Sin las comunidades locales, será muy difícil operar en Las Bambas," *Gestion*, June 2, 2014; Oficina de Gestión Social, MINEM, "Reporte No. 17: Fondos Sociales," August 31, 2015, http://www.minem.gob.pe/minem/archivos/file/Gestion%20Social/Fondo%20Social/2015/Informe%20n%C2%B0%2017%20Segundo%20informe%20cuatrimestral%202015.pdf (accessed June 27, 2016).

54 Specific regulations include the Environment Code of 1990, the Law to Promote Investments in the Mining Sector of 1991 (Legislative Decree 708), and the General Law of Mining in 1992.

55 SENACE, "SENACE inicia hoy oficialmente sus funciones de evaluación de estudios de impacto ambiental detallados y actuará como ventanilla," December 28, 2015.

56 OEFA, "OEFA ordena a Minera Chinalco Perú S.A. detener aquellas actividades causantes de vertimientos en lagunas de Junín," March 28, 2014.

57 OEFA, "El OEFA consta que Minera Chinalco Perú S.A. cumplió con detener la descarga de efluentes que vertían hacia dos lagunas de Junín," March 29, 2014; "Chinalco Says It Has Resumed Some Operations at Peru Mine," *Reuters*, April 4, 2014.

58 MINAM organized a series of conferences about environmental management in mining activities. See MINAM, "Se inicia Ciclo de Conferencias sobre Gestión Ambiental de las Actividades Minero-Energéticas," August 20, 2014.

59 This transaction was later scrutinized by anti-corruption investigators in China and Peru. In 1995, Shougang chairman Zhou Guanwu was forced to resign and his son Zhou Beifang given a suspended death sentence on corruption charges related to Shougang operations. See "Corruption Case Is Seen Signaling China Struggle," *Los Angeles Times*, February 21, 1995. In 2001 a Peruvian congressional commission investigated alleged corruption by Fujimori government officials in this sale, but no charges were brought. A summary of the investigation of privatization cases can be found in Peru National Congress, http://www4.congreso.gob.pe/comisiones/2002/CIDEF/index1b.html (accessed June 27, 2016). More details can also be found in Peru National Congress, "Comisión Investigadora de Casos de Corrupción cometidos en la década de 1990–2001," June 2002, http://www4.congreso.gob.pe/comisiones/2002/CIDEF/oscuga/informecideffinal.pdf (accessed June 27, 2016).

60 For more on Shougang's arrival to Peru, see Gonzalez Vicente, "Political Economy of Sino-Peruvian Relations"; and Irwin and Gallagher, "Chinese Mining Investment in Latin America." Company officials interviewed for this project say that 171 workers were brought from China for one year only. See also interview with Kong Aimin, Lima, May 19, 2014.

61 "Trabajadores de minera Shougang en huelga indefinida en busca de mejores salarios," *La República*, September 21, 2015.

62 Peter Nolan, *China and the Global Economy: National Champions, Industrial Policy and the Big Business Revolution* (New York: Palgrave, 2001). See also Gonzalez Vicente, "Political Economy of Sino-Peruvian Relations"; and Irwin and Gallagher, "Chinese Mining Investment in Latin America."

63 Interview with Kong Aimin, Lima, May 19, 2014.

64 Irwin and Gallagher, "Chinese Mining Investment in Latin America."

65 Sanborn and Torres, *La economía china*, pp. 190–202.

66 "矿企海外遇阻," 今日中国, July 30, 2012; and "秘铁: 首钢的整合之痛," *Sina*, September 17, 2013 explore some of the socio-cultural challenges Chinese companies experience when investing overseas, as well as some suggestions on how to improve relations with the local communities and authorities in the host countries.

67 Cynthia Sanborn and Victoria Chonn Ching, "Making Way for Mines: Chinese Investment in Peru," *ReVista, the Harvard Review of Latin America*, vol. XIII, no. 2 (Winter 2014).

68 "中铝秘鲁项目投运为中国海外最大铜矿," *Xinhua*, December 12, 2013.

69 In September 2014, the company had reduced its short-term production figures by 56 percent owing to delays caused by various factors, including a shortage of adequate power supply, problems with its equipment, ore quality, and community relations challenges. See "Toromocho solo produjo 31 mil toneladas de cobre a Julio," *El Comercio*, Portafolio, September 9, 2014, p. B4. Also see note published by Chinalco on production and benefits, http://www.chinalco.com.pe/es/producci%C3%B3n-y-beneficios (accessed June 27, 2016).

70 "Volcan, Ferreryros y Chinalco se consorcian para ejecutar Obras por Impuestos en Junín," *Gestión*, March 19, 2014.

71 Sanborn and Chonn Ching, "Making Way for Mines."

72 Interviews with: Alan Dabbs, Silvia Matos, and team from Social Capital Group, Lima, January 21, 2014; Silvia Matos, consultant from Social Capital Group, Lima, January 8, 2013; and Rubén Villasante, Social Capital Group, Nueva Morococha, January 23, 2014.

73 The emergency report can be found in Instituto Nacional de Defensa Civil (INDECI), "Peligro de movimiento en masa en el distrito de Morococha—Junin," Reporte de Peligro no. 202. See also INDECI, "Declaratorias de estado de emergencia a nivel nacional 2013–2014," last updated December 2013, http://sinpad.indeci.gob.pe/UploadPortalSINPAD/CONSOLIDADO%20DEE%202013-2014%20EC%20 21.01.14.pdf (accessed June 27, 2016).

74 "Restablecen servicio de energía eléctrica en Morococha antigua," *SERVINDI*, March 6, 2014.

75 Interviews with Marcial Salomé Ponce, Mayor of Morococha, Nueva Morococha, January 24, 2014, and with the inhabitants of Nueva Morococha (names withheld on request), Nueva Morococha, January 24, 2014.

76 Dan Collins, "Latest Chinese Mine in Peru Offers New Living Standards for Residents," *CCTV America*, January 4, 2016.

77 This section draws from our own work, Sanborn and Chonn Ching, "Making Way for Mines" and Sanborn and Chonn Ching, "Chinese Investment in Peru's Mining Industry," and from Rebecca Ray, Kevin Gallagher, Andres Lopez, and Cynthia Sanborn, *China in Latin America: Lessons for South–South Cooperation and Sustainable Development* (Boston, MA: Boston University, Centro de Investigación para la Transformación, Tufts University, and Universidad del Pacífico, 2015).

78 Sanborn and Chonn Ching, "Making Way for Mines"; Sanborn and Chonn Ching, "Chinese Investment in Peru's Mining Industry"; and Ray et al., *China in Latin America*.

79 Concession of Hidrovía Amazónica Project had only one qualified bidder, a Chinese firm (China Communications Construction Company—CCCC), on January 28, 2015, but subsequently halted in February 2015 as a result of the demand for prior consultation with the native communities along the route. The consultation was conducted in September 2015, and a new concession process was opened in December 2015, though as of May 2016 there was still no bid awarded. See Barbara Fraser, "Why Consulta Previa Is among the Most Divisive Issues in Peru," *America's Quarterly*, http://www.americasquarterly.org/content/why-consulta-previa-among-most-divisive-issues-peru; and Proinversión (2016), "Hidrovía Amazónica—Second Calling," http://www.proyectosapp.pe/modulos/JER/PlantillaProyecto.aspx?ARE=0&PFL=2&JER=8332&SEC=22.

80 For example, according to Patricia Castro Obando, about 40 Chinese universities have established their own research centers in Latin American issues related to culture, economy, trade, politics, and law. Some 90 Chinese universities teach Spanish. Peru has four Confucius institutes supported by China to offer Chinese language study, six private universities with some kind of exchange program with China, and one university-based Center for Peru–China Studies, which focuses on economics, business, and international relations, at the Universidad del Pacífico, founded in 2013. See Castro Obando, "La onda académica en China." See also Patricia Castro Obando, "Universidades privadas desembarcan en China," *El Comercio*, October 26, 2015.

81 Sanborn and Chonn Ching, "Chinese Investment in Peru's Mining Industry," pp. 20–23.

82 "Las Bambas: Comunidades no dan el brazo a torcer," *SERVINDI*, February 12, 2015.

83 This case is examined more closely in A. Bebbington et al. (2012), *Industrias extractivas, conflicto social y dinámicas institucionales en la región andina* (Lima: IEP, 2012); Sanborn and Torres, *La economía china*; and Sanborn and Chonn Ching, "Making Way for Mines."

PART II

Development Trends Since the Turn of the Millennium

A Critical Assessment

7

AFTER THE CHINA BOOM

What Now for Latin America's Emerging Economies?

Carol Wise[1]

Introduction

It would be difficult to exaggerate the sea change that has occurred within Latin America's emerging economies (EEs) as a result of China's phenomenal rise within the international political economy over the past two decades. Although a great deal of ink has already been spilled over the explosion of trade and investment ties between China and the region's top four emerging economies (Argentina, Brazil, Chile, and Mexico) during the 2000s,[2] in this chapter I analyze the experience of these Latin American countries (LAC) by situating them in a broader political economy context. In doing so, I focus on three main themes: the *dynamism* that has underpinned this relationship from 2003 up through the 2013 slowdown in Chinese growth and demand; the *debates* that have emerged concerning the nature of this burgeoning economic bond; and the question of dependence, i.e., Latin America's potential over-*dependence* on the Chinese market.

In terms of dynamism, we see the rapidly growing China–LAC ties as one of the most compelling cross-Pacific trends currently underway. Indeed, recent research conducted by IDB economist Ambrogio Cesa-Bianchi and his colleagues found that "the long-run impact of a Chinese GDP shock on the typical Latin American economy has increased three times since 1990."[3] During the period from 2003 to 2013, or what our colleague Kevin Gallagher refers to as the "China Boom,"[4] China's GDP shock was decidedly positive for the three South American EEs, but much less so for Mexico. Following China's 2001 entry into the World Trade Organization (WTO), its heavy demand for commodities to fuel a new development phase triggered the biggest commodity lottery that the LAC region had seen in a century. Up until 2013, Argentina,

TABLE 7.1 Annual Commodity Price Trends in Real Dollars, 2000 to Mid-2015

Date	Copper ($/metric ton)	Crude oil ($/bbl)	Soybeans ($/metric ton)	Iron ore ($/dry metric ton unit)	Fishmeal ($/metric ton)
2000	2,279.38	35.48	266.26	36.19	519.11
2001	2,061.05	31.80	255.73	39.22	635.53
2002	2,060.54	32.94	281.00	38.73	800.60
2003	2,234.60	36.30	331.58	40.13	767.05
2004	3,370.60	44.38	360.48	44.57	762.81
2005	4,194.64	60.88	313.20	74.11	833.43
2006	7,475.17	71.49	298.74	77.10	1,296.99
2007	7,459.13	74.52	402.44	128.88	1,233.63
2008	6,764.19	94.32	508.43	151.69	1,101.86
2009	5,338.61	64.02	452.94	82.91	1,275.37
2010	7,534.78	79.04	449.80	145.86	1,687.50
2011	8,103.66	95.47	496.29	153.99	1,411.24
2012	7,400.30	97.60	549.67	119.43	1,448.33
2013	6,913.32	98.13	507.66	127.63	1,647.37
2014	6,482.35	87.94	464.47	91.56	1,613.98
2015	5,833.01*	59.80*	408.00*	63.00*	1,490.00*

Source: World Bank Global Economic Monitor (GEM), http://databank.worldbank.org/data/views/variableselection/selectvariables.aspx?source=global-economic-monitor-%28gem%29-commodities (accessed January 18, 2016).

Note: *Real data only available on annual basis, data available through M6 2015, nominal value for July (M6) 2015 used.

Brazil, and Chile saw a spike in prices for soya, fishmeal, iron ore, copper, tin, zinc, and oil, all of which are abundant to varying degrees in these countries (see Table 7.1). Mexico, too, enjoyed high prices on its oil over this period, even if it sells little directly to China. In all, as of 2013, China accounted for 10 percent of LAC's exports and 16 percent of its imports; total China–LAC trade increased 22-fold between 2000 and 2013.[5]

A second feature of dynamism concerns China's foreign direct investment (FDI) in the LAC region, which has taken off in two of these Latin American EEs (Argentina and Brazil) in ways that were simply unimaginable a decade ago (see Tables 7.2 and 7.3). To date, the bulk of Chinese FDI has been channeled through the Cayman and British Virgin Islands, mainly for tax purposes, which makes it difficult to gauge the precise amount that has actually been invested in the economies under discussion. However, research to date does suggest that the bulk of these investments and the loans that have accompanied them have gone toward resource extraction.[6] There are, however, some signs that Chinese FDI is branching into the manufacturing sector in Brazil and the financial sector in Argentina, where China's Industrial and Commercial Bank (ICBC) has purchased an 80 percent equity share in Argentina's Standard Bank.[7] Even if the pattern is a lopsided one, LAC is now the destination of about 15 percent of

TABLE 7.2 China's Outward FDI Stocks to Four Latin Emerging Economies and Two Regions, 2003–14

	Latin America (US$m)	Argentina (US$m)	Brazil (US$m)	British Virgin Islands (US$m)	Cayman Islands (US$m)	Chile (US$m)	Mexico (US$m)
2003	4,619.32	1.05	52.19	532.64	3,690.68	0.75	97.18
2004	8,268.37	19.27	79.22	1,089.38	6,659.91	1.48	125.29
2005	11,469.61	4.22	81.39	1,983.58	8,935.59	3.71	141.86
2006	19,694.37	11.34	130.41	4,750.40	14,209.19	10.84	128.61
2007	24,700.91	157.19	189.55	6,626.54	16,810.68	56.80	151.44
2008	32,240.15	173.36	217.05	10,477.33	20,327.45	58.09	173.08
2009	30,595.48	169.05	360.89	15,060.69	13,577.07	66.02	173.90
2010	43,875.64	218.99	923.65	23,242.76	17,256.27	109.58	152.87
2011	55,171.75	405.25	1,071.79	29,261.41	21,692.32	97.94	263.88
2012	68,211.63	897.19	1,449.51	30,850.95	30,072.00	126.28	368.48
2013	86,095.93	1,658.20	1,733.58	33,902.98	42,324.06	179.04	409.87
2014	106,111.13	1,791.52	2,832.89	49,320.41	44,236.72	195.83	541.21

Source: Authors' calculation based on Comprehensive Economic, Industry and Corporate Data (CEIC), http://www.ceicdata.com/ (accessed October 15, 2015).

Chinese FDI (versus 65 percent for Asia).[8] At the very least, this is a noteworthy step toward LAC's longstanding quest to diversify its global economic ties.

The upshot of these buoyant trade and FDI flows is that China has become an important engine of growth for Latin America. This became apparent when the four emerging economies considered in this chapter rebounded along with

TABLE 7.3 China's Outward FDI Flows to Four Latin Emerging Economies and Two Regions, 2003–14

	Latin America (US$m)	Argentina (US$m)	Brazil (US$m)	British Virgin Islands (US$m)	Cayman Islands (US$m)	Chile (US$m)	Mexico (US$m)
2003	1,038.15	1.00	6.67	209.68	806.61	0.20	0.03
2004	1,762.72	1.12	6.43	385.52	1,286.13	0.55	27.10
2005	6,466.16	0.35	15.09	1,226.08	5,162.75	1.80	3.55
2006	8,468.74	6.22	10.09	538.11	7,832.72	6.58	−3.69
2007	4,902.41	136.69	51.13	1,876.14	2,601.59	3.83	17.16
2008	3,677.25	10.82	22.38	2,104.33	1,524.01	0.93	5.63
2009	7,327.90	−22.82	116.27	1,612.05	5,366.30	7.78	0.82
2010	10,538.27	27.23	487.46	6,119.76	3,496.13	33.71	26.73
2011	11,935.82	185.15	126.40	6,208.33	4,936.46	13.99	41.54
2012	6,169.74	743.25	194.10	2,239.28	827.43	26.22	100.42
2013	14,358.95	221.41	310.93	3,221.56	9,253.40	11.79	49.73
2014	10,547.39	269.92	730.00	4,570.43	4,191.72	16.29	140.57

Source: Authors' calculation based on CEIC data, http://www.ceicdata.com/ (accessed October 13, 2015).

China from the 2008–09 global financial crisis (GFC) in 2010, while most of Europe is still mired in low growth and financial instability. Although the shocks that hit the region in 2008 were financial in nature, the recovery was trade-led, and China was largely the leader.[9] At the same time, the Chinese government signed currency swap agreements with Argentina (2009) and Brazil (2012) to facilitate bilateral trade and lower transaction costs, and it negotiated a loan-for-oil agreement with Brazil in 2009. China's provision of liquidity to the region has been further formalized under an arrangement between the Export–Import Bank of China and the Inter-American Development Bank (IDB), which China joined in 2009. This consists of the establishment of a US$1.8 billion Latin American Fund to spur equity investments in the region's infrastructure, medium-sized enterprises, and natural resources.

This narrative thus far has focused on China's rapid rise in the LAC region as a positive GDP shock, but Cesa-Bianchi and his colleagues also caution that a slowing of Chinese growth could be destabilizing "if and when China's growth begins to slow significantly, especially if this happens before the United States and the euro area have fully recovered from the global crisis."[10] With China's 2015 growth rate estimated at about 6.9 percent of GDP, this latter scenario is now plainly in view. As a result, debates about this bust–boom–bust cycle for LAC are flourishing. In this chapter I zero in on two main political economy debates that have basically been resurrected from much earlier times: (1) the pioneering work of Raúl Prebisch (the first director of the United Nations Economic Commission on Latin America, or ECLAC) on unequal exchange, which became a mainstay of the dependency school's emphasis on the international system as the perpetuator of underdevelopment; (2) the classic framework of Max Corden and Peter Neary on the "resource curse," also known as the "Dutch disease,"[11] which shows how new natural resource discoveries or favorable price changes in one commodity can adversely affect other sectors of the economy, namely manufacturing.[12]

These two terms together have become buzz words for a new era of dependency in the LAC region. However, upon reviewing these debates, I argue that they may partially apply in select circumstances, but fail to capture the overall effects of the rise of China in contemporary Latin America. First, trends in global trade and investment since 2013 suggest that a number of countries and subregions are struggling in the face of China's slowing growth and demand. Latin America, it seems, has no pride of place in terms of being more economically dependent on China than any of these other countries, including some within the OECD bloc.[13] Second, I argue here that it is less a matter of LAC's increased structural dependence on China that endangers growth and development in these EEs, but rather a case of path dependence, whereby current policy choices are limited by "an initial set of institutions that provide disincentives to productive activity."[14] Not surprisingly, for these LAC EEs, the winding down of the China boom has caused longstanding institutional fragilities to float right back to the surface.

Dynamism

Macroeconomic Prudence versus Microeconomic Doldrums

At the turn of the new millennium there was little to suggest that a take-off was in the making for Latin America's emerging economies. The U.S. had yet to rebound from the 2000 dot.com bust when the 9/11/01 terrorist attacks hit New York and Washington, and this worked to prolong a global recession. The data on average GDP growth rates for the four Latin American EEs in Table 7.4 ranged from dismal (Argentina) to lackluster (Brazil) between 2000 and 2002. However, in 2004 China's trade with all four countries began to climb quickly, the result being LAC's abrupt exit from the global recession and a higher pace of average aggregate growth than in the OECD bloc.

The five-year span between 2003 and 2008 was a brief golden age for all four EEs in Table 7.4. All four had deepened their financial markets, reduced external debt, and built up large arsenals of foreign exchange reserves.[15] For once, inflation was running in the single-digit range. With brisk Chinese demand spurring a petroleum price boom, Mexico rebounded on the strength of global oil prices, despite exporting little of its own oil supply to China. For Argentina, Brazil, and Chile, the combination of China's annual average growth rate of 9 to 10 percent during this period and the increase in capital inflows due to the U.S. Federal Reserve Bank's low interest rate policy provided the stimulus for high aggregate growth and an impressive leap in per capita GDP. Despite the vociferous turn away from the Washington Consensus, particularly in Argentina and Brazil, this period reflected the strength of institutional reforms that had been implemented in the 1990s in the realm of banking, finance, and macroeconomic policy making.[16]

The 2008–09 global financial crisis further tested the extent to which macroeconomic policy approaches had been institutionalized across Latin America. Perhaps for the first time ever, the combination of a fiscal surplus, banking sector reform, and a large foreign exchange cushion positioned policy makers within

TABLE 7.4 Comparative Macroeconomic Performance for Four LAC EEs, 2001–14 Averages

Country	GDP (% annual growth)	GDP per capita (% annual growth)	Gross capital formation (GCF) (% of GDP)
Argentina	3.80	2.71	18.06
Brazil	3.24	2.07	19.46
Chile	4.00	2.84	22.52
Mexico	2.13	0.69	22.35

Source: World Development Indicators, http://databank.worldbank.org/data/home.aspx (accessed October 29, 2015).

all four of the EEs in Table 7.4 to respond to the crisis with counter-cyclical policies that eased the pain of adjustment. But Alejandro Izquierdo and Ernesto Talvi also warned that the high growth rates (averaging 6 percent regionally in 2003–07 versus a 3 percent historical average rate of growth) which made the consolidation of macroeconomic reforms possible were driven largely by booming commodity prices and Chinese demand.[17] Latin America's quick recovery from the crisis correlates with a rebound in these prices and the prospect that Chinese-driven demand in such raw material sectors as soybeans, iron ore, and copper could remain steady for some time.[18]

However, we now know that this particular story ended rather abruptly. As Table 7.1 showed, prices on these commodities began to tumble in 2013, with crude oil plunging from about US$100 per barrel in 2013 all the way down to below US$30 a barrel in January 2016.[19] Wishful thinking aside, all booms of this nature inevitably come to an end. For Argentina and Brazil the result has been deep economic recession; Chile and Mexico have fared better in the midst of this price freefall, but there now remains the question of how to kickstart higher sustainable growth in the post-boom era. With the aura of plenty quickly fading, Figure 7.1 offers a glimpse of where these LAC EEs stand on the World Bank's Global Competitiveness Index as of 2016.[20] The indicators displayed in the figure are considered especially important for attracting FDI, achieving efficiency gains, and sustaining higher growth. The results for Argentina and Brazil are disheartening:

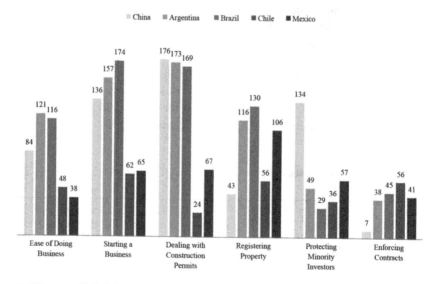

FIGURE 7.1 Global Competitiveness Index (CGI)

Source: Doing Business, Economy Rankings.

Note: Lower numbers mean higher rates of competitiveness.

on four of the six measures in the figure, neither makes it into the top 100 countries. Chile is the clear front-runner, with Mexico running in a distant second place. Chile aside, it would be difficult to put a positive spin on these numbers.

It was on this very question of competitiveness and microeconomic restructuring that Washington Consensus reforms based on deeper liberalization and deregulation had stalled in the late 1990s in Argentina, Brazil, and Mexico. During the first phase of market reform in the early 1990s the gains from macroeconomic stabilization in terms of fiscal, monetary, and currency reform were compelling. Yet a stark reality of this period was the failure of per capita growth and employment creation to keep pace with these positive aggregate returns. The microeconomic agenda was postponed, as incumbent politicians handed off these onerous reform tasks to their successors, and a series of financial crises in the late 1990s threatened to erode the macroeconomic stability that had been so hard won. The 2000–03 global recession exacerbated these trends until, seemingly out of nowhere, the commodity lottery struck; China suddenly became a crucial intervening variable for all four Latin American EEs analyzed here.

The following brief country sketches highlight the profound but highly variable effects that this evolving economic relationship with China has had on development strategies in each of these four countries. The analysis shows that there is no single China–Latin America political economy profile, but rather a set of preliminary outcomes that vary according to a given country's factor endowments and institutional landscape, and the development trajectory underway when Chinese trade and investment began to take off in Latin America in the early 2000s.

Country Sketches: Varieties of Capitalist Development in China–LAC Relations

Mexico

The rise of China in LAC has placed Mexico on the defensive since the late 1980s. At that time, a conscious effort had been made to rely much less on the country's primary exports and to harness its labor surplus to an outward-oriented industrial sector which now forms the backbone of higher-tech manufacturing under the North American Free Trade Agreement (NAFTA). However, in one of the earliest and most comprehensive reports on China–Latin America relations in the 2000s Robert Devlin and his co-authors point to Mexico as a potential "loser" as a result of its high export similarity index (ESI) with China and the strong overlap in goods that both China and Mexico are exporting to the U.S. market.[21]

Indeed, by 2003 China had displaced Mexico as the second most important U.S. trade partner; over the period 2000–05 Mexico had increased its share of U.S. imports by 25 percent, while China's share of U.S. imports grew by

143 percent;[22] by 2011, 31 percent of all U.S. imports from Mexico were deemed
to be under "direct threat" from Chinese competition in the U.S. market, and
some 46 percent of Mexico's manufacturing exports to the U.S. were classified in
this same category.[23] Apart from this head-on competition from China in the U.S.
market, China accounted for around 16 percent of Mexico's imports in 2013 but
just 2 percent of its exports.[24] In contrast to the South American EEs, Mexico does
not have an ample supply of oil or other raw materials to sell to China, the result
being a burgeoning manufacturing trade deficit with China in the 2000s.

The irony for Mexico is twofold. First, Mexico was the only country in
this group that exported high value-added goods to China in the 1980–2000
period; however, in the 2001–14 period, that figure had dropped from an
average of 35 percent of Mexico's exports to China (which, again, total about
2 percent of its total exports) in the earlier period to 27 percent during the boom
years (2003–13). Second, Mexican policy makers spent the last 25 years working to diversify the country's exports away from primary products. Although
they largely succeeded, they took the market route toward restructuring and
did so via Mexico's entry into NAFTA in 1994. Under NAFTA, Mexico's
expectation was that, by liberalizing its trade and investment regimes, it could
count on U.S. FDI and the heightened competition from U.S. imports to force
a restructuring of the domestic industrial sector.[25] Industrial policy was tapered
off, and the tough tasks of technology acquisition and adaptation were basically
turned over to foreign companies operating in export production zones located
in central and northern Mexico.

This said, Figure 7.2 shows that Mexico is the only Latin American EE that
comes close to China in terms of the revealed comparative advantage (RCA) of
its manufacturing sector;[26] it has certainly outpaced Brazil on this measure, but is
also struggling to regain the competitiveness peak it had reached at the outset of
the 2000s. Mexico's high ranking in Figure 7.2 raises two key questions. First,
why has Mexico registered the slowest growth rate over the past 15 years within
the group of Latin American EEs considered here (see Table 7.4)? Second, why
can't Mexican manufactured exports hold their own against Chinese competitors in the U.S. market? After all, from 1994 to 2002 Mexico enjoyed very
privileged access to the U.S. market under NAFTA, maintained a competitive
exchange rate, and continues to face much lower tariffs there than does China.

Hindsight suggests that Mexico's entry into NAFTA has been as much a
burden as a blessing. Back in the early 1990s newly converted neoliberal technocrats sought NAFTA entry as a way to permanently lock in market reforms
and implement new ones. But NAFTA membership also transmitted the U.S.
commitment to laissez-faire, and a fickle one at that, into Mexico's technocratic
psyche and superimposed this doctrine onto a dysfunctional congress and political party system; it additionally cemented the country's overwhelming trade and
investment dependence on the U.S. market. In 2011, 89 percent of Mexican
exports that incorporate imported inputs were destined for the U.S. market.[27]

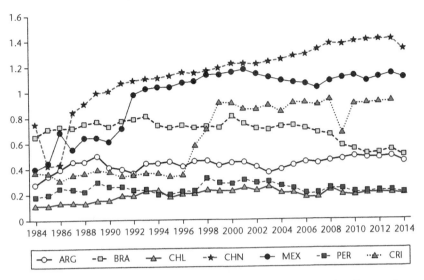

FIGURE 7.2 Manufacturing RCA for China and Five LAC Emerging Economies

Source: Calculation based on WDI database.

Note: RCA refers to Revealed Comparative Advantage Index. If RCA>2.5, industry's competitiveness is the highest. If 1.25<RCA<2.5, its competitiveness is high. If 0.8<RCA<1.25, its competitiveness is lower. If RCA<0.8, industry's competitiveness is weak.

Having harnessed the country's economic fate to NAFTA, Mexican politicians and policy makers have spent most of the 2000s crafting protectionist tariffs on Chinese manufacturing imports and stalling on the completion of essential reforms. As recently as 2012, this reform lag included fiscal policy, utility inputs, oil production, labor markets, anti-trust, and education[28]—all of which are essential if the country is to climb the industrial ladder on a par with China. Mexico's development model in place at the turn of the century could thus be described as "pseudo-neoliberal" in the sense that fiscal policy and monetary policy have remained tight and the country has entered into a network of ten FTAs with 45 countries.[29] Yet trade protectionism toward non-FTA members is rampant, and market-strengthening structural reforms continue to languish.

Despite Mexico's obvious geographic advantage over China, the latter has gradually eclipsed Mexico in the U.S. manufacturing market by virtue of its lower *overall* costs and by actively deploying public policy in the expansion, upgrading, and infusion of technology into its manufacturing sector.[30] The World Economic Forum's *Global Competitiveness Report 2013–2014* further refines the differences between China and Mexico: With regard to those indicators (FDI and technology transfer, local supplier quality, and sophistication of production processes)[31] that reflect an industrial model like Mexico's, with its strong orientation toward FDI operating in export processing zones, Mexico readily outshines China in the rankings. Conversely, on those indicators (capacity for innovation, company spending on R&D, availability of scientists and engineers, venture capital availability, and ease of access to business loans)[32] that capture the development of an endogenous industrial model like China's, one that is steadily accruing value-added and absorbing new technologies,[33] China basically leaves Mexico in the dust.

Chinese FDI to Mexico lags far behind that of Argentina and Brazil (see Tables 7.2 and 7.3), with a modest presence in computers (Lenovo) and autos (Golden Dragon), but this is not for lack of trying. There is, in fact, ample room to expand Chinese FDI into Mexico, especially given its proximity to the U.S. market. Yet, for any number of reasons, there are few planned projects in the making. While some Mexican industrial producers are the first to admit that they have benefited from the purchase of China's cheaper intermediate inputs,[34] China's deepening presence in Mexico's domestic manufacturing sector in the 2000s found the bulk of producers there completely unprepared to face the competition. A key issue is that Mexico has yet to strike a positive chord in its dealings with China, including the abrupt cancellation in 2014 of a nearly US$4 billion contract with a Chinese-led consortium to build a bullet train in Mexico.[35] The project collapsed amidst allegations of executive-level corruption in the bidding process on the Mexican side.

Brazil

Political and economic elites in Brazil, which is now ranked as the world's sixth largest economy, have converged around a gradualist strategy that has incorporated market norms into a developmental capitalist framework. The prevailing development model at the turn of the century could best be described as state capitalist, whereby market norms have been gradually adopted since the early 1990s. As with Mexico, Brazil's banking and financial sector reforms have been impressive, as indicated by its successful response and timely recovery from the 2008–09 global financial crisis and its coveted investment-grade rating up through December 2015.[36]

But all of the various ways of measuring the impact of China on Brazil suggest that the situation is worlds apart from that which Mexico now faces vis-à-vis China in both its home market and the U.S. From 2000 to 2011, for example, bilateral trade between China and Brazil grew by more than 2,000 percent, and Brazil has run a trade surplus with China for most of this period.[37] And yet Brazil's growth abruptly slowed in 2011 and slumped into an official recession in 2015. This suggests that currency reform, including a floating exchange rate and sustained macroeconomic stabilization, is perhaps a necessary condition for growth but not entirely sufficient. In this respect, Brazil's thick regulatory and bureaucratic overhang reflects the extent to which this version of the developmental capitalist model is still too much of a drag on growth. Whereas the average South American rate of government spending as a percentage of GDP is about 26 percent, on the eve of the current slowdown Brazil's stood at about 40 percent.

The pattern of China–Brazil bilateral trade is based on traditional comparative advantage: Brazil exports mainly raw materials to China and imports back manufactured intermediate goods that are increasingly higher in technological content. This has raised a number of sticking points for Brazil. For example, in 2006 its volume of raw material exports surpassed that of manufactured goods for the first time since the early 1990s; and Brazilian industrial producers are feeling the pinch from Chinese competition in both domestic and third country markets such as Chile and Venezuela.[38] Brazil's low level of trade openness is also out of step with Chile and Mexico. For example, Brazil ranks at 71 on a scale of 1–100 (with 100 being the most open trade regime), which is about 10–14 points less open than Chile and Mexico.[39] This partly reflects the efforts of both Argentina and Brazil to cushion themselves from trade competition within the context of the Southern Cone Common Market (Mercosur, which includes Argentina, Brazil, Paraguay, Uruguay, and Venezuela, launched in 1995.

André Nassif argues that Brazil's comparatively higher trade barriers reflect how "the country has sacrificed higher and more productive growth over the past twenty years due to the partial and incomplete nature of its microeconomic reforms."[40] However, with the rapid rise of China in LAC since 2000, and for perhaps the first time in the post-World War II era, the Brazilian industrial sector has not been able to entirely shelter itself from the fierce competition that Chinese manufactured imports are now presenting. Until 2014, currency over-valuation had been a damper for Brazil's manufactured exports, which have been more expensive on global markets than those from countries with more competitive exchange rates and price structures. Jenkins and Barbosa also note that Brazil has considerable room to expand high value-added exports to the rest of the world, as its exports as a share of GDP remain quite low.[41]

Brazilian-style state capitalism has also been a drag on private sector investment, which registered just 12.8 percent of long-term financing in 2012, while the state-owned development bank (BNDES) accounted for around 72.4 percent.[42] The backdrop is that: capital has been abundant but interest rates are sky-high as a deterrent to inflation; investment and productivity are flat, as Brazilian private investors have gone abroad in search of better deals; and, bolstered by an overvalued currency for most of the 2000s, domestic consumer spending until 2012 averaged around 60 percent of GDP. Whereas today's problem is ostensibly the inability to channel the mass of resource rents into productive ventures, this has been exacerbated by an accounting scandal that erupted in 2014 at Brazil's semi-public (60 percent state-held) oil firm, Petrobras, where an alleged US$22 billion in bribes, money laundering, and rogue contracts had been siphoned off by the country's powerful economic interests and political elites.

Although Brazil's stalling of growth is partly due to China's economic slow-down and the related negative GDP shock, as well as the related plummet in prices for iron ore and oil, it also has to do with the country's slow progress on reforms that are key to higher growth and productivity gains (see Figure 7.2). The implosion of Petrobras has also weighed heavily on the economy. Once the sixth largest company in the world by market capitalization, Petrobras accounts for roughly 10 percent of Brazil's GDP. In 2007 Brazil had announced the discovery of some 20 to 110 billion barrels of oil in deep-water "pre-salt" reserves off the country's coast.[43] Petrobras raised US$70 billion in 2010, one of the biggest share sales in LAC history, as oil prices were booming. Having lost its investment-grade rating in the wake of the scandal, the company's shares are down 39 percent from where they were in 2014.[44] Brazil's overall debt rating has also dropped from investment grade to just above junk status. Perhaps more than any other economic event within the EEs, the sudden and shocking fall of Petrobras has clearly signaled the end of the boom.

Still, in contrast with Mexico's comparatively bleak positon with regard to the rise of China, Brazil–China economic relations have a distinct upside: Chinese FDI in Brazil towers over that in the other LAC emerging economies (see Tables 7.2 and 7.3).[45] Despite China's concentration of FDI in extractive projects in LAC, Brazilian firms have succeeded in setting up joint ventures with top Chinese firms (Huawei, Chery, China South Industries Group) in manufacturing. This prospect is obviously not enough to pull Brazil out of its deep recession. It is, however, an important incentive for Brazilian policy makers to buckle down in implementing those stalled reforms which are essential for jump-starting growth.

Argentina

Since the launching of the 1991 Convertibility Plan Argentina has run the full gamut from neoliberal (1991–2001) to developmental or heterodox economic policy approaches (2001 to present). With the country's 2001 default on some US$100 billion in government-held debt and the collapse of the decade-long currency board (which tightly pegged the Argentine peso to the U.S. dollar) in 2002, the situation could not have looked more bleak. Growth was down by nearly 11 percent in 2002, and inflation, which had been reduced to single digits through the 1990s, spiked to 30 percent that same year. By imposing a unilateral restructuring on about 75 percent of the country's outstanding external debt, the government reduced its debt service burden from 8 percent to 2 percent of GDP.[46] This, along with a more competitive exchange rate and significant financial reforms implemented in the 1990s, set the stage for what looked to be a modest recovery. However, Argentina's growth rebounded to nearly 9 percent of GDP in 2003 and would go on to average 7 percent annually between 2003 and 2011. As with Brazil, in 2003 Argentina suddenly began to thrive under the thrust of brisk Chinese demand and the resulting high world prices for its main commodities (soybeans and crude petroleum).

In the decade from 2002 to 2011 China advanced to become Argentina's second most important trading partner (after Brazil), and total trade between the two countries had increased nearly 12-fold to about US$17 billion dollars in 2011.[47] Argentina, moreover, is second only to Brazil as a destination for Chinese FDI in the 2000s (see Tables 7.2 and 7.3), the bulk of it concentrated in natural resources (e.g., oil, iron, wood, gas, copper, gold, and lithium).[48] In the first few years following the Argentine default, the country's leaders embraced China as a new political and economic ally now that Argentina had basically frozen itself out of Western capital markets and international financial institution (IFI) relations had similarly cooled. And, although perhaps not to the extent that Argentina had hoped, China has become a source of alternative financing. First was the aforementioned US$10 billion currency swap in 2009, and in 2010 China put up US$10 billion in loans and rolling stocks to modernize Argentina's railway system.[49] Yet tensions have gradually arisen as Argentina has sought (unsuccessfully) to increase the value-added of its primary exports to China, for example to ship soybean oil rather than solely raw soya beans;[50] moreover, Argentina has filed numerous anti-dumping complaints against China over the past few years on everything from bicycle tires, to textiles, to shoes.[51]

Nevertheless, I would argue that China's economic importance to Argentina is far from trivial. It was, after all, Chinese demand that breathed new life into the collapsed Argentine economy beginning in 2003. More recently, the investment side of the relationship has picked up considerably, as Argentina now accounts for some 40 percent of Chinese FDI to the region. On the less favorable side, Argentina's foreign exchange earnings from high commodity prices, combined with the burst of FDI from China, prompted a populist-style spending spree. Whereas Brazil's ability to productively invest its windfall earnings is mostly a matter of dense over-regulation and bureaucratic bungling, Argentina engaged in one of Latin America's more dramatic episodes of capital squandering during the China boom.

The country's fiscal and current accounts deteriorated, inflation again hit double digits, and the government resorted to import, price, and capital controls. As of 2010 the Argentine government began dipping into Central Bank reserves to cover its expenditures, the result being a precipitous US$12 billion drop in reserves between 2010 and 2012. Argentine trade protectionism has been such that the country even imposed import licenses and tariffs, and filed anti-dumping complaints against its own Mercosur partners, especially Brazil, on washing machines, television sets, transformers, and glass products.[52] At the current juncture, to speak of Argentina's competitiveness, or even a development model proper, is a moot point, as the country's performance in Figure 7.1 indicates. However, Argentina's growing economic ties with China suggest that it could muddle along with macro-profligacy, high inflation, and sub-optimal returns for some time to come.[53] The outcome of the country's December 2015 presidential race showed, however, that the electorate has a much brighter future in mind. The departure of populist Peronist President Cristina Fernández in late 2015 and the inauguration of Mauricio Macri, a more cautious and economically astute executive, gives good reason to hope that the country can make its way back to some semblance of a sane economic policy. Already, Argentina has settled with the hold-out creditors from the 2001 default, and global markets responded warmly to a 2016 debt issue of more than US$15 billion.[54]

Chile

Chile is the most open, market-oriented, and trade-dependent of the four Latin American EEs analyzed here, and the negotiation of FTAs has been an integral part of its development strategy since the 1990s. This partially explains Chile's favorable response to China's invitation to negotiate a bilateral FTA, implemented in 2006. However, Chile has cultivated a strong relationship with China that dates back to the administration of socialist President Salvador Allende (1970–73). For example, Chile was one of LAC's most active supporters of China's 1970 entry into the United Nations, and China's bid to accede to the WTO in 2001, and it was the first country in the LAC region to offer the PRC "market economy" status. The fact that Chile already had an FTA in place with the U.S. enabled China to tread softly without appearing to upstage U.S. ties and interests in the Western Hemisphere.

The Chile–China FTA speaks directly to the latter's resource scarcity in copper, iron ore, and other minerals. Raw materials thus constitute the bulk of Chile's exports to China. Chile's trade with China has quadrupled under this FTA, now in place for a decade, and China is now the country's top destination for exports.[55] At just US$196 million (see Table 7.2), Chile's FDI inflows from China have been exceedingly modest; this is partly due to the fact that FDI in copper is China's main interest and Chilean copper is largely state-held. China sweetened the FTA deal by accepting numerous exceptions in the Chilean domestic manufacturing sector. For China, these market access concessions to Chile represented such a minuscule percentage of its total trade in manufactured exports that the sacrifice was worth making in order to secure a steady supply of commodities from Chile.

Chile's decision to negotiate an FTA with China was underpinned, first, by the growing conviction that domestic producers should be trying harder to export non-traditional and higher value-added products to the Chinese market and, second, by the goal of attracting Chinese FDI into efficiency and market-seeking investments, as opposed to resource-seeking investments limited to mineral extraction.[56] An FTA with China also raised the prospect that Chile could be transformed into a dynamic transport and service hub for transpacific trade.[57] As Latin America's stellar performer for two decades and a seasoned negotiator of numerous other FTAs—including those with Japan, the U.S., the EU, and India—Chile offered China the opportunity to seal a fairly easy deal while at the same time securing a steady supply of copper from the world's top producer of this ore.

In principle, both Chile and China saw eye to eye on the merit of the FTA as a means to: branch into new product lines; create economies of scale; increase outward investment in both directions; and facilitate access to the markets of third countries, Chile in East Asia and China in South America.[58] In practice, this FTA has mainly spurred trade in primary goods, although Chilean wine exports to China are now second only to those of the EU.[59] With its exceptions in textiles and garments, and some major appliances, the Chile–China FTA also opened the back door for industrial policy.[60] Whereas most other Western Hemisphere FTAs have strong provisions for increased market access in manufacturing sectors, Chilean negotiators were able to completely exclude 152 "sensitive products" from this FTA while obtaining immediate duty-free access to the Chinese market for 92 percent of Chile's products covered by the agreement.[61] While just six of Chile's abundant agricultural exports were initially covered by the FTA, Chilean policy makers have subsequently succeeded in securing market access for tropical fruits, rendering Chile second only to Thailand in the export of tropical fruits to China.[62] More than 90 per cent of Chile's imports from China are manufactured goods, with over 42 per cent ranking as medium- and high-tech.[63] These higher-tech imports grew by more than 900 percent between 2003 and 2011.[64]

China's exceedingly low levels of non-mining investment and services trade with Chile suggest that the promotion of market- and efficiency-seeking investments were of less concern from the Chinese standpoint. With Chile's prompting, the two governments did sign the Supplementary Agreement on Trade in Services of the Free Trade Agreement in 2008,[65] and in 2012 they completed an agreement on investment. Of note here are the very few limitations set by Chile in terms of market access for services and national treatment for investors compared with China's thick list of restrictions concerning Chile's access to its services market, in particular. At the end of the day it seems safe to say that Chile has done well in securing a deal that has cushioned both sides from wild swings in copper prices over the next two decades, even if the FTA shows weak promise as a venue for diversifying into a pattern of more dynamic and competitive exchange between the two countries.[66]

Debates

The phenomenal "rise" of China has breathed new life into the field of development economics, and it has invoked the application of past concepts to the present situation. As mentioned in the introduction to this chapter, I will focus here on two main debates: (1) unequal exchange, which emphasized the chronic price swings and negative terms of trade for commodity exporters in the LAC region during the early post-World War II period and became a mainstay of the dependency school's emphasis on the international system as the perpetuator of underdevelopment; and (2) the "Dutch disease"[67] or "resource curse," related to a country's over-dependence on commodity exports at the expense of the industrial sector and sound macroeconomic policy making. Neither of these classic arguments entirely fits any of the China–LAC relationships just reviewed. Below, I explain why, while also offering a 21st-century rendition of them but also applying these terms where appropriate.

Unequal Exchange and the Shadow of the Past?

Some of the very best scholars now writing on the political economy of China–Latin America relations have expressed concern that today's pattern of exchange harks back to the turn of the last century, a time when LAC's primary exports to the North were offset by the import of manufactured and intermediate capital goods back from the developed countries.[68] Yet, whereas the earlier experience with this pattern of trade inspired policies of import-substitution industrialization and a widespread critique concerning the unfavorable terms of trade for the region—as the price of manufactured imports continued to rise while commodity exports were plagued by cyclical price downturns—the structural conditions that now prevail within most of these economies are radically different. With the exception of Chile, considerable inroads have been made with industrialization in the LAC EEs, and manufactured goods accounted for some 47 percent of regional exports in 2013.[69] Moreover, for all but Mexico the terms of trade during the China boom were highly favorable (see Figure 7.3). This is the good news.

The downside of this story is that, although forward linkages in terms of manufactured exports have clearly improved in LAC, backward linkages to the domestic market are still too weak. This is the case with Mexico, for example, where manufacturing production is tied to FDI to the extent that local producers of intermediate goods are still not competitive as suppliers in these production zones—hence the ease with which China has slipped into markets for intermediate inputs in Argentina, Brazil, and Mexico. Put simply, those intermediate goods that producers in all three of these LAC EEs are importing from China are higher in knowledge, value-added, and technological content, and they are more competitively priced. As shown in Figure 7.2, LAC EEs have not kept pace with the competitiveness gains that China has registered in its manufacturing sector over the past 20 years, advances which are the result of highly focused expenditures and policies that have promoted science, technological adaptation, advanced education in hard science fields, and research and development since the early 1980s.[70]

Based on his econometric analysis, Jaime Ortiz argues that LAC "has reached a point in its production possibilities frontier at which it is not feasible to further increase its level of output unless technology and innovation come into play.

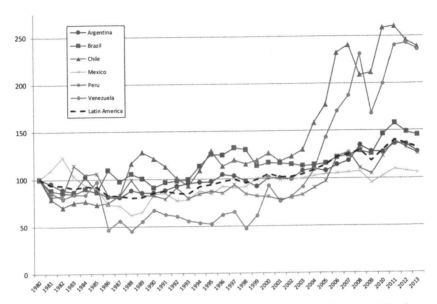

FIGURE 7.3   Evolution of the Terms of Trade (Goods Only) in Argentina, Brazil, Chile, Mexico, Peru, and Venezuela, 1980–2013

Source: ECLAC—CEPALSTAT, renormalized to 1980.

Latin America must broaden its productivity base, move into more sophisticated endeavors, and diversify its export basket to gain market share."[71] Despite their propensity for import-substitution and protectionism, even the earlier theorists of unequal exchange advocated technology adaptation, the strengthening of backward linkages, and export diversification.[72] LAC countries are perhaps more pressed than ever before to quickly climb the value-added production ladder and to articulate a longer-term vision for a growth model based on efficiency, innovation, and competitiveness.[73] It's the delay in going full speed ahead with the necessary policies and further reforms that is placing a major drag on LAC's post-boom growth.

"Dutch Disease" Latin American-style?

Apart from a brief window from 2004 to 2006, exceptionally low interest rates have been a mainstay of U.S. monetary policy since 2000—including the U.S. Fed's near zero interest rate policy that prevailed from December 2008 through late 2015.[74] Conversely, LAC's interest rates have been much higher, as domestic price spikes still lay just below the surface in these inflation-prone countries. This encouraged massive capital inflows to some LAC EEs in the 2000s[75] and, when combined with the aforementioned commodity price boom, the accumulation of unprecedented levels of foreign exchange reserves. One consequence was the considerable overvaluation of LAC currencies (until the wave of depreciations triggered by the abrupt devaluation of the Chinese yuan in August 2015), a trend which has been referred to as a case of "financial Dutch disease" within the LAC EEs.[76] Whereas the original version of the Dutch disease referred to the deleterious effect of a boom in natural gas prices in the late 1950s, including currency appreciation, industrial decline, and job losses, LAC's manufactured exports and sizable industrial sector suggest that it would be premature to diagnose a generalized case of traditional Dutch disease or resource curse in the region.

But the resource curse also concerns the nature of macroeconomic policy management during a foreign exchange bonanza. In days of old, the cluster of macroeconomic policies that embellished the resource curse—trade protectionism, financial repression, fiscal profligacy, and overvalued exchange rates—readily set the stage for a full-blown balance-of-payments crisis once commodity prices began to tumble. However, the GFC unveiled the substantial macroeconomic, financial sector, and trade reforms that have been undertaken by LAC countries over the past two decades.[77] The combination of a fiscal surplus, banking sector reform, and a large foreign exchange cushion indeed positioned Latin American policy makers to respond to the crisis with counter-cyclical policies that eased the pain of adjustment. I would argue that these reform advances also helped to fend off the old-fashioned balance-of-payments implosions that used to erupt in the wake of a commodity price boom. Venezuela, which has obstinately refused to move forward on modernizing its domestic financial institutions, provides the counter-factual case here, as that heavily dependent oil producer is imploding now that petroleum prices have fallen through the floor.

Still, the South American LAC countries are not out of the woods in terms of falling prey to a case of financial Dutch disease. Argentina, for example, rode out the 2002 devaluation with a fairly competitive exchange rate up until 2009, at which point this pattern dramatically reversed. Currency appreciation, dwindling central bank reserves, and increasing resort to financial repression all reflected the onset of financial Dutch disease, if not worse.[78] Brazil, too, fell prey to financial Dutch disease, as the Brazilian real had been steeply overvalued up until the aforementioned Chinese devaluation in 2014.[79] Although Brazil is still a formidable industrial exporter, Brazilian manufacturing has taken an extra hit from the resource curse during the 2000s. The more powerful industrial groups in Sao Paulo have blamed this trend on Chinese manufactured exports to Brazil, and hence the Brazilian government's move to ratchet up protectionist measures against China.[80] But financial Dutch disease also kicked in here as an unduly strong currency simultaneously favored manufactured imports and penalized exporters in this sector during the height of the 2003–13 boom.

To be clear, financial Dutch disease is just one possible outcome in this scenario. Chile, for example, has been hit even harder by falling commodity prices and the drop in Chinese demand post-2013, although policy makers there weathered this storm much better than their South American neighbors. Guillermo Perry and Alejandro Forero attribute the success of both Chile and Peru to:

> a combination of higher previous TFP (total factor productivity) growth in industry in Peru and Chile and to two macro policy factors that miti-gated the extent of real exchange rate appreciation in both countries: first, they were the only two countries in the region that kept a fiscal surplus during the boom . . . and second, they accumulated larger fractions of reserves to GDP than the rest.[81]

These same authors add that Chile and Peru also undertook the most significant counter-cyclical fiscal interventions in the throes of the GFC, but also tapered these policies down to pre-crisis levels once the recovery was underway. Brazil, and to a lesser extent Argentina, simply continued to spend in the post-crisis period.

Although perhaps counter-intuitive, it is the small, open economies—or least likely cases if you will—which have done better in the 2000s. Going back to the data in Figure 7.1, Chile has made by far the most notable reform progress in the 2000s. Argentina and Brazil have been backsliding on reforms in the 2000s, and Mexico has basically been treading water. And yet, in varying degrees, all four of these EEs continue to face longstanding obstacles to achieving higher sustainable growth. The attainment of sound macroeconomic stability (for all but Argentina) is the big triumph of the past two decades, but the remaining list of reform tasks lingers, and is hardly new.[82] These challenges include: historically low rates of investment and productivity; insufficient innovation by firms; poor quality of public infrastructure; lack of access to financial services; and numerous other vari-ables that are crucial for sustainable growth (e.g., government effectiveness, rule of law, control of corruption). How is it that the more things appear to change, the more they seem to stay the same?

(Path) Dependence?

Despite the broad use of this term to describe all that is potentially wrong with the developing world, it does provide a helpful framework for comparative political economic analysis. The doom-and-gloom aspect of path dependence, which holds that the impacts of past decisions tend to shape the perceived range of policy choices for the present and the future, can be overly deterministic. However, in his seminal work on this topic, Douglass North reminds us that path dependence need not be "a story of inevitability in which the past neatly predicts the future."[83] Rather, the restructuring of political and economic insti-tutions can lower the barriers to reform and open the way for new leadership, organizational change, and policy innovation. This is inevitably a gradual, long-term process, one marked by discontinuities or critical junctures.[84] Over time, "Decisions become embodied in socio-economic structures, political institutions, and rules that subsequently mold the preferences and behavior of individuals, thereby enhancing (or reducing) the probability of certain outcomes."[85]

Latin America has had no shortage of discontinuous events and critical junctures over the past few decades. The most dramatic turning point for all four of the LAC countries considered here would be the external debt shocks that hit the region in 1982.[86] From there followed the collapse of import substitution, the widespread trend toward political liberalization, and the pursuit of market reforms. Critical political (authoritarian lapses, as in Argentina in 1987 or Peru in 1992) and economic (hyperinflation, currency crises, debt defaults) junctures punctuated the recent history of all four countries in the post-1982 period. Although the GFC was undoubtedly a major global event, LAC was able to ride this out on China's shirt tails. However, taken together it is the rapid rise of China in LAC in the 2000s, the 2003–13 commodity price boom, and now the collapse of those prices and the slowing of Chinese growth and demand which constitute the biggest shock since 1982. In the parlance of path-dependent analysis, in what ways have these critical junctures worked to restructure (or deter) political and economic institutions, lower (or raise) the barriers to reform, and open (or close) the way for new leadership, organizational change, and policy innovation?

Of the four LAC countries analyzed here, only Argentina has fallen prey to the path of inevitability in which institutions that previously provided disincentives to productive activity have continued to do so. By virtue of having hit the commodity lottery in the 2000s, Argentina has had ample room to reform those institutions and correct for those policy errors that provoked a massive financial crisis in 2001–02. Political leaders and policy makers, moreover, could have crafted a restructuring strategy to address the country's massive reform deficit. Instead, this opportunity was lost. To put this another way, in 1991 the size of the Argentine economy was 50 percent that of China's, but by 2011 it had dwindled to just 6.1 percent.[87] Again, the complementarity of the China–Argentina economic relationship is such that Argentina's commodity exports will be in demand indefinitely, meaning that the country has a longer-than-usual horizon for muddling through and achieving much less than is warranted by its rich natural resource abundance and factor endowments. And yet the election of President Macri on a more centrist ticket opens up still another opportunity for the country to overturn this pessimistic scenario.

Both Brazil and Mexico have moved considerably outside of their traditional development paths based on import-substitution industrialization and financial repression over the post-World War II era. Although the respective routes that each has taken to achieve macroeconomic stabilization and industrial restructuring are markedly different, each has sought to head in the same steady upward direction. The data in Figure 7.1 confirm that Mexico has moved more quickly than Brazil on a competitiveness agenda, although both trail behind Chile on the majority of policy indicators for competitiveness. If anything, the rise of China has confirmed how much such policies matter: in 1991 Brazil's total GDP was 107.3 percent the size of China's, but just 33.9 percent in 2011; Mexico's total GDP was 82.8 percent the size of China's in 1991, but a mere 15.8 percent in 2011.[88] A main response toward China by both Brazil and Mexico has been to raise tariffs through the roof on Chinese goods coming into these markets. Yet the Brazilian economist Alexandre Barbosa cautions that "China's ascent cannot serve—as the vague concept of globalisation once did—as an excuse for fatalistically giving up on national development and regional integration. On the contrary, it makes these policies more urgent than ever."[89] Clearly, the reform lag in both countries confirms that there still exist "disincentives to productive activity" in each.[90]

Whereas Brazil and Mexico are still struggling against the "inevitability" of sub-optimal economic performance, Chile has stuck firmly to the open-economy, macro-prudent development path that it embarked on some 40 years ago. As Figure 7.1 showed, the country has made impressive inroads in the way of institutional modernization and policy innovation. By negotiating a bilateral FTA with China, Chile has secured greater access to that market, and won some modest relief for domestic producers in those sectors heavily exposed to competition from Chinese imports. In terms of macroeconomic performance during the boom and post-boom periods, Chile has also successfully fought against financial Dutch disease and sought to pursue a development path that builds on reform successes in the way of institutional modernization and policy innovation.

Conclusions

In this chapter I have taken an early stab at assessing the pre-boom, boom, and post-boom phases in China's relationship with four LAC EEs. In the pre-boom period we saw that growth and economic dynamism were essentially flat for all but Chile. Argentina was in dire straits, Mexico was still hampered by the U.S. dot.com bust and recession, and Brazil was in the midst of electing its first Labor Party candidate (who turned out to be truly progressive on social policy but also friendlier than expected toward Wall Street). There were few signs that the dawn of the new millennium would constitute a critical juncture for these LAC EEs. Alas, China's entry into the WTO, the recovery of the U.S. economy, and rising growth rates in both the OECD and the EEs all converged; the 2008–09 global financial crisis notwithstanding, China's 9–10 percent average growth rates until 2012 kicked off the biggest commodity lottery in more than a century. These LAC EEs reduced debt, amassed large arsenals of foreign reserves, and (more or less) put their fiscal houses in order.

These similarities aside, the four country sketches revealed both the diversity of responses to the boom and the very different ways in which these EEs fared according to domestic institutions, factor endowments, and the development trajectory that a given country found itself on when the boom hit. These findings are somewhat counter-intuitive: Mexico, given its membership in NAFTA and the OECD, as well as its formidable industrial base and oil reserves, fared the worst in terms of average annual GDP growth from 2001 to 2014. What's worse, its average annual rate of per capita GDP growth during this period was downright abysmal. Hindsight shows that the country's efforts to "lock in" newly minted market reforms by joining NAFTA in 1994 were misguided, and that the growth losses from delaying structural reforms needed to bolster the market have been exponential. The tight wage compression reflected in Table 7.4 is simply not a recipe for success.

As a small open economy that depends heavily on a wide range of primary exports, in yesteryears Chile would have been the most likely to crash in the post-boom phase. However, as with the East Asian EEs, Chile has shown that delayed development is not a terminal illness. Rather, policy makers and political leaders there have stuck tenaciously to a strategy of institutional innovation and prudent macro- and microeconomic management. Table 7.4 shows that during the China boom Chile registered the highest rates of average annual growth, per capita growth, and gross capital formation as a percentage of GDP. In 2010 it became the 31st country to be admitted to the OECD bloc. Argentina and Brazil, while holding their own on these same performance indicators from 2001 to 2014, now find themselves mired in deep recession. Policy makers in Brazil took their eyes off the prize and now have considerable catching up to do on the reform front. For Argentina, unfortunately, the China boom afforded the country just enough rope to hang itself; the way back to some semblance of development is now in the hands of a new administration intent on turning this situation around.

As for the usefulness of earlier paradigms like unequal exchange and Dutch disease, I would not rule these out entirely. However, both must be viewed through a 21st-century lens. Whereas earlier reference to unequal exchange applied to commodity exporters with low levels of industrial development, the cases of Argentina and Brazil confirm that this dynamic can set in even when a country has achieved a sizable level of industrial capacity and exports. In short, China has upped the ante exponentially at the microeconomic level for these EEs, showing that there are no shortcuts to achieving high growth via investment, productivity, and efficiency gains; moreover, the decade-long boom in commodity prices, trade, and capital inflows offered these countries unprecedented room to maneuver. Some were obviously able to take better advantage of it than others.

As for Dutch disease, the earlier emphasis on manufacturing sector decline during a commodity price boom misses the mark. As I mentioned earlier, LAC's average level of manufactured exports was roughly 47 percent in 2013.[91] There is, however, evidence of financial Dutch disease, especially in the macroeconomic policies of Argentina and Brazil. Massive capital inflows, soaring commodity prices, and the accumulation of unprecedented levels of foreign exchange reserves contributed to the overvaluation of LAC currencies until the wave of downward exchange rate adjustments that followed the devaluation of the Chinese yuan in 2014. This trend toward overvaluation was most dramatic in Brazil and Argentina post-2009. Now, with capital flows reversing, commodity prices dropping, and the tapping of foreign reserves in both countries, policy makers in each are faced with the task of repairing the damage inflicted by financial Dutch disease—and this on top of the laundry list of reforms that are still pending.

Finally, I turned to the path-dependence framework as a way of elucidating not the automaticity of policy failure and the repetitious barriers to reform but rather the considerable leeway for human agency that these LAC countries have been afforded by the rise of China in Latin America. For Argentina, Brazil, and even Mexico, an exit from the current slowdown will require much more than advancing on the kinds of institutional reforms laid out in Figure 7.1. Traditional issues like bureaucratic streamlining, building infrastructure, and ramping up manufactured exports are part of the answer. But the key to sustainable growth will be a very rigorous housecleaning and overhaul of those domestic institutions that continue to provide disincentives to productive activity.

Notes

1 A previous version of this chapter was published in *Latin American Policy*, vol. 7, no. 1 (2016), pp. 26–51. The author thanks Scotty Huhn, Hannah Kwon, and Vijeta Tanden for their superb research assistance and several anonymous reviewers for their extremely helpful comments and feedback.
2 See, for example, R. Evan Ellis, *China in Latin America: The Whats and Wherefores* (Boulder, CO: Lynne Rienner, 2009); Alicia Bárcena and Osvaldo Rosales, *The People's Republic of China and Latin America and the Caribbean: Towards a Strategic Partnership* (Santiago: Economic Commission for Latin America and the Caribbean, 2010); Rhys Jenkins, "China's Global Expansion and Latin America," *Journal of Latin American Studies*, vol. 42, no. 1 (November 2010), pp. 809–837; Kevin P. Gallagher and Roberto Porzecanski, *The Dragon in the Room: China and the Future of Latin American Industrialization* (Stanford, CA: Stanford University Press, 2011); and Adrian H. Hearn and José Luis León-Manríquez, eds., *China Engages Latin America: Tracing the Trajectory* (Boulder, CO: Lynne Rienner, 2011).
3 Ambrogio Cesa-Bianchi, M. Hashem Pesaran, Alessandro Rebucci, and Tengteng Xu, "China's Emergence in the World Economy and Business Cycles in Latin America," *Economía*, vol. 12, no. 2 (2012), p. 32.
4 Kevin Gallagher, *The China Triangle: Latin America's China Boom and the Fate of the Washington Consensus* (New York: Oxford University Press, 2016).
5 Economic Commission for Latin America and the Caribbean (ECLAC), *First Forum of China and the Community of Latin American and Caribbean States* (Santiago: ECLAC, 2015), p. 23.
6 Enrique Dussel Peters, *China's Evolving Role in Latin America: Can It Be a Win–Win?* (Washington, DC: Atlantic Council, 2015).
7 Economic Commission for Latin America and the Caribbean (ECLAC), *Foreign Direct Investment in Latin America and the Caribbean 2012* (Santiago: ECLAC, 2013), p. 27.

8   Eduardo Daniel Oviedo, "Argentina Facing China: Modernization, Interests, and Economic Relations Model," *East Asia*, vol. 30, no.1 (2013), p. 27.

9   Su Zhenxing and Yong Zhang, "Guoji jinrongweiji beijingxia de Zhongla jingmao hezuo" [An analysis of economic cooperation and trade between China and Latin America in the context of the international financial crisis], *Ladingmeizhou he Jialebi fazhan baogao 2009–2010* [Development report of Latin America and the Caribbean 2009–2010] (China: Social Sciences Academic Press, 2010).

10 Cesa-Bianchi et al., "China's Emergence in the World Economy and Business Cycles in Latin America," p. 4.

11 This term first appeared in a 1973 article in *The Economist* and referred to the decline of the Dutch manufacturing sector due to the discovery and development of natural gas in the late 1950s. As high natural gas prices triggered a foreign exchange boom and, in turn, the currency appreciated while industrial exports and jobs languished.

12 Max Corden and Peter Neary, "Booming Sector and De-industrialization in a Small Open Economy," *Economic Journal*, vol. 92 (December 1982), pp. 825–848.

13 Sarah Gordon, "Fears Grow That Few Can Escape China's Tremors," *Financial Times*, January 20, 2016, p. 16.

14 Douglass North, *Institutions, Institutional Change, and Economic Performance* (Cambridge, UK: Cambridge University Press, 1990), p. 99. Also see James Mahoney, *The Legacies of Liberalism: Path Dependence and Political Regimes in Central America* (Baltimore, MD: Johns Hopkins University Press, 2001), pp. 3–28.

15 Data that reflect these trends can be found in Carol Wise, Leslie Armijo, and Saori Katada, "The Puzzle," in Carol Wise, Leslie Armijo, and Saori Katada, eds., *Unexpected Outcomes: How Emerging Markets Survived the Global Financial Crisis* (Washington, DC: Brookings Institution Press, 2015).

16 Ibid., pp. 15–20; Manuel Pastor and Carol Wise, "Good-bye Financial Crash, Hello Financial Eclecticism: Latin American Responses to the 2008–09 Global Financial Crisis," *Journal of International Money and Finance*, vol. 52 (April 2015), pp. 200–217.

17 Alejandro Izquierdo and Ernesto Talvi, *Policy Trade-offs for Unprecedented Times: Confronting the Global Crisis in Latin America and the Caribbean* (Washington, DC: Inter-American Development Bank, 2009), p. 5.

18 Gallagher and Porzecanski, *Dragon in the Room*, pp. 25–26.

19 Clifford Kraus, "Oil Glut Grows and Takes a Toll on the Economy," *New York Times*, January 16, 2016, p. A1.

20 This index averages a country's percentile rankings on ten topics—starting a business, dealing with construction permits, getting electricity, registering property, obtaining credit, protecting investors, paying taxes, trading across borders, enforcing contracts, and resolving insolvency—giving equal weight to each topic. See http://doingbusiness.org/rankings (accessed January 25, 2016).

21 Robert Devlin, Antoni Estevadeordal, and Andrés Rodríguez-Clare, eds., *The Emergence of China: Opportunities and Challenges for Latin America and the Caribbean* (Cambridge, MA: Harvard University Press, 2006). Also see Juan Ignacio Martínez Cortes and Oscar Neme Castillo, "La ventaja comparativa de China y México en el mercado estadounidense," *Comercio Exterior*, vol. 54, no. 6 (2004), pp. 516–528.

22 Ralph Watkins, "Meeting the China Challenge to Manufacturing in Mexico," in Enrique Dussel Peters, Adrian Hearn, and Harley Shaiken, eds., *China and the New Triangular Relationships in the Americas* (Miami, FL: Center for Latin American Studies, University of Miami, 2013), p. 38.

23 Kevin P. Gallagher and Enrique Dussel Peters, "China's Economic Effects on the U.S.–Mexico Trade Relationship: Towards a New Triangular Relationship?" in Enrique Dussel Peters, Adrian Hearn, and Harley Shaiken, eds., *China and the New Triangular Relationships in the Americas*, pp. 18–19.

24 Gallagher and Dussel Peters, "China's Economic Effects on the U.S.–Mexico Trade Relationship," p. 15.

25 Carol Wise, "Unfulfilled Promise: Economic Convergence under NAFTA," in Isabel Studer and Carol Wise, eds., *Requiem or Revival? The Promise of North American Integration* (Washington, DC: Brookings Institution Press, 2007).

26 Also see Gallagher and Porzecanski, *Dragon in the Room*, p. 68.

27 Watkins, "Meeting the China Challenge to Manufacturing in Mexico," p. 43.

28 Wise, "Unfulfilled Promise."

29 See http://www.promexico.gob.mx/en/mx/tratados-comerciales (accessed January 28, 2016).

30 Robert Devlin, "China's Economic Rise," in Riordan Roett and Guadalupe Paz, eds., *China's Expansion into the Western Hemisphere: Implications for Latin America and the United States* (Washington, DC: Brookings Institution Press, 2008), pp. 137–139.

31 Klaus Schwab, ed., *The Global Competitiveness Report 2013–2014* (Cologny, Switzerland: World Economic Forum, 2013), pp. 512, 525, 530.

32 Ibid., pp. 503, 504, 534, 536, 539.

33 Bikramjit Sinha, "Increasing Industrialization of R&D in China," in Amiya Kumar Bagchi and Anthony P. D'Costa, eds., *Transformation and Development: The Political Economy of Transition in India and China* (New Delhi: Oxford University Press, 2012).

34 Author's interview with Armando Vega, Production Director, DJO Global, Tijuana, Baja California, Mexico, August 6, 2013; author's interview with Rafael Solorzano, Former Director, Secretariat of Economic Development, Tijuana, Baja California, Mexico, August 5, 2013.

35 Dussel Peters, *China's Evolving Role in Latin America*, pp. 18–20; also see Tracy Wilkinson, "Mexico Cancels Deal with Chinese-led Consortium to Build Bullet Train," *Los Angeles Times*, November 7, 2014, http://www.latimes.com/world/mexico-americas/la-fg-mexico-china-bullet-train-20141107-story.html (accessed May 25, 2015).

36 "Brazil Stripped of Investment Grade Rating as Crisis Deepens," *Reuters*, December 16, 2015, http://www.reuters.com/article/us-brazil-ratings-fitch-idUSKBN0U00A R20151217 (accessed January 17, 2016).

37 Daniel Cardoso, "China–Brazil: A Strategic Partnership in an Evolving World Order," *East Asia*, vol. 30, no. 1 (2013), pp. 31–51.

38 Rhys Jenkins and Alexandre de Freitas Barbosa, "Fear of Manufacturing? China and the Future of Industry in Brazil and Latin America," *China Quarterly*, no. 209 (March 2012), p. 77.

39 Leslie Armijo, Carol Wise, and Saori Katada, "Lessons from the Country Case Studies," in Carol Wise, Leslie Armijo, and Saori Katada, eds., *Unexpected Outcomes: How Emerging Markets Survived the Global Financial Crisis*, p. 220.

40 André Nassif, "Brazil and India in the Global Economic Crisis," in Sebastian Dullien, Detlef J. Kotte, Alejandro Márquez, and Jan Priewe, eds., *The Financial and Economic Crisis of 2008–2009 and Developing Countries* (New York: United Nations, 2010).

41 Jenkins and Barbosa, "Fear of Manufacturing?"

42 Seth Colby, "Brazil's Second-Best Financial Strategy," *Americas Quarterly*, vol. 7, no. 2 (Spring 2013), pp. 34–5.

43 Susana Moreira, "The Impact of Brazil's Expanding Hydrocarbon Reserves and Its Relations with the US and the PRC," in David Zweig and Yufan Hao, eds., *Sino-U.S. Energy Triangles: Resource Diplomacy under Hegemony* (New York: Routledge, 2015), pp. 185–187.

44 BloombergBusiness, "Petrobras Hits Drilling Snag at Brazil's Biggest-ever Oil Find," February 10, 2015, http://www.bloomberg.com/news/articles/2015-02-10/petrobras-said-to-interrupt-drilling-at-biggest-brazil-discovery (accessed October 2, 2015).

45 Rhys Jenkins, "China and Brazil: Economic Impacts of a Growing Relationship," *Journal of Current Chinese Affairs*, no. 1 (January 2012), pp. 26–9.
46 Ignacio Labaqui, "Living within Our Means: The Role of Financial Policy in the Néstor and Cristina Fernandez de Kirchner Administrations," Paper presented at the Latin American Studies Association Annual Meeting, San Francisco, May 2012.
47 "China–Argentina Trade, Investment Ties Booming," *Xinhua News Agency* (Beijing), May 8, 2013.
48 Ruben Laufer, "Argentina–China: New Courses for an Old Dependency," *Latin American Policy*, vol. 4, no. 1 (2013), pp. 123–43.
49 "China/Argentina: China, Argentina Sign 10-bln USD Rail Deal," *Asia News Monitor* (Bangkok), July 14, 2010.
50 Oviedo, "Argentina Facing China," p. 26.
51 "Latin America/China: Global Crisis Boosted Trade Ties," *Oxford Analytica Daily Brief Service*, September 15, 2010.
52 Laura Gómez-Mera, *Power and Regionalism in Latin America: The Politics of Mercosur* (Notre Dame, IN: University of Notre Dame Press, 2013), p. 17.
53 Albert Fishlow, "Crying for Argentina," *Foreign Policy*, March 11, 2013.
54 Benedict Mander, "Argentina Rekindles Its Relationship with Wall Street," *Financial Times*, May 12, 2016, http://www.ft.com/intl/cms/s/2/6aeb9ae2-17aa-11e6-b8d5-4c1fcdbe169f.html#axzz493Czp2OZ (accessed May 18, 2016).
55 ECLAC, *First Forum of China and the Community of Latin American and Caribbean States*, p. 28.
56 These insights are based on author's confidential interviews conducted in Santiago, Chile during June 2011 with a range of protagonists in the public and private sectors. Former Chilean trade negotiator Osvaldo Rosales offered particularly helpful insights.
57 Jian Yang, "China's Competitive FTA Strategy: Realism on a Liberal Slide," in Mireya Solís, Barbara Stallings, and Saori Katada, eds., *Competitive Regionalism: FTA Diffusion in the Pacific Rim* (Basingstoke, UK: Palgrave Macmillan, 2009), p. 230.
58 Stephen Hoadley and Jian Yang, "China's Cross-Regional FTA Initiatives," *Pacific Affairs*, vol. 80, no. 1 (Summer 2007), p. 333.
59 Author's interview with Andreas Pierotic, Prochile (Export Promotion Bureau), Chilean Embassy in Beijing, April 1, 2015.
60 Carol Wise, "Tratados de libre comercio al estilo chino: los TLC Chile–China y Perú–China," *Apuntes: Revista de Ciencias Sociales*, no. 71 (2013), pp. 161–188.
61 Jonathan R. Barton, "The Chilean Case," in Rhys Jenkins and Enrique Dussel Peters, eds., *China and Latin America: Economic Relations in the Twenty-First Century* (Bonn: German Development Institute, 2009), p. 244.
62 Author's interview with Andreas Pierotic, Prochile (Export Promotion Bureau), Chilean Embassy in Beijing, April 1, 2015.
63 Barton, "Chilean Case."
64 Wise, "Tratados de libre comercio al estilo chino," pp. 170–171.
65 This agreement covers business services (e.g., engineering, architecture, financial auditing, and advertising), computers and related services (e.g., software implementation, data processing, and hardware installation), real estate, research and development, telecommunications, and manufacturing services. For a summary go to http://fta.mofcom.gov.cn/topic/enchile.shtml.
66 Carol Wise, "Playing Both Sides of the Pacific: Latin America's Free Trade Agreements with China," *Pacific Affairs*, vol. 89, no. 1 (2016), pp. 98–99.
67 See note 10.
68 See, for example, Jaime Ortiz, "Déjà Vu: Latin America and Its New Trade Dependency…This Time with China," *Latin American Research Review*, vol. 47, no. 3 (2012), pp. 175–90; Juan Carlos Gachúz, "Chile's Economic and Political Relationship with China," *Journal of Current Chinese Affairs*, vol. 41, no. 1 (January 2012), pp. 150–51; and Rubén Gonzalez-Vicente, "The Political Economy of Sino-Peruvian Relations: A New Dependency?" *Journal of Current Chinese Affairs*, vol. 41, no. 1 (2012), pp. 98–131.

69 CEPALSTAT, "Exports of Manufactured Products According to Their Share in the Total: Latin America and Caribbean," 2014, http://interwp.cepal.org/sisgen/ConsultaIntegrada.asp?IdAplicacion=6&idTema=119&idIndicador=1911&idioma=i (accessed October 16, 2015).

70 See Sunil Mani, "Have China and India Become More Innovative since the Onset of Reforms in the Two Countries?" in Amiya Kumar Bagchi and Anthony P. D'Costa, eds., *Transformation and Development: The Political Economy of Transition in India and China* (New Delhi: Oxford University Press, 2012); and Gallagher and Porzecanski, *Dragon in the Room*, chap. 3.

71 Ortiz, "Déjà Vu," p. 188.

72 Raúl Prebisch, *The Economic Development of Latin America and Its Principal Problems* (New York: United Nations, Department of Social Affairs, 1950).

73 Devlin, "China's Economic Rise," pp. 137–9.

74 Alan Blinder, *After the Music Stopped* (New York: Penguin, 2013).

75 From 2009 to 2014 some US$2.2 trillion dollars flowed into the top 15 emerging markets. See James Kynge, "Emerging Market Capital Outflows Hit US$600 Billion as Strong Dollar Takes Its Toll," *Financial Times*, May 8, 2015, p. 13.

76 Mauricio Cardenas, "Curbing Success in Latin America," April 14, 2011, http://www.brookings.edu/opinions/2011/0414_curbing_success_cardenas_yeyati.aspx (accessed July 5, 2011).

77 Pastor and Wise, "Good-bye Financial Crash, Hello Financial Eclecticism."

78 Guillermo Perry and Alejandro Forero, "Latin America: The Day After. Is This Time Different?" Documentos CEDE 46, Centro de Estudios sobre Desarrollo Económico, University of the Andes, Bogotá, December 2014, pp. 18–22.

79 Carol Wise and Maria Antonieta del Tedesco Lins, "Macro-prudence versus Macro-profligacy: Brazil and Argentina in the Face of the Global Financial Crisis," in Carol Wise, Leslie Armijo, and Saori Katada, eds., *Unexpected Outcomes: How Emerging Markets Survived the Global Financial Crisis.*

80 Jenkins, "China and Brazil," pp. 26–9.

81 Perry and Forero, "Latin America: The Day After," p. 22. Total factor productivity is the portion of output that is not explained by the inputs to production but rather by the efficiency gains realized from these inputs in the overall production process.

82 See, for example, Sebastian Edwards, *Crisis and Reform in Latin America: From Despair to Hope* (Washington, DC: World Bank, 1995); and Inter-American Development Bank (IDB), *The Age of Productivity: Transforming Economies from the Bottom Up* (Washington, DC: IDB, 2010).

83 North, *Institutions, Institutional Change, and Economic Performance*, pp. 98–9.

84 Mahoney, *Legacies of Liberalism.*

85 Terry Lynn Karl, *The Paradox of Plenty: Oil Booms and Petro-States* (Berkeley, CA: University of California Press, 1997), p. 13.

86 Edwards, *Crisis and Reform in Latin America*; Armijo et al., "Lessons from the Country Case Studies."

87 Oviedo, "Argentina Facing China," p. 17.

88 Ibid.

89 Alexandre de Freitas Barbosa, "Rising China and Its Impacts on Latin America: Strategic Partnership or a New International Trap?" Paper presented at the VIII Reunión de la Red de Estudios de América Latina y el Caribe sobre Asia-Pacífico, Bogotá, August 22–28, 2008, p. 22.

90 North, *Institutions, Institutional Change, and Economic Performance*, p. 99.

91 CEPALSTAT, "Exports of Manufactured Products According to Their Share in the Total."

8

THE AGROPOLIS

South America, China, and the Soybean Connection

Mariano Turzi

Introduction

The strategic relevance of agricultural products has been undervalued relative to other natural resources such as gold, silver, and oil. Since the mid-20th century, oil has been regarded as the most critical commodity. Nevertheless, agricultural commodities are a much more vital class of goods for Latin American economies. World demand for agricultural commodities is driven by four "Fs": food, feed, fuel, and finance. Demand for food is closely related to demographics: the global population is growing by around 80 million people per year. The first billion was achieved in 1804. From 1804 to 2012, the world's population grew by 600 percent, to 7 billion. In 2009, renowned agronomist Norman Borlaug estimated that over the next 50 years the world would have to produce more food than it has in the past 10,000 years.

The second "F," feed, is mostly attributable to the rise of emerging economies, with a particular focus on Asia. When living standards rise, so does the demand for meat and dairy products. As people from Brazil, China, and India move out of poverty and into the burgeoning global middle class, they diversify their diets to include more vegetable oils, meat, and dairy products. Not only are there more people in these countries, but also more people eating pork, chicken, and beef. Against this backdrop, soybeans have become one of the most essential inputs in the global food system. The soybean contains 83 percent flour and 17 percent oil. When oil is extracted, the remaining residue is known as soybean cake, meal, or pellets. The latter has a vegetable protein concentrate of around 42 to 44 percent. Soybean cake has found its strongest application as fodder for the industrial raising of farm animals, also known as "factory farming."

Soybeans can also be processed for human consumption in a variety of ways: soy meal, soy flour, soy milk, soy sauce, soy oil, tofu, and the textured vegetable protein lecithin (found in a variety of vegetarian foods intended to substitute for meat). Soybean oil is the world's most widely used edible oil and has several industrial applications. Soybeans are thus a highly efficient crop: about 40 percent of the calories in soybeans are derived from protein, compared with 25 percent for most other crops. This means the return per dollar spent is relatively higher than is the case with other oilseeds. For lower-income families, soy has become an essential component for covering daily caloric requirements inexpensively. Because livestock can be fed more efficiently with soybean-based feed, the massive spread of the crop has made chicken, beef, and pork cheaper and more readily available worldwide.

In China, a shift towards modern livestock production has boosted soy demand. Because of the high "proteic return" of soybeans, the proportion of soybean meal used in Chinese feed mix has gradually risen in the last decade as farmers have increased the protein content of livestock feed. To this day, most Chinese pork meat is produced by small farmers, with modern operations accounting for only about 30 percent of the country's production. However, modern hog farms use even higher concentrations of soybean meal in their feed, so the government's policy transition towards larger operations is expected to maintain high demand levels for soybeans well into the future.

The third factor pushing up demand for grain production is fuel. The debate about peak oil and the subsequent expectations that oil prices will remain relatively high, plus the risk of supply shortages, has triggered a growing demand for energy from the biofuels industry. Supported by policy mandates, countries are seeking to diversify their energy sources by incorporating renewables into their development plans. The Food and Agriculture Organization of the United Nations (FAO) estimated in 2013 that prices for biofuels will continue to rise (by 16 to 32 percent in real terms when compared with the previous decade) over the next ten years. This too has heightened the demand for soybeans.

The financial component of demand is more indirect and controversial, but nevertheless equally important. Since 2000, there has been a 50-fold increase in dollars invested in commodity index funds. After the 2008–09 financial crisis global investors, seeking safe hedges for their portfolios, turned commodities into an asset class. Back in 2003, the commodities futures market totaled US$13 billion. In the first two months of 2008, US$55 billion flowed into commodity markets, and by July 2008 US$318 billion had been invested in agricultural commodities.[1] By 2012, commodity-based assets had risen to a record US$412 billion. The financialization of commodity markets is self-perpetuating: as new investment products, food derivatives, and indexed commodities create speculative opportunities in grains, edible oils, and livestock, price increases have inevitably followed. Although food inflation and price volatility have increased alongside commodity speculation, there is still no conclusive evidence on the impact of food sector financialization on prices.[2] The reverse can also happen: by November 2014, total commodity assets under management had declined to $276 billion. Withdrawals from commodity index-linked investments between January and November 2014 were 125 percent larger than in 2013.

This chapter analyzes the determinants of Chinese demand for agricultural products in Latin America. With a focus on soybeans, it then describes the economic and political conditions of South American supply, taking into account the region's historical experience with a trade model based on commodity exports. The chapter goes on to explore the emerging structure and pattern of China's rapidly expanding relationship with South America within the context of the contemporary international political economy. The chapter highlights the domestic-level impacts of this relationship, as a new vector of international integration and regional dis-integration, on governance structures within the agricultural sector of three countries: Argentina, Brazil, and Paraguay.

International demand has empowered the resource and agricultural sector in the three countries, albeit in different ways and magnitudes. For example, in Brazil local governance is much stronger, allowing for effective integration of state institutions with resource sector interests and could thus be labeled as a case of *coordination*. In Paraguay, power asymmetries and weak initial institutional conditions within the agricultural sector have constituted a case of *colonization*, marked by collusion between special interests, both domestic and foreign. Finally, Argentina is a case of centralized state institutions and a conflictive pattern of *confrontation* between state actors and those operating within the resource sector. Similar to the findings reported in other chapters within this volume, the political economic impact of China's entry into South America is largely conditioned by actors, interests, and institutions within the countries considered here. There is, in other words, a variety of impacts related to China's intense demand for South American food commodities in the 2000s.

Chinese Demand

The McKinsey Global Institute estimated in December 2013 that more than 1.8 billion people will join the ranks of the world's consuming class by 2025.[3] The impetus for this rise of the global consumer class is the economic growth of India and China, and both will continue to drive demand for food. This represents a historically unprecedented structural shift in the world economy. The industrialization of these countries is happening at about ten times the speed that the United Kingdom experienced during its Industrial Revolution during the 19th century, and at around 200 times the scale.

The agricultural dimension of this shift is made vivid by the sheer numbers: China is a leading producer, consumer, and importer of agricultural commodities. For example, China produces over 30 percent of the world's cotton and rice and more than 20 percent of its corn. China produces over 20 percent of the world's soybean meal and, according to its General Administration of Customs, China's soybean edible oil imports rose 9 percent year on year to 5.98 million tons in the first three quarters of 2013.[4] This indicates the country's widening gap in edible oil supply and its increasing dependence on the world market for soybean and oil consumption. Chinese per capita consumption averaged 18.5 kilograms of edible soy oil in 2012, compared with 11 kilograms in 2001. The China National Grain and Oils Information Center forecasts that this figure will rise to 23 kilograms between 2017 and 2022.[5] China imports 54 percent of all soybeans and 28 percent of soybean oil from other countries, even though it is a main global producer of both. Still, China alone was responsible for half of the worldwide increase in consumption of soybean oil and a third of the increase in demand for soybeans in the period 2007–09.[6] FAO expects the country to reach an oilseed production level of 83 million tons by 2022, a 41 percent increase, which will account for some 59 percent of global trade.[7]

In 1995, China produced 14 million tons of soybeans and it consumed roughly the same amount, essentially achieving self-sufficiency. In 2012, China was still producing about the same amount. However, its domestic consumption had risen by 400 percent, to 70 million tons. As a result, China imported 58 million tons of soybeans in 2012, mostly from the United States, Brazil, and Argentina. Since 1978, grain production in China has increased 93 percent, from 305 million tons in 1978 to 590 million tons in 2012. Over this period, oil crop production also rose, but consumption consistently outpaced production (see Figures 8.1 and 8.2), limiting China's attempts at self-sufficiency. According to the *OECD–FAO Agricultural Outlook 2013–2022*, the U.S. Department of Agriculture (USDA) projects soybean consumption in China to surpass 100 million tons in 2020.[8]

Food security has been a key policy priority in China. It is based on the historical memory of Mao's Great Leap Forward in 1958–61, which sought to rapidly industrialize and collectivize the Chinese economy along communist lines, thereby ensuring continued Communist Party rule and legitimacy. One unfortunate result was the Great Famine of 1959–61.[9] For China's leaders—many of whom lived through the famine—dependency on world markets for food staples was considered perilous and a potential trigger for widespread social unrest. Subsequent support for grain (corn, wheat, and rice) production through subsidies led to a rapid and massive increase in grain harvests while domestic soybean production remained comparatively stagnant.

Agricultural self-sufficiency remains a national goal for China. Both the 12th Five-Year Plan for National Economic and Social Development of the People's Republic of China (2011–15) and the National Modern Agriculture Development Plan (2011–15) have set the top priorities as: "ensuring general self-sufficiency in food production" and "safeguarding national grain security." In March 2015, the National Development and Reform Commission (NDRC), in charge of the 13th Five-Year Plan (2016–20), pointed out that it would maintain agriculture as a priority, accelerating agricultural modernization, and productivity, raising food safety standards, and expanding rural development to

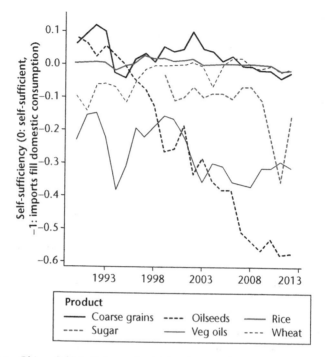

FIGURE 8.1 China: Self-Sufficiency for Major Commodities

Source: OECD and FAO, *OECD–FAO Agricultural Outlook 2013–2022*.

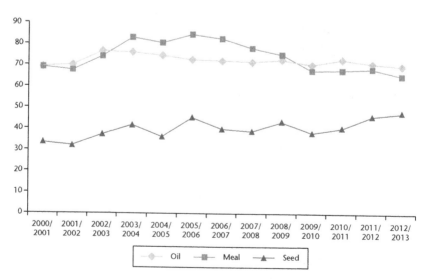

FIGURE 8.2 Percentage of Global Soybean Exports, MERCOSUR

Source: Author's calculation based on USDA data.

benefit farmers and raise rural living standards. In his March 2015 "Report on the Work of the Government"[10] Premier Li Keqiang stated that grain output had increased for the 11th consecutive year; moreover, the income of rural residents grew faster than that of urban residents for the fifth year running. This is a longstanding trend, dating back to 1995, when the Chinese government decided to forgo self-sufficiency in soybeans. The result was the so-called "two markets, two resources" approach to food security, wherein China worked to improve domestic production capacity in staple foods while seeking to control production, processing, and logistics for commodities like soy which cannot be supplied domestically in sufficient quantities (see Chapter 5 by Guo and Myers in this volume). According to the Earth Policy Institute,[11] had China chosen to produce all of the 70 million tons of soybeans it consumed in 2012, it would have had to shift one-third of its land away from grain and into soybeans, forcing it to import 160 million tons of grain—more than a third of its total consumption.

Agricultural trade increased considerably when China joined the World Trade Organization (WTO) in 2001, as the partial opening of its agricultural sector cleared the way for a surge in soybean imports. This effectively freed some 28 million hectares of arable land, thereby facilitating self-sufficiency in corn, wheat, and rice production. With one-fifth of the world's population, high-income growth, and burgeoning food consumption, China now has a major influence on world markets and prices. In the coming years, China will nonetheless face considerable challenges even in grain self-sufficiency (see Figure 8.1). This is due to its high level of economic growth and increased resource constraints on production, land degradation, water depletion, and greater production variability.

China's agricultural and trade policy choices have effectively linked national and international interests. Agricultural liberalization has catalyzed domestic interests. For example, during the 2013 annual session of the National People's Congress (NPC), representative Sun Bin, a farmer from the northeastern province of Heilongjiang, pleaded for government protection against cheaper, genetically modified (GM) soybeans from overseas. Heilongjiang accounts for about one-third of China's annual soybean output, producing up to 18.4 million metric tons annually. The province's soybean planted area shrank by 40 percent in just three years, from 4.7 million hectares in 2009 to 2.53 million hectares in 2012. National Committee member Zhao Yusen similarly argued against the activities of multinational grain companies such as Cargill, Monsanto, ADM, and Bunge during a recent Chinese People's Political Consultative Conference meeting. These firms have been accused of manipulating the price of soybeans in world markets and using a strategy of underpricing soybean supply to China in order to out-price domestic players and take over China's soybean industry.

The efforts to defend the domestic soybean industry are revealing for a couple of reasons. First, this signals the continuing trend towards plurality of participation (new actors and interests) in the policy-making process in China.

Vertical and horizontal (*tiao* and *kuai*) pluralization has resulted in a form of decentralization.[12] Second, this indicates that political, economic, and geographic cleavages within Chinese society are fast becoming fault lines for constituency formation. In a weakly institutionalized setting, policy implementation and resource mobilization—both material and symbolic—are largely determined by interests over institutions.

Following the global financial crisis of 2008–09, the Chinese government began adjusting its development model in order to "rebalance" the economy. At the macro level, the rebalancing meant moving away from a reliance on fixed asset investments and exports to stimulate economic growth, and instead promoting higher rates of domestic consumption as a share of GDP. Emphasizing domestic consumption over exports also implies micro-level changes. According to the 12th Five-Year Plan, these include reducing long-term reliance on cheap labor and low value-added manufacturing and shifting into higher value-added production based on technology-intensive industries, innovation, and research and development.

For agricultural products, this means securing long-term supply agreements for low-value inputs and fostering domestic processing by local companies. This policy trend points toward the use of dominant buyer positions to leverage price advantages, as Chinese firms enjoy unique cost advantages because of relationships with state-owned banks, tariffs meant to advance local processing, and supply contracts backed by government guarantees. As Guo and Myers note in Chapter 5, China is increasingly promoting the internationalization of its agricultural firms. The China National Cereals, Oils and Foodstuffs Corporation (COFCO) and Beidahuang are such examples, where government promotion consists of tax incentives, subsidies, credit, low-interest loans, and/or high-level diplomatic support.[13] Chinese firms are attempting to integrate the value chain upstream and downstream, increasingly investing in all phases of production in order to expand capacity, reduce costs, and diversify risk. Firms like Noble Group, Chongqing Grain Group, Sanhe Hopeful, and China National Heavy Machinery Corporation have all invested in factories, pressing plants, mills, and other agriculture-related infrastructure in Latin America. China's current goal is to vertically integrate supply and promote higher value-added production.

South American Supply

As China attempts to feed its growing population, as well as a rising middle class with increasingly diverse food tastes, the value of Chinese agricultural trade (imports and exports) has increased from US$27.9 billion in 2001 to US$155.7 billion in 2012, an average annual growth rate of 17 percent. The trade dependence of Chinese agriculture has also increased, from 15 percent in 2001 to 21 percent in 2011. The net trade deficit in agriculture and food in 2012 reached US$31 billion, a 67 percent increase over 2011.

China's soybean imports are almost exclusively sourced from the Western Hemisphere. China's customs authorities reported in November 2013 that the country's soybean imports increased by 3 percent from January to October 2013 over the same period in 2012. In the world market for soybeans, the Southern Cone Common Market (MERCOSUR) countries—which include Argentina, Brazil, Uruguay, Paraguay, and Venezuela—account for almost 40 percent of global soybean trade and well over 60 percent in soybean meal and soybean oil. Together, these countries have the potential to form an agriculture-based platform from which to increase competitiveness, bolster regional integration, and play a greater role in the global economy. Needless to say, such an effort could also help to improve domestic economic stability in these countries.

For South American agricultural producers, this massive Chinese demand-side shift for soy-based products has transformed the structure of their domestic agricultural sectors and shifted the distribution of factors of production. Politically, China's booming demand has empowered new political factions and greatly affected national patterns of policy-making in these countries. Despite the hopeful prospects arising from CELAC (the Community of Latin American and Caribbean States) and the first China–CELAC Summit held in Beijing in January 2015, the region as a whole is not integrated into one encompassing regional trade agreement. Rather, countries share memberships through a complex web of multiple agreements that are likely to restrict the scope of production and foster fragmentation across the region. In light of this, MERCOSUR—despite its institutional weaknesses and lackluster record to date—would be the most likely platform for the sub-regional integration of agriculture-based production in the Southern Cone countries analyzed in this chapter. South American leaders, however, have yet to fully embrace a plan for coordinated regional action.

MERCOSUR's share of global soybean exports is depicted in Figure 8.2. Globally, soybean export concentration has decreased slightly since the 1970s, but the United States and Brazil have been responsible for more than 80 percent of total world exports for the past four decades. At the same time, Argentina has consistently been the third largest global exporter of soy. For South American producers—especially Brazil and Argentina—China has rapidly emerged as the most important market for their soy exports, as domestic food demand and feed demand have rapidly increased there.

However, it is important to note that overall GDP growth rates in Argentina and Brazil are far less dependent on China than the high soy export figures might imply. In fact, exports to China are worth less than 2 percent of GDP for both Brazil and Argentina. This low figure confirms that trade plays a relatively small role in the Brazilian and Argentine economies. Both have low export-to-GDP ratios—around 9 percent and 18 percent, respectively. In these countries, fewer products are exported to China than to other regions and countries of the world.[14] The Southern Cone profile of exports to China is concentrated in raw materials, accounting for 59.6 percent of total exports, followed by natural-resource-based manufactures, processed mineral products, and agro-industrial goods. For Argentina and Brazil, soybeans constitute just 7.5 percent and 5.6 percent of each country's total exports, respectively. Yet the figures are much higher for soybean exports to China when calculated as a percentage of total exports to China, which amount to 71 percent and 23.2 percent, respectively. Soybean exports to China as a percentage of total commodity exports to China are higher still—82.6 percent for Argentina and 64.6 percent for Brazil. These numbers confirm that the agricultural sectors in both countries are indeed dependent on China as an export market (see Figure 8.3).

Historically, resource-driven countries have not been able to sustain strong GDP growth rates for longer than a decade. Even those that have appeared to put their economics on a healthier longer-term growth trajectory have rarely managed to transform that growth into broader economic prosperity. Is the soybean boom just the newest version of the traditional Latin American model of integrating with the international economy as a commodity exporter? Growth based on "star" products has in the past led countries in the region into commodity bubbles that went bust when international conditions shifted. Nobody in Manaus would have anticipated that Brazil's quasi-monopoly over the world rubber market would be destroyed by Malaysian rubber production. But rubber exports from Ceylon and Malaysia grew from 4 tons in 1900 to over 70,000 tons by 1914. By 1919, that figure reached 400,000 tons, and Brazilian rubber exports plummeted to just one-eighth of global supply.

Latin America's recent economic history offers humbling lessons and cautionary tales about placing too much hope in primary exports. Commodities producers are entirely susceptible to price and demand shocks, which inevitably occur. Dependence on commodity exports detracts from product diversification and fosters an unbalanced pattern of development. This so-called "resource

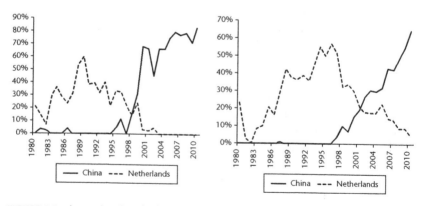

FIGURE 8.3 Argentina (on the left) and Brazil (on the right): Exports of Soybean to Main Partners

Source: BBVA Research, *Evaluating Latin America's Commodity Dependence on China*, Economic Analysis, Working Paper Number 13/05 (Hong Kong: BBVA Research, January 2013).

curse," moreover, inevitably spills over to the political arena, creating a cycle of political polarization, nationalist rhetoric, populist policies, and institutional instability. This has been the effect, for example, on oil producers like Ecuador and Venezuela, as the drop in oil prices in late 2014 wreaked havoc on the political economy of both countries.

Over the past decade, Argentina has become disproportionately dependent on Chinese demand for its soybeans. This is because China accounts for a very high share of the country's total soy exports (82.6 percent in 2012) and because Argentina's soybean exports only account for 8 percent of world oilseed supply. Argentina actually holds a much stronger position in soy meal and soy oils. Even so, the country's vulnerability to Chinese demand for its soybeans became especially evident in 2009, when China cut off all imports of Argentine soy in response to a bilateral trade dispute. Its dominant importer position means that China enjoys a great deal of leverage over Argentina at this point in time. Brazil's soybean producers also remain highly dependent on China, although less so than in Argentina. If South American soybean chains remain integrated at just the national level—as is currently the trend—countries in the region will continue to compete against each other and lose bargaining power vis-à-vis China.

The concentration of exports in a small number of primary products means that the South American countries are likely missing opportunities for deeper engagement in the Chinese market. Leveraging the current economic momentum through deeper regional integration of soy production could enable South America to avoid the risk of "re-primarization" or falling back into a pattern of low value-added production. Excessive primarization is not only detrimental to South American development, it is also risky for China. Negative balances in manufacturing trade have prompted South American governments to enact restrictions on the importation of Chinese industrial goods and to employ protectionist measures against foreign manufactured imports, even if this means breaching their WTO obligations.[15] As of December 2012, for example, Argentina and Brazil were some of the leading countries to file anti-dumping complaints against China at the WTO, with Brazil ranking fourth (with 89 initiations) and Argentina fifth (with 62 initiations) in the WTO complaint rankings. In 2013, Brazil initiated a total of 38 anti-dumping investigations, 10 of which were directed at China.[16] In 2014, it initiated 66 anti-dumping investigations, with China being the target in 16 of these, accounting for the highest proportion of cases. Political mobilization in response to manufacturing trade deficits with China has led to "China scapegoating" in some countries in the region. The reality, however, is that the positive effects of commodity exports on the terms of trade for these countries have contributed to a windfall in tax revenues, rendering the revenues earned from trade with China increasingly important.

The current pattern of China–South America trade has been further exacerbated by the low levels of manufacturing productivity and competitiveness in both Argentina and Brazil, not to mention the ability of powerful political coalitions in both countries to exert pressure for protectionist measures. In both countries, labor-urban-industrial coalitions have effectively mobilized, especially in the context of national elections, and secured numerous measures to help cushion the domestic manufacturing sector from Chinese competition. This is especially the case for labor-intensive "light" industries such as textiles, clothing, toys, plastic manufactures, and the like. Interestingly, capital goods and intermediate inputs for industrial production account for a sizeable share of Chinese exports to South America. In the case of Argentina, 50 percent of imports from China are capital goods. Despite the potential for China's higher-quality capital inputs to increase productivity in these countries, politicians have succumbed to protectionist demands and income transfers in order to cement their "winning coalition" in the labor-urban-industrial sector.[17]

A New Vector of Integration?

There are some incipient signs of an increasingly integrated agro-industrial network emerging in the Southern Cone, based on seeding, processing, and trading companies. I have labeled it "the Soybean Republic,"[18] which includes Argentina, Brazil, Paraguay, and Uruguay. All four of these countries are increasingly woven into a global system of food production and consumption, with emerging Asia and China as the main hub. This reflects a structural feature of contemporary global capitalism: the increasing fragmentation of production across countries and its (re)organization along supply and value chains.[19] The analysis of global commodity chains, i.e., the interlinking of dispersed activities in a single industry across geographic boundaries, elucidates how patterns of trade and production are being rapidly transformed.

When applied to the agricultural sector, global value chains (GVCs) exhibit succinct characteristics. GVC analysis begins with the acceptance of international and (bi-)regional business networks as the main departure point. Owing to liberalized international trade, foreign investment, and advanced technologies, Latin America's agricultural exports have acquired transnational reach. However, these global agricultural chains are highly asymmetrical, since they integrate small growers in developing countries into global sourcing networks with large multinational players in the market. The latter have the advantage of flexibility, lower prices, and diversified products, all of which enables them to simultaneously integrate production at different locations and within a number of overlapping systems. Within international agricultural markets, actors—state and/or corporate—on the demand side capitalize on the fragmentation of production on a global scale because they are constantly evaluating sourcing strategies. The offshoring decisions of suppliers can rapidly change. This allows for financial profits based on short-term volatility. Moreover, it can be devastating to suppliers, deleterious to domestic political economy structures, and destabilizing to national politics.

Latin American industrial policies have yet to take into account the new international production realities of GVCs when dealing with the PRC. A coordinated, bi-regional GVC-oriented industrial policy between Latin America and China would focus on the intersection of global, national, and local actors; at the same time, it should take into account the interests, power, and reach of firms on both producer and consumer sides. A deeper understanding of GVCs and a wider adoption of commercial policies to support these could significantly improve Latin America's bargaining position within the global agri-food chain. This is especially so with respect to both China and the traditional big agricultural traders like Cargill, Monsanto, ADM, and Bunge.

Politically, this means that the governance of agri-business concerns is much more global and corporate, as opposed to the national and public production modes now operative in the countries considered here. In short, market power has shifted in favor of retailers and against producers. In advanced and emerging economies, retailers and supermarket chains have grown ever larger. Chemical multinational companies (MNCs) have integrated vertically, generating a commanding production structure through the use of scientific and technological (proprietary) knowledge to advance the sale of their agrochemical products. They have united with traders and processors to leverage scale advantages to establish dominant buying positions on well-known consumer brands. This power shift has also occurred between producing and consuming nations. China is perfectly positioned to reap advantages on both ends, corporate and consumer. Closer coordination along the supply and production chain has led to consolidation among fewer, larger, and more diversified suppliers.

From the standpoint of the national political economy, participation in global value chains depends on whether a given country is a user of foreign inputs (upstream links) or a supplier of intermediate goods and services that are used in the production of other countries' exports (downstream links). According to the OECD's GVC Participation Index 2013, Argentina and Brazil are around 10 percent in upstream links and just over 30 percent on the downstream side. Historically, Latin American industrial policies have targeted particular industries or firms. This has been justified on grounds ranging across strategic importance (natural resources like oil, natural gas, and minerals), national security (military procurement, essential medicines, basic foodstuffs), exceptional opportunities for forward and backward linkages with domestic suppliers (such as the automotive industries in Mexico and Brazil), or the support of "infant industries," which in time—and with due protection—would ideally become internationally competitive national champions. These import-substitution (ISI) development strategies and policies sought to recreate entire supply chains within a national territory. In contrast, global value chain analysis—as a development paradigm and a guiding policy principle—accepts international production networks as a structural starting point and advocates domestic industrial policy as the most efficacious way to forge creative extra-territorial, multi-nodal patterns of production.

By opening to multi-level networks, GVC analysis stresses the importance of positioning production modes within global value chains. When applied to the South American agricultural sector, this paradigm promises to create a new vector for regional integration. However, this is no minor challenge, as the domestic political economy structures within the agricultural sectors of South American producers vary widely.

The different social and political cleavages surrounding soybean production in the South American countries have generated specific national political economy arrangements and policy responses. This has given rise to differing patterns of institutional governance of this resource, mainly according to the level of centralization and control attempted by the public sector in each country. Below I briefly review how these dynamics have crystallized around the recent soybean price boom in Brazil, Argentina, and Paraguay:

- *Brazil.* The Brazilian case is one in which local governance is allowing for effective integration of state institutions with resource or sector interests (*coordination*). Since resources are managed at the local level in Brazil, this situation has empowered governors and municipalities over the federal government, generating an alliance with multinational trading companies that serves their financial and political independence vis-à-vis the central urban power forces. With rural constituencies, politicians such as Mato Grosso state governor Blairo Maggi—also the largest individual soybean producer in the country—have an incentive to manage resources responsibly and with relative political, rather than ecological, sustainability. Dualization of the economy is evident, and a higher relative degree of institutional strength has helped to prevent conflicts from escalating to the levels observed in Paraguay.

- *Argentina.* Argentina is a case of centralized state institutions exhibiting a conflictive pattern of *confrontation* with actors in the resource sector. Argentina has a more atomized agrarian economic structure, which has acted as a buffer against the emergence of economic dualization. Thus power is also much more dispersed among actors in the winning coalition. A more flexible land tenure system is at the core of a broader base of producers. However, the Peronist-run urban labor-based coalition was pitted against the countryside as the centralist structure of state financing determined it was politically more profitable to extract rents from the agricultural sector. The Argentine export tax on soybeans acts as a covert incentive for exporting meals and oil.

- *Paraguay.* In Paraguay the agricultural sector has achieved de facto decentralization by state capture, taking advantage of power asymmetries and weak initial institutional conditions; there has been *colonization* by a collusion of special domestic and foreign interests. Paraguay exhibits a dire pattern of dual economic development, where indigenous and landless peasants are systematically marginalized. The soybean model of production is secured by institutions captured by private economic interests. In this case, there is a coalition of colonizing interests: multinational companies and Brazilian and brasiguayo landowners overwhelmingly supported by the Paraguayan landlords. The geographically flexible model of soybean trading and processing has also created hierarchical relations between the three countries.

These differing political economy strengths and weaknesses are being used by international companies to incorporate the three countries in a global division of agricultural labor, itself a link in a wider and deeper agri-food chain. Multinational companies have decided it is more cost effective to build processing capacity in Argentina and bring the beans from Paraguay. Because there are so few players that can afford such capital-intensive developments, Paraguay loses the rents that would accrue from exporting a higher value-added product instead of the raw bean. China itself has been racing to get to the top of this high-stakes global game of corporate-concentration, scale-driven competitive scenario. China's 2014 purchases of Nidera and Noble Agri by COFCO point in the direction of China becoming a multinational corporate player in Latin America's grain sector. With China becoming a platform for Asian export to developed countries, Nidera has a comprehensive storage and logistics network in the producing regions of Argentina, Brazil, and Uruguay, as well as in other South American countries. Thus, now COFCO establishes a commanding global presence in grain storage, logistics, and processing facilities.

Argentina, Brazil, and Uruguay all have laws that limit foreign ownership of agricultural land. However, these are national-level norms. There is no regional-level institutional entity under MERCOSUR that could generate regional norms, for example. This would not only strengthen and facilitate cooperation between the South American countries by enforcing agreements and reducing transaction costs, but it would facilitate the monitoring of compliance on the part of Chinese companies and other foreign actors. This is of critical importance, given the highly asymmetrical relations between China and South America. Sub-regional institutionalization under MERCOSUR could provide a sound framework for prudent, practical foreign policy-making. The weaker side would act in accordance with the power disparities, yet safeguard at least some of its autonomy through regional integration. Furthermore, South America could use this sector-specific drive toward regional integration to bargain its way into higher value-added agricultural or even (agro-)industrial chains. This would offer the extra benefit of creating investment and trade flows via integration into corporate supply chains.

So far, Latin America's integration into global supply chains has been overwhelmingly organized and determined by large multinational, western corporations. The aforementioned 2014 COFCO purchases point toward a new trend: increasingly, the integration of South America—mainly led by agricultural products—into global value and supply chains centered in Asia, managed by Asian MNCs, but with aims and strategies determined by domestic political economy structures. In this regard, it is important to clarify a common misconception in the literature that uses "value chain" and "supply chain" interchangeably. However, the difference is significant, especially in terms of the impact. Supply chains focus on the stages that transform a raw material into a finished product or service and its delivery to end users, a map of the transfer of a commodity from one economic agent to another. The notion of value chain focuses on the value-added at different stages of transfer. From an international political economy perspective, stakeholders involved in agricultural commodity value chains linking China to Latin America are not only adding value, but competing for markets, profits, and surplus.

The Path Ahead

Demographic and environmental factors are projected to make buyers increasingly more dependent on and South American sellers more competitive in the international agricultural market. Just as the rise of U.S. economic might was made possible by a steady, secure supply of oil from the Middle East, the rise of China necessitates the purchase of soybeans from South America. Achieving deeper, higher-quality economic integration with Asia's emerging economies is not an easy task. Asian countries have a tariff-escalation system: the higher the value added to primary goods, the higher the protection. So, diversifying the export basket into higher value-added goods in order to move beyond basic trade complementarity implies a certain level of disruption of the domestic political economy structure in China, since those protective measures respond to domestic political economy coalitions and conditions. For China to lower tariffs on higher value-added agro-industrial products (e.g., soy oil) would be a challenge to the Chinese model of development and governance. However, as this model is increasingly put to the test, it is not out of the question for China to loosen constraints in this area.

How the Southern Cone countries will adjust to a rapidly changing regional and global political economy remains to be seen. In May 2013, Chile, Colombia, Mexico, and Peru launched the Pacific Alliance, a new trade group or regional bloc in South America. The main goal is to increase trade with fast-growing Asian nations. This has opened up new geopolitical and geo-economic fault lines in the region. For example, Legler argues that current Latin American regionalism—as manifested in and promoted by ALBA, CELAC, and UNASUR—is giving rise to an authentic "regional political economy," one that is redefining state–society and state–market relations away from neo-liberalism and toward a renewed statism and developmentalism.[20] It is unclear how much of this regional drive has been supported by the recent commodity bonanza, and reinforced by ideological affinities between "new left" governments in the region.

Trade deals could provide opportunities for increased participation in global value chains if these agreements foster the formation of international supply chains. Although it makes sense that highly integrated countries would be more likely to share international production networks, not all integration schemes create the conditions to support production networks among countries. With MERCOSUR becoming more protectionist, politicized, and stagnant in the 2000s, its member nations are attempting to play a stronger leadership role in the absence of this so-called integration framework. How can Latin American trade policies and agreements make better use of global value agricultural chains with China? The answer is to maximize the concrete gains and to minimize the risks as best possible. In other words, if competitive weaknesses are not addressed and improved in all economic sectors within these countries, this could further cement the asymmetries between China and Latin America. Agricultural regional integration could act as a product-based vector for the aggregation of interests throughout the region, helping to reduce fragmentation while at the same time softening the asymmetric position vis-à-vis Asian buyers. For its part, China's grain policy is focused on two variables, supply security and price stability, neither of which collides in principle with a more productive and coordinated regional strategy in South America.

Conclusions and Policy Implications

During the past decade, Latin America has been one of China's most dynamic trading partners. China's trade has grown faster with Latin America than with any other region, growing twice as fast as China's total global trade from 2005 to 2010. Commodities—agricultural and otherwise—constitute the vast majority of this trade. Producers in South America (Brazil, Argentina, and Paraguay) and buyers in Asia (China in particular) are locked into a mutually interdependent relationship poised to grow in the future as a result of demographic and economic factors in emerging Asia. China has crafted an international agricultural policy that seeks security of supply and avoids price volatility, and which is largely focused on South American producers.

Booming trade with China has influenced South American soy producers in numerous ways. It has created new political, social, economic, and environmental challenges, and also redistributed national power across regions and sectors. In line with findings reported in other chapters within this volume, this new relationship is being shaped by actors, interests, and institutions within the Latin American countries. This is verified by political economic realities now emerging within the agricultural soybean-producing countries studied in this chapter. Brazil with its stronger federalism and local governance is proving capable of *coordinating* Brazilian state institutions with resource sector interests. Paraguay sits at the opposite end of the continuum, as power asymmetries vis-à-vis its neighbors and weak initial institutional conditions surrounding the agricultural sector have induced collusion between special interests and a pattern of de facto *colonized* governance. Finally, Argentina's agricultural sector has been relatively successful in climbing the international value chain through the export of soybean oil and meal, but politically this sector has been locked into *confrontation* between centralized state institutions and domestic producers. The novel contribution of this chapter has been the specification of the agricultural sector in the Southern Cone as a new vector of international integration (between producers) and a potential source of regional dis-integration (with China being the pulling force).

In a world of increased production fragmentation and economic reorganization around global chains, export competitiveness depends on the sourcing of efficient inputs and on access to final producers and consumers abroad. China has successfully expanded into agricultural value chains in Latin America and will continue to do so for profit and for national security motives. Agricultural producers in these Southern Cone countries have realized that participation in global value chains can provide opportunities to industrialize at a faster pace than in the past, and to increase trade opportunities and the prospects for trade diversification. But there is much too little effort on the side of Latin American producers to improve competitiveness and diversify the production structure, or to access technological and/or managerial knowledge from their Chinese counterparts. This passivity will have direct and dire consequences on South American development results, for example in the realm of economic equality, political transparency, social development, and environmental sustainability. Those international agricultural political economy links now being created with China are not serving to redistribute the added value in favor of resource-abundant countries. On the contrary, the so-called complementarity model is replacing western-MNC dominance by eastern-SOE preponderance. But complementarity leaves the value capture and distribution unchanged, relegating South American producers to the lower, less profitable links in the chain. This goes to the heart of the resource curse, whereby natural-resource-rich economies get locked into excessive commodity dependence, exposure to international price volatility, lack of diversification, and—ultimately—an unbalanced pattern of development.

There will be little room for "win–win" strategies in such a "lose–lose" scenario. Creating governance structures that align national policies of governments and corporate interests of firms will be critical for both China and South America. Evident over the past decade is the emergence of a consolidated soybean complex, with the potential to develop into a single, regional commodity chain that can override production practices that prevailed up until the turn of the millennium. This integrated production entity has yet to be institutionalized, and economic modernization has outpaced political institutionalization.[21] From an international political economy standpoint, the effective management of this phenomenon will eventually require new institutional frameworks to guarantee long-term credible commitments. Thus, there are too few signs of a regional-level attempt to coordinate policies to address the challenges discussed in this chapter. South American producers need to rethink industrial policy in the 21st century and the vital role it could play in the economic development of the agricultural sector as it is now evolving.

Notes

1 Frederick Kaufman, "How Goldman Sachs Created the Food Crisis," *Foreign Policy*, April 2011.
2 Among the studies which find that financialization does not actually cause commodity prices to rise are: George M. Korniotis, "Does Speculation Affect Spot Price Levels? The Case of Metals with and without Futures Markets," Working Paper no. 2009-29, Board of Governors of the Federal Reserve System, May 2009; L. Kilian and B. Hicks, "Did Unexpectedly Strong Economic Growth Cause the Oil Price Shock of 2003–2008?" *Journal of Forecasting*, vol. 32, no. 5 (2012), pp. 385–394; and S. Irwin and D. Sanders, "The Impact of Index and Swap Funds on Commodity Futures Markets," OECD Food, Agriculture and Fisheries Papers, 2010, doi:10.1787/5kmd40wl1t5f-en. Studies suggesting there is empirical evidence of such a link include: T. Kawamoto, T. Kimura, K. Morishita, and M. Higashi, "What Has Caused the Surge in Global Commodity Prices and Strengthened Cross-Market Linkage?" Bank of Japan Working Paper Series no. 11-E3, 2011; B. Buyuksahin and M.A. Robe, "Speculators, Commodities and Cross-Market Linkages," *SSRN Electronic Journal*, n.d., doi:10.2139/ssrn.1707103; K. Tang and W. Xiong, "Index Investment and Financialization of Commodities," *SSRN Electronic Journal*, n.d., doi:10.2139/ssrn.1571987; and C.L. Gilbert and S. Pfuderer, "The Financialization of Food Commodity Markets," in R. Jha, R. Gaiha, and A.B. Deolalikar, eds., *Handbook on Food: Demand, Supply, Sustainability and Security* (Cheltenham, UK: Edward Elgar, 2014), pp. 122–48.
3 McKinsey Global Institute, "Global Flowers in a Digital Age: How Trade, Finance, People, and Data Connect the World Economy," April 2014.
4 Zhong Nan, "Soybean Imports from US Soar," *China Daily*, December 11, 2013, http://usa.chinadaily.com.cn/2013-12/11/content_17168646.htm (accessed July 1, 2016).
5 Zhao Ruixue, "The Peony's Blossoming Business," *China Daily*, January 1, 2014, http://usa.chinadaily.com.cn/2014-01/01/content_17209268.htm.
6 Osvaldo Rosales and Mikio Kuwayama, "China and Latin America and the Caribbean: Building a Strategic Economic and Trade Relationship," ECLAC, 2011, http://www10.iadb.org/intal/intalcdi/PE/2012/11001en.pdf (accessed July 1, 2016).
7 Niu Shuping and Fayen Wong, "Rising Food Demand to Put Pressure on Global Prices—FAO/OECD," *Reuters*, June 5, 2015, http://www.reuters.com/article/2013/06/06/food-fao-idUSL3N0EI09Y20130606 (accessed July 1, 2016).
8 OECD and FAO, *OECD–FAO Agricultural Outlook 2013–2022* (Paris and Rome: OECD and FAO, 2013).
9 See Frank Dikotter, *Mao's Great Famine: The History of China's Most Devastating Catastrophe, 1958–1962* (New York: Walker Publishing Company, 2010).
10 Delivered at the Third Session of the 12th National People's Congress on March 5, 2015 and adopted on March 15, 2015: "Report on the Work of the Government," *Xinhua*, March 16, 2015, http://news.xinhuanet.com/english/china/2015-03/16/c_134071473.htm (accessed July 1, 2016).
11 Lester R. Brown, "China's Rising Soybean Consumption Reshaping Western Agriculture," *Earth Policy Institute Data Highlights*, January 8, 2013.
12 David M. Lampton, "Chinese Politics: The Bargaining Treadmill," *Issues and Studies*, vol. 23, no. 3 (March 1987), pp. 11–41.

13 Margaret Myers, "China and Latin America Agricultural Workshop: Background Reading," Inter-American Dialogue, 2013, http://www.thedialogue.org/uploads/CLWGAgricultureWorkshop-BackgroundReading.pdf (accessed July 1, 2016).

14 World Customs Organization (5,052 tariff lines).

15 This has hurt China, but also other countries. For example, on January 26, 2015 the WTO Appellate Body issued a report on the case "Argentina: Measures Affecting the Importation of Goods" (DS438, DS444, DS445), WTO, May 4, 2015, https://www.wto.org/english/tratop_e/dispu_e/cases_e/ds438_e.htm (accessed July 1, 2016). Paradoxically, China was not involved, as complainants in this case were the European Union, Japan, and the United States.

16 "Argentina: Measures Affecting the Importation of Goods."

17 Bruce Bueno de Mesquita, *The Logic of Political Survival* (Cambridge, MA: MIT Press, 2003), p. 51.

18 Mariano Turzi, "The Soybean Republic," *Yale Journal of International Affairs*, Spring–Summer 2011, http://www.ucema.edu.ar/conferencias/download/2011/10.14CP.pdf (accessed July 1, 2016).

19 A supply chain is normally defined as a group of economic units which provide a range of tangible and intangible value-adding activities that bring a good or service along from its conception, through the different production phases, and on to consumers. The aim is to minimize the costs (labor, inputs, transport, and communication) of the total system while also maximizing its efficiency. The term "supply chain" refers to the network of a particular firm, while the term "value chain" is more commonly used in a broader context to refer to an entire industry.

20 Thomas Legler, "The Rise and Decline of the Summit of the Americas," *Journal of Iberian and Latin American Research*, vol. 19, no. 2 (2013), pp. 179–193. The Alianza Bolivariana para los Pueblos de Nuestra América (ALBA) is defined as an integration platform intended to achieve integral development for Latin America and the Caribbean through a process of integration inspired by the likes of Simon Bolivar and Jose Marti. Established in 2004, UNASUR, or the Union of South American Nations, is an intergovernmental body modeled after the European Union. CELAC is the Community of Latin American and Caribbean States, which was founded in 2010.

21 Samuel Huntington, *Political Order in Changing Societies* (New Haven, CT: Yale University Press, 1968).

9

CENTRAL AMERICA, CHINA, AND THE US

What Prospects for Development?

Rolando Avendaño and Jeff Dayton-Johnson[1]

What does the vertiginous economic emergence of China mean for development prospects in the countries of Central America (El Salvador, Costa Rica, Guatemala, Honduras, Nicaragua, and Panama)? Has rapid growth in China been a bane or boon for these Central American countries? Were they harder hit by the 2008–09 economic downturn in the United States than their neighbors in South America, whose China trade has been much more vigorous? What are the longer-term implications of Central America's economic relationship with China versus the United States? This chapter explores these questions by analyzing Central America's trade relations with China, contrasting those relations with Central America's trade with the United States.[2]

We begin with a quantitative assessment of Central America's trade patterns with China. Though the countries of the isthmus are marked by considerable economic heterogeneity, many (Guatemala, Honduras, Panama) continue to be highly dependent on primary product exports, particularly coffee, bananas, and sugar, with some mineral production. Unlike the commodity exporters of South America, Central American countries export goods for which there is little demand in the Chinese market. Thus these countries remain tightly linked to the US economy. The beneficial impact of the so-called "China effect" on hard commodities has not reached Central America, where exports are focused on soft commodities. A second group of Central American countries—El Salvador, Nicaragua, and to a certain extent Guatemala—have seen important increases in manufactured exports, particularly *maquila* (assembly plant) exports to the US. We analyze evidence that suggests these exports face increased competition from Chinese exports of similar goods, particularly textiles. Costa Rica's recent rise in the export of microprocessors to China and the US alike represents an exceptional case of dynamism in the region's export history.

We situate Central America's China trade in the broader context of foreign direct investment (FDI) flows and official development assistance (ODA) flows from China to the countries of the region. We then consider whether Central America's feeble trade with China has been depressed by the sub-region's role in the diplomatic rivalry between mainland China and Taiwan: with the exception of Costa Rica, which broke from the pack in 2007, all Central American countries officially recognize and maintain diplomatic relations with only Taiwan. From there follows a comparative analysis of the sophistication and capability of Central American export sectors, using new insights from the "product space" literature. This confirms the picture of trade patterns drawn earlier in the chapter: namely, highly concentrated export baskets with little diversification of export markets.

Central America in the Global Economy

When it comes to their place in the world trading system, Central American countries exhibit a surprising heterogeneity, which is a microcosm of the rich diversity of Latin America as a whole (see Figure 9.1). El Salvador, Guatemala, Honduras, and Nicaragua are poorer than the average Latin American country; moreover, Guatemala, Honduras, Nicaragua, and Panama are more dependent upon commodity exports than the Latin American average. Lower per-capita income tends to be associated with lower levels of manufactures in a country's export basket, but there are exceptions: El Salvador, though poorer than the average, has a share of manufactured exports that is higher than Mexico's; Panama, while not a strong manufactured goods exporter, has higher per-capita

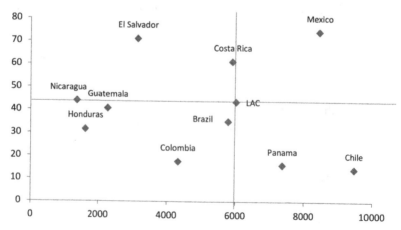

FIGURE 9.1 Share of Manufacturing Exports and GDP per Capita

Source: World Development Indicators, World Bank.

Note: Average values, 2009–11. Horizontal and vertical bars mark the average values for Latin America and the Caribbean. GDP per capita in constant 2005 USD.

income than the average Latin American country (note that these trade data consider only trade in goods, not services).

Economic growth rates in Central American countries from 2003 to 2008 were respectable—per-capita GDP expanded by 4 percent or more per annum over the five years. But these rates were relatively unspectacular compared with those of the seven largest economies of Latin America, which experienced growth rates of GDP per capita above 6 percent. The post-crisis years have proven more difficult for several economies in Central America. Guatemala, Honduras, and Nicaragua were the most adversely affected, with per-capita GDP growth rates dipping below 2 percent. Among the LAC-7 countries,[3] only Venezuela has experienced similarly depressed growth since 2009. As with the remainder of Latin America, and other developing economies, Central America's post-crisis growth rates have been lower than those observed during the pre-crisis years.

In contrast with the case in the average Latin American economy, the share of exports as a percentage of GDP in the Central American countries is higher; this is not surprising, given that most of the Central American economies are smaller than the average for the Latin American region. Since the beginning of the 2000s, total exports in Latin America have represented about 20 to 25 percent of total output. In the case of Costa Rica (47 percent), Honduras (60 percent), and Panama (79 percent), this share has been more important, illustrating one difference with other economies in the region. Small economies in Central America are more open but also more vulnerable to trade shocks. The export share of the Latin American economies—Central American countries among them—did not grow much in the first decade of the new century. But the composition and destination of exports have changed substantially for some countries in this sub-region.

Total Central American exports have grown little (as a share of GDP) over the last decade, but the composition of export baskets has changed somewhat (see Figure 9.2a). For all six countries, the four main exports by country remained the same between 2000 and 2011. Coffee exports, for example, maintained a similar share of exports for coffee-exporting countries (Guatemala, Honduras, El Salvador). More interestingly, the share of manufactured goods has increased in Costa Rica and Nicaragua, while *maquila* exports in El Salvador have fallen. This composition illustrates the heterogeneity of Central American countries: whereas Guatemala, Honduras, and Panama can certainly be considered commodity exporters, the export profile of Costa Rica, El Salvador, and Nicaragua is more diverse and includes both commodities and manufactured goods. However, product-level information regarding the leading exports confirms the importance of primary products even in the more manufacturing-oriented economies of the region (see Figure 9.2b).

It has become commonplace to advise countries that primarily export commodities to diversify their export baskets to reduce exposure to global price swings.[4] How dependent are countries in Central America on a single export

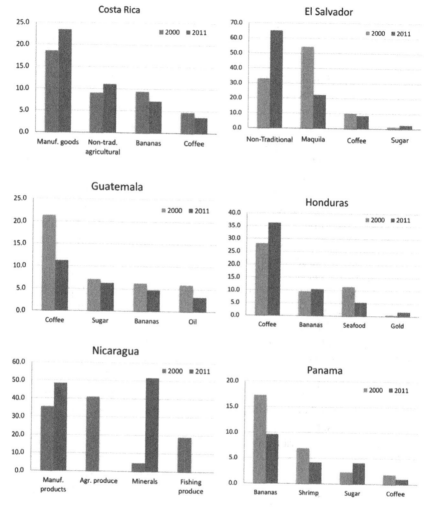

FIGURE 9.2A Main Exported Products as Share of Total Exports in Central America, 2000–2011

Sources: UN Comtrade, 2012; Nomenclature SITC Revision 3.

or a small number of exported goods? A more detailed estimation of export concentration provides the level of product concentration that characterizes Central American economies (see Figure 9.3). In this regard, most countries in the region have maintained low levels of concentration: that is to say, a more diversified basket of commodities (as is the case for El Salvador, Guatemala, and Honduras) compared with oil and mineral exporters (Venezuela, Chile). As we will see below, a low level of product concentration in exports is desirable, but not sufficient, for economic development.

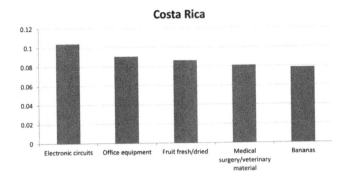

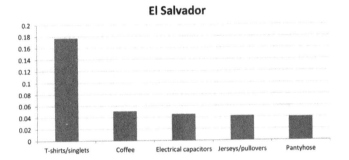

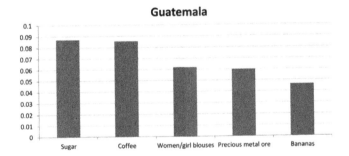

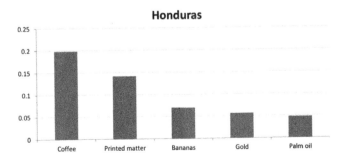

FIGURE 9.2B *(continued)*

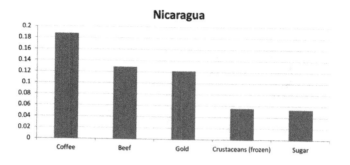

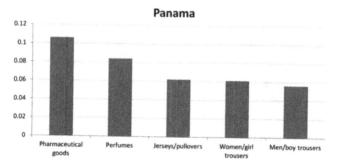

FIGURE 9.2B Disaggregated Information on Central American Exports, 2011

Sources: UN Comtrade, 2012; Nomenclature SITC Revision 3.

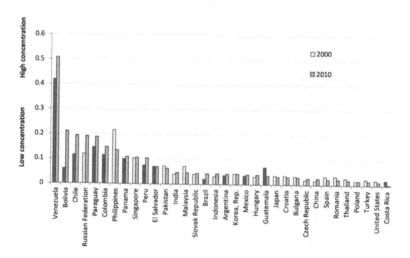

FIGURE 9.3 Latin America Herfindahl–Hirschman Index by Product, 2000 and 2010

Source: Based on UN Comtrade.

Note: The Herfindahl–Hirschman Index is estimated as the squared sum of market shares of exports of country *i* to country *j* on all four-digit levels of goods, corrected by the number of exported goods. See the Annex for details. Nomenclature SITC Revision 3, 2012.

The US–Central America Trade Relationship

The diversification of export destinations in many South American countries—particularly increased trade with China—is credited with dampening the shock of the global financial crisis (GFC) that erupted in 2008. The severity of this shock in Mexico, for instance, has been blamed on that country's ever-deepening trade and financial integration with the US.[5] Central American countries are in this regard closer to the Mexican end of the continuum. The dominant role of the US as the main importer of Central American goods (Figure 9.4) has not diminished during the last decade.[6] Indeed, the US has become even more important as an export destination for Nicaragua and, to a lesser extent, Guatemala. Costa Rica, El Salvador, and Panama, meanwhile, have increased export shares to other partners, including neighboring countries, Europe (Netherlands, Germany), and marginally China. In contrast to this Central American pattern, for most LAC-7 economies China has become a strategic destination of their exports (Figure 9.5).

From 2006 to 2009, all of the countries included in this chapter except for Panama entered into the Dominican Republic–Central America–United States Free Trade Agreement (CAFTA-DR). It has been argued that the fear of increasing Chinese competition in the US market was an important argument for the Central American and Dominican administrations to join this agreement.[7] Yet, in contrast to the boost in US–Mexico trade following the adoption of the

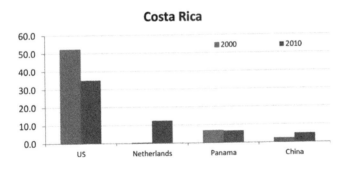

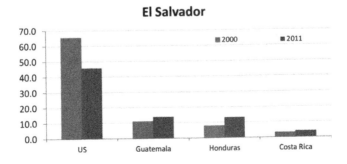

FIGURE 9.4 *(continued)*

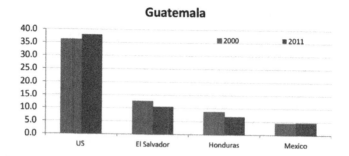

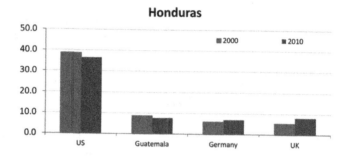

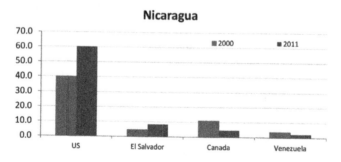

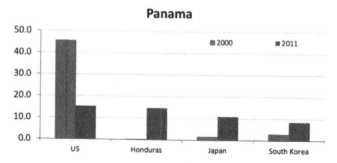

FIGURE 9.4 Main Destination of Central American Exports, 2000 and 2010

Sources: UN Comtrade, 2012. Nomenclature SITC Revision 3.

Note: Data for Costa Rica are for 2000 and 2009.

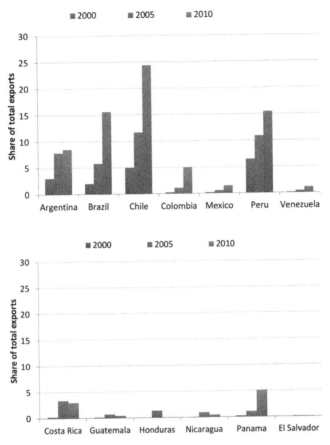

FIGURE 9.5   Exports to China as Percentage of Total Exports, 2000, 2005, and 2010

Source: UN Comtrade, 2012.

North American Free Trade Agreement in 1994, CAFTA-DR has witnessed an anemic trade response, in part because the agreement coincided with the eruption of the GFC which sprang from the US financial sector (refer to Figure 9.6).

In fact, while 73 percent of CAFTA-DR exports flowed to the US in 2000, by 2010 that fraction had fallen to 43 percent. Only Costa Rica and Nicaragua enjoyed increases in their exports to the US. In fact, export values for both countries had tripled in nominal terms by 2010, relative to 2000–08 levels. Nicaragua has followed in the footsteps of El Salvador and Guatemala and moved into *maquila*-type manufacturing, as well as selling traditional agricultural products to the US market. Costa Rica, meanwhile, exports more sophisticated manufactured goods to the US, including integrated circuits and specialized aircraft motors. For the other CAFTA-DR countries, the composition of exports to the US has been much less dynamic.[8]

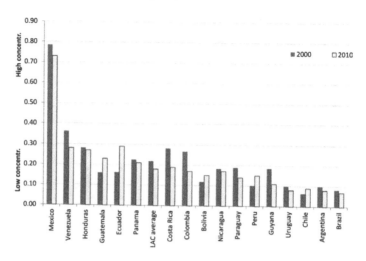

FIGURE 9.6 Herindahl–Hirschmann index by destination, 2000–2010

Source: Based on UN Comtrade.

Note: The Herfindahl–Hirschman Index is estimated as the squared sum of market shares of exports of country *i* to country *j* on all four-digit levels of goods, corrected by the number of exported goods. See the Annex for details. Nomenclature SITC Revision 3, 2012.

The low concentration of trade partners for Central American countries is also captured in the Herfindahl–Hirschman Index, computed by export destination (see Figure 9.6). This indicator gives us an estimation of the number and distribution of exports among trade partners with each country. Mexico, for example, is highly concentrated in terms of destination, with more of its exports targeting the US. However, Honduras, Guatemala, Panama, and Nicaragua exhibit much lower levels of dependence on a single trade partner, in a range similar to that of the average Latin America economy. In fact, export concentration (by destination) decreased between 2000 and 2010 for Latin America as a whole.

A Descriptive Analysis of Central America's Trade with China

There is a popular view, perhaps oversimplified, of the implications of China's rapid growth and industrialization for Latin America and the Caribbean. In this view, the countries of the region fall into two categories. On the one hand, there are the commodity-exporting countries of South America, led by Argentina, Brazil, Chile, and Peru, whose export performance weathered the GFC that began in 2008 thanks to vigorous Chinese demand for their exports. On the other hand, there are countries with export baskets that closely resemble China's export profile, and this second group has increasingly suffered from fierce Chinese competition in third-country markets. This latter group, moreover, depends critically on the US market for its exports, a market still emerging from the effects of the GFC.

This second group of countries has thus had to cope with a much higher level of competition from China, including the ability to attract FDI, and this has dampened their productive capacity in the medium term. In the long run, this trend implies their exclusion from global value chains and other opportunities for productive upgrading. The dichotomy is further complicated by the fact that countries can fall into both categories. Brazil, most notably, has benefited from high commodity prices and seen an increasing loss of market share to China in third markets.

Where do the Central American countries fit with regard to this scenario?[9] The question is not frequently posed, but the answer could be important for policy makers in the countries of the isthmus. In particular, if breakneck Chinese growth and its associated demand for commodity exports can serve as a motor for economic growth elsewhere in the developing world, few parts of Latin America stand in greater need of such a motor than the largely poor Central American economies. At the same time, if a dependence upon primary-product exports slows long-term development achievements, then perhaps Central American policy makers should look askance at this putative opportunity.

While the effect of China's increasing demand for Latin American goods has not dramatically modified the contribution of exports to GDP in Central América, it is illustrative to compare the exports to China as a share of total exports across different countries (see Figure 9.6). Chile, Peru, and Brazil have strengthened their trade bonds with China, with a much higher contribution of their total exports going to China. Currently, more than 50 percent of Chilean copper is destined to satisfy China's demand for this metal as an input for infrastructure development, construction, industrial equipment, and transportation. In contrast, the export profile of Central America's core economies shows that the share of exports to China is minuscule: only Costa Rica and to some extent Panama have increased their exports to China, with these shares hardly reaching 5 percent of total exports.

A closer look at the trade competition patterns between Central America and China is provided by comparing their trade structures at a disaggregated level. We begin by looking at widely used coefficient of conformity (CC) and coefficient of specialization (CS) indices. These suggest that the average trade competition of Central American countries with China is relatively low: Costa Rica, El Salvador, Guatemala, Honduras, and Panama all show more complementarities than competition with China's export basket (see Figure 9.7). More recent indicators from 2010 (see Figure 9.8) show basically the same result; in comparison with other emerging regions—notably Central Europe and East Asia—the competition for Central American countries with China is low. Later in this chapter, we consider an alternative index that addresses criticisms of the CC and CS indices.

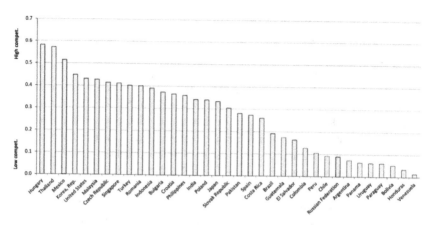

FIGURE 9.7 Evolution of Export Competition with China for Selected Countries, 2000–2009

Source: Based on WITS Database, 2012.

Note: CS and CC coefficients calculated with exports of country *i* and exports of country *j* (China). The coefficient of specialization and coefficient of conformity are measures of the level of trade competition between two economies. The competition level is determined by the similarity of export baskets between these countries, with competition being high (tends to 1) when export structures are similar, and competition being low (tends to 0) when export structures are complementary. See Annex for more details.

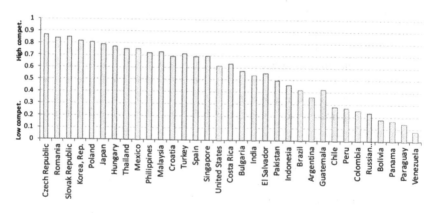

FIGURE 9.8 Export Competition with China for Selected Countries, 2010

Source: Based on WITS Database, 2012.

Note: CS and CC coefficients calculated with exports of country *i* and exports of country *j* (China). The coefficient of specialization and coefficient of conformity are measures of the level of trade competition between two economies. The competition level is determined by the similarity of export baskets between these countries, with competition being high (tends to 1) when export structures are similar, and competition being low (tends to 0) when export structures are complementary. See Annex for more details.

Central America and China have complementary export baskets because several of the Central American countries are primarily commodity exporters, while China is a massive exporter of manufactures. Could Central American economies benefit from China's rapidly increasing demand for primary goods? This requires an explicit analysis of the compatibility of Chinese imports and Central America's main primary exports. The picture that emerges is not very encouraging. Honduras, Panama, and Costa Rica export goods substantially different from those imported by China. There are few potential complementarities to be exploited for these countries by targeting the Chinese market (see Figure 9.9).

However useful export similarity indices (ESI), such as the coefficients of conformity and specialization, are to compare export structures, they do not tell the complete story. Indeed, these indicators must be corrected to account for the effect created by the scale differential between the economies being compared. While all six Central American countries considered in this study accounted together for a sub-regional GDP of US$313 billion in 2013, China's output for the same year was 42 times larger. To better correct for the scale effect, and following the work of Rhys Jenkins,[10] instead of comparing the proportion of total exports we focus on the proportion of exports for which China is globally competitive. The Index of Competitive Threat (ICT) for a given country is

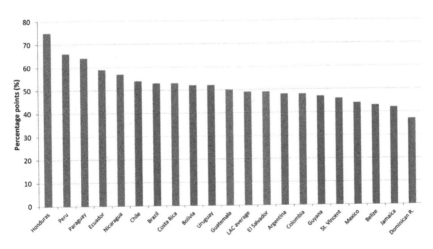

FIGURE 9.9   Index of Competitive Threat for Latin American Countries, 2000–2012

Sources: Authors' calculation based on Rhys Jenkins, "Measuring the Competitive Threat from China," Research Paper no. 2008/11, UNU-WIDER, School of Development Studies, University of East Anglia, UK, February 2008, and Comtrade, 2014.

Note: The Index of Competitive Threat is estimated as the percentage of sectors (for all four-digit sectors in STIC Revision 3 classification) where China exhibits growth in excess of global export growth over the period 2000–2012.

therefore a percentage of goods in the production and export of which China is globally competitive.[11] To identify the goods where China is competitive, we estimate the sectors for which China's exports have grown faster than world exports over the period 2000–2012.[12]

Not surprisingly, the Indices of Competitive Threat suggest increasing competition for some Central American nations when comparing the goods for which China is more competitive. The strongest increase in competition takes place in Honduras, with a 47 percent increase in the ICT index. By 2008, four of the top five Latin American countries that faced a competitive threat from China in the US market were located in Central America and the Caribbean (El Salvador, Guatemala, Honduras, and Dominican Republic). Interestingly, having a high ICT in this period confirmed that Central American countries were specialized in products for which China had captured a significant share of the US market in 2001. Growth patterns in the Central American textile and clothing industry during this period, in particular, explain this increasing competition.

As mentioned before, ESI-type indices focus on the similarity of export structures and can miss a fundamental element of the analysis. Even if China's export share in a specific product is declining, and a Latin American country exports this product, it does not necessarily mean a decline in competition. As Chinese exports have grown rapidly over the last decade, the apparent loss of *comparative* advantage can hide an increase in China's *competitive* advantage in the product.[13]

While the role of China in the global demand for commodities has been studied in detail, less work has been devoted to understanding the impact of this demand on *global commodity prices*. From the perspective of the Central American countries, the straightforward channel through which China's effect has been perceived in the region is the increasing demand for raw materials and eventually competition in third markets. This does not mean that Central America is not affected by other side effects of China's growth. As a price-taker of imported commodities such as oil and metals, the Central American countries have been indirectly affected by China's considerable influence on commodity prices, which, even after the boom between 2001 and 2008, persists today.

The effect of China on commodity prices is a reflection of its demand for both non-renewable (oil, copper, iron ore, zinc) and agricultural (coffee, soybeans, sugar, meat products) commodities. While domestic suppliers, until the beginning of the century, provided some of these goods, the share of China's consumption was relatively low and started to increase rapidly. There are, indeed, other factors associated with the evolution of commodity prices, and the peak levels registered over the last decade do not respond solely to the increasing demand of China or other economies. Supply-side effects, such as climatic factors, resource discoveries, depletion of reserves, and the so-called "financialization" (and associated speculation) of commodity-related industries, have also affected the growth of prices.

Jenkins estimates the *China effect* on global commodity prices by calculating how large the demand for a certain commodity would be if China's demand had grown at rates similar to those of the rest of the world.[14] The results show that the Chinese effect was strongest in four metals (iron, copper, aluminum, and zinc). These estimates show that the growth of Chinese demand is believed to have increased the price of these commodities by at least 40 percent. For other commodities, mostly agricultural, the effect of Chinese demand is considered to be below 10 percent of the price. Taking into account the main commodity exports of Central American economies (sugar from Guatemala, coffee from Honduras, Nicaragua, and El Salvador), it is clear that the China effect on commodity prices has been more significant for hard-commodity exporters than for agricultural exporters.

The distinction between the China effect for hard and soft commodities is reflected in export earnings for Latin American countries. The large effect on earnings is captured on metals, where China's price effect was more pronounced, including crude oil, iron ore, copper, aluminum, and zinc. Agricultural products like coffee, sugar, and bananas, where Central American exports are concentrated, experienced a much milder effect from China's demand (Table 9.1). In short, the commodities that Central American countries export, including coffee and bananas, have not significantly benefited from increasing demand or prices.

TABLE 9.1 Estimated Impact on Net Export Earnings for Central America

Central America			*South America*		
	Minimum	*Maximum*		*Minimum*	*Maximum*
Costa Rica	−7.5	−13.3	Argentina	6.9	11.9
El Salvador	−19.0	−37.0	Bolivia	23.8	40.0
Guatemala	0.1	3.4	Brazil	11.9	16.0
Honduras	1.6	3.6	Chile	28.8	47.8
Nicaragua	−7.5	−14.9	Colombia	3.3	9.1
Panama	−7.6	−9.3	Ecuador	7.9	17.4
			Mexico	6.7	16.2
			Paraguay	4.4	7.2
			Peru	29.3	48.2
			Uruguay	−3.9	−9.4
			Venezuela	10.1	21.4
Central America	−4	−6	South America	13.3	23.8
Latin America	13	23.3			

Source: Jenkins, "China Effect on Commodity Prices and Latin American Export Earnings," based on UN Comtrade.

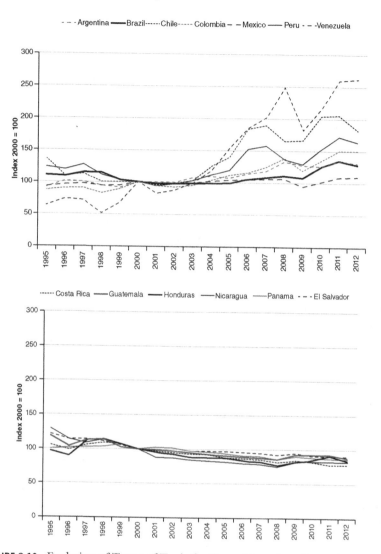

FIGURE 9.10 Evolution of Terms of Trade for Central American Countries

Source: Authors' calculation, based on data from UN Comtrade.

Note: The vertical axis in each panel is an index equal to 100 in 2000.

Both the effect on commodity prices and export earnings derived from Chinese economic growth have clearly benefited other Latin American countries over Central America. This is also reflected in the evolution of terms of trade, which is the ratio of a country's export prices to the prices of its imports (see Figure 9.10). Whereas hard-commodity exporters like Chile, Peru, and Venezuela have enjoyed advantageous terms of trade for most of the 2000s, the story for Central America is quite the opposite. Whatever positive effect China may have had on soft commodities, and therefore on Central American export prices, this has not offset the costs these countries have had to pay for hard-commodity imports (oil and gas in particular)

An additional dimension to consider is the level of *intra-industry trade* present within the Central American region. This refers to the volume of exchange in products belonging to the same industry. The Vollrath Index is typically used to measure the degree of comparative advantage that derives from intra-industry trade. This measures each country's exports and imports relative to global exports and imports in each sector. Values above 1 indicate a comparative advantage for the country in that specific sector. Table 9.2 summarizes these results, highlighting in red those sectors where comparative advantage is higher. Although countries like Chile, Colombia, Peru, and Venezuela have developed a pattern of specialization over the last decade, the Central American countries have not.

Beyond Trade: Aid and Investment

Just as Central America's trade flows are tilted overwhelmingly toward the US, so too are other international resource flows, including foreign direct investment and official development assistance. Although Chinese FDI flows to some parts of Latin America and the Caribbean now rival those of the US, this is simply not the case in Central America. Enrique Dussel Peters reports that 78 percent of the nearly US$27 billion of realized Chinese FDI in Latin America and the Caribbean flowed to Brazil and Argentina alone, and perhaps another 8 percent flowed to tax havens in the Caribbean.[15] Information from China's Ministry of Commerce (MOFCOM) and the *Statistical Bulletin of China's Outward Investment* report that Panama is an exception in the region in that it has significant levels of Chinese FDI, despite not having diplomatic relations with Beijing.

China's Going Global Investment Index, proposed and calculated by the Economic Intelligence Unit, shows that, out of 67 countries, Chile (22nd), Brazil (26th), Mexico (30th), and Costa Rica (32nd) are the most attractive Latin American destinations for Chinese firms. US FDI in Central America, while volatile from country to country and year to year, remains relatively important. In some years, US FDI has exceeded US$1 billion in Costa Rica, El Salvador, and Panama.

Official development assistance, meanwhile, has dwindled in importance for Latin America and the Caribbean, although some Central American countries are still recipients of aid from the Development Assistance Committee (DAC) of the Organisation for Economic Co-operation and Development (notably from the US and Spain). The primary recipient of US ODA switches from year to year among the poorest countries of the region: El Salvador, Guatemala, Honduras, and Nicaragua. Indeed, in some years, US ODA exceeds US FDI flows to some

TABLE 9.2 Vollrath Index of Comparative Advantage in Selected Latin American Countries, 2000–2010

2000

Product code	Argentina	Brazil	Chile	Colombia	Mexico	Peru	Venezuela	Costa Rica	Guatemala	Nicaragua	Panama	El Salvador
Food and live animals	2.45	1.32	1.46	0.95	-0.68	7.56	-3.38	1.99	2.47	3.86	7.74	11.74
Beverages and tobacco	1.39	1.74	2.45	-0.68	0.54	-1.87	-1.65	-1.10	1.25	0.25	1.41	-0.70
Crude materials excluding food/fuels	1.04	1.87	3.25	0.38	0.79	2.26	-1.42	0.57	1.19	0.80	0.06	-1.42
Mineral fuels/lubricants	1.77	-2.08	-2.64	3.60	0.25	-0.13	4.29	-2.52	-0.60	-0.55	1.19	-0.78
Animal/vegetable oils/fats/waxes	3.41	0.78	-2.04	-1.00	-0.90	1.19	-2.01	1.41	-0.20	-1.46	-0.60	-0.31
Chemicals/products	-0.68	-0.77	-0.62	-0.50	-0.89	-2.58	-2.41	-0.80	-0.05	-3.43	-1.26	-2.02
Manufactured goods	0.00	1.03	1.44	-0.20	-0.28	0.52	-0.91	-0.63	-0.14	-1.86	-0.84	-0.39
Machinery/transport equipment	-0.78	0.24	-2.27	-1.74	0.87	-3.92	-3.92	0.82	-2.34	-4.55	-6.20	-3.25
Miscellaneous manufacturing	-1.15	0.27	-1.69	0.12	0.88	0.74	-2.72	0.43	0.25	-0.69	0.20	0.71
Other commodities	0.96	8.69	1.52	-1.06	-3.33	2.20	-3.50	-1.44		0.35	-4.81	4.29

2010

Product code	Argentina	Brazil	Chile	Colombia	Mexico	Peru	Venezuela	Costa Rica	Guatemala	Nicaragua	Panama	El Salvador
Food and live animals	8.00	3.36	9.11	11.09	3.56	4.74	-3.42	3.71	2.68	4.43	6.77	5.28
Beverages and tobacco	1.72	1.02	1.04	-2.02	0.55	-2.65	-2.83	-0.76	0.43	0.49	1.00	0.30
Crude materials excluding food/fuels	2.66	3.52	3.49	1.38	0.39	3.59	-0.08	0.57	1.59	0.07	0.53	-0.65
Mineral fuels/lubricants	0.14	0.70	-1.77	3.34	0.91	0.51	5.88	-2.22	0.17	-0.44	-1.05	-0.46
Animal/vegetable oils/fats/waxes	4.21	1.29	-0.78	1.48	-1.15	1.40	-3.60	2.23	2.23	1.79	3.35	0.15
Chemicals/products	1.43	-0.10	-0.16	-0.95	-0.65	-2.08	-3.13	0.61	-0.70	-3.39	0.16	-1.50
Manufactured goods	-0.67	-0.21	2.00	-0.61	-0.31	0.14	-1.81	-0.34	-0.37	-2.25	-1.10	0.14
Machinery/transport equipment	-0.92	-0.85	-2.78	-3.12	0.92	-4.17	-4.09	-0.43	-2.99	-4.11	-7.41	-2.45
Miscellaneous manufacturing	-1.68	-0.98	-1.59	-0.56	0.30	-0.24	-3.93	1.27	1.67	-0.42	-1.97	3.24
Other commodities	-0.32	-1.94	-1.86	-0.40	-1.30	1.44	-5.48	-3.32	-4.75	0.51	-0.76	-0.45

Source: Authors' calculation, based on UN Comtrade, 2013.

Note: Highlighted numbers reveal comparative advantage for the indicated country in that product. See the Annex for details.

countries in the sub-region. In terms of share of the recipient country's gross national income (GNI), Nicaragua is the main aid recipient in Central America: in 2011, total aid from OECD members to that country reached 4.73 percent of GNI, much higher than the second main recipient, El Salvador, with 1.11 percent of GNI.[16]

Much less is known about the portfolio of Chinese development assistance. In Chapter 4 in this volume Barbara Stallings has extrapolated estimates of Chinese aid to Latin America and the Caribbean from a slim set of data sources. With the exception of Costa Rica, which received concessional official loans ranging from US$180 million to nearly US$1 billion for a variety of infrastructure-related projects following its diplomatic recognition of Beijing in 2007, she reports no Chinese aid to Central America.

Taiwan, the People's Republic of China, and Central America

Central America's trade with mainland China is potentially complicated by the diplomatic rivalry between China and Taiwan. Only 22 countries now maintain diplomatic relations with Taiwan, and 11 of those are countries in Central America and the Caribbean.[17] Of the six countries covered in this chapter, only Costa Rica has broken relations with Taipei and established formal relations with Beijing, in 2007. A bilateral FTA with China followed Costa Rica's switch in 2011.[18] During the 2010s, Taipei negotiated bilateral FTAs with Panama (2004), Guatemala (2006), and Nicaragua (2008). Despite sporadic high-level contacts over several years between Panama and Beijing, and the clear interest Chinese firms have expressed in bidding on improvements to Panama's canal, for obvious reasons the Taiwan–Panama FTA has been the main conversation stopper.

For decades, the smaller economies of the region may have judged that their bet was Taiwan, as Taipei rewarded their diplomatic loyalty with generous development assistance and other economic links as part of Taiwan's so-called "checkbook diplomacy." But, as the ink was just drying on the Taiwan–Panama FTA, the election of the Kuomintang party in 2008 augured the end of Taipei's generous checkbook diplomacy. Apart from these Taiwan–Central America FTAs, Lee Ming argues that those countries that continue to recognize Taipei are important to the latter because they represent scarce diplomatic support, but not important to Beijing because they have so few important natural resources.[19] Others contend that the checkbook diplomacy aspect of Taiwan's economic relations with these small developing countries is overly simplistic and fails to acknowledge other dimensions of Taiwanese diplomacy in the isthmus, including in the domains of public health and education.[20] Even if some Central American countries would like to recognize Beijing, China has rebuffed those offers in the name of its One-China policy. China's more recent effort to maintain the cross-strait truce is another consideration.

In light of our analysis of the structure of China–Central America trade, it is difficult to see how normalized relations between Beijing and the Central American republics would have fundamentally changed the patterns of China–Central America trade presented here. Again, the principal Central American soft-commodity exports have not experienced the same kind of price growth that hard commodities used for Chinese industrialization have enjoyed. At the same time, more non-traditional exports from the region to China may not be impeded by the diplomatic impasse. To the extent that ever more Central American exports come from affiliates of transnational corporations (TNCs), particularly from the US, those TNC global value chains and clients have a lot to do with export destinations. That is particularly clear in the case of Costa Rica, where exports to Asia, notably including China and Taiwan, have been closely linked to exports of microchips by Intel's plant in the country (established in 1997).

The relationship between FTAs and bilateral trade and investment flows, moreover, is not straightforward. Table 9.3 reveals that Central American exports to both Taiwan and China are generally small in volume, though volatile from one year to the next, and that exports to Taiwan exceed those to China for most countries in most years. In 2012, Salvadoran and Nicaraguan exports to Taiwan were around five times as large as those to China. However, Costa Rica—the only country in the isthmus with a preferential trade agreement with China—continues to export more to Taiwan than to China.[21]

Wise elaborates on the counter-intuitive nature of some FTAs with her analysis of the other two Chinese FTAs in the region—the China–Chile FTA of 2006 and the China–Peru FTA of 2009. She argues that Chilean and Peruvian policy makers were not solely motivated by a desire to lower trade barriers.[22] Rather, in exchange for securing the outflow of mineral exports sought by China, negotiators in Chile and Peru were able to protect some domestic sectors from competition with Chinese manufactured goods. Wise surmises that Chinese negotiators judged this a reasonable trade-off because of the relatively small size of the Latin American industrial sectors in question, and in light of the critical need of Chinese industry for copper and iron exports from these countries. While the first consideration (a small domestic market size) implies the possibility of some policy space for Central American trade negotiators, the second (vast supplies of critical mineral wealth) does not. Thus far, Costa Rica is the only country in the isthmus to find a loophole vis-à-vis China.

While every case is seemingly unique, at least two features of the China–Costa Rica FTA can be deemed as such. First are the sizable side-payments that Costa Rica extracted from China for recognizing the PRC over Taiwan in 2007, including the implementation of the China–Costa Rica FTA in 2011. Other diplomatic highlights include: China's purchase of US$300 million in Costa Rican bonds in 2008; in 2009, the launching of a US$1.5 billion mixed capital venture between the Chinese National Petroleum Corporation (CNPC)

TABLE 9.3 Central American Trade with China and Taiwan, 2001–12

	Costa Rica	El Salvador	Guatemala	Honduras	Nicaragua	Panama
Central American exports to China (US$ millions)						
2001	13.8	0.1	0.4	0.5	0.4	3.2
2002	33.4	0.9	4.8	0.5	0.2	2.0
2003	88.6	5.1	3.7	2.5	0.1	12.2
2004	162.7	3.6	19.4	8.1	2.6	10.9
2005	240.7	2.9	36.7	17.0	8.2	10.2
2006	556.9	6.5	29.9	13.6	1.7	13.4
2007	835.1	7.0	58.2	19.4	6.2	68.0
2008	613.0	7.1	31.8	n.a.	5.4	49.1
2009	765.5	2.6	30.2	42.2	3.7	20.3
2010	268.8	3.3	34.9	n.a.	8.2	36.1
2011	214.9	2.0	27.9	n.a.	16.4	40.5
2012	326.7	3.7	34.7	n.a.	10.6	n.a.
Central American exports to Taiwan (US$ millions)						
2001	1,705.7	183.0	418.1	209.0	233.0	376.0
2002	1,692.3	181.7	395.4	207.7	232.2	371.5
2003	89.7	2.5	1.3	1.1	0.7	7.5
2004	1,880.1	203.9	437.2	225.0	262.6	378.8
2005	118.5	9.7	22.6	16.4	7.5	26.8
2006	1,391.1	158.5	362.3	185.7	221.7	311.4
2007	252.8	32.9	61.6	60.0	46.4	122.8
2008	126.8	20.2	29.6	37.3	31.6	69.8
2009	998.6	116.6	256.3	111.3	166.6	152.3
2010	228.1	21.8	75.6	28.2	43.6	49.3
2011	295.9	64.3	75.8	35.5	57.0	46.6
2012	395.2	15.8	73.4	38.9	57.6	40.0

Sources: WITS Comtrade (for China Statistics) and Taiwan Bureau of Foreign Trade (for Taiwan statistics), 2013.

and Costa Rica's national oil refinery company for the construction of new refineries; and China's donation of US$83 million for the construction of a new soccer stadium in San Jose, completed in 2011. Soft loans from China for highway construction, solar energy, an industrial park, and numerous other ventures are still in the pipeline.[23]

Second, and in distinct contrast with its neighbors in the sub-region, Costa Rica has developed an impressive intra-industry high-tech manufacturing sector over the past two decades. To date, more than 30 percent of this cross-border trade and production is conducted with the US, versus just 3.3 percent with China. Yet 84.5 percent of the latter trade is in higher value-added electrical and electronic equipment. Approximately 26 percent of Costa Rica's imports from

China are in the same sectors, indicating that the possibilities for the expansion of intra-industry trade and cross-border production in high-tech operations between the two countries are strong.

The timeline on the China–Costa Rica FTA is admittedly too short to attribute the country's dynamic trade with China to the FTA. Costa Rica's high value-added exports to China have arguably had more to do with Intel's exports of microprocessors to China. Indeed, microprocessors constituted 20.6 percent of Costa Rican exports in 2013, making them the country's number one export overall.[24] In 2012, Costa Rica's principal exports to China were processors and controllers (78 percent of total exports to China), followed by light sockets, plugs, and power outlets (4.3 percent of total exports).[25] The leading primary product exported to China, concentrated orange pulp, made up only 3.7 percent of the total. At the same time, the FTA can be expected to deepen these trends. At this point, Costa Rica's export bundle to China is higher in technology, value-added, and manufactures than is Brazil's.

China as a Driver of Growth

How should Central American trade policy makers respond to China's emergence as the motor of global growth? Can trade with China be marshaled in support of economic transformation and a move up on the technology and value-added production curve? As is evident from Chapter 7 in this volume by Wise, few Latin American economies have achieved this goal. Productivity levels in the region have remained stagnant for years, explaining in part the low income of the region relative to the industrialized economies.[26] Recent research has explored the relationship between export structure and productive transformation. The "product space" literature focuses on the "aggregate value" of exports as a way of categorizing relationships between export industries, in order to evaluate the export profile of a specific country over time.[27]

Researchers have found that two dimensions in particular provide an informative perspective on a given country's positioning of itself in world trade. The first is the degree of sophistication of a country's export basket[28] (EXPY in Figure 9.11), which indicates the *complexity* of the goods the country exports. The second dimension, *capability*,[29] measures the variability of goods produced by a country, taking into account how frequently these goods are produced in other countries. In other words, the capability measure combines a measure of product diversification (how many goods are exported) with a measure of uniqueness (how different the country's export basket is from that of the rest of the world). Both measures have been demonstrated to be statistically accurate predictors of GDP growth in this empirical literature.

Figure 9.11 depicts the relationship between EXPY (sophistication of exports) and the capabilities index (capacity to produce new products) for a number of selected economies between 1965 and 2009. The US has particularly high values

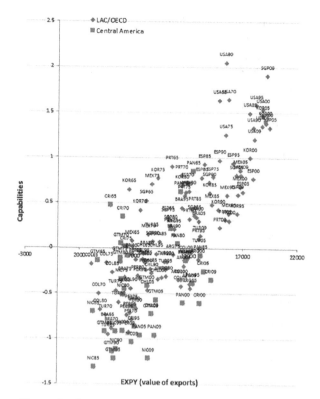

FIGURE 9.11 Export Sophistication and Capacity, Various Countries, 1965–2009

Source: Jankowska et al., *Product Space and the Middle-income Trap.*

Note: Definitions of the variables provided in the text. See the Annex for more details.

of both variables over many years; South Korea and Singapore have high values of both in recent years, after substantial increases in both dimensions over time. The results for Central American countries are striking. Most countries of the region are concentrated in low-sophistication goods. However, the trajectories over time differ from country to country, reflecting the heterogeneity within Central American trade noted earlier in this chapter.

In Costa Rica, and to some extent Guatemala, the level of sophistication of exports increased between 1965 and 2009, with a concurrent fall in the capability index. Panama, on the other hand, experienced an increase in the sophistication of exports up to 2000, which decreased thereafter, together with its capability index (indeed, Panama in 1965 had higher values of both dimensions than any other Central American country–year observation in Figure 9.11). In the case of Nicaragua the increase in sophistication has not been accompanied by higher capabilities. The picture emerging from the product space methodology is that Central American countries have marginally increased the sophistication levels of their exports, but their capabilities remain low. This suggests that their capacity for upgrading towards higher value-added goods is still constrained, even if the basket of goods they export is more diversified (see Figure 9.3).

In the area of international trade, Central American countries face many of the same challenges today that they did before China's rise in the early 1990s. Some of these problems are more acute today, perhaps as a result of China's emergence. These challenges include: (1) high levels of specialization and, for some countries, increased competition; (2) the low value-added and unsophisticated nature of their exports; and (3) the ever slimmer prospects for product upgrading.

Policy makers have focused on horizontal policies, such as infrastructure and innovation, to tackle some of the challenges posed by the China effect. Better infrastructure, in particular, could contribute to the strengthening of Latin America's competitive trade position overall. Investment in infrastructure in most countries remains low, which undermines competitiveness.[30] The state of trade-related infrastructure is likely to be most important for countries that compete with China in third markets. In this connection, the Latin American business press regularly reports that it takes longer or costs more (or both) to ship a container from some Latin American port to the US than it does from China, because of poor-quality infrastructure. The Logistics Performance Index (LPI) provides a snapshot of weak and strong points for countries in trade logistics, based on a survey of operators (global freight forwarders and express carriers). Most Central American countries score poorly in terms of competitiveness and logistics, and lag behind Southeast Asian economies like Vietnam, Thailand, or Malaysia.[31]

Despite the heterogeneity of countries' trade characteristics, this comparative analysis of export sophistication and capacity reveals a group of countries with low levels of both overall, tied to rather poor performance on the infrastructure and logistics side. This confirms the descriptive statistics discussed above in the section "The US–Central America Trade Relationship," which depicted—in spite of some changes in the composition of some countries' export baskets—a relatively high and unchanging concentration of export markets (i.e., the US) and of exported products. This somewhat disappointing performance in export sophistication and capacity, moreover, does not bode well in an environment of growing competition with Chinese goods in third markets, as analyzed in the section "A Descriptive Analysis of Central America's Trade with China."

Conclusion

In the current debate surrounding China's impact on Latin American development, Central America seems doubly cursed: largely trapped in a trade structure of primary product export dominance, with relatively low value-added, but at the same time not profiting from vigorous Chinese demand for its exports—unlike the South American countries—and perhaps suffering from Chinese competition, as is the case with Mexico. Our systematic assessment of Central America's trade, in the larger context of changing Latin American patterns of trade, uncovers a truth that is somewhat more nuanced than that pessimistic interpretation, but largely confirms that there is little in China's rise likely to benefit Central American countries at present.

Among the nuances in the story is the heterogeneity of Central American countries. In fact, the larger Latin American dichotomy of booming economies selling primary products to China, on the one hand, and struggling manufactures exporters competing with China, on the other, is partially reproduced in miniature among the countries of the isthmus—but only partially. There is a group of primary product exporters (Guatemala, Honduras, and Panama) selling mainly coffee, sugar, and bananas, goods that are not in demand in China on a par with certain minerals or extensively farmed crops.[32] Whether changing consumption patterns in the Chinese middle class, for example, will drive up demand for these Central American commodity exports in the medium to longer term remains to be seen.

There is also a group of mixed manufactures exporters: Costa Rica, El Salvador, Nicaragua. All of these countries also export primary products but have substantial industrial exports as well. Compared with Mexico, however (the textbook case of a country that suffers from competition with Chinese trade), the figures reported in this chapter suggest that competition with China is not particularly acute (except for Guatemala and El Salvador).[33]

China's booming growth certainly presents opportunities for some Central American businesses and some Central American investment projects, and there will be even more such opportunities in the future. But, in the aggregate, Central America has largely remained on the sidelines of the explosion of China–Latin America trade and investment and with the exception of Costa Rica is quite likely to remain relegated to the sidelines. Changes in cross-strait tensions between Taipei and Beijing could, if anything, be bad news for Central American countries, as Taipei's willingness to underwrite development projects is likely to flag, even despite new political developments on the island and Taiwan's recently negotiated FTAs with Panama, Guatemala, and Nicaragua.

There remains, perhaps, one sphere of economic influence which is more diffuse and difficult to detect, but this could have an impact on Central America's prospects. We refer to the increasing success of the Chinese development model in the marketplace of ideas, even supplanting the long-standing supremacy of the liberal "Washington Consensus" with a "Beijing Consensus."[34] More than a few policy makers and opinion leaders in Latin America have been emboldened by China's success to promote new development strategies in their own countries. While these challenges to the Washington Consensus orthodoxy resemble Chinese economic policy making imperfectly at best,[35] they nevertheless represent a new willingness to innovate or at least dust off discarded policy prescriptions from the past. Among the measures under discussion are a more activist industrial policy and more generous social transfers. If these debates encourage

Central American policy makers to consider productive and efficient alternatives to the low value-added export-drive development model, this could be a beneficial—although quite indirect—consequence of China's rise.

In the meantime, the critical tasks for Central American development strategies are not fundamentally changed by the China factor. In terms of trade, lowering the cost of trade via infrastructure investments could stimulate existing trade ties. More generally, the overarching economic policy priorities of all Latin American countries in the next decade are most certainly those of Central America as well: reducing economic inequality and its associated disastrous consequences and raising productivity.

Annex

A series of technical measures and concepts used in this chapter are defined here for convenience.

Coefficients of Specialization and Conformity

Comparing trade structures is a common means of studying the impact of trade on a specific economy. Coefficients of specialization (CS) and conformity (CC) have been developed to make such a comparison, though their use has sometimes met with criticism in the trade literature. It has been noted that these indicators do not always account for the relative importance of each good in world markets and that the approach pays no attention to the size of the economies in question. Moreover, intra-industry trade in intermediate goods is not captured by a study of trade structures. To respond to these weaknesses, several alternatives have been envisaged, including a general equilibrium framework assessing the trade impact and the use of a revealed comparative advantage index accounting for differences in market size. It should be added that most of these approaches have reached similar conclusions.

This chapter uses two different approaches for comparing trade structures. First, both CS and CC coefficients are calculated. Two modified indicators, using both exports and imports, are also proposed (namely CSm and CCm). Second, an indicator of relative comparative advantage (RCA) is constructed to verify the robustness of results.

The coefficients of specialization and conformity are traditionally calculated as follows:

$$CS = 1 - \frac{1}{2}\sum_n \left| a_{it}^n - a_{jt}^n \right|$$

$$CC = \frac{\sum d_{it}^n d_{jt}^n}{\sqrt{\sum_n (a_{it}^n)^2 \sum_n (a_{jt}^n)^2}}$$

where a_{it}^n and a_{jt}^n represent the share of good n in total exports of country i and j in period t. In the examples provided in this chapter, China is measured against a sample of Latin American and other emerging economies. If two countries (i,j) have exactly the same exporting structure, then both indices are equal to 1 and potential trade competition is high. In the opposite case, if there is no coincidence, both indices equal 0. To ensure consistent results, two separate indices are employed. Coefficients are calculated yearly for the period 2000–2005. The data source is Comtrade (UNCTAD, World Integrated Trade System), and the three-digit Standard International Trade Classification (Revision 3) has been used.

Relative Comparative Advantage Index

The Vollrath Relative Comparative Advantage (RCA) Index[36] is calculated as follows:

$$RCA_{s,t}^c = \ln(RXA_{s,t}^c) - \ln(RMA_{s,t}^c)$$

where

$$RXA_{s,t}^c = \frac{(X_{s,t}^c)/(X_{-s,t}^c)}{(X_{s,t}^{-c})/(X_{-s,t}^{-c})} \quad RMA_{s,t}^c = \frac{(M_{s,t}^c)/(M_{-s,t}^c)}{(M_{s,t}^{-c})/(M_{-s,t}^{-c})}$$

The term $X_{s,t}^c$ represents the exports of country c in sector s at time t; $X_{-s,t}^c$ represents the exports of country c in all sectors except s, at time t, and successively. The Vollrath RCA Index addresses some of the flaws found in other indices (e.g., the Balassa Index of Revealed Comparative Advantage), especially because it takes into account both the supply and demand sides on each sector. A positive value of the Vollrath Index reveals a comparative advantage, whereas negative values indicate a comparative disadvantage.

Herfindahl–Hirschman Index

The Herfindahl–Hirschman Index is calculated as follows:[37]

$$HH = \frac{\left(\sum_{j=1}^{n} p_j^2 - \frac{1}{n} \right)}{1 - \frac{1}{n}}$$

where $p_j = x_{ij}/X_i$ represents the market share of country j on the exports of country i in its total exports (X_i). The squared sum of all shares is also known as the Herfindahl–Hirschman Index. Given that shares are weighted by the number of observations, the Herfindahl–Hirschman Index is adopted, allowing different sets of goods and destinations to be compared.

Index of Competitive Threat

Following Jenkins,[38] the Index of Competitive Threat is defined as the share of exports in a country's export basket in which China is globally competitive. To define which are the products in which China is competitive, we consider those products where China's exports (to the world) have grown faster than the country's exports (to the world). This differs slightly from Jenkins's definition of Dynamic Index of Competitive Threat (DICT), to the extent that it does not compare China's exports to world exports but to the country's exports. In this way, the indicator highlights those products where China has surpassed, in growth rate, the country's exports.

PRODY and EXPY Indices

The PRODY and EXPY, two key concepts in the product space literature, are two basic measures of sophistication for a product or for a set of products. For the PRODY, the index is composed of a weighted average of the per-capita GDP of the countries that export it, weighted by the RCA of that country and product. In other words, the PRODY represents the income level associated with that product. A high PRODY corresponds to goods that are exported by high-income countries. The indicator is calculated as:

$$Prody_i = \Sigma_c [\text{RCA}_{ci} . \text{GDP}_c]$$

with x_{ci} being the total exports i in country c, and X_c the total value of exports for country c.

The EXPY is an estimate of the degree of sophistication of a country's export basket. The definition of EXPY corresponds to a weighted average of the PRODY of the goods exported by a country, weighted by the relative export shares.[39]

$$Expy_c = \Sigma_i \left[\frac{x_{ci}}{X_c} \right] Prody_i$$

Both the PRODY and the EXPY are used in the product space literature to determine which products (and which countries' export basket) contain a higher degree of sophistication.

Capabilities

In the product space literature, the notion of *capability* is derived from two main concepts: the *diversity* of goods of a country's export basket and the *ubiquity* of the goods it produces.[40] The first concept is related to the diversification of exports of the country, already discussed above. The more products a given country exports, the more abundant capabilities are in that country. The second concept measures the "rareness" of the goods that the country is exporting in comparison to world exports. The less ubiquitous a good is, the more capabilities the country has for producing this good. Products that are exported by relatively few countries, i.e., are not ubiquitous, seem to require many or very particular capabilities.

Using the "method of reflections,"[41] these two sources of information are combined using a bipartite network representation of countries and products, in which countries and products are connected if a country has an RCA greater than one in that product category.

$$K_{c,0} = \sum_p M_{cp}$$

$$K_{p,0} = \sum_c M_{cp}$$

$$K_{c,N} = \frac{1}{K_{c,0}} \sum_p M_{cp} K_{p,N-1}$$

$$K_{p,N} = \frac{1}{K_{p,0}} \sum_c M_{cp} K_{c,N-1}$$

The iteration of the above equations provides information about product sophistication and country capabilities. The values are normalized afterwards (a zero capability value indicates that the country has the same capabilities as the world average).

Notes

1 A version of this chapter was previously published in *Pacific Affairs*, vol. 88, no. 1 (March 2015) and reflected in the OECD/ECLAC/CAF, Latin America Economic Outlook 2016: Toward a New Partnership with China, Paris: OECD Publishing, 2015.
2 The authors gratefully acknowledge the constructive collaboration of the editors, as well as other contributors to this volume, in the completion of this chapter. A companion paper that emerged from our research project was published in 2015 ("Central America, China, and the US: What Prospects for Development?" *Pacific Affairs*, vol. 88, no. 4, pp. 813–47, December 2015). That paper pays more attention to the economic relations between China and Central American countries beyond trade (i.e., foreign direct investment and official development assistance). The 2015 paper furthermore compares in greater detail all of those relations, trade included, with US–Central American relations.
3 Argentina, Brazil, Chile, Colombia, Mexico, Peru, and Venezuela.
4 For Latin American countries, this advice dates back at least to the seminal report of the UN Economic Commission for Latin America (CEPAL) entitled *The Economic*

Development of Latin America and Its Principal Problems (Lake Success, NY: United Nations, 1949), which went further and recommended import-substituting industrialization.

5 Gerardo Esquivel, "Mexico's Recovery from the Global Financial Crisis," in Carol Wise, Leslie Armijo, and Saori Katada, eds., *Unexpected Outcomes: How the Emerging Economies Survived the 2008–09 Global Financial Crisis* (Washington, DC: Brookings Institution Press, 2015).

6 Victor Bulmer-Thomas provides a historical overview of the development of Central America's commodity-based export structure, and of the role of the US as its principal export destination, in *The Political Economy of Central America since 1920* (Cambridge, UK: Cambridge University Press, 1987).

7 Rhys Jenkins, "China's Global Growth and Latin American Exports," WIDER Research Paper 2008/104 (2008).

8 Jeff F. Hornbeck, *The Dominican Republic–Central America–United States Free Trade Agreement (CAFTA-DR): Developments in Trade and Investment* (Washington, DC: Congressional Research Service, April 2012).

9 There are by now many studies of the economic relationship between China and Latin America. Among these are: Alex E. Fernández Jilberto and Barbara Hogenboom, eds., *Latin America Facing China: South–South Relations beyond the Washington Consensus* (Amsterdam: Centre for Latin American Research and Documentation and New York: Berghahn Books, 2010); K.C. Fung and Alicia García Herrero, eds., *Sino-Latin American Economic Relations* (London: Routledge, 2011); Kevin P. Gallagher, "A Catalyst for Hope: China's Opportunity for Latin America," in Javier Santiso and Jeff Dayton-Johnson, eds., *Oxford Handbook of Latin American Political Economy* (Oxford, UK: Oxford University Press, 2012); and Adrian H. Hearn and José Luis León-Manríquez, eds., *China Engages Latin America: Tracing the Trajectory* (Boulder, CO: Lynne Rienner, 2011).

10 This point is made by Rhys Jenkins, "Measuring the Competitive Threat from China for Other Southern Exporters," *World Economy*, vol. 31, no. 10 (2008), pp. 1351–66; and Jenkins, "China's Global Growth and Latin American Exports."

11 See Annex for the definition of the ICT.

12 This is the approach used by Manuel Albaladejo and Sanjay Lall, "China's Competitive Performance: A Threat to East Asian Manufactured Exports?" *World Development*, vol. 32, no. 9 (September 2004), pp. 1441–66.

13 Jenkins, "China's Global Growth and Latin American Exports."

14 Rhys Jenkins, "The China Effect on Commodity Prices and Latin American Export Earnings," *CEPAL Review*, 103 (April 2011).

15 Enrique Dussel Peters, "Characteristics of Chinese Overseas Foreign Direct Investment (OFDI) in Latin America (2000–2012)," *Contemporary International Relations*, vol. 23, no. 5 (2013), pp. 105–29.

16 OECD.Stat. Refer also to Table 3 of Rolando Avendaño and Jeff Dayton-Johnson, "Central America, China and the US: What Prospects for Development?" *Pacific Affairs*, vol. 88, no. 4 (2015).

17 Taiwan's diplomatic relationship with Central American countries is analyzed, for example, by Colin R. Alexander, *China and Taiwan in Central America: Engaging Foreign Publics in Diplomacy* (New York: Palgrave Macmillan, 2014); and Mario Esteban Rodríguez, "Batalla diplomática entre China y Taiwán: las paradojas de Costa Rica y Nicaragua," Paper presented at the conference China, América Latina y el Caribe: condiciones y retos en el siglo XXI, Facultad de Economía, UNAM, Mexico, May 2012.

18 The China–Costa Rica FTA is analyzed by Carol Wise, "Playing Both Sides of the Pacific: Latin America's Free Trade Agreements with China," *Pacific Affairs*, vol. 89, no. 1 (2016).

19 See Lee Ming, "Cross Taiwan Straits Relations and Ma Ying-Jeou's Policy of Diplomatic Truce," in Kevin G. Cai, ed., *Cross-Taiwan Straits Relations since 1979: Policy*

Adjustment and Institutional Change across the Straits, Series on Contemporary China, vol. 28 (Singapore: World Scientific Publishing, 2011), pp. 200–1.

20 See Alexander, *China and Taiwan in Central America*.

21 The figures in Table 9.3 may not be strictly comparable. The Chinese data come from the WITS/UN Comtrade data base, the data source for most international trade research; because Taiwanese data in the Comtrade data base can be spotty, we have reported figures from Taiwan's Bureau of Trade.

22 Carol Wise, "Tratados de libre comercio al estilo chino: los TLC Chile–China y Perú–China," *Apuntes: Revista de Ciencias Sociales*, vol. 71 (2012).

23 Wise, "Playing Both Sides of the Pacific."

24 Costa Rica, Ministry of Foreign Trade statistics, http://www.comex.go.cr/estadisticas/exportaciones.aspx (accessed June 27, 2016).

25 Figures from the Costa Rican Foreign Trade Promotion Agency (PROCOMER), courtesy of the Costa Rican embassy in Washington, DC.

26 Christian Daude and Eduardo Fernández-Arias, *On the Role of Productivity and Factor Accumulation in Economic Development in Latin America and the Caribbean*, Working Paper 290 (Paris: OECD Development Centre, 2010).

27 Ricardo Hausmann, J. Hwang, and Dani Rodrik, "What You Export Matters," *Journal of Economic Growth*, vol. 12, no. 1 (2007), pp. 1–25; C.A. Hidalgo, B. Klinger, A.L. Barabási, and R. Hausmann, "The Product Space Conditions the Development of Nations," *Science*, vol. 317, no. 5837 (2007), pp. 482–7; and Anna Jankowska, Arne Nagengast, and José Ramón Perea, *The Product Space and the Middle-Income Trap: Comparing Asian and Latin American Experiences*, Working Paper 311 (Paris: OECD Development Centre, 2012).

28 For details of the estimation of the indices, see Hausmann et al., "What You Export Matters"; and Anna Jankowska et al., *Product Space and the Middle-Income Trap*, as well as the Annex to this chapter.

29 A.C. Hidalgo and Ricardo Hausmann, "The Building Blocks of Economic Complexity," *Proceedings of the National Academy of Sciences*, vol. 106, no. 26 (2009), pp. 10570–75.

30 OECD, *Latin American Economic Outlook 2008* (Paris: OECD Development Centre, 2007); and OECD, *Latin American Economic Outlook 2013* (Paris: OECD Development Centre, 2012).

31 World Bank Logistic Performance Index.

32 Margaret Myers and Yang Zhimin outline in greater detail economic and policy-driven factors in China likely to increase Chinese demand for minerals and some agricultural products including soya: "¿Qué significará el 12° Plan Quinquenal de China para las relaciones sino-latinoamericanas?" *Apuntes: Revista de Ciencias Sociales*, 71 (2012). Shaun K. Roache analyzes the impact of Chinese demand on global commodity prices generally, and finds that Chinese impact is in many ways still smaller than US impacts on those prices, though the effects of Chinese demand are growing and are particularly important for oil and some base metals: *China's Impact on World Commodity Markets*, Working Paper WP/12/115 (Washington, DC: International Monetary Fund, 2012). The quantitative question of Chinese demand on commodity prices is considered more specifically from the Latin American perspective by Yu Yongzhen, *Identifying the Linkages between Major Mining Commodity Prices and China's Economic Growth: Implications for Latin America*, Working Paper WP/11/86 (Washington, DC: International Monetary Fund, 2011); and Andy Powell, ed., *The World of Forking Paths: Latin America and the Caribbean Facing Global Economic Risks*, Latin America and the Caribbean Macroeconomic Report (Washington, DC: Inter-American Development Bank, 2012), chap. 3. Lucio Castro, meanwhile, contrasts low-value commodity specialization in Latin America with higher-value forms of commodity specialization found in other developing economies (e.g., in Southeast

Asia): "Variedades de primarización, recursos naturales y diferenciación: el desafío de Sudamérica en la relación con China," *Apuntes: Revista de Ciencias Sociales*, 71 (2012).

33 Competition with China may be more pronounced than the statistics suggest: it could be that commodity prices, unusually high at present, obscure the degree of competition in other sectors such as textiles, in the computation of the various indices considered above.

34 John Williamson, who coined the term "Washington Consensus," considers the new policy prescriptions in "Is the Beijing Consensus Now Dominant?" *Asia Policy*, 13 (2012).

35 The Chinese development model since 1979 has been widely analyzed in numerous studies: Barry J. Naughton's *The Chinese Economy: Transitions and Growth* (Cambridge, MA: MIT Press, 2006) is a succinct account, while Pranab K. Bardhan's *Awakening Giants, Feet of Clay: Assessing the Economic Rise of China and India* (Princeton, NJ: Princeton University Press, 2010) critically assesses the conventional wisdom behind versions of China's rapid economic growth.

36 Thomas L. Vollrath, "A Theoretical Evaluation of Alternative Trade Intensity Measures of Revealed Comparative Advantage," *Weltwirtschaftliches Archiv*, vol. 127, no. 2 (June 1991), pp. 265–80.

37 We follow Mikio Kuwayama and José Durán, *La calidad de la inserción internacional de América Latina y el Caribe en el comercio mundial*, CEPAL Serie Comercio Internacional no. 26 (Santiago: Comisión Económica para América Latina y el Caribe, May 2003).

38 Rhys Jenkins, "Measuring the Competitive Threat from China," Research Paper no. 2008/11, UNU-WIDER, School of Development Studies, University of East Anglia, UK, February 2008.

39 The definition is derived from that used by Hausmann et al., "What You Export Matters."

40 See also Hidalgo and Hausmann, "Building Blocks of Economic Complexity"; and Jankowska et al., *Product Space and the Middle-income Trap*.

41 Hidalgo and Hausmann, "Building Blocks of Economic Complexity."

10

WHO WANTS WHAT FOR LATIN AMERICA?

Voices For and Against the China-Backed Extractivist Development Model

Adam Chimienti and Benjamin Creutzfeldt

Introduction

President Xi Jinping's opening speech at the first ministerial meeting between China and the Community of Latin American and Caribbean States (CELAC) in January 2015 is the most recent example of China's official state rhetoric towards that region.[1] The "Beijing Declaration" issued at the China–CELAC Forum reaffirmed China's win–win, South–South strategy, which dates back to the earliest days of the People's Republic and was expressly established in the government's 2008 "China Policy Paper on Latin America."[2] President Xi's announced goals of increasing China–LAC trade to US$500 billion and Chinese foreign direct investment (FDI) in LAC to US$250 billion reflects the rapidly growing political and economic ties between China and Latin America. However, while governments have welcomed and even sought these growing commitments, civil society organizations, mainly indigenous and environmental, have responded with skepticism or outright opposition. Our examination of the unfolding outcomes of China's growing involvement in three Andean countries—Ecuador, Colombia, and Peru[3]—serves to disaggregate both the region and the preliminary effects of Chinese economic forces.

In Latin America, where the US government and its multinationals have played a major role for decades, we consider the data and effects of China's more recent entry into the Andean sub-region. A review of the main issues that define Chinese involvement in Colombia, Ecuador, and Peru, focusing on aid, trade, lending, and investment, is then followed by a discussion of how each of these countries has fared in managing its bilateral relations with China. We conclude by discussing how civil society and environmental and social issues might be shaping these bilateral relationships.

We focus on these three Andean countries because they share similar endowment factors and have close trade and investment ties with the US, as well as rapidly growing ties with China.[4] All three countries have long been engaged in an extractivist development model, and all three are under pressure to step up environmental and social safeguards with regard to exploration and production. At the same time, the cases diverge in terms of economic policy choice, with Peru and Colombia both being more market-oriented economies and members of the Pacific Alliance (which includes Chile, Mexico, Colombia, and Peru). The embrace of free trade agreements (FTAs) by Colombia and Peru has resulted in remarkably open economies, though many critics of neoliberalism question how much this is benefiting these countries as a whole. Ecuador, by contrast, claims to have moved away from neoliberalism and dismisses free trade, but many question if this is more rhetorical than factual owing to its historical reliance on foreign capital,[5] evident in a new trade agreement with the European Union and its growing economic dependence on China. Regardless of economic policy preferences, we suggest that China's trade, aid, and investment in these countries has given them greater room to maneuver in the management of their respective political economies. Studying these cases can help illuminate China's interactions with resource-rich countries and their peoples in broader terms.[6]

An analysis of these three Andean case studies enables us to better understand the China–LAC relationship in three important ways. First, it provides insights into three dynamic economic cases, all rich in natural resources but with distinct development strategies. Second, it offers a view of different sectors within those countries where China is having a profound effect, be it mining in Peru, petroleum and electricity generation in Ecuador, or coal and oil in Colombia. Third, by looking at these different sectors in LAC, we can begin to disaggregate China's effect and understand the motives and reactions of the various actors involved on the ground in these countries.[7]

China's Involvement in the Andean Region

China has looked to LAC from much the same perspective as that from which it has engaged with Southeast Asia and Africa: by offering financial assistance for some chronically underdeveloped nations in these regions. The Andean sub-region holds rich deposits of oil, gas, and minerals, and its geographical location renders it a logical gateway for Chinese products into the region, as well as exports back to China and the Asia Pacific. Political leaders and economic actors in the Andean sub-region have been eager for their countries to play this role, most notably Chile and, more recently, Peru, whose former President Ollanta Humala, while meeting with the new Chinese Premier Li Keqiang, stated he wanted his nation to serve as a bridge of understanding between China and LAC.[8]

Peru was the first test case for China. The Hierro Peru mine was purchased by China's state-owned Shougang Company in 1992. The PRC's relations with Peru have been strong ever since this Andean nation became the third country in South America, following Chile, to officially recognize the PRC in November 1971.[9] Colombia and Ecuador waited to officially acknowledge Beijing until after Washington switched its recognition from Taiwan to the PRC in 1979. Ecuador's ties with China stand out for the loans-for-oil deals that have been struck between the two. These loans are part of a bilateral strategy to advance mining, crude extraction, refinement, and delivery, as well as a general upgrade of infrastructure in this small, but remarkably endowed, country. This and other lending ranks Ecuador as one of China's biggest borrowers within Latin America. Beyond trade, Colombia's relationship with China has been less pronounced, although both sides have touted the possibility of negotiating a bilateral FTA. Peru's Shougang deal reflected an obvious effort by the Chinese government to diversify its range of primary exporting partners. Although Peru, like its LAC neighbors, has sought greater diversification in Chinese FDI, the country's rich minerals sector remains the big draw for China. However, a former vice-minister of energy and mines urges a careful review of these figures, pointing out that investments continue to grow and that China is expanding its involvement in the country.[10]

The LAC region as a whole is looking to attract more investment and sectoral diversity in Chinese ventures, and China has indicated it will be looking to invest considerably significant sums in the medium term. One study estimates that China's overall FDI outflows could reach as much as US$1 to $2 trillion by 2020,[11] and Latin America should be well positioned to capture a healthy portion of these funds:[12] first, because relations are rapidly advancing and familiarity is growing; and, second, China needs to diversify its massive foreign exchange holdings. However, the Economic Commission on Latin America and the Caribbean (ECLAC) cautions that the bulk of Chinese FDI will flow into extractive industries in LAC, rather than cutting-edge investments.[13] The coincidence of China's Going Out strategy and much of LAC's growing diplomatic distance from the US, as well as the waning of the Washington Consensus, is certainly a call for new perspectives on political economic strategies. However, Chinese demand and LAC's supply of a range of rich natural resources makes it difficult to envision concrete alternatives.

Of the three Andean countries considered here, the heavily state-directed nature of China's development path resonates most with Ecuador. Under the current administration of President Rafael Correa, Ecuador's national development plans and augmented social spending reflect this affinity.[14] However, in contrast with China, Ecuador is highly dependent on foreign loans to maintain this statist thrust.[15] What is more, since 2005 the Ecuadorian leadership has made a point of steering clear of Washington-led free trade initiatives. Peru and Colombia are relatively more open economies, both having signed an FTA with the US. But both have reduced their levels of dependence on the US, thanks largely to the entry of China into the region.

Against this backdrop, the PRC denies any political element to its involvement in the LAC region, insisting that China seeks a value-free and stable relationship with its partners in the region. Furthermore, as historian Yinghong Cheng has remarked, China is by no means a perfect development model, as it has sacrificed social progress and environmental safety for economic advancement, and has used anti-neoliberal rhetoric to protect its giant SOEs as essential players in the country's development.[16] The sizable role played by Chinese SOEs in the Andean region also demonstrates their importance in managing resources and building the infrastructure needed to enable the shipment of goods between China and the Andean sub-region. But there have also been setbacks on this front. For example, an attempted expansion of the port of Manta in Ecuador caught the attention of a private Chinese firm, a subsidiary of the Fortune 500 Hutchison Whampoa Limited. Yet this project ultimately stalled amidst multiple political, economic, and geographic realities.[17] The project entailed the building of a corridor from Manta that would have extended to Manaus in the Brazilian Amazon.

To what extent are Chinese corporate activities, in fact, an extension of Beijing's foreign policy strategy? China's energy security is a national priority, and its huge foreign currency reserves, coupled with state ownership of the energy and infrastructure firms, make a strong case for a national agenda. However, it is simplistic to think of Chinese firms as "zombies without regard for their own economic well-being,"[18] and Beijing's call for its companies to "Go Out" is not so much a central strategy as a broad call to spread their wings globally. Many analysts focus on national interests, but for Chinese enterprises, whether state-owned or not, trade and investment are often only loosely linked to government policy. As Fornés and Butt Philip write, "Chinese MNEs investing in Latin America do so for largely instrumental commercial reasons, and not at the behest of the Chinese government." What's more, there is now "evidence that Chinese [corporate] interests are also acquiring strategic assets for market-seeking purposes."[19] Others echo this point by highlighting the importance of SOE executives in this decision-making process and their need to adhere to local rules, ensuring a positive reputation for their firms.[20] It is probably more useful to consider the interdependence of national interests and state-owned firms in priority sectors in China as not being so dissimilar from the situation in the US, where Congress intervened in 2005 to prevent the takeover of Unocal by China's state-owned oil company (CNOOC), citing national security as the main concern.

Perhaps more important is the notion that there are officials operating within elite academic and decision-making bodies in Beijing who fear that many of the Chinese SOEs that have *gone out* are taking too many risks. Leading Chinese environmentalist Hu Tao recently explained that it is essential to remember that Chinese firms are certainly not altruistic institutions, though they must pay careful attention to their image in the world.[21] Meanwhile, others specifically warn against taking a "top-level" approach in which Chinese companies and governments only consult with officials, a source of frustration for stakeholders based close to Chinese projects. Engaging communities and civil society organizations at the grassroots level and building a system to manage social risks is regarded as a means for reducing tension and potential conflicts, especially for countries with historically weak institutions, where efforts should be coordinated to avoid alienating the public—which may already have a problematic relationship with the government.[22] There are increasing calls to mitigate the risks associated with Going Out and to vet current guidelines from Chinese banks and other institutions.[23] Indeed, human rights advocates and environmentalists in LAC have confirmed they are in regular contact with potential environmental allies in China and are seeking to expand those ties.

China's Trade with the Sub-Region

Overall, trade with China has gained in importance for the region and for the Andean sub-region in particular. In 2010, China became the world's largest exporter and was well on its way to becoming the world's largest importer.[24] And, while Peru, Ecuador, and Colombia are all still strongly oriented toward the US market, China seeks to offer something of an alternative. As the world's largest importer of fuel and minerals, China is rapidly increasing its presence in the Andean region.

Figure 10.1 shows that Peru leads the way in total trade with China, and the latter has now become Peru's most important partner in total trade. It is also the only country considered here that has signed FTAs with both the US (2009) and China (2010), as well as with the EU, Japan, Canada, and others, making its economy one of the most open in the region. Despite having signed an FTA with the US, Colombia is still one of the most closed of Latin America's principal economies.[25] Colombia is frequently acknowledged as having a strong manufacturing base, and while it is the most industrially diverse country in the Andean Community, these firms are dominated by powerful conglomerates that form monopolies or oligopolies and tend to bias government institutions and initiate protectionist measures.

According to figures published by Colombia's National Administrative Department of Statistics (DANE), non-renewable commodities constitute almost 20 percent of Colombia's GDP and 72 percent of its recorded exports.[26] The country sent 38.5 percent of its exports to the US market in 2011, while China accounted for around 3.6 percent of Colombian exports. In terms of Colombia's imports, the US is its leading partner, representing 25 percent, and China second with 15 percent of the national total.[27] The other way around, however, Colombia represents a mere 0.2 percent of China's total imports, consisting almost exclusively (95 percent) of commodities with no added value.

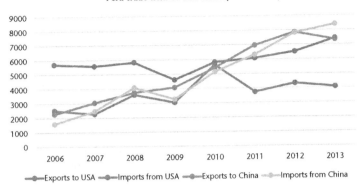

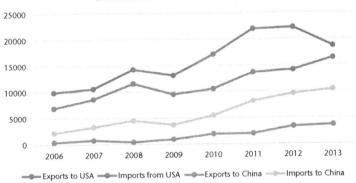

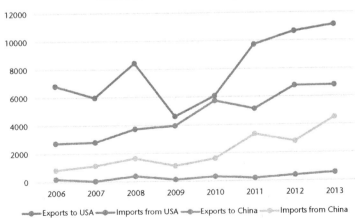

FIGURE 10.1 Comparison of US and Chinese Trade with Peru, Ecuador, and Colombia, 2006–2013

Source: UN Comtrade (with Peru, Colombia, and Ecuador).

Bilateral commercial relations are set to expand, mainly around the government's so-called mining locomotive, which is focused on mineral exploitation. When it comes to trade, Ecuador is not a priority for China in terms of volume, yet China sees considerable potential here and has taken an active role in the country in terms of investment and loans for oil. Currently, oil and crude, followed by bananas and cut flowers, are the main Ecuadorian exports. These primarily go to the US—nearly 45 percent in 2013—with most of the rest sold to the LAC region (Chile, Colombia, and Panama) or to Japan and Russia. The US also leads the way in Ecuador's imports—25 percent in 2013—but China is the second most important source of imports, at 16.7 percent.[28]

While China has gained in its share of imports from these three Andean countries combined, the US has either declined in significance (Peru and Colombia) or remained static (Ecuador). Ecuador has increasingly relied on intra-regional destinations for its goods, while China and the US have become slightly less important as export markets. Over the same period, Colombia has sent moderately more of its exports to the Asia-Pacific region and the EU, while seeing a slight decline in its exports to LAC and a relatively large move toward decreasing its dependency on the US market. Colombia's exports to the US fell by more than 10 percent over the past decade, including in the lead-up to the implementation of the Colombia–US FTA in 2012.[29]

Chinese Aid to the Sub-Region

Chinese aid to LAC has been a subject of great speculation. As Barbara Stallings points out in Chapter 4 in this volume, this is due to the withholding of some information and a view of aid and investment that diverges significantly from that of traditional Western methodology. For our purposes, we define aid as any assistance coming from China that may be classified as concessional loans or otherwise designed to improve infrastructure or assist in the delivery of basic services to recipient countries. As mentioned earlier, it is not entirely clear how much China gives and where it invests.[30] The idea that cooperation is a key element of its relationship with other developing countries is steeped in a tradition that has been briefly touched upon above. To dismiss the rhetoric is to miss the point, as Varrall elaborates on in her ground-breaking work on Chinese development. Officials interviewed by the authors all shared that China presents an alternative source of income and loans founded on genuine solidarity and the search to overcome similar dependencies.[31] Moreover, Varrall argues that these perceptions shape development assistance decisions and will continue to do so for the foreseeable future.[32]

Using the most current data gathered from the China–Latin America Finance Database, we determined that there are 76 loan agreements that have been signed between Chinese sources and their partners in the sub-region. Spread out largely amongst 15 countries over the last decade, these loans represent an annual average of US$793 million across the 15 recipient countries. As Table 10.1 shows, our three countries received widely divergent amounts from China over the past seven years:

- US$230 million for Peru (considerably below the average);
- US$1,080 billion for Ecuador (well above the average);
- roughly US$7.5 million for Colombia (a mere fraction of the average).

In terms of loans, Peru receives a fairly even spread from the IDB, the World Bank, China, and the US. The total amount coming from China is confusing, as its loans are based on commercial interest rates, which are not typically characterized as development assistance according to the OECD. As for overseas development assistance (ODA), Peru has received significant amounts from the US in recent years. Chinese loans are a relatively new source of finance for Peru and, at roughly 22 percent of the total, make up more than double the ODA coming from the US. The IDB and World Bank, which account for roughly a third of the total from major sources of lending, are still just a bit ahead of Chinese loans to Peru.

Colombia has borrowed mainly from the World Bank and the IDB, while loans originating from the US are less significant and follow the pattern across the region. In other words, they are based on peace and security,[33] with democracy, human rights, and governance, and education and social services running a distant second and third. Loans from China, however, are negligible. This is in part due to Colombia's comparatively better credit rating, which has enabled it to attract loans at interest rates that give the China Development Bank (CDB) little or no competitive edge. In fact, the CDB closed its Bogota office after several years of fruitless activities. China's Prime Minister Li Keqiang visited Bogota in May 2015 and was accompanied by a delegation of senior CDB staff, indicating that CDB may get back into the lending game in Colombia.

Ecuador's credit line received a much needed boost from China after it defaulted on US$3.2 billion of foreign debt in 2008 and a government audit that found domestic laws had been violated, as well as US Securities and Exchange Commission regulations.[34] This came amidst a rejection of neoliberal policies by the Ecuadorian government and a reduced role in US drug interdiction, which had been the basis for US development assistance and preferential treatment for Ecuador.

China's Investments in the Andean Sub-Region

When it comes to Chinese investment in the Andean sub-region (see Table 10.1), these data can also be problematic, mainly owing to the fact that China doesn't publish this information. As mentioned earlier, there is also the problem of a conceptual overlap between Chinese lending and investing.

Peru has historically been a major destination for Chinese investments, primarily in minerals such as copper and iron ore (Shougang Hierro Peru is the country's sole iron ore producer). Two of the most recent investments are amongst the most significant thus far:

1. Peruvian oil and gas assets by CNPC's SAPET in 2013 for US$2.6 billion. This marked a new era for Chinese FDI in the Peruvian energy industry, with an additional US$2 billion slated over the next ten years in Peruvian oil fields and a natural gas pipeline project in the southern region of the country.[35]
2. A Chinese consortium led by a subsidiary of China Minmetals Corporation paid US$5.8 billion in cash for Glencore Xstrata's Las Bambas copper mine, marking the largest mining transaction in Peruvian history (which took place between two foreign firms entirely outside of the country). This is expected to double Peru's copper production, while significantly boosting China's presence in the Peruvian mining industry.[36]

Colombia's FDI inflows from China are only a fraction of a percentage of the investment coming into the region, though published figures diverge.[37] These figures are likely to grow if Colombian officials and private entrepreneurs learn to respond more adequately to China's declarations of interest.[38]

Ecuador's funding from China began in earnest around 2009, and has featured the aforementioned loans as prepayments for oil and financing for major hydroelectric projects, as well as a combination of loans and investments in the oil sector and copper mines (see Table 10.1). Most recently, Chinese banks announced a 30 percent investment in what may soon become the largest infrastructure project in the country's history, the Refinería del Pacífico on its central coast. This project would reportedly satisfy Ecuador's petroleum needs and allow for an increase in its oil exports to China and Asia.[39]

China's Impact on Development in the Andean Region

Having signed FTAs with the US, neither Peru nor Colombia is willing or able to turn away from Washington along the lines of a more combative Ecuador. Even so, the three countries are clearly seeking to diversify their economic and diplomatic relations. China is a natural partner, owing to the structural complementarity of factor endowments between China and all three countries. The question remains, however, as to the ability of these countries, and the civil societies of which they are composed, to work compatibly with Chinese companies and other PRC representatives on the ground in the context of ongoing investments and development projects.

Colombian President Santos, for example, sought to follow in the footsteps of Chile and Peru with the negotiation of an FTA with China. However, the Colombian government's commitment to conduct a feasibility study for a

TABLE 10.1 Major Chinese Investment Projects in Peru, Ecuador, and Colombia since 2005

Country	Subsector	Sector	Quantity (US$ million)	Partner or target	Share	Investor	Year
Peru	Copper	Metals	$190	Monterrico Metals plc	79.9% total (45%, 35%, 20%)	Zijin, Tongling, Xiamen C&D	2007
Peru	Copper	Metals	$790	Peru Copper	100%	Chinalco	2007
Peru	Copper	Metals	$450	Northern Peru Copper	100%	Minmetals and Jiangxi Copper	2007
Peru	Copper	Metals	$2,160	N/A	N/A	Chinalco	2008
Peru	Steel	Metals	$990	N/A	N/A	Shougang Group	2009
Peru	Steel	Metals	$100	Cardero	N/A	Najinzhao	2009
Peru	Copper	Metals	$2,500	N/A	N/A	Minmetals	2010
Peru	Agriculture	Agriculture	$820	Copeinca	98%	China Fishery	2013
Peru	Oil	Energy	$2,600	Petrobras	N/A	CNPC	2013
Peru	Copper	Metals	$5,850	Glencore	N/A	Minmetals	2014
TOTAL			$16,450				
Ecuador	Oil	Energy	$1,420	EnCana	N/A	CNPC and Sinopec	2005
Ecuador	Copper	Metals	$650	Corriente Resources	100%	China Railway Construction and China Nonferrous	2009

(continued)

TABLE 10.1 *(continued)*

Country	Subsector	Sector	Quantity (US$ million)	Partner or target	Share	Investor	Year
Ecuador	Hydro	Energy	$2,300	N/A	N/A	Sinohydro	2010
Ecuador	Hydro	Energy	$670	Hidropaute	N/A	Gezhouba	2010
Ecuador	Oil	Energy	$610	N/A	N/A	CNPC and Sinopec	2010
Ecuador	Hydro	Energy	$270	N/A	N/A	Three Gorges	2010
Ecuador	Hydro	Energy	$210	Celec	N/A	Power Construction Corp	2011
Ecuador	Hydro	Energy	$470	Celec	N/A	Harbin Electric International	2011
Ecuador	Copper	Metals	$2,040	N/A	N/A	China Railway Construction and China Nonferrous	2013
TOTAL			$8,640				
Colombia	Oil	Energy	$430	Omimex	50%	Sinopec	2006
Colombia	Coal	Energy	$240	N/A	N/A	Sinomach	2011
Colombia	Gas	Energy	$980	Total	N/A	Sinochem	2012
TOTAL			$1,650				

Source: Heritage Foundation, *China Global Investment Tracker.*

TABLE 10.2 Investment Totals in the Region

Country	Global FDI flows (2005–12) (US$m)*	Chinese FDI flows (2005–14) (US$m)**	US FDI flows (2005–12) (US$m)***
Peru	$8,209	$559	$5,943
Ecuador	$3,720	$930	$671
Colombia	$79,492	$335	$8,946

Sources: *United Nations Conference on Trade and Development; **Comprehensive Economic, Industry and Corporate Data (CEIC); ***FDI flows by partner country, World Bank Data.

Note: Data from 2005 to 2012 summated (all data available).

possible China–Colombia FTA has thus far come to naught. Domestic critics have begun to speculate about what such a treaty could mean for Colombian industries, and recent strikes and disruptions across the nation have been directed at the failure of extant FTAs to protect the livelihoods of small-scale farmers. The trend under Santos has been to continue opening the Colombian economy, and the Chinese government's push to increase its overall investment while spreading risk within the region would seem to dovetail neatly with this plan.[40] But growing public awareness of the effects of current agreements may translate into considerable resistance from those already struggling at the lower levels of the real economy.

For China to effectively carry out its stated aims in the Andean sub-region, it will have to learn how to better broker with the increasingly organized and cohesive grassroots networks that have sprung to life around the complex extraction and related infrastructure projects that it is now promoting. China must also realistically assess the risks and navigate the legal and regulatory frameworks now evolving within the governments of Colombia, Ecuador, and Peru. For instance, a prior consultation law concerning such projects was passed in Peru in 2011, and indigenous leaders who lobbied for it are demanding that the government and foreign investors respect this law. Regarding prior consultation initiatives such as the one legislated in Peru, Macintyre[41] argues that, without clear guidelines or procedures, these attempts will mostly be gratuitous. One Peruvian indigenous community president expressed his early disappointment with the Peruvian law in the following statement:

> When the government says that the company has a plan for a dialogue with the population, it is confirming that the state will not listen to the indigenous population [and] if they impose their model of development on us, we will have to appeal to the [InterAmerican Commission on Human Rights], for opposing the democratic will of the people.[42]

Former President Humala of Peru, aside from his occasional calls for diversification, stated rather ambitiously at the inauguration of the Toromocho open-pit copper mine that this was the start of a new era: "Today, the government is promoting mining that is socially responsible, mining that puts people first."[43] And yet, Peruvian anthropologist Javier Torres Seoane argues that Peru's leaders are continuing the decades-old practice of approving any projects they want notwithstanding local community concerns, claiming: "The problem is that the state has not established clear norms or procedures."[44]

Not surprisingly, economic considerations weigh heavily in government decisions, even when such decisions imply betrayals of trust and ideals that helped garner electoral support for national politicians. One such example was the collapse in August 2013 of Ecuador's initiative to forgo drilling for oil in Yasuni National Park in exchange for financial contributions from around the world, equivalent to a portion of the expected revenues.[45] While citizen concerns may not be their top priority, Chinese firms must tread carefully and learn to balance their commercial and strategic interests with responsibilities and social realities rarely experienced on their home terrain. As Gu et al.[46] point out, the PRC is aware "that international stability and positive international perception of its global rise are important preconditions for a smooth domestic transition process. This makes China sensitive to external criticism and amenable for a constructive engagement with western countries." However, the question remains as to whether Chinese firms can carry off complex negotiations and societal intermediation as they seek to deepen their presence in the Andean region.

Owing to the proximity of indigenous communities to major Chinese natural resource concessions in Peru, a smooth working relationship between company and community is becoming a major factor in the fate of a given project. Peru's 1993 hydrocarbons law ensured foreign capital entry into the national mining sector, and this has been reinforced within the various FTAs that Peru has signed, including the China–Peru FTA. Perhaps this sheds light on why, despite the populist rhetoric that underpinned his election campaign, President Humala has not proven much different from his predecessors.

More recently, there has been some progress made in reducing poverty and inequality in Peru—poverty has dropped by 11.5 percent since 2008, down to 25.8 percent of the population in 2012 according to World Bank statistics. While the Humala government has committed to diversifying the economy and ensuring that taxes from the mining sector go toward expanding access to water, electricity, education, health, and other social services, delivering these public goods across the country's socioeconomic divide has been quite challenging.[47] One optimistic vision is that China could play a positive role in reshaping the nature of these extractive realities and what they mean for the local communities affected by them.

Still, the weak record of foreign extractive firms in Peru has been linked to the government's own lax approach to regulation, as exemplified in the dual role played by the Ministry of Energy and Mines (MINEM) as both promoter of mining and enforcer of environmental regulations. Sanborn and Torres note that fears about the behavior of Chinese firms are often generated by their multinational competitors and a media eager to sensationalize what a "rising China" means (see chapter by Sanborn and Chonn in this volume).[48] Yet interviews conducted by Gallagher and Irwin with an Aluminum Corporation of China (Chinalco) manager based in Peru reveal that at least some Chinese firms are moving toward socially responsible investment practices.[49] In fact, there appears to be a learning curve: with its Toromocho copper mine project Chinalco has benefited from the earlier negative lessons of the Shougang iron mine and even hired Western executives to deal with the concerns of the surrounding communities.

The learning curve required of Chinese enterprises is still quite steep, however. Although many manufacturing and trading firms in Colombia rely on imports from China, the perception persists that Chinese industry, along with the political and social structures it represents, constitutes a threat to the status quo. This perception has led to anti-Chinese demonstrations reminiscent of those in small towns in Mexico, though less violently manifested.[50] While some joint ventures have adapted to local conditions and are maintaining a low profile, the Chinese owners (Sinochem) of Emerald Industries in Colombia soon inadvertently offended the local population, leading to heavy media criticism and even kidnappings.[51]

In Ecuador, we see a government that is increasingly interested in challenging the role of multinationals, using enhanced oversight to benefit as many groups as possible. Despite these efforts, there are clear battles brewing over oil and mineral concessions around the country, and the perception among opposition groups and international observers is that Ecuador is merely replacing its dependency on Western multinationals and primary commodities with Chinese firms unwilling to ensure, or incapable of ensuring, environmental safety. For example, according to LAPOP data, 46 percent of Ecuadorians surveyed believe that the US is a better partner versus 38 percent who prefer China. When it comes to general influence on their country, 61 percent of Ecuadorians surveyed believe China is a positive influence, but that number drops to 56.8 percent when the influence is specifically related to the influence of Chinese businesses in Ecuador.[52]

These business interests include Ecuador's nascent mining industry. One former vice-minister and current advisor to a Chinese mining company, for instance, argues that Chinese acquiescence to the Ecuadorian government's strong demands is an important factor. The challenge, as biologists, environmental economists, and NGO and community leaders point out, lies mainly in the environmental impact assessments and consultation process that demand committed institutional actors and methods. If these actors and methods are not adequately prepared, responsive, or independent, and many opponents to extractivism in the region claim they are not, then there is the need for these shortcomings to be addressed by all concerned parties.

Two independent contractors preparing environmental and social impact assessments for different megaprojects in the region have shared their apprehensions about government agencies with which they work, alleging a lack of coordination, experience, and knowledge of the major local issues.[53] Such concerns have been reiterated by Santiago Espinosa, a highly regarded biologist working in the Ecuadorian Amazon under the auspices of the Ministry of the Environment after discovering an oil leak by Repsol on the border of Yasuni National Park in 2008. As the discovery and development phases of projects have been seen as lacking legitimacy, this has become a problem that the Ecuadorian government has sought to minimize or deny.[54] One local indigenous leader angrily explained that the constitutionally required consultation process over Chinese mining had been a sham: "Who was consulted? Maybe this guy over there was consulted and maybe a few others were consulted, but no one here [indicating local indigenous leaders who had gathered for the meeting] was. You haven't bought copper. You've bought problems."[55]

The high prices of commodities in the 2000s and the lucrative tax revenues that derive from large-scale resource extraction make it more probable that public policy in all three Andean countries will have to attend more closely to the societal challenges that we have discussed here. Moreover, the build-up in foreign exchange reserves and primary budget surpluses allowed these countries to launch social programs and poverty reduction initiatives. There could be, in other words, something in this for everyone, including China, although it is incumbent upon all stakeholders in this new evolving China–LAC scenario to carry their weight and act accordingly.

Conclusion

This chapter has illustrated how the nature of China's evolving ties with three Andean countries fits with the general South American theme of economic complementarities in factor endowments and China's voracious appetite for natural resources to support its economic development. These Andean cases stand apart from the emerging economies in the region, for example Argentina, Brazil, and Mexico, in that civic groups, social movements, and indigenous communities have all been recognized as formidable actors on the national political stage. This civil society aspect disproportionately shapes the relationship of the Andean nations with China and thus adds a new twist to China's heightened interest in and ability to extract primary commodities from the LAC region. Chinese investors and officials, who have not had their feet held closely to the fire on their own authoritarian home turf, are now being contested. When Chinese actors display the best of intentions, Chinese business relations with local people in these Andean countries rarely succeed because of limitations within the firm's governance structure; most often in control are "older technocrats without international education and more susceptible to bureaucratic culture," those who are less capable of engaging in an effective dialogue with local groups.[56] Ironically, at this point it is unclear whether the Chinese government actually has the leverage to compel its globally engaged SOEs to comply with its goals and principles.[57]

Yet, as many analysts of this burgeoning China–LAC relationship have pointed out in this volume and beyond, much of the responsibility to ensure that rising standards are enforced falls on the shoulders of the host governments. Each is being affected by its own problematic history and by the uncontrollable forces of global markets. Only after considering these factors can we adequately explain the distinct country approaches described above to Chinese investment and loans with an extractivist focus.

While it may be Chinese capital that is significantly contributing to this new, risky push into extractives and is arguably hampering efforts to diversify these economies, it is the pressure of global markets that is responsible for projects that are being rushed into production phases. This may be most obvious in Peru, where a long history of economic issues and fragmentation, as historian José Luis Renique has argued, has led to the export-oriented structure of the national economy benefiting the interests of Lima at the expense of the Sierra.[58] This invariably shapes ties with China, as Chinese investments entering the extractives sector can be extraordinarily patient and wait for social conflicts to dissipate in a way that even some of the largest investors cannot.[59] Speeding up the approval process and weakening environmental laws that were an early trademark of the Humala government[60] will likely complicate matters later down the road for the various stakeholders.

Ecuador's decision to embrace China, coupled with rebuttals to the global economic order, involves various key industries and feeds into National Plans that explicitly serve domestic needs. Success for Correa's early governance scheme could only have been feasible by envisioning a much larger role for Chinese funds and, hence, Chinese firms. Yet, under pressure to move the projects into production as a result of a drop in commodity prices, Correa recently admitted that allowing excessive influence of social movements in shaping much of the celebrated 2008 Constitution was the biggest mistake he has made since becoming president.[61]

Colombia's approach to China is markedly different, and we must concede that it is not entirely clear why exactly. While the extractivist focus of the economy is similar to that of the other two countries, the political situation is invariably complicated by its aversion to left-wing politics owing to a decades-long armed struggle and the attendant horrors of such civil conflict. China has made many attempts to engage with Colombia, but these have simply not paid off in the same way as they have in other countries across the region.

It remains to be seen whether the lofty goals of a new internationalism embedded in recent Chinese history can genuinely be achieved. It is also rather uncertain at this stage how political debates over extractivism in the sub-region and beyond will affect the viability of projects that are increasingly impacting communities that have historically been marginalized. However, China's dependence on massive primary commodity imports from the region promises to become a permanent feature of China–LAC relations for years to come. China thus has every incentive to make the relationship work, even if it must do considerably more to bring it up to true international standards. Morón and Sanborn[62] suggest that this is already happening, for example, in the directives of Chinese state development banks to improve economic efficiency and performance with concern for the environment and labor. In the case of Ecuador, the government is making the most of Chinese commitments to upgrade the country's infrastructure, education, and health, and to reduce unemployment and poverty. Yet the question of sustainability lingers owing to the social and environmental dangers inherent in an extractives-based agenda, regardless of the government's best intentions.[63]

Certain unsavory realities persist about the nature of resource extraction and the problems it engenders. The leadership required to navigate a nation's path through the price fluctuations, endemic corruption, environmental problems, resistance from civil society, and difficulties involved in institution building may lie beyond the realm of possibilities for any one country. It does appear, however, that the purported principles of China's aid, trade, and investment with the developing world are sincere and offer an opportunity for the leaders of twenty-first-century South America to set in motion processes and structures that can help to mitigate the social and environmental ills of the resource curse, paving the way instead for long-term sustainable development.

Notes

1 Xi Jinping, "Gongtong puxie zhongla quanmian hezuo huoban guanxi xinbianzhang" [共同谱写中拉全面合作伙伴关系新篇章, Jointly write a new chapter in Latin America comprehensive cooperative partnership relations], *Xinhua*, January 8, 2015, http://news.xinhuanet.com/world/2015-01/08/c_1113929589.htm (accessed March 12, 2015).
2 See China, "Beijing Declaration of the First China–CELAC Forum Ministerial Meeting," January 21, 2015, http://www.chinacelacforum.org/chn/zywj/t1230231. htm (accessed March 3, 2015); and China, "China's Policy Paper on Latin America and the Caribbean," *Xinhua*, November 8, 2008, http://news.xinhuanet.com/english/2008-11/05/content_10308117.htm (accessed February 10, 2015).
3 Bolivia has been omitted from this study of Andean countries because of its relatively smaller GDP, population size, and low volume of inward FDI.
4 Venezuela and Bolivia constitute an important part of the discussion around the new age of extractivism and Chinese investment in Latin America; moreover, both are similar to Ecuador in terms of embracing Chinese investment and rejecting the neoliberal model. Bolivia, a landlocked nation with a significantly smaller economy and population, is limited in both its wealth of resources and its access to global markets; Venezuela's economy, significantly larger than the others, is based almost entirely on oil exports, much of which have been used as a political mechanism to reduce a regional dependence on Western institutions. With respect to China, both are outliers

in the extent of Chinese trade, aid, and investment, with Bolivia mainly distinguished by its limitations and Venezuela by its advanced oil industry, which has allowed populism and political maneuvers that are of questionable long-term benefit for the country.

5 The Ecuadorian government's rhetoric on free trade has been assailed by former ministers and founders of the ruling party Alianza Pais.

6 Hongbo Sun, "Lamei youqi touzi huanjing: zhengce, shichang ji fengxian" [拉美油气投资环境: 政策、市场及风险, Latin America's petroleum investment environment: policies, markets and risks], *Guoji Shiyou Jingji* [国际石油经济, International petroleum economics], 2014, pp. 1–2, 117–24.

7 Prudence Ho and Yvonne Lee, "Chinese Miners Compete for Las Bambas Project in Peru," *Wall Street Journal*, September 30, 2013, http://online.wsj.com/news/articles/SB10001424052702303918804579106273770828920 (accessed March 1, 2016); Rubén González-Vicente, "Development Dynamics of Chinese Resource-Based Investment in Peru and Ecuador," *Latin American Politics and Society*, vol. 55, no. 1 (2013); Gastón Fornés and Alan Butt Philip, *The China–Latin America Axis: Emerging Markets and the Future of Globalisation* (London: Palgrave Macmillan, 2012).

8 Thomas Narins, "China's Eye on Ecuador," *Global Studies Journal*, vol. 4, no. 2 (2012), pp. 295–308: Chen Weihua and Li Xiaokun, "Xi Visits 'Gateway to Latin America,'" *China Daily*, June 10, 2011, http://usa.chinadaily.com.cn/epaper/2011-06/10/content_12672857.htm (accessed May 19, 2015); "Humala presenta Perú como 'puente' entre China y Latinoamérica," April 8, 2013, http://www.publimetro.co/mundo/humala-presenta-peru-como-puente-entre-china-y-latinoamerica/lAmmdh!3X6k2RP9N n2CkhsEaMB@ng/ (accessed May 23, 2016).

9 Adam McKeown, *Chinese Migrant Networks and Cultural Change: Peru, Chicago, and Hawaii, 1900–1936* (Chicago: University of Chicago Press, 2001); Chang Kim Shi, "Lamei diqu huaren yimin yu Yindu yimin de bijiao fenxi" [拉美地区华人移民与印度移民的比较分析, Chinese and Indian immigration to the Latin American region in comparison], Guangzhou, Guangdong, 2006.

10 Based on a personal interview in Lima, Peru on February 15, 2014.

11 Daniel H. Rosen and Thilo Hanemann, *An American Open Door? Maximizing the Benefits of Chinese Foreign Direct Investment*, Asia Society Special Report, 2011, http://asiasociety.org/files/pdf/AnAmericanOpenDoor_FINAL.pdf (accessed March 1, 2016).

12 China, "Zhongguo yu Lamei he Jialebi guojia hezuo guihua (2015–2019)" [中国与拉美和加勒比国家合作规划 (2015–2019), Cooperation plan between China and the countries of Latin America and the Caribbean (2015–2019)], China–CELAC Forum, January 21, 2015, http://www.chinacelacforum.org/chn/zywj/t1230230.htm (accessed March 3, 2015).

13 Miguel Pérez Ludeña, "Is Chinese FDI Pushing Latin America into Natural Resources?" *Columbia FDI Perspectives*, vol. 63 (2012).

14 Secretaría Nacional de Planificación y Desarrollo (SENPLADES), "Plan Nacional para el Buen Vivir," 2013–17, http://www.buenvivir.gob.ec/versiones-plan-nacional#tabs1 (accessed March 1, 2016).

15 Personal interview conducted with the Secretary of National Planning at SENPLADES in Quito, Ecuador, January 23, 2014.

16 Yinghong Cheng, "The 'Socialist Other': Cuba in Chinese Ideological Debates since the 1990s," in Julia C. Strauss and Ariel C. Armony, eds., *From the Great Wall to the New World: China and Latin America in the 21st Century* (Cambridge, UK: Cambridge University Press, 2012), p. 215.

17 Narins, "China's Eye on Ecuador," p. 303.

18 Gregg B. Johnson and Jesse T. Wasson, "China, Latin America, and the United States: The Political Economy of Energy Policy in the Americas," in Carrie Liu Currier and Manochehr Dorraj, eds., *China's Energy Relations with the Developing World* (New York: Continuum, 2011), p. 133.

19 Fornés and Butt Philip, *China–Latin America Axis*, p. 75.

20 Daojiong Zha,"Chinese Perceptions of Investing in Australia—Professor Zha Daojiong,"
  February 27, 2013, http://www.lowyinstitute.org/news-and-media/videos/chinese-
  perceptions-investing-australia-dr-zha-daojiong (accessed March 14, 2015).
21 This idea was expressed in a conversation between the authors and Hu Tao, who has
  been described as having an insider's perspective on China's environmental policy,
  March 11, 2014 in Lima, Peru.
22 This event, co-sponsored by China's Global Environmental Institute and the UK's
  International Institute for Environment and Development (IIED), took place on
  March 31, 2014, and the minutes were translated by IIED's Xiaoxue Weng.
23 Hongxiang Huang, "As China Goes Out, It Needs to Look Within: On Reforms
  of State-Owned Enterprises," June 23, 2012, http://chinaopenmic.com/as-china-
  goes-out-it-needs-to-look-within-on-reforms-of-state-owned-enterprises (accessed
  March 14, 2015); Ciprian N. Radavoi and Yongmin Bian,"Why China Should Regulate
  Its Overseas Investors' Environmental Behavior," *Beijing Law Review*, vol. 5 (2014), pp.
  22–33, http://file.scirp.org/pdf/BLR_201432109163556.pdf (accessed June 5, 2016);
  Chinese Academy for Environmental Planning,"The Ministry of Commerce and the
  Ministry of Environmental Protection Jointly Issue the 'Environmental Protection
  Guide to Foreign Investment Cooperation,'" March 28, 2013, http://www.caep.org.
  cn/english/ReadNewsen.asp?NewsID=3582 (accessed September 15, 2015).
24 "How to Get a Date: The Year When the Chinese Economy Will Truly Eclipse
  America's Is in Sight," *Economist*, December 31, 2011, http://www.economist.com/
  node/21542155 (accessed June 3, 2016).
25 Mauricio Reina and Sandra Oviedo, "Colombia and Asia: Trying to Make Up for
  Lost Time," in Cynthia J. Arnson, Jorge Heine, and Christine Zaino, eds., *Reaching
  across the Pacific: Latin America and Asia in the New Century* (Washington, DC: Woodrow
  Wilson Center, 2014), pp. 253–91.
26 Ibid.
27 "Colombia: Economic Indicators," *Trading Economics*, www.tradingeconomics.com/
  colombia/indicators (accessed October 12, 2013).
28 For the 2013 percentages on bilateral trade, we relied on UN Comtrade data.
29 Osvaldo Rosales and Mikio Kuwayama,"China and Latin America and the Caribbean:
  Building a Strategic Economic and Trade Relationship," ECLAC, 2011.
30 Kevin Gallagher and Amos Irwin, "China's Economic Statecraft in Latin America:
  Evidence from China's Policy Banks," *Pacific Affairs*, vol. 88, no. 1 (2015); Enrique
  Dussel Peters, *Chinese FDI in Latin America: Does Ownership Matter?* Working Group
  on Trade and Environment in the Americas Discussion Paper no. 33 (Medford, MA:
  Tufts University, 2012).
31 Interviews conducted by the authors in Ecuador and Colombia between September
  2013 and June 2014.
32 Merriden Varrall, "Chinese Views on China's Role in International Development
  Assistance," *Pacific Affairs*, vol. 86, no. 2 (2013), p. 254.
33 Although military aid cannot strictly be considered ODA, some peace and security
  initiatives, such as those related to the US-funded Plan Colombia, have sometimes
  been categorized as ODA. For more on this, see the declassified document from the
  OECD,"ODA Casebook on Conflict, Peace and Security Activities," at http://www.
  oecd.org/dac/incaf/39967978.pdf (accessed June 10, 2016).
34 Neil Watkins and Sarah Anders, "Ecuador's Debt Default," *Foreign Policy in Focus*,
  December 15, 2008, www.ips-dc.org/articles/ecuadors_debt_default_exposing_a_
  gap_in_the_global_financial_architecture (accessed June 10, 2016).
35 Chen Aizhu, Judy Hua, and Anthony Boadle,"Petrobras Sells Peru Unit to PetroChina/
  CNPC for $2.6 Billion," Reuters, November 13, 2013, www.reuters.com/article/
  2013/11/13/us-petrochina-petrobras-acquisition-idUSBRE9AC0CU20131113
  (accessed June 12, 2016); Patricia Velez and Marco Aquino, "China CNPC Sees to

Invest at Least $2 Billion in Peru after Petrobras Deal," *Fecima*, May 28, 2014, https://www.fecima.com/utilities/item/55159-update-2-china-cnpc-sees-to-invest-at-least-2-bln-in-peru-after-petrobras-deal. (accessed March 17, 2015).

36 This perspective is based on personal correspondence with Cynthia Sanborn after the Las Bambas deal was finalized in mid-April 2014.

37 Reina and Oviedo, "Colombia and Asia"; and Edgar Vieira Posada, ed., *La transformación de China y su impacto para Colombia* (Bogota: CESA, 2013).

38 An expression of such interest is evident in the article "哥伦比亚: 中国企业投资的理想之地" [Colombia: ideal investment location for Chinese enterprises], November 9, 2012, http://news.hexun.com/2012-11-09/147798009.html (accessed March 1, 2016).

39 "La Refinería del Pacífico estará lista en cuatro años," *El Telégrafo*, July 1, 2013, www.telegrafo.com.ec/economia/item/la-refineria-del-pacifico-estara-lista-en-cuatro-anos.html (accessed March 14, 2015).

40 Information provided by senior staff at the Colombian embassy in Beijing, February 14, 2015.

41 Martha Macintyre, "Informed Consent and Mining Projects: A View from Papua New Guinea," *Pacific Affairs*, vol. 80, no. 1 (2007), pp. 49–65.

42 Magali Zevallos Rios, "Setback in the Implementation of the Prior Consultation Law," *Latin America Press*, May 24, 2013, www.lapress.org/articles.asp?art=6831 (accessed March 14, 2015).

43 "Humala: Tras Toromocho, el Perú se consolidará como una potencia minera," *El Comercio*, December 10, 2013, http://elcomercio.pe/economia/peru/humala-toro mocho-peru-se-consolidara-como-potencia-minera-noticia-1671249 (accessed March 14, 2015).

44 Interview conducted in Lima, Peru on November 13, 2013.

45 "Rafael Correa anunció la liquidación de los fideicomisos del Yasuní," *El Comercio*, August 15, 2013.

46 Jing Gu, John Humphrey, and Dirk Messner, "Global Governance and Developing Countries: The Implications of the Rise of China," *World Development*, vol. 36, no. 2 (2008), pp. 274–292.

47 Benjamin Dangle, "Hope in the Andes," *Counterpunch*, June 8, 2011, www.counterpunch.org/2011/06/08/hope-in-the-andes/ (accessed March 14, 2015); and Margaret Boland, "Corporate Conquistadores: Peru's Mineral Extraction Industry Boosts Economy while Rural Poor Continue to Suffer," *Council on Hemispheric Affairs*, July 12, 2013, http://www.coha.org/corporate-conquistadores-perus-mineral-extraction-industry-boosts-economy-while-rural-poor-continue-to-suffer/ (accessed March 15, 2015).

48 Cynthia A. Sanborn and Víctor Torres, *La economía china y las industrias extractivas: desafíos para el Perú* (Lima: Centro de Investigación e la Universidad del Pacífico y CooperAcción, 2009).

49 Gallagher and Irwin, "China's Economic Statecraft in Latin America."

50 Adrian Hearn, "Harnessing the Dragon: Overseas Chinese Entrepreneurs in Mexico and Cuba," in Julia C. Strauss and Ariel C. Armony, eds., *From the Great Wall to the New World: China and Latin America in the 21st Century* (Cambridge, UK: Cambridge University Press, 2012), pp. 111–133.

51 Kidnappings by the FARC and other guerrilla groups in Colombia have for some time been less politically motivated and instead driven by the potential income derived.

52 Elizabeth J. Zechmeister, Mitchell A. Seligson, Dinorah Azpuru, and Kang Liu, "China in Latin America: Public Impressions and Policy Implications," *Latin American Public Opinion Project: America's Barometer*, 2012, www.vanderbilt.edu/lapop/news/032813.AB-China-WWC-PPT.pdf (accessed March 14, 2015).

53 These interviews were conducted in Ecuador in late 2013 and early 2014, and the subjects wish to remain anonymous.

54 Rebecca Ray and Adam Chimienti, "A Line in the Equatorial Forests: Chinese Investment and the Environmental and Social Impacts of Extractive Industries in Ecuador," GEGI Discussion Paper, June 2015, http://www.bu.edu/pardeeschool/files/2014/12/Ecuador1.pdf (accessed May 23, 2016).

55 The Shuar meeting with Chinese representatives of Ecuacorriente took place on January 26, 2014 and was published on Youtube on February 5, 2014. It can be viewed at www.youtube.com/watch?v=ebWkp9YY7BU.

56 Huang, "As China Goes Out, It Needs to Look Within."

57 Dussel Peters, *Chinese FDI in Latin America.*

58 José Luis Renique, *Incendiar la pradera: Un ensayo sobre la revolución* (Lima: La Siniestra ensayos, 2015).

59 David Stringer, "Glencore Copper Mines Seen Top of China's Asset Shopping List," *Bloomberg Business*, September 30, 2015, http://www.bloomberg.com/news/articles/2015-09-30/glencore-copper-mines-seen-top-of-china-s-asset-shopping-list (accessed November 19, 2015).

60 Ryan Dube, "Peru's Economic Proposals Trigger Environmental Concerns," *Wall Street Journal*, June 26, 2014, http://www.wsj.com/articles/perus-economic-proposals-trigger-environmental-concerns-1403804824 (accessed November 19, 2015).

61 Ecuador Inmediato, "Presidente Correa: Mayor error cometido en estos años fue permitir que Alberto Acosta sea president de la constituyente," August 31, 2014, http://www.ecuadorinmediato.com/index.php?module=Noticias&func=news_user_view&id=2818768950 (accessed November 19, 2015).

62 Eduardo Morón and Cynthia Sanborn, *The Pitfalls of Policymaking in Peru: Actors, Institutions and Rules of the Game* (Washington, DC: Inter-American Development Bank, April 2006), p. 55.

63 For examples of this, see the Plan Nacional para el Buen Vivir, 2013–2017 and the more recent Transformacion de la Matriz Productiva, which emphasize the extraction projects, planned and actual, as merely a bridge to an alternative future economy based on knowledge.

11

CHINA–BRAZIL ECONOMIC RELATIONS

Too Big to Fail?

Dawn Powell

Introduction

China's entry into the World Trade Organization (WTO) in 2001 marked a new phase of economic activity in the Western Hemisphere, as WTO membership better enabled China to pursue trade and investment relationships with Latin American countries. In the following decade, China's emergence in Latin America—principally, Chinese demand for commodities—helped to boost the aggregate welfare of the resource-rich countries of the Southern Cone, and even aided in ameliorating the impact of the 2008–09 Global Financial Crisis on these economies.

This trend is particularly poignant when studying the relationship between Brazil and China. Brazil recovered quickly from the crisis, in part as a result of China's sustained purchase of iron ore, soybeans, and petroleum, which kept the economy afloat in spite of plummeting US and European demand. In 2009, China surpassed the US to become Brazil's single largest trading partner. While the world scaled back on investment and Brazilian gross capital formation (GCF) remained at a mere 20 percent of GDP, China accounted for about US$12.7 billion in direct investment in Brazil in 2010 alone.[1] Despite the onset of slower growth since 2011, nearly 1 percent of Brazil's 2.7 percent GDP growth that year was driven by Chinese demand.[2] Even in the midst of recent headwinds—the readjustment of the Chinese economy and a full-blown recession in Brazil—it is apparent that China will remain an important driver of global growth and a key partner for Brazil.

Other countries in South America that possess seemingly similar economic complementarities with China, such as Chile and Peru, have proactively pursued trade integration. Both countries signed separate bilateral free trade agreements

(FTAs) with the US, and each followed up by entering into a bilateral FTA with China. It is important to note that within their respective FTAs with China both Chile and Peru were successful in negotiating exclusions for sensitive products, such as textiles, shoes, and electronics, a crucial political victory considering the labor-intensity of these sectors.[3] Although the Sino-Brazilian trade and investment relationship has produced more winners than losers on the Brazilian side, an FTA with China has not been on the policy radar screen. In spite of significant advances in trade liberalization under the administrations of President Fernando Henrique Cardoso and President Luiz Inácio Lula da Silva, and high-level discourse in favor of South–South trade, Brazil has opted for a statist approach to development, keeping its markets relatively closed over the past few decades. Moreover, in 2004 Brazil failed to ratify China's bid for market economy status at the World Trade Organization (WTO), which would be the first step toward any conceivable FTA negotiations.

Throughout this chapter, I will focus on the domestic actors behind these and other important policy developments in the China–Brazil relationship. While trade and investment ties with China have presented rich opportunities for Brazil, those domestic groups that are most exposed to Chinese competition have called for a more protectionist economic policy stance. Increased Chinese presence has been met with resistance from the Brazilian manufacturing sector, and in recent years, from 2010 to 2012 in particular, industrial groups harnessed their political power to pressure the government into adopting a series of protectionist policies. A closer look at this domestic political conflict over the *entrada chinesa* in Brazil, and its policy ramifications, reveals a less than ideal picture of China–Brazil economic ties.

For the most part, the early literature on China–Latin America relations emphasized that the Southern Cone countries, in particular, have benefited from economic ties with China owing to their complementary factors of endowment.[4] These analyses are based mainly on the explosion of trade and investment as an indicator of stronger overall ties with China. As Maciel and Nedal have highlighted, when focusing on the sheer magnitude of trade and investment ties and diplomatic visits, the China–Brazil bilateral relationship appears to be moving in a positive direction. But these same authors also note that Brazil's expanding economic ties with China have been met with strong resistance on the home front.[5] In fact, political discourse across Latin America has also highlighted the negative aspects of the region's relationship with China, including the threat to local industries and growing fears of dependency.[6] For example, Gallagher and Porzecanski have documented how the manufacturing sector across the region is being upstaged by China in both domestic and third markets.[7] However, a reconciliation of these competing narratives—the positive and negative views—can be found in Jenkins and Barbosa's assessment of China's impact on Brazilian industry; they argue that domestic claims of "deindustrialization" are still more dramatic than the data actually portray.[8]

There is still no comprehensive study that assesses how the political economy of Brazil has been affected through its deepening bilateral relationship with China, and how this might be shaping Brazil's economic development trajectory overall. This chapter intends to fill the gap in the current literature by answering the following question: How has the Brazilian political debate influenced the China–Brazil relationship and what are the prospects for further integration between the world's second and seventh largest economies?[9] My premise is that Brazil's relationship with China is best understood on a domestic rather than a regional level. In building this argument I draw on the work of Maciel and Nedal,[10] who assert that these increasing economic ties have triggered "domestic political reverberations" that complicate the furthering of the relationship between Brazil and China.[11] I begin by identifying those key domestic political actors in Brazil which have shaped its trade and investment policies toward China. More specifically, I seek to understand how and why those within the few protection-dependent industrial sub-sectors have succeeded in casting Sino-Brazilian ties in such negative terms. After an overview of this debate, I delineate those sectoral winners and losers which have emerged within the Brazilian political economy as a result of this rapidly growing Sino-Brazilian economic relationship. I also identify the self-proclaimed losers that have sought protection from Chinese competition and seek to explain how their concerns have emerged as a powerful roadblock in the formation of a closer, more productive economic partnership.

This research draws on various sources, including trade and investment flows, antidumping data, news stories in the Brazilian and international press, statements drawn from lectures, conferences, and business events in Rio de Janeiro and São Paulo, and interviews with scholars, government officials, and key protagonists within the private sector. Included in this analysis is a case study of a proposed Chinese investment in Brazil, which is based on primary sources, field interviews, and observations at the site of a planned Chinese investment in the Brazilian soybean industry. An overriding question addressed throughout the chapter is the ways in which domestic politics are influencing the China–Brazil relationship and how the dynamics of bilateral ties are affecting Brazilian development.

The *Entrada Chinesa:* Mapping the Brazilian Political Debate and the Shift towards Increased Protectionism

Although the numbers suggest a relationship in which Brazil benefits from closer economic ties with China, the domestic political climate has not welcomed the *entrada chinesa*. The Brazilian political reaction to increased trade and investment ties with China can be summarized by the emergence of two popular and parallel narratives: first is the neocolonialism or primarization debate; second is that over the deindustrialization of the Brazilian economy due to heightened competition from China. Below, I review each of these debates in turn.

Neocolonialism and Primarization: Brazilian Exports to China

The sheer magnitude of Brazil's increased trade with China stoked fears of dependency in Brazil. In 2001, total trade (the sum of imports and exports) between the two countries amounted to just US$3.2 billion. A decade later, in 2011, total trade reached US$77 billion, an increase of over 2,000 percent.[12] What's more, Chinese demand for commodities drove price increases for Brazilian products such as soybeans and iron ore, leading to Brazil's trade surplus. This, in turn, contributed to the country's increased reserves, which provided funding for the expansion of public investments, and a decade of impressive growth.[13] Even though China contributed substantially to Brazilian growth throughout this period, Brazil's single largest trading partner became the subject of a wide range of criticism on the home front—even in 2010, the year that Brazil registered a record 7.5 percent growth rate.

In Brazil, China has been accused of neocolonialism, or the "primarization" of the Brazilian export basket to China, 80 percent of which is raw materials (iron ore, soy, oil, and to a lesser extent cellulose).[14] While this simplified classification does not take into account the research and technology involved in oil exploration, mining, and agribusiness, it is clear that Brazilian exports to China are largely centered around commodities. Thus, a common theme that now underpins public discourse is the need to diversify Brazil's exports to China to include more higher value-added goods. Although this is a noble aspiration, Brazil lacks the institutional structure to produce industrialized goods at competitive prices vis-à-vis China, as demonstrated by the World Economic Forum's 2014–2015 Global Competitiveness Index, in which China ranked 28th and Brazil ranked

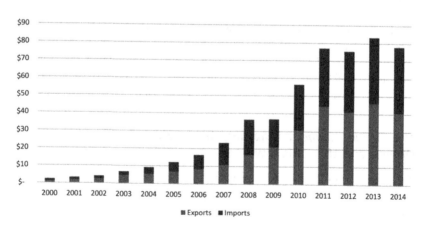

FIGURE 11.1   China–Brazil Trade (Exports and Imports in US$ billions, 2000–2014)

Source: Ministério do Desenvolvimento, Indústria e Comércio Exterior (MDIC).

57th out of 143 economies,[15] as well as the World Bank's ease of doing business ranking, which places Brazil in 116th place.[16] This is due in large part to the *custo Brasil*: a complex tax system, outdated labor laws, and daunting infrastructure bottlenecks.

Beyond the desire to diversify the Brazilian export basket, the "primarization" debate reflects fears of dependency and vulnerability due to increased exposure to fluctuations in commodity prices and demand.[17] From 2008 to 2013, however, high commodity prices led to a positive reversal in the terms of trade, contrary to Raúl Prebisch's original thesis that emphasized the declining terms of trade for developing countries that depend on primary exports. Brazil's relative vulnerability to external shocks such as the Global Financial Crisis was mitigated by two main factors: a diversified set of trading partners, including the export of industrial goods to much of its own region (trade with China constituted an average of 16 percent of Brazil's international trade from 2009 to 2014); and its economy being buoyed by robust domestic demand.[18]

One of the effects of increased China–Brazil trade was the appreciation of the real[19]—which reached a peak of R\$1.56 to the dollar in July 2011—as high primary commodity prices and large foreign reserves placed upward pressure on the exchange rate. The stronger currency instilled concerns that Brazil might be succumbing to Dutch disease, an appreciating exchange rate signifying less competitive prices for exports of manufactured goods. Exporters and manufacturers lobbied for policies to reverse the strengthening of the real.[20] It was feared that Brazil was exporting primary goods to China at the expense of its national industry, which was experiencing additional pressure from the import of higher value-added goods from China. Concerns of an overvalued currency have become less relevant, as the real has since depreciated significantly, reaching a low of R\$4.17 in September 2015.

While the onset of a recession in Brazil can be partially attributed to a slowing of Chinese demand and with this lower commodity prices, it would be premature to assert that slowing growth is due to an overdependence on China. Homegrown fiscal mismanagement—from rampant overspending to outright corruption in the public sector—has also played a large role in triggering Brazil's recent economic woes. Brazil has much work to do following the end of the commodity boom, as Wise writes in Chapter 7 in this volume, which will prove crucial for improving the competitiveness of the country.

Deindustrialization: Brazilian Imports from China

Intertwined with this fear over Dutch disease is a deindustrialization narrative that also surfaced in Brazil, where the flood of Chinese imports is viewed as a threat to the future of national industry. Although imports of industrial goods have increased, during the boom years overall industrial production also increased to meet domestic demand.[21] At any rate, the supposed deindustrialization of Brazil cannot be solely attributable to China. Contrary to popular perception, consumer goods represent just a fraction of Chinese imports, while intermediate and capital goods constitute the mainstay of Brazil's import basket from China. In 2011, approximately half of Brazilian imports from China were either capital or intermediate goods.[22] These include intermediate products such as television parts, bicycle pedals, and polyester thread for the manufacture of textiles.[23]

Brazilian industry buys these inputs at competitive prices, which lowers the costs of production.[24] The data suggest that, "rather than being a competitive threat in the market for final consumer goods, imports from China may be a source of increased profits for Brazilian producers through providing access to cheaper equipment, intermediate inputs, and parts and components."[25] While it is not clear whether this is contributing to the modernization of Brazilian industry or simply disrupting domestic supply chains, it does seem that the negative aspects of China's penetration into the domestic market are exaggerated, while the benefits have been underplayed. On this point, the influx of cheap Chinese imports has helped meet consumer demand and placed downward pressure on prices. Owing to a history of high inflation, which was controlled with the launching of the Real Plan in 1994, the Brazilian government employs an inflation-targeting strategy. Barring Chinese imports would be counter-productive to the government's constant struggle to hold inflation down.

The final aspect of the deindustrialization narrative is the fear that manufacturing jobs are being transferred from Brazil to China, as expressed in this 2011 headline in a reputable Brazilian newspaper: "China Advances in New Sectors and Destroys Jobs."[26] Despite this claim, at the time the data showed decreasing rates of unemployment in Brazil, which reached a historic low of 4.7 percent in December 2011.[27] Two 2011 studies revealed that, in addition to low levels of unemployment, there was even a shortage of qualified workers to fill the available job postings. According to a Federation of Industries of Rio de Janeiro (FIRJAN) study, thousands of jobs in Brazil were unfilled owing to the lack of qualified candidates. Of the 600 factories interviewed for the study, at the time 60 percent were hiring, but of these over 53 percent had failed to find the right candidate for a given job after a six-month search.[28] Another study, released by the National Industries Confederation (CNI), revealed that the lack of a qualified workforce affects 69 percent of companies in the industrial sector.[29]

Both FIRJAN and CNI emphasized that this problem could be attributed to the Brazilian government's lack of investment in quality education at all levels. An ill-prepared workforce, with the average Brazilian worker having completed just six years of formal schooling, significantly limits the country's growth.[30] Beyond a shortage of engineers with university degrees, a large number of candidates lack basic math and Portuguese skills, as "only half of Brazilian students who enter high school go on to graduate."[31] While the underlying problem of low levels of investment in education remains unaddressed, the deindustrialization narrative has used China as a scapegoat for the threat of manufacturing jobs moving offshore.

Diversity of Chinese Investments in Brazil

The surge in Chinese investment exacerbated Brazil's fears of a neocolonial relationship in the making. From 1990 to 2009, Chinese investment in Brazil amounted to just US$255 million. In 2010, however, US$12.7 billion in investment was confirmed, and another US$23 billion was announced.[32] The dollar amounts of these early investments were mostly composed of projects in Brazil's natural resource sectors, which are more capital intensive than manufacturing ventures. Yet, despite the seeming preponderance of Chinese investment in natural resources, a closer look at these investments in Brazil reveals that a range of deals in manufacturing and infrastructure are also underway.[33]

According to the China–Brazil Business Council, the majority of Chinese investments announced from 2007 to 2012 were market-seeking, with less than a third related to natural resources. While in 2010 Chinese investments in Brazil were indeed more focused on natural resources, a second wave of investment, which began in late 2010 and continued through 2012, is characterized by the efforts of Chinese companies to sell their products to an expanding consumer market in Brazil, and to use Brazil as a base from which to export to the rest of Latin America.[34] Not only do Chinese investments seek to capitalize on the appetite of the Brazilian consumer for Chinese cars, motorcycles, and so on, but they also seek out strategic acquisitions or "long-term investments in critical infrastructure assets," as in the case of State Grid's investment in electrical power distribution.[35]

Despite the diversity of Chinese investments and the opportunities these present, the focus of domestic political debates has remained on investments in the natural resource sectors and been cast negatively as furthering the "primarization" of the Brazilian export basket. Yet in order for Brazil to reap the benefits that China has to offer—including, but not limited to, capital and technology transfer—"regulatory and public opinion challenges must be managed in a sophisticated and effective manner."[36] Unfortunately, as I will discuss further in the following section, special interest groups have influenced public opinion and Brazil's policy toward China—and not necessarily for the better.

Winners and Losers on the Brazilian Side

In this section I delineate the winners and the losers in the trade game (see Table 11.1) and their respective domestic lobbying efforts for or against deeper relations with China. As the voices of the losers are louder, the Brazilian domestic political debate over the influx of Chinese investments and imports

TABLE 11.1 Pro and Anti-China Sectoral Actors in the Political Debate

Winners		Losers	
Commodity exporters to China	*High-technology exporters to China*	*Import-competing sectors*	*Protection-seeking sectors*
Mining	Aeronautics	Toys	Machines
Agribusiness: soy	Refrigeration	Shoes	Electronics
and cellulose	Motors	Textiles	São Paulo-based
Oil			industry

has prompted policymakers to opt for protectionist measures to compensate for the perceived asymmetries of the relationship. What is more, the Brazilian government not only shifted its China policy to address the domestic distributive conflicts faced by the import-competing sectors (the true losers), but also doled out subsidies and enacted import tariffs for the sectors that claim they are under threat, inhibiting the pursuit of the structural reform agenda that Brazil must pursue in order to increase its long-term competitiveness.[37]

The clear winners in the relationship are the primary commodity exporters, recipients of Chinese investment, and businesses that have successfully entered the Chinese market. The primary commodity sectors rode the wave of increased demand for Brazilian resources by supplying China with the materials it needed to fuel its growth. Brazilian producers in this sector also welcomed Chinese investment to facilitate the exportation of their products to the Chinese market. The winning sectors are as follows: mining, petroleum, agribusiness (mainly soy), logistics, and infrastructure. The pro-China actors include two of the largest companies in Brazil, often referred to as "national champions": Vale, the mining giant funded heavily by the Brazilian National Development Bank (BNDES); and Petrobras, the state-run oil company.

The case of the latter company, embroiled in a multibillion-dollar graft and corruption scandal since early 2015, illustrates how the commodity boom also opened up new opportunities for rent-seeking and outright theft in commodity-rich emerging economies like Brazil. Petrobras's significant decline in value—shares that traded on the NYSE for approximately US$40 each in the first quarter of 2011 plunged to the US$4 range in the third quarter of 2015—has shaken the Brazilian economy. While this was driven by depressed oil prices and a grim sector outlook, the country's largest corruption scandal also played a part. The boom times created an opportunity for Petrobras and a cartel of service providers (mostly construction companies) to engage in a kickback scheme, as the systematic overcharging of the state-controlled giant raised no red flags in the midst of a high oil price environment. Petrobras executives are estimated to have siphoned approximately US$3 billion throughout the *Lava Jato* operation, pocketing bribes and also channeling funds to elected officials, most of whom belong to Mr. da Silva and his successor

Ms. Rousseff's Workers' Party.[38] The unfolding investigations have revealed the lavish lifestyles of public officials and private sector executives, funded by stolen cash that flowed through phantom companies and into offshore accounts in elaborate money-laundering schemes.

While corruption is widespread and embedded at all levels of Brazilian society, with the country ranking 69 out of 175 countries on Transparency International's Corruption Perceptions Index, the magnitude of this corruption scandal has rocked Brazilians' already meager trust of public institutions.[39] The case of Petrobras—a winner in the China–Brazil trade relationship—is one example of how Brazil's downward spiral was in part self-inflicted; during the boom years, Brazil not only failed to capitalize on the opportunity to invest in structural reforms, but also took a huge step backwards.

Also among the winners are the most prominent actors in favor of closer China–Brazil ties: companies that have entered the Chinese market. One such company is Embraer, a leading manufacturer of airplanes, along with other companies such as WEG, the producer of electronic motors, and Embraco, the refrigeration company, all of which sell their products in China.[40] The winners are very loosely organized into a pro-China lobby through the China–Brazil Business Council, yet for various reasons that I will address later they have as yet been unsuccessful in influencing the government to pursue a more cohesive and constructive China strategy.

Apart from the more obvious aforementioned winners, Brazilian consumers and state governments are also benefiting from China's increased presence in the country. On the whole, trade with China puts downward pressure on consumer prices, and low-priced goods from China offer more Brazilians the opportunity to increase their standard of living. For instance, the Chinese automobile company Chery produces a QQ model that proved to be an affordable alternative for Brazilians, as it was the cheapest "complete" car in Brazil before a 30 percent tax was enacted in 2011.[41] On the local level, state governments compete to attract Chinese investments—such as Chinese car factories—in order to create jobs and increase economic activity in their regions. They also benefit from the increase in tax revenues these companies bring. It could even be argued that to a certain extent Brazilian industry wins as well. As previously mentioned, a large portion of Chinese imports is intermediate goods—or inputs to the production process—which contribute to lower prices and therefore strengthen the competitiveness of Brazilian consumer goods.[42]

In spite of the benefits China offers Brazil, the losers in the trade game have proved louder than the winners. In line with the literature on the political economy of protectionism, the losers have a greater capacity to organize owing to the smaller size of the group, their clear homogeneous policy preferences, and the fact that they tend to be geographically concentrated.[43] Those sectors of the Brazilian economy that are subject to, or see themselves as under threat of, Chinese competition are as follows: toys, textiles, shoes, automobiles, machines, electronics, and miscellaneous manufacturing. These import-competing sectors are represented by their respective sectoral industrial associations: ABIT (textiles), ABRINQ (toys), ABICALÇADOS (shoes), ABIMAQ (machines), and ABINEE (electronics). These associations are in practice special interest groups. In addition to standard lobbying activities, they have frequently voiced their concerns in the press, thereby setting a negative tone for the debate on how Brazil must adapt to the rise of China. For instance, in early 2012, ABINEE released a study revealing the negative impacts of Chinese cell phones on domestic industry, and called for protectionist measures. ABIMAQ has also pleaded for protection on many accounts, its director admitting: "It is an illusion to think that we can sell manufactured goods to China. Brazil is not a competitive country."[44]

At the height of increased trade and investment flows with China, powerful São Paulo-based industry touted a Sinophobic line of political debate, blaming China for triggering a trend of deindustrialization. It was FIESP—the São Paulo state federation of industry—that successfully lobbied to thwart Brazil's granting market status to China at the WTO in 2004. Then, starting in 2010, this influential group effectively pressured the government to adopt a number of protectionist measures.[45] Over time, Brazilian industry has become accustomed to protection. A history of import-substitution industrialization fostered a misperception among industrialists that competitiveness was not of high importance because the domestic market was already reserved for their products.[46] Yet, in today's world, Brazilian industry is faced with increasingly globalized production processes, and protectionism is not an effective means to address the drivers of such low levels of competitiveness.

Brazilian industry employs a significant number of workers and as a result has considerable political power. However, the question remains as to the extent to which Brazil's factories are under threat from Chinese imports (with the exception of the toy industry, which has been hit the hardest, and to a lesser degree the shoe and textile industries). Other sectors have lost market share to Chinese companies without experiencing a significant slowdown in production. While more research is needed to determine China's role in the supposed decline of industrial activity in Brazil, there is ample evidence that some of Brazil's competitiveness challenges are homegrown.

Nevertheless, the losers have fueled Sinophobia in Brazil and successfully influenced the government to adopt protectionist policies. A selection of domestic headlines from 2011 and early 2012 reveals the severity of this problem: "Businessmen demand defensive measures against China," "Ambassador says that Brazil will adopt specific measures against the Chinese," and—the most dramatic—"Brazil becomes a Chinese colony."[47] The anti-China political climate flourished in part because of Brazil's lack of China specialists, which has only recently begun to improve. On top of a shortage of leaders capable of making well-informed, balanced decisions on China policy, the academic infrastructure for aspiring Sinophiles is threadbare: in late 2011, there were just two university-level courses offered on China in all of Brazil. This knowledge gap allowed the voices of special interest groups to dominate the political debate, which in turn engendered a rise of protectionist measures in Brazil.

Government Response: A New Wave of Protectionism

Throughout her first term in office, President Dilma Rousseff listened to these worries of neocolonialism and deindustrialization, and took note of the various industry groups filing antidumping cases and lobbying for various other forms of protection against Chinese competition. When Rousseff made her first international trip as President in April 2011, China was her destination, and the theme of her visit was "Beyond complementarities," a nod to the pleas of the industrial lobby to rebalance the China–Brazil relationship. With the agenda of diversifying away from the export of Brazilian commodities and the import of Chinese manufactured goods, Rousseff, ignoring the dynamism already present in the bilateral economic exchange, sought to remedy the "one-sided" nature of the relationship with a dose of protectionism.

In direct response to the pressures of industry groups, the government enacted a range of protectionist measures in the form of increased taxes and non-tariff barriers on Chinese imports, coupled with local content rules and subsidies for local production. Aside from accusations of dumping into the Brazilian market, currency measures grew in number, with the argument that a strong real and weak renminbi was giving China an advantage over Brazilian products in both domestic and third markets. The biggest problem with this shift towards protectionism is that these measures offer nothing in the way of economic restructuring and therefore are highly unlikely to improve Brazil's long-term competitiveness. As Table 11.2 depicts, throughout the course of Rousseff's first year in office, her administration passed (or was considering) 40 protectionist measures to shield Brazilian industry from the "avalanche" of imported goods, in large part from China.[48]

To protect local industry from Chinese imports, the Brazilian government has enacted a large number of antidumping and safeguard measures.[49] A brief analysis of WTO data on antidumping measures reveals that, from the beginning of 1995 to the end of 2014, Brazil took 197 actions (an average of nearly ten per year), of which 28 percent were directed at China. Despite the Rousseff administration's tougher stance on antidumping, Brazil remains in fifth place in the world for reported antidumping measures against China. Some scholars, such as Vera Thorstensen, a professor at FGV São Paulo, argue that Brazil must use WTO rules to its advantage and increase the number of defensive measures to protect its industry.[50] This tool has its limits, however, because, if all the antidumping measures demanded by the private sector were adopted, only a fraction (4 percent in 2011) of all Brazilian imports would be affected.[51] Moreover, filing more antidumping suits risks provoking the Chinese to enact their own

TABLE 11.2 Main Protectionist Policies Enacted, 2010–2014

Policy	Date	Description	China as target
Reinterpretation of land law	August 2010	Further restrictions on foreigners' purchase of farmland	Largely in response to Chinese announcements of interest in buying land for soy and corn production
Antidumping actions	Ongoing throughout period	From January 2012 to December 2014, 86 actions enacted	28 percent historically directed at China
Currency controls	Ongoing throughout period	Under Rousseff government, eight exchange rate measures passed	Compensate for overvalued real and undervalued renminbi
Tax on industrial products (IPI) on automobiles	September 2011	30-plus percent tax on cars with less than 65 percent local content	Chinese companies—Chery, JAC Motors, and Lifan—announced they would construct factories in Brazil, but must pay tax in the meantime
Bigger Brazil industrial stimulus plan	August 2011; additional measures in April 2012	Increased number of trade investigators. Decreased taxes for local industry. Latest measure increases taxes on foreign goods	Protect domestic industry from flow of competitive Chinese imports

Source: Author's compilation of protectionist measures based on announcements in the Brazilian and international press and WTO data.

import restrictions, as was the case with China's blockade of Argentine soybean oil in 2010, as well as previous phytosanitary restrictions China enforced against Argentine beef. Rousseff's defensive trade policy risked similar trade retaliation measures by China.

Perhaps the most hard-hitting protectionist measure was the 30 percent increase in the tax on industrial products (IPI) for imported cars, announced by Rousseff in September 2011 and effective until the end of 2012.[52] As a result, some models had to pay an IPI tax of 55 percent, plus import tariffs. The measure affected automobiles that have less than 65 percent local content, which principally pertains to Chinese cars. The international press cried foul on Brazil's blatant protectionist move, as the measure was largely believed to violate WTO rules.[53] Furthermore, Brazilian consumers were the ultimate losers in this story, as they pay exceedingly high prices for automobiles owing to other taxes in place aside from this IPI hike; for instance, to purchase a Toyota Corolla, a Brazilian consumer shells out approximately 150 percent more than a US consumer.[54]

In reaction to the IPI tariff, Chinese car companies—Chery, JAC Motors, and Lifan—confirmed their plans to build factories in Brazil and integrate into the Brazilian auto parts production chain, but in the meantime their imported cars were subject to this tax. Ironically, the Chinese automobile companies required to build factories in order to better access the Brazilian market had trouble finding reasonably priced inputs to construct the factories themselves. Reports indicate that Chery, in particular, in building its first integrated factory outside of China in the state of São Paulo, imported 60 to 70 percent of the construction materials from China, as, even with the shipping and logistics costs and import taxes, in the end it was cheaper to import construction materials from China than to buy them locally.[55] This is just one example of the magnitude of Brazil's structural inefficiencies.

In August 2011, the Rousseff government revealed the Bigger Brazil plan, an industrial policy which allocated R$25 billion in tax refunds for exporters in the shoe, textile, furniture, and software industries, as well as an increase in the number of trade investigators to protect borders and violations of intellectual property.[56] Experts have concluded that these types of measures, no matter how comprehensive, are not enough to save Brazilian industry, as "Brazil's deindustrialization and competitiveness challenges can be attributed to more than just Chinese trade and competition."[57] In spite of the critics, in April 2012 the government announced a R$60.4 billion continuation of this industrial stimulus package. The majority was allocated to BNDES, for the purpose of extending corporate credit to strategic industries at lower interest rates (ironically, beneficiaries of these below-market-rate loans include Vale and Petrobras, two of Brazil's biggest exporters to China, a strategy that hardly promoted the diversification of Brazil's export basket). The plan also included measures that require the government to buy "Made in Brazil" products, even if they are more expensive, as well as increased taxes on imports. These stimulus packages were seen as largely political moves, unsupported by many economists, perhaps because Brazil lacks not an industrial policy but rather an innovation policy.[58]

In addition to direct measures and grand industrial plans, Brazil also led a currency war against what Rousseff called a monetary tsunami from the developed countries, or "currency dumping."[59] After her government passed eight domestic measures to combat currency appreciation, Rousseff, still unsatisfied, took her fight to the WTO. There, she proposed an antidumping measure against those countries accused of printing large amounts of money and dumping it in the developing markets, a proposal highly criticized by China.[60] Because the undervalued renminbi and the overvalued real were seen as the perfect storm for the demise of the Brazilian export industry, Brazil's Minister of Finance, Guido Mantega, explained that Brazil had to maintain a "dirty float," manipulating the exchange rate to defend itself in a global currency war.[61] However, as has become clear in recent years, a favorable exchange rate in and of itself will not solve Brazil's problems of competitiveness. Even with the significant depreciation of the real in 2015, Brazil still has a range of complex but essential battles to face: reining in inflation, lowering interest rates, reducing taxes on industry, improving infrastructure, educating the workforce, and investing in research and development.

Nevertheless, a wave of protectionism swept Brazil, stimulated in large part by domestic industry's opposition to the increasing Chinese presence. In the following section I analyze one of the first measures in this wave of protectionism, the reinterpretation of a land purchase law, largely in reaction to Chinese companies attempting to secure access to Brazilian farmland for soy production.[62]

Case Study: Chinese Investment in Agribusiness[63]

Starting in April 2010, various Chinese state-owned enterprises (SOEs) announced their interest in purchasing agrarian land in the Brazilian midwest, especially in the state of Goiás, as well as in the country's new agricultural frontier known as Mapitoba, composed of states in the north and northeastern regions of Brazil: Maranhão, Piauí, Tocantins, and Bahia. One of these firms, Chongqing Grain Group, proposed the purchase of a large tract of land in western Bahia—between 100,000 and 200,000 hectares depending on the report, a significant acquisition in a state with only 368,888 hectares of foreign-owned land at the time[64]—for the purpose of soy production.[65]

Largely in reaction to these announcements, the Ministry of Defense and the Federal Prosecutor's Office (AGU) flagged the purchase of land by foreigners as a national security issue.[66] In August 2010, under then President Luiz Inácio Lula da Silva, the AGU reinterpreted Law 5.079, which increased barriers for foreigners purchasing rural property in Brazil. The new interpretation of the 1971 legislation restricted the purchase of farmland by all foreign businesses and individuals, as well as Brazilian companies that have over 50 percent foreign ownership or foreign-controlled decision-making bodies.[67] In addition, all foreign land purchases became subject to the review of the National Institute of Colonization and Agrarian Reform (INCRA).[68]

These new restrictions on foreigners seeking to purchase Brazilian property, meant to prevent Chinese investors from buying large tracts of land, represent one of the most contradictory features of the China–Brazil relationship. Brazil's competitive advantage in agribusiness, combined with its infrastructure bottlenecks (for instance, just 14 percent of Brazil's roads are paved[69]), reveals the simultaneous potential and need for investment in this sector. Diplomats, business leaders, and academics all agree that agribusiness is the sector with the most synergies and potential for growth in the China–Brazil relationship.[70] Yet, at the height of the political uproar, former Finance Minister Antônio Delfim Netto stoked fears that "the Chinese have bought Africa and now they're trying to buy Brazil."[71] However, a visit to the site of the first large-scale Chinese investment in Brazilian agribusiness shows that not only were the Chinese playing by the rules but also, on a local level, state governments worked to proactively attract Chinese capital, as Brazil has much to gain from these investments. As the national investment climate has deteriorated for a number of macro- and micro-economic reasons, it remains to be seen whether Brazil will manage to reap the benefits that Chinese capital has to offer.

On a fundamental level, Brazilian officials have questioned the role of the Chinese government in promoting foreign direct investment (FDI). In 2010, when Chinese companies announced their interest in buying land in Brazil for soybean cultivation, these potential investments were not interpreted as market-seeking business transactions, but rather as "land grabbing." It was feared that Chinese SOEs were on a strategic mission to buy up land around the world in order to guarantee a constant food supply for the growing Chinese population. Nedal sums up this popular argument in Brazil: "Chinese FDI is qualitatively different from that of traditional sources because of the controlled nature of the Chinese economy . . . and the close association between the investing companies and the Chinese state."[72] Even Sergio Amaral, a former trade minister and former president of the China–Brazil Business Council, subscribed to this view: "The expansion of trade and of investment is very beneficial for the country, with one qualification. Sometimes you don't know whether the investments are looking for Brazil as a market or whether they correspond to strategic purposes of the Chinese government."[73] As described in detail in Chapter 5 by Guo and Myers, while some Chinese agricultural firms may in fact be investing in the name of food security, others are purely motivated by profit. The fear over land grabs, however, eclipsed this more nuanced reality, and the stated intention of Chinese SOEs to buy land to harvest soybeans and ship them back to China was viewed as a threat to Brazilian sovereignty and national security.[74]

While China's business motives were ignored in the political debate over the AGU's reinterpretation of the land law, concerns mounted that any Chinese investment in the Brazilian natural resource sector was just another step in reaffirming a neocolonial relationship.[75] Chongqing Grain Group's revised investment proposal to build an industrial soy complex, near Barreiras in western Bahia, was categorized as a natural resource investment, despite the industrial nature of the project, the high-tech aspects of modern soy production, and the fact that the plant is slated to produce soy oil, which is considered a value-added export when compared to the grain itself.

In an attempt to demystify these arguments in the Brazilian political debate over a Chinese land grab, I conducted field interviews and paid a visit to this site of Chinese investment in Brazilian agribusiness.[76] According to agribusiness experts in the soy-rich region of western Bahia in northeastern Brazil, the objective of Chinese companies seeking to purchase land was to cut out the intermediary in trading transactions and to establish more control over the price of the commodity they are buying in increasing quantities.[77] This is in line with the global trend in Chinese outbound investment: a preference for investments that allow for control over the entire production chain. Currently, China purchases Brazilian soy from the American agribusiness giants Archer Daniels Midland, Bunge, and Cargill, all of which are well established in Brazil.

When one takes a closer look at the case, it becomes clear that, at least on the state level, Brazil is slowly learning to develop a more proactive China strategy. In May 2010, Bahia was the first state in Brazil to open a government office in Shanghai, with the intent of forming business relationships and attracting investments. Shortly thereafter, according to Dr. Jairo Vaz, the Superintendent of Agribusiness of the Government of Bahia at the time, the state hosted more than six trade commissions consisting of 20 to 30 Chinese authorities and business groups—Chongqing Grain Group among them—all interested in buying land for agricultural production. The government of Bahia countered with proposals of industrial development that would still enable the Chinese access to the soy they desired, and this strategy worked. In a meeting with government officials in Salvador, the capital of Bahia, in March 2011, Chongqing Grain Group announced an investment in the western part of the state. The official letter of intent was signed in April 2011 at the BRICS summit in Hainan, China.[78]

With an initial investment of US$300 million, Chongqing Grain Group, through its Brazilian subsidiary Universo Verde, plans to construct an industrial soy complex just outside the city of Barreiras in western Bahia. Following the model that American agribusiness firms Cargill and Bunge have already established in the region, Chongqing Grain Group intends to make advance purchases of soy from Brazilian producers, and then clean and process the soybeans to produce soybean oil, adding value to the product on Brazilian rather than Chinese soil. The investment could reach up to R$4 billion, including the following proposed projects: six other factories, including a cotton plant; a railway to the coast; and a modern port to facilitate exportation. To close the deal, the mayor of Barreiras presented the Chinese with a fiscal incentive, negotiating with a local landowner and business to donate 100 hectares of land for the construction of the plant. In an ironic turn of events, the Chinese did not even need to buy any land, because the local government actually gave them a piece.[79]

In order to hold on to the parcel of land donated by the mayor, it was a condition that Chongqing Grain Group construct the plant within three years. Although the political ceremony announcing the official launch of the project was held in June 2011, Chongqing Grain Group was only granted the much-awaited environmental permits in March 2012. This was a necessary step, as the failure to obtain environmental licensing could have put an end to the project, as was the case with the planned Vale and Baosteel joint venture that fell through in 2009. Chongqing Grain Group experienced a delay in part because the parcel of land donated for the construction of the plant contains a legal reserve that, under Brazilian law, cannot be deforested.

What at first appeared to be minor delays subsequently turned into a stalled process. Four years after the signing of the letter of intent, construction had still not officially begun.[80] There have been no public reports announcing the project's abandonment nor pinpointing the possible reasons for such a significant delay. Although the government of Bahia has a vested interest in seeing that this project is realized in order to pave the way for future investments, the alarming narrative that accompanied its development unfolded in parallel with the deterioration of the regulatory environment on a national level. The regulatory restrictions introduced in 2010 led to a drop in investment levels and threatened the prospects for future deals. Just one year after the reinterpretation of the land purchase law, it was estimated that US$15 billion in prospective agricultural investments would no longer materialize.[81] In particular, Chinese investments in the Brazilian natural resource-based sectors decreased from 12 projects in 2010 to just five in 2011 and 2012 combined.[82]

Moreover, the new restrictions on land purchases by foreigners scared away investors from the US and Europe, those whom the Brazilian cellulose and agribusiness industries had been longing to attract. As a result, proposed changes based on reciprocity were debated in Brazilian Congress.[83] It was argued, for example, that Chinese investors should be banned from buying any land in Brazil, as China does not permit Brazilians (or any foreigners) to own land on Chinese soil. A clause restricting foreign state-owned companies was also proposed, which would have targeted the majority of Chinese investments in Brazilian agribusiness. If the political debate over the past few years is any indication of the potential consequences of this selective welcoming of FDI, Chinese investments will be denied, while American and European investments will be permitted. This legal limbo has bred investor uncertainty, in many cases leading to the withdrawal of proposed projects, and foreign investors with investment plans continue to wait until the law is made clear.[84]

The Brazilian legislative subcommittee originally had until March 2012 to pass a new land law, but owing to a logjam in Congress the topic was archived, only to return to the agenda in 2015. Meanwhile, the agribusiness lobby (SRB) brought its case to the Supreme Court in May 2015, arguing that the 2010 reinterpretation of Law 5.709 violates the Constitution, as all Brazilian companies—whether foreign-owned or not—should receive the same treatment. The SRB also claimed that the repercussions were detrimental to national development, stating that it sought to reverse the measure in order to attract foreign investors, reportedly with a potential caveat for the Chinese as well as sovereign wealth funds.[85] A bill proposing more relaxed restrictions for the purchase of land by foreigners—with the exclusion of sovereign wealth funds—was fast-tracked for an urgent vote in Congress in September 2015, although as of June 2016 a decision had still not been reached. If approved, foreign companies would be able to purchase up to 100,000 hectares of farmland.[86] Although the topic remains highly controversial, a new, foreign-investor-friendly land law is now closer to being introduced than at any other time in the past several years. Attracting agribusiness investments would be a welcome development in light of the current recession in Brazil, yet given the sensitivity of foreign land ownership there is still a great deal of uncertainty over the potential reversal of the 2010 reinterpretation.

In the current scenario, which lacks both regulatory clarity and a track record of success, investors are waiting on the sidelines. This is true for other companies looking to make agribusiness investments throughout Brazil and for Chongqing Grain Group itself, as the total of R$4 billion in potential investments in other agro-industrial projects and infrastructure, such as the east–west railway, will only materialize if the first project goes smoothly. The government of Bahia hosted a delegation of Chinese business leaders at the state's first "Chongqing Day" in December 2013, evidence of efforts to continue a partnership with Chongqing Grain Group in the agribusiness, infrastructure, and tourism sectors, despite the stalled status of the first project.[87] The successful realization of the initial Chongqing Grain Group investment would establish a much-needed track record for Chinese investments in Brazilian agribusiness, and would pave the way for future investment flows. As this case unfolds, and potential shifts in the regulatory environment come to fruition, the future of Chinese investments in Brazilian agribusiness will become clear.

This case study demonstrates that Brazil has much to gain from Chinese capital—industrial growth, value-added exports, job creation, and improved infrastructure—and therefore Brazilian officials and Congress should focus on lowering barriers to doing business rather than creating a murky investment environment. However, the political climate has fostered the further complication of the regulatory environment for Chinese investment and FDI in general, compromising investors' perceptions as a result. This is a price that Brazil cannot afford to pay, especially considering its meager GCF levels.

Conclusions

In this chapter I have analyzed both the political debate and the numbers to conclude that Brazil is falling short of capturing the benefits presented by China's increasing presence in the region. The data present clear aggregate benefits for Brazil, yet domestic interest groups have blocked the formation of a policy that would allow all Brazilians to reap these benefits. Instead of rising to the occasion by increasing its own competitiveness in the international marketplace, Brazil has reverted to old development patterns by implementing protectionist policies.

For the time being, powerful special interests are likely to continue to hamper Brazil in taking full advantage of the opportunities presented by expanded ties with its biggest trading partner, a trend that does not bode well for the future of Brazilian economic development. The case study presented here shows that the state of Bahia is an example of a domestic actor actively promoting trade and attracting FDI, yet the political climate has impeded these initiatives from reaching a national scale. In fact, the recent reactionary wave of protectionist measures has slowed the influx of investments and their accompanying benefits. By failing to forge a more productive economic relationship with China, Brazil risks being left behind as other economies integrate and foreign investors flag the country as an unstable place for their investments.

There are any number of ways that Brazil can adapt to a rising China. The decreasing competitiveness of manufacturing industries highlights the possibility of liberalizing uncompetitive sectors in the short term, although this would be considered political suicide in the context of Brazil's powerful industrial lobby. Perhaps more within reach are long-term structural improvements such as investments in innovation, technology, research and development, and education, as well as tax reform. Brazil could also continue to diversify its trading partners by pursuing a more liberal economic strategy via the formation of preferential trade agreements within the region and with other emerging economies.[88] Like its neighbors Chile and Peru, Brazil could open up its economy through bilateral trade deals, thereby allowing its firms to increase their global competitiveness.[89] Furthermore, much deeper regional integration within the Mercosur bloc could be a powerful way to increase leverage vis-à-vis China, especially with regard to the Brazilian and Argentine soy industries, as Turzi highlighted in Chapter 8 in this volume.

Blaming China for Brazil's low levels of competitiveness, however, has proved unproductive, serving only to delay the recognition that many of Brazil's development roadblocks are homegrown. Anna Jaguaribe, Director of the Institute of Brazil–China Studies (IBRACH), explains succinctly why China has become such a sensitive subject in Brazil: "The debate about China is a debate about Brazil." In other words, using China as a scapegoat has given policymakers an excuse to delay difficult structural and fiscal reforms. Exaggerating China's influence in Brazil masks the true challenges the country faces: Brazil's lack of competitiveness is a result of insufficient levels of investment in research and development and education, high taxes on businesses, complex labor laws, an under-qualified workforce, infrastructure bottlenecks, poor-quality public services, and institutionalized corruption, among other structural challenges. At the root of these issues is the fact that GCF remains consistently low, hovering around 20 percent of GDP on average from 2001 to 2014,[90] which has inhibited progress in addressing structural issues and led to decelerated growth.

To tackle the necessary reforms, the Brazilian government must both increase public investment and encourage private investment by clearly establishing the rules of the game and ditching counter-productive interventionist policies. Increased public investment requires reining in government spending on generous public sector benefits and pensions; a politically unpopular policy in the short term, such fiscal reform remains elusive. Former President Mr. da Silva lost a window of opportunity to reallocate the public budget, created by high commodity prices and a current account surplus.[91] With the end of the commodity super-cycle and recent political instability, however, came much less room to maneuver. Thanks to rising inflation and unemployment, a massive corruption scandal at the state-run oil company, and bloated spending on the World Cup and Olympics in lieu of investment in improved education and healthcare, nationwide protests erupted and Ms. Rousseff's approval ratings reached a record low. In May 2016, she was suspended, as she faces an impeachment trial for her misrepresentation of the public budget; needless to say, Ms. Rousseff's hands are tied.

Although interim President Michel Temer has made clear his plans to restructure the budget, a necessary step to improve the Brazilian economy over the long term, his government's ability to implement these reforms remains dependent on maintaining both a fragile coalition and public support in a fragmented Brazil, as well as dodging any accusations of wrongdoing in the ongoing *Lava Jato* investigations. The interim government's market-friendly rhetoric certainly contrasts with the protectionist agenda lauded by Ms. Rousseff, yet it remains to be seen whether special interest groups will continue to overshadow the country's policies on foreign trade and investment relations. While the market reacted optimistically to the suspension of Ms. Rousseff, the road to reform will likely prove long and at times painful owing to the complex nature of the obstacles Brazil must overcome.

Especially in this current negative growth environment, it is all the more important that tangible, proactive efforts are made to encourage and comfort the private sector investor, both domestic and foreign. By complementing GCF, FDI can play an important role in helping Brazil to overcome its development challenges and pave the way for stable growth. At the Comissão Sino-Brasileira de Alto Nível de Concertação e Cooperação (COSBAN) meeting in Beijing in November 2013, Chinese officials reiterated their plans to continue investing in Brazil, yet asked the Brazilian government to facilitate the entry of new investments by minimizing red tape.[92] Therefore, first and foremost, Brazil must simplify its regulatory regime.

The future of Brazilian economic development relies upon increasing competitiveness through a series of domestic reforms, economic liberalization, and the fostering of a regulatory and political environment that welcomes a flourishing trade and investment relationship with China and other economies. The sooner that policymakers and politicians set their sights on tackling these tasks, the closer Brazil can come to realizing its full economic potential.

Notes

1 China–Brazil Business Council (CEBC), "Investimentos Chineses no Brasil: uma nova fase da relação Brasil–China," May 2011.
2 Kate Mackenzie, "China as the World's (Unreliable) Importer," *Financial Times*, March 26, 2011.

3 Carol Wise, "Playing Both Sides of the Pacific: Latin America's Free Trade Agreements with China," *Pacific Affairs*, vol. 89, no. 1 (2016).
4 Robert M. Devlin, Antoni Estevadeordal, and Andrés Rodríguez-Clare, eds., *The Emergence of China: Opportunities and Challenges for Latin America and the Caribbean* (Washington, DC: Inter-American Development Bank, 2006); R. Evan Ellis, *China in Latin America: The Whats and Wherefores* (Boulder, CO: Lynne Rienner, 2009); Javier Santiso, ed., *The Visible Hand of China in Latin America* (Paris: OECD, 2007).
5 Rodrigo Tavares Maciel and Dani K. Nedal, "China and Brazil: Two Trajectories of a 'Strategic Partnership,'" in Adrian H. Hearn and José Luis León-Manríquez, eds., *China Engages Latin America: Tracing the Trajectory* (Boulder, CO: Lynne Rienner, 2011).
6 Matt Ferchen, "China–Latin America Relations: Short-Term Boon or Long-Term Boom?" *Chinese Journal of International Politics*, vol. 4 (2011), pp. 55–86.
7 Kevin P. Gallagher and Roberto Porzecanski, *The Dragon in the Room: China and the Future of Latin American Industrialization* (Stanford, CA: Stanford University Press, 2010).
8 Rhys Jenkins and Alexandre de Freitas Barbosa, "Fear for Manufacturing? China and the Future of Industry in Brazil and Latin America," *China Quarterly*, no. 209 (March 2012), pp. 59–81.
9 World Bank data by nominal GDP, 2014.
10 Maciel and Nedal, "China and Brazil."
11 Dani Nedal, "Commentary: Chinese Investment in Brazil," *Harvard Asia Quarterly*, vol. XIII, no. 1 (Spring 2011), pp. 20–23.
12 MDIC data.
13 Interview with Marcelo Nonnemberg, Rio de Janeiro, July 4, 2011.
14 China–Brazil Business Council (CEBC), "Oportunidades de comercio e investimento na China para setores selecionados," 2015.
15 World Economic Forum, *The Global Competitiveness Report (2014–2015)*, http://reports.weforum.org/the-global-competitiveness-report-2013-2014/.
16 World Bank data, http://doingbusiness.org/rankings (accessed June 2015).
17 Jenkins and Barbosa, "Fear for Manufacturing?" pp. 59–81.
18 MDIC data.
19 The real (plural reais) is the currency of Brazil, abbreviated as R$.
20 "Juggling Technocrats and Party Hats," *Economist*, October 15, 2009.
21 Interview with Marcelo Nonnemberg, Rio de Janeiro, July 4, 2011.
22 MDIC data.
23 Interview with Luiz Augusto de Castro Neves, Rio de Janeiro, July 5, 2011.
24 Maciel and Nedal, "China and Brazil."
25 Rhys Jenkins, "China and Brazil: Economic Impacts of a Growing Relationship," *Journal of Current Chinese Affairs*, vol. 41, no. 1 (2012), pp. 21–47.
26 "China avança em novos setores e destrói empregos," *Valor Econômico*, April 5, 2011.
27 IBGE data.
28 "Pesquisa comprova: há empregos, mas falta mão de obra qualificada," *O Globo*, July 11, 2011.
29 "CNI: falta de mão de obra apta afeta 69% das empresas," *O Estado de São Paulo*, April 6, 2011.
30 Ibid.
31 McKinsey Global Institute, *Connecting Brazil to the World: A Path to Inclusive Growth* (McKinsey & Co., May 2014).
32 CEBC.
33 There is a lack of consistent data here, but for a more detailed account of Chinese investments in Brazil please refer to the China–Brazil Business Council's studies: "Chinese Investments in Brazil," May 2011; and "An Analysis of Chinese Investments in Brazil: 2007–2012," August 2013. The latter concludes that, from 2007 to 2012, Chinese companies announced 60 projects in Brazil, totaling US$68.4 billion, of which 39 projects, or US$24.4 billion, are confirmed.

34 "Chineses no Brasil," *Sinocultura Industrial*, February 18, 2011.

35 Charles Ho and Lap Chan, "Commentary: The Investments of China's State-Owned Enterprises in Brazilian Infrastructure," *Harvard Asia Quarterly*, vol. XIII, no. 1 (Spring 2011), pp. 16–19.

36 Ibid.

37 Carlos Pereira and Joao Augusto de Castro Neves, *Brazil and China: South–South Partnership or North–South Competition?* Policy Paper no. 26 (Washington, DC: Brookings Institution, March 2011).

38 David Segal, "Petrobras Oil Scandal Leaves Brazilians Lamenting a Lost Dream," *New York Times*, August 7, 2015.

39 While the recent imprisonment of prominent perpetrators is a positive development, as wealthy Brazilians have traditionally been above the law, Brazil has a long road ahead on the quest to strengthen its democratic institutions.

40 Interview with Edison Renato, Rio de Janeiro, July 5, 2011.

41 Claudio de Souza, "'Fofinho,' Chery QQ custa R$ 22.990 para ser o carro mais barato do Brasil," *UOL*, April 28, 2011.

42 Interview with Luiz Augusto de Castro Neves, Rio de Janeiro, July 5, 2011.

43 Jeffry A. Frieden, Manuel Pastor Jr., and Michael Tomz, eds., *Modern Political Economy and Latin America: Theory and Policy* (Boulder, CO: Westview Press, 2000).

44 "Brasil vira colônia da China, diz presidente da Abimaq," *O Estado de São Paulo*, April 28, 2011.

45 Pereira and de Castro Neves, *Brazil and China*.

46 Interview with Luiz Augusto de Castro Neves, Rio de Janeiro, July 5, 2011.

47 "Empresários cobram defesas contra a China," *Estado de São Paulo*, March 14, 2011; "Embaixador diz que Brasil adotará medidas específicas contra chineses," *Valor Econômico*, February 29, 2012; and "Brasil vira colônia da China diz presidente da Abimaq," *Agencia Estado*, April 28, 2011.

48 Raquel Landim, "Dilma baixa 40 medidas protecionistas e os empresários querem bem mais," *O Estado de São Paulo*, March 26, 2012.

49 Jenkins and Barbosa, "Fear for Manufacturing?"

50 "Defesa tímida contra a China," *Valor Econômico*, May 24, 2011.

51 "Brasil propõe taxa extra de importação para compensar 'dumping' cambial," *Estado de São Paulo*, September 19, 2011.

52 Iona Texeira Stevens and Joe Jeahy, "Brazil Gets Protectionist on Auto," *Financial Times*, September 16, 2011.

53 "Brazil's Trade Policy: Seeking Protection," *Economist*, January 14, 2012.

54 McKinsey Global Institute, *Connecting Brazil to the World*.

55 "Chery importa vigas da China para fábrica em Jacareí," *Estadão*, October 21, 2013.

56 Samantha Pearson, "Brazil Steps Up Fight against Imports," *Financial Times*, August 2, 2011.

57 Kim Covington, "Assessing Dilma Rousseff's Approach to Chinese Competition," Event Summary, Inter-American Dialogue, August 29, 2011.

58 Interview with Marcelo Nonnemberg, Rio de Janeiro, July 4, 2011.

59 "Brasil propõe taxa extra de importação para compensar 'dumping' cambial."

60 "China critica proposta de política monetária apresentada pelo Brasil na OMC," *Estado de São Paulo*, November 27, 2012.

61 "Mantega admite 'flutuação suja,'" *Valor Econômico*, October 24, 2012.

62 Jamil Chade, "China negocia terras para soja e milho no Brasil," *O Estado de São Paulo*, April 27, 2010.

63 This section draws heavily on my article "The Dragon's Appetite for Soy Stokes Brazilian Protectionism," beyondbrics blog, *Financial Times*, October 10, 2011.

64 INCRA data.

65 "China compra terras no Brasil," *O Estado de São Paulo*, August 3, 2010.

66 Pereira and de Castro Neves, *Brazil and China*.

67 This differential treatment of Brazilian companies, whether Brazilian or foreign-owned, is widely considered to be unconstitutional. Article 171 of the Constitution allows for the preferential treatment of Brazilian companies with local shareholders, but does not permit discrimination against Brazilian companies with foreign share-holders. For more on this topic, see "Aquisição de Terras por Estrangeiros no Brasil: Uma Avaliação Jurídica e Econômica," Núcleo de Estudos e Pesquisas do Senado, June 2012.

68 Ariovaldo Umbelino de Oliveira, "A questão da aquisição de terras por estrangeiros no Brasil—um retorno aos dossiês," *Agrária*, no. 12 (2010), pp. 3–113.

69 McKinsey Global Institute, *Connecting Brazil to the World*.

70 "Investimentos Chineses no Brasil: 2007–2012," Presentation at a CEBC event, Rio de Janeiro, August 2, 2013.

71 "China compra terras no Brasil."

72 Nedal, "Commentary," pp. 20–23.

73 Solana Pyne, "China's Brazilian Shopping Spree," *Global Post*, November 22, 2010.

74 Sarah Arnott, "Fears of Chinese Land Grab as Beijing's Billions Buy Up Resources," *Independent*, October 2, 2010.

75 Jean-Pierre Langellier, "Encontro de países emergentes em Brasília gera apelos contra o 'neocolonialismo' chinês," *Le Monde*, April 16, 2010.

76 This field research took place in August 2011.

77 "China Wants to Buy Directly from Brazilian Farmers, Avoid Intermediation," *MercoPress*, August 16, 2011.

78 "Grupo chinês vai investir R$4 bi em processamento de soja na Bahia," *O Estado de São Paulo*, March 18, 2011.

79 Interview with Dr. Jairo Vaz, Bahia, Salvador, August 16, 2011.

80 Gustavo de L.T. Oliveira, "Chinese and Other Foreign Investments in the Brazilian Soybean Complex," BICAS Working Paper, April 2015; Caroline Stauffer, "Big Chinese Soy Project in Brazil: So Far, Just an Empty Field," *Reuters*, April 4, 2014.

81 "Protectionism in Brazil: A Self-Made Siege," *Economist*, September 24, 2011. Also, Agroconsult and MB Agro, *Impactos Econômicos do Parecer da AGU (Advocacia Geral da União), que impõe restrições à aquisição e arrendamento de terras agrícolas por empresas brasilei-ras com controle do capital detido por estrangeiros*, April 2011.

82 Claudio Frischtak and Andre Soares, "China–Brazil Two-Way Investment Flows," Presentation at CEBC Conference, São Paulo, November 21, 2012.

83 Denize Bacoccina, "Proibição seletiva," *Isto é Dinheiro*, August 26, 2011.

84 Joe Leahy, "Investors in Brazil Feel Tied on Land Issue," *Financial Times*, March 25, 2012.

85 Caroline Stauffer, "Sociedade Rural contesta veto à compra de terras por estrangeiros," *Reuters*, April 16, 2015.

86 Patricia Comunello, "PL de compra de terras por estrangeiros tem votação de urgên-cia," *Jornal do Comércio*, November 18, 2015.

87 "Chongqing Day em Salvador vai debater investimentos chineses na Bahia," *Imprensa Seagri*, September 26, 2013.

88 Pereira and de Castro Neves, *Brazil and China*.

89 "Brazil's Future, Has Brazil Blown It?" *Economist*, September 28, 2013.

90 World Bank data.

91 "Reform, Reality Dawns: Slower Growth and an Assertive New Middle Class Will Force Political Change," *Economist*, September 28, 2013.

92 "China pede mais agilidade para investir," *Valor Econômico*, November 11, 2013.

CONCLUSION

Final Reflections on the China–Latin America Relationship

José Luis León-Manríquez

The 11 chapters in this volume employ diverse methodologies and theoretical perspectives to examine the political economy of China–Latin America relations. In the process, the volume's authors provide a more nuanced approach to the study of this evolving relationship than is typical in the existing literature. As in other volumes on this topic, attention is paid throughout to well-documented trends in Chinese trade and foreign direct investment (FDI) in the region. The authors confirm that the China–Latin America economic relationship continues to be characterized in many cases by asymmetric trade and highly concentrated FDI from China. The volume also goes to great lengths to examine the effects of a wide range of sub-state actors (e.g., Chinese state-owned enterprises, policy banks, individual ministries in China and Latin America, economic interest groups, and organized crime networks) and extra-regional actors (e.g., the United States and Taiwan) with regard to the China–Latin America relationship. The chapters range from individual country and sub-regional studies to analyses of the effects of external actors and conditions on the region as a whole.

One main contribution of this collection of political economy chapters is how it portrays the complex interplay between states and markets. In Part I of the volume China is viewed not as a singular actor in Latin America but as the aggregate of a diverse network of banks, companies, and bureaucracies, each with its own (though sometimes complementary) interests. Part II of the book examines the many domestic and regional dynamics in Latin America which shape relations with China—from Brazil's anti-China lobbies to the reactions of indigenous communities in the Andean region. The wide range of actors and issues examined in both parts is summarized in Table 12.1.

Together, the chapters offer rich diversity in approach and perspective. Several common themes include: (1) the ongoing asymmetries in the China–Latin

TABLE 12.1 Levels of Analysis, Actors, and Issues in the China–LAC Relationship

Levels of analysis	Actors		Issues	Chapters
	China	*Latin America*		
Regional	—	CELAC, IDB	Cooperation, foreign policy	1, 2
Sub-regional	—	Mercosur, CARICOM, Central America, Andean countries	Trade and FDI policies, joint diplomacy, integration	7, 8, 9, 10
Extra-regional	—	United States	Trade, investment, aid, security, political influence	2, 9
National	Chinese government (MOFA, MOFCOM), policy banks (CDB, China Eximbank), China Investment Corporation	Latin American Ministries of Trade, Foreign Affairs, Defense, Education	Aid, trade, industrial and innovation policies, FTAs, bilateral investment treaties (BITs), diplomatic relations, military linkages, infrastructure	1, 2, 3, 4, 5, 6, 10
Subnational	Chinese SOEs (CNPC, Minmetals, Chinalco, Shougang, COFCO, Chongqing Grain Group, Beidahuang), local governments	Latin American SOEs (Petrobras, PDVSA, CODELCO, Enami), local governments	FDI (energy, minerals, food production), joint ventures	1, 3, 5, 6, 8, 11
Non-state legal	Private firms, business chambers	Private firms, business chambers (FIESP, ABIC, UIA), social movements, environmental groups	FDI, protectionist measures, anti-mining movements, environment, labor rights	5, 8, 9, 10, 11
Non-state illegal	Chinese organized crime	LAC mafias	Human trafficking, drugs, contraband, money laundering, piracy	2

Source: Author's elaboration.

Notes: CELAC: Community of Latin American and Caribbean States; IDB: Inter-American Development Bank; CARICOM: Caribbean Community; MOFA: China's Ministry of Foreign Affairs; MOFCOM: China's Ministry of Commerce; COFCO: China National Cereals, Oils and Foodstuffs Corporation; PDVSA: Petróleos de Venezuela, S.A.; CODELCO: Corporación Nacional del Cobre in Chile.

America economic relationship; (2) industrial policies and protectionist tendencies in certain Latin American countries; (3) the effect of the commodity cycle on
economic growth and policy-making; and (4) transparency issues in the China–
LAC relationship. Below I address each of these in turn.

Economic Asymmetries

As Wise and Myers explain in the Introduction, Chinese engagement has not
uniformly penetrated the various sub-regions of Latin America. South American
commodity exporters, such as Argentina, Brazil, Chile, and Peru, have enjoyed
a closer relationship with China, based on the export of oil, copper, iron ore,
and fishmeal, which account for more than 80 percent of the region's total
exports to China. Soybeans and iron ore account for almost four-fifths of
Brazilian exports to China.

Yet, as Avendaño and Dayton-Johnson in Chapter 9, as well as Wise in
Chapter 7, indicate, Mexico and some Central American countries maintain
huge trade imbalances with China and continue to be adversely affected by the
flood of Chinese goods into their domestic markets and into niches of the U.S.
market that they once dominated. Central American nations are increasingly
importing Chinese manufactured goods, but experience little demand for their
exports from China. Only Costa Rica and Panama export more than 5 percent
of their total to China. Avendaño and Dayton-Johnson find that exports from
four Central American countries also face an intense "competitive threat" in
third markets, mainly the U.S.

Economic asymmetry is perhaps most evident in the Mexico–China relationship. Mexico is the most industrialized country in Latin America (see Table 12.2),
but Mexican exports to China are mainly composed of foodstuffs and minerals.

TABLE 12.2 Manufactured Exports as a Percentage of Total Exports, 2000 and 2014, for China and selected LAC countries

Country	2000	2014
Argentina	32	32
Brazil	58	35
Chile	16	14
Colombia	32	18 (2013)
El Salvador	21	76
Guatemala	32	39
Mexico	84	79
Peru	20	15
China	*88*	*94*

Source: World Bank, World Development Indicators, 2015, http://datos.bancomundial.org/
indicador/TX.VAL.MANF.ZS.UN.

As Wise indicates in Chapter 7, Mexico's trade deficit with China has yet to improve despite its negative impact on bilateral relations. However, she attributes this to Mexico's over-reliance on foreign firms and market norms to transfer the technology and know-how necessary to rise to the challenge that China is presenting to Mexico's industrial producers. A more cohesive and strategic set of public policies is called for in this case.

Chinese doors are not closed to LAC industrial exports. In Chapter 7, Wise points to China's FTA with Chile (entered into effect in 2006) as a WTO-plus agreement that opens the door for Chilean industrial exports to China. Nevertheless, the degree of industrialization in Chile is very low and even decreasing. In short, Chile does not produce the kind and quality of industrial goods that Chinese producers seek to buy. Wise concludes that this FTA basically succeeded in contractualizing a traditional comparative advantage model between Chile and China which basically cushions both sides from wild swings in copper prices.

Many of the authors argue the need for a much more proactive Latin American industrial upgrading as a means to compete more effectively in global trade. According to Wise in Chapter 7, China's own rise was largely "the result of highly focused expenditures and policies that have promoted science, technological adaptation, advanced education in hard science fields, and research and development since the early 1980s." In the Introduction, Wise and Myers argue that LAC countries are perhaps more pressed than ever before to quickly climb the value-added production ladder. But the low levels of R&D reported in Table 12.3 continue to hamper LAC growth and industrial development.

TABLE 12.3 R&D Expenditures in Select LAC and Asia-Pacific Countries, 2000 and 2012

Country	2000 (% of GDP)	2012 (% of GDP)
Argentina	0.44	0.65
Brazil	1.02	1.21
Chile	0.31 (2007)	0.42 (2010)
Colombia	0.11	0.17
El Salvador	0.08 (1998)	0.03
Guatemala	0.04	0.05
Mexico	0.31	0.43 (2011)
Peru	0.11	0.15 (2004)
Australia	1.57	2.39
China	0.90	1.98
Korea, Republic of	2.30	4.04 (2011)
New Zealand	0.97 (1999)	1.27 (2011)

Source: World Bank, World Development Indicators, 2015, http://data.worldbank.org/indicator/ GB.XPD.RSDV.GD.ZS?page=2&order=wbapi_data_value_2006%20wbapi_data_value%20 wbapi_data_value-first&sort=asc.

Argentina and Brazil have sought to improve R&D, as mentioned by Powell in Chapter 11. In Chapter 7, Wise states that Chile has been debating means by which to increase its value-added exports, including efforts to strengthen technological capabilities. As indicated in Table 12.3, Argentina, Brazil, and Chile have indeed increased their investment in R&D as a share of GDP. In the last few years, Brazil has provided generous incentives for overseas graduate study, and Argentina has raised the wages of scholars in public universities. These policies fall short of addressing critical competitiveness challenges, however. Although a differentiation of production is evident in some LAC countries, the overwhelming majority of natural resource exporters in LAC have low levels of R&D investment. In contrast, Australia, Canada, New Zealand, and even Malaysia and Thailand are swiftly increasing value-added in their agricultural sectors.

Beyond trade-related asymmetries there are imbalances in the overall relationship between China and the Latin American countries. The word "relationship" implies two-way interaction, but the bulk of engagement in the China–Latin America relationship is driven by Chinese entities, as documented in Part I of this book. The "one-way" nature of the China–LAC relationship has changed very little in recent decades. It is true that trade has increased substantially in aggregate terms, but, beyond commodity exports, LAC value-added industrial exports and FDI in China are merely symbolic. There are a few clear examples of substantial LAC investment in China, such as Brazil's Embraer factory established in Harbin or the joint venture between China National Petroleum Corporation (CNPC) and Petróleos de Venezuela (PDVSA) to build a US$9 billion oil refinery in Guangdong, but these are few and far between.

Economic complementarity and competition generally explain the various asymmetries evident in the China–Latin America relationship, as supported by the contributions to this volume and other recent literature on China–LAC. The diverging paths in the relationship between China and various Latin American countries can be explained in large part by comparative advantage. Other key factors include influence by external actors such as the United States, as Ellis indicates in Chapter 2, and the distinctly different institutional and public policy landscape that has evolved in LAC versus China.

Industrial Policy and Protectionist Tendencies in Latin America

Given the diversity of political and economic systems in LAC, the policy responses of individual countries to China have varied considerably, although protectionist reactions have been fairly common among the region's major manufacturers. Wise (Chapter 7), Turzi (Chapter 8), and Powell (Chapter 11) demonstrate that in the last decade LAC industrialists have pressed for a panoply of protectionist measures, frequently endorsed by politicians. Manufacturing associations invoke unfair competition, state subsidies, dumping, and an undervalued renminbi. They have also complained bitterly about the imposition of non-tariff barriers to LAC manufactured goods in China.

As Powell indicates in Chapter 11, Brazil responded to China's growing presence in the region with the Bigger Brazil plan, an ambitious policy to develop export capacity in manufacturing industries. In Brazil, the state has met the demands of the Federation of Industries of the State of Sao Paulo (FIESP) and other special interest groups. According to Powell, from the beginning of 1995 to the end of 2014 Brazil took 197 actions, of which 28 percent were directed at China. Among Latin American countries, Brazil, along with Argentina and Mexico, has led anti-Chinese dumping complaints at the WTO.[1] Distrust and defensive attitudes also permeate the agricultural sector. In Chapter 11, Powell examines Brazil's decision in 2010 to reinterpret its land law to restrict the foreign purchase of Brazilian land. In Chapter 5, Guo and Myers refer to similar Argentine legislation, enacted in 2011. In both countries, this recent legislation was implicitly directed toward China.

Aside from these protectionist policies, the very different policy responses heralded by Pacific Alliance members (Mexico, Colombia, Peru, and Chile) are perhaps related to their favorable prospects as members of the pending Trans-Pacific Partnership (Colombia is still in the queue to join). There is little indication of coherent China-related policy elsewhere in the region. None of the bigger LAC emerging economies (Argentina, Brazil, and Mexico) has formulated a cohesive or constructive strategy for coping with the China challenge in the Western Hemisphere. Diplomatic rhetoric and "strategic alliances" with China are pervasive, but it is virtually impossible to find a mirror document to the *Policy Paper on Latin America and the Caribbean*, which was published by the Chinese government in 2008.

Beyond the normative claim that LAC should try to improve its technological capacities and modest growth of R&D investments in some countries, there is very little evidence that a comprehensive innovation policy is indeed underway across the region. If prospects for upgrading in Argentina, Brazil, Mexico, Chile, and Peru are modest, then in the Central American and Caribbean countries they are bleak. In the innovation field, the LAC trajectory is radically different from that of East Asia.

In addition, as Creutzfeldt argues in Chapter 1, LAC countries "remain relatively unprepared and largely unaware of what their neighbors are doing with regard to China." In Chapter 8, Turzi postulates that the sub-regional integration of soy producers in South America could reduce the risks of re-primarization and low value-added production, but real collective action has yet to emerge. In Chapter 9, Avendaño and Dayton-Johnson find scant evidence of Central American initiatives for dealing with the Chinese, whether individually or as a sub-region. As Avendaño and Dayton-Johnson note, this complacency has been compounded by the fact that the majority of these countries have resisted China's "One-China" policy and continue to recognize Taiwan diplomatically. The China–CELAC Forum, established in 2014, has done relatively little thus far to catalyze LAC into forming a more aligned position vis-à-vis China.

The region's relative affluence in the 2000s hasn't led to effective economic policy-making. Despite huge resources obtained by positive external shocks in the 2000s, no country in LAC (with the probable exception of Chile) under-took a comprehensive reorganization of the state apparatus or established a full-fledged meritocratic civil service. It is true that some "islands of efficiency"[2] remain within central banks and ministries of finance, energy, and foreign affairs, but the bulk of LAC is still beholden to the spoils systems or political clien-telism. Brazil's "car wash" scandal involving massive graft in the state oil com-pany (Petrobras) is a painful reminder on this point. Argentina, Ecuador, and Venezuela employed the fiscal resources obtained via positive external shocks to enhance distributive policies through the creation of patron–client networks. Populist politics remained alive and well throughout this period. Although Wise, in Chapter 7, notes improvements in the rule of law, effectiveness of gov-ernment, and quality of regulations in Chile, countries such as Argentina, Brazil, Mexico, and Peru devolved in critical areas.

Even in the most economically liberal LAC countries (e.g., those belonging to the Pacific Alliance), which have the capacity to curb inflation, achieve fiscal balance, negotiate FTAs, and attract FDI, the ability to enforce global standards cannot be taken for granted. Sanborn and Chonn Ching drive this point home well in Chapter 6 on Chinese investment in Peruvian mining. Douglass North's theory of "path dependency," as quoted by Wise in Chapter 7, highlights how "an initial set of institutions [can] . . . provide disincentives to productive activ-ity." It is evident that many LAC countries are indeed constrained by "path-dependent" trajectories, along with low levels of state efficacy.

China's "New Normal" and LAC

Another common theme in this volume involves the cycle of high prices for natural resources that ran from 2003 to 2013, which constitutes the biggest commodity lottery that the LAC region has seen in more than a century. In the Introduction, Wise and Myers explain that, owing in large part to Chinese demand for their commodities, countries such as Argentina, Brazil, Chile, and Peru were able to avoid the worst effects of the global financial crisis in 2008–2009.[3] In Chapter 11, Powell writes that rising commodity prices "led to a positive reversal in the terms of trade, contrary to Raúl Prebisch's original thesis that emphasized the declining terms of trade for developing countries that depend on primary exports."

Other contributors paint a bleaker image of the region's commodity depend-ence, suggesting that the massive export of commodities by LAC countries reinforces old patterns of insertion into the world economy. In Chapter 8, Turzi contends that "Historically, resource-driven countries have not been able to sustain strong GDP growth rates for longer than a decade. Even those that have appeared to put their economics on a healthier longer-term growth trajectory have rarely managed to transform that growth into broader economic prosperity."

Natural resources can become a "devil's gift," as Mexican poet Ramón López Velarde wrote in 1921. The positive shocks due to skyrocketing prices of commodities create incentives to avoid or defer strategic institutional, industrial, and/or fiscal reforms. Overdependence on primary exports may bring about a "resource curse," as explained in different chapters of this book. By definition, all booms are eventually followed by busts, a harsh reality that LAC once again faces. The pending questions are numerous. For example, will the new global economic constraints offset the undeniable social advancements made in the region in the past two decades? Is LAC in fact incapable of circumventing the cycle of commodity-related booms and busts?

The answers to these questions will depend in some part on the future of the Chinese economy, among other factors. In October 2010, the Central Committee of the Communist Party of China (CCP) announced the approval of the 12th Five-Year Plan (FYP) from 2011 to 2015. According to the document, China would pursue, among other goals, an average annual GDP growth of 7–8 percent. In the 13th FYP (2016–2020), released in March 2016, the Chinese government intends to enhance economic reforms and technical innovation, to deepen the anti-corruption campaign launched by President Xi Jinping after taking office in 2013, to strengthen internal consumption, and to achieve a GDP growth of 6.8 percent. Clearly, the days of two-digit growth have ended. Be it the Chinese government, consultancy firms, or international organizations, nobody is forecasting growth rates higher than 7 percent for China.[4]

Unsurprisingly, China's "new normal" in GDP growth has caused considerable concern in many LAC countries, especially following news of slowing Chinese trade. Between July 2014 and July 2015, China's exports declined 8.3 percent and imports fell 8.1 percent.[5] Continued slowing in China's GDP growth will have consequences not only for LAC but also in Africa and Southeast Asia, regions that also benefited from the China-generated boom in commodity prices in the 2000s. As Wise points out in Chapter 7, the LAC region is not alone in expressing fears about excessive dependence on the Chinese market. However, the widespread impact of China's slowing growth confirms that it is now a global concern, for developed and developing countries alike.

If the U.S. and the European Union do not achieve substantial growth in the coming years, and if China's GDP falls even below official forecasts, it is reasonable to expect especially negative effects on LAC.[6] The Economic Commission for Latin America and the Caribbean (ECLAC) forecast for LAC growth was adjusted from 2.2 to −0.3 percent between January and October 2015.

By October 2015, the forecasts for Argentine, Brazilian, and Venezuelan GDP growth were 1.6, −2.8, and −6.7 percent, respectively.[7] Prices for some LAC commodities are still at their 2004–2006 levels, but are well below their 2010–2012 peak. Crude oil and mineral markets have been hit the hardest. Crude oil fell from US$105.01 per barrel in 2012 to US$42.70 in late 2015, iron ore from US$167.75 to US$47.00 per dry metric ton over the same period, and copper from US$8,828.19 in 2011 to US$4,800.00 per metric ton in 2015. The drop in prices for soybeans, soybean oil, fishmeal, and meat is less dramatic.

Despite the gloomy outlook, some analysts assert that LAC should stick to its comparative advantages—namely, its vast abundance in natural resources. Alejandro Werner, head of the Western Hemisphere division of the IMF, recommended that LAC "not bet against nature,"[8] suggesting that, even if international commodity prices return to the pre-boom levels, China and other Asian emerging economies will continue to demand Latin America's rich array of primary goods. Some of the chapters in this volume support this line of reasoning. In Chapter 8, Turzi explains that China produces 14 million tons of soybeans but consumes 70 million tons per annum. In a similar vein, Guo and Myers in Chapter 5 forecast that demand for wheat and corn will rise from 470 million tons today to 560 million tons in 2025. New patterns of food consumption in China will mean sustained demand for meat, milk, fish, vegetables, and fruit, much of which will come from Latin America. It seems clear, however, that the economic boom enjoyed during the 2000s has come to an end.

Minimal Transparency

A constant theme throughout this volume is the lack of reliable and systematic information on specific aspects of the China–LAC relationship. In Chapter 2, Ellis raises this issue of low transparency in ongoing interactions between China and the U.S., and Chimienti and Creutzfeldt in Chapter 10, as well as Sanborn and Chonn Ching in Chapter 6, repeatedly return to this information gap. Whereas trade can be measured with some certainty thanks to sources such as U.N. Comtrade, Chinese aid, FDI, and finance to LAC governments are exceedingly difficult to calculate. The lack of data in these areas is a formidable methodological challenge. Some of the authors have admittedly employed "economic archeology" and investigative journalistic techniques to collect data and derive conclusions from incomplete or fragmentary information.

Gallagher and Irwin (Chapter 3), Stallings (Chapter 4), and Guo and Myers (Chapter 5) all reported difficulties in finding systematic data on Chinese loans, aid, and FDI in LAC. In some cases figures are out of date and in others data are published for only a single year, making it difficult to track variations over time. In other cases, concepts and accounting styles differ from conventional practices. Chinese statistical sources frequently blend finance and foreign aid (Gallagher and Irwin in Chapter 3; Stallings in Chapter 4) and FDI and foreign aid (Chimienti and Creutzfeldt in Chapter 10), for example. At least from the evidence presented in the book, it seems almost impossible to reconstruct the flows of aid, investment, and loans using figures provided by the statistical systems of the LAC countries.

Chinese transparency is showing some slow signs of improvement, however. Sanborn and Chonn Ching (Chapter 6) and Chimienti and Creutzfeldt (Chapter 10) report that, in the wake of Shougang Hierro's major setbacks in Peru, more recent Chinese investors in the country's mining sector have sought to adhere closely to local standards and to engage more with local communities. Moreover, Sanborn and Chonn Ching report that in 2013 Chinese mining firms in Peru expressed interest in participating in the Extractive Industries Transparency Initiative (EITI). Although economic forecasts are cloudy in the Asia-Pacific region, we should expect positive progress with respect to Chinese compliance and growing adherence to international norms.

A Bright Future for China and Latin America?

Future gains from China's presence will depend largely on the development of government policies that capture the economic benefits of China's presence and invest them in growth-promoting sectors and social development. This is a daunting prospect as growth slows on both sides of the Pacific, but one that is more promising than the current model of commodities dependence. Government policy-making in the coming years will no doubt be influenced by rapidly changing political conditions in Latin America. The results of the Argentine presidential elections in November 2015 and the Venezuelan congressional election in December 2015 were surprising victories for the political opposition in these countries. The Brazilian Senate voted in May 2016 to suspend President Dilma Rousseff and begin an impeachment trial against her. Governments of all forms will be looking to manage deteriorating economic conditions and related political fallout. The next few years will be critical in terms of assessing the long-term viability of the China model, the resilience of LAC economies to negative external shocks, and the strength of the world economy in an era of slowing Chinese growth.

Notes

1 On the specific case of Mexico's protectionist pressures, see Romer Cornejo, Francisco Haro-Navejas, and José Luis León-Manríquez, "Trade Issues and Beyond: Mexican Perceptions on Contemporary China," *Latin American Policy*, vol. 4, no. 1 (2013), pp. 57–75.
2 This concept is widely explained in Barbara Geddes, *Politician's Dilemma: Building State Capacity in Latin America* (Berkeley: University of California Press, 1994).
3 This finding is confirmed by the chapters in José Luis León-Manríquez, ed., *Crisis global, respuestas nacionales: La Gran Recesión en América Latina y Asia Pacífico* (Montevideo: CEPAL/ALADI/CAF, 2015).

4 Owen Haacke, "Understanding China's 13th Five-year Plan," *China Business Review*, February 12, 2015, http://www.chinabusinessreview.com/understanding-chinas-13th-five-year-plan/ (accessed December 4, 2015).

5 William Kazer, "China Exports, Imports Slump in July," *Wall Street Journal*, August 18, 2015.

6 León-Manríquez, *Crisis global, respuestas nacionales*, p. 29.

7 "Crecimiento de América Latina se contraerá −0.3% en 2015: Cepal," *El Economista*, October 5, 2015.

8 Quoted by Eduardo Porter, "Slowdown in China Bruises Economy in Latin America," *New York Times*, December 16, 2014.

CONTRIBUTORS

Rolando Avendaño is a research associate at the OECD Development Centre. Prior to joining the Centre, he worked with the OECD Economics Department on macroeconomic policy. He completed a Master's degree in International Economics at University of Paris Nanterre, and a Master's in Economic Policy Analysis at the Paris School of Economics (Ecole Normale Supérieure). He is now finishing a PhD in Economics at the Paris School of Economics and has authored several manuscripts and working papers on remittance flows and development economics.

Adam Chimienti is a PhD candidate at the Institute of China Asia Pacific Studies at National Sun Yat-sen University in Taiwan. He received his MA in International Relations from St. John's University and his BA in History and Sociology from Queens College, City University of New York. His research interests center on Chinese–Ecuadorian relations, and the environmental and social issues which stem from major extractive projects throughout the Andean region. He has written several articles on Chinese foreign investment and contemporary issues in Latin America.

Victoria Chonn Ching is a doctoral student at the University of Southern California. She was formerly a Researcher at the Centro de Investigación de la Universidad del Pacífico (CIUP) and Assistant to the Director of the Peru–China Center at Universidad del Pacífico in Lima, Peru. She has interned at the National Committee on U.S.–China Relations in New York, and has provided research assistance to different public-sector agencies. She holds an MA in Chinese Studies and a BA in Political Science and Asian Languages and Civilizations from the University of Michigan.

Benjamin Creutzfeldt is Resident Postdoctoral Fellow on Sino-Latin American-U.S. Affairs with the Foreign Policy Institute at the Johns Hopkins School of Advanced International Studies. Prior to that he was advisor to the Director of International Affairs at the Bogotá Mayor's Office and lecturer for Chinese politics at Los Andes University in Bogotá, Colombia. He received his PhD in Political Studies from Externado University in Colombia on the subject of China's foreign policy towards Latin America. An expert in Chinese antiques, he also spent several years working as an auctioneer at Christie's after receiving his Master's degree from SOAS, University of London.

Jeff Dayton-Johnson is Vice President for Academic Affairs and Dean of the Middlebury Institute of International Studies at Monterey. A development economist, he has published three books on the political economy of Latin America. Prior to joining the Institute, he spent seven years as a senior economist at the Organisation for Economic Co-operation and Development (OECD) in Paris, where he was the first Head of the Americas Desk at the OECD's Development Centre. Prior to that, he was a tenured Associate Professor of Economics and International Development Studies at Dalhousie University in Canada. He holds a PhD in Economics from the University of California, Berkeley, and received his undergraduate education in Latin American studies at Berkeley and the Universidad Nacional Autónoma de México.

R. Evan Ellis is a research professor of Latin American Studies at the Strategic Studies Institute of the U.S. Army War College. His research focuses primarily on Latin America's relationships with China as well as other non-Western Hemisphere actors, including India, Russia, and Iran. He holds a PhD in political science from Purdue University with a specialization in comparative politics. He has published over 110 works, including *China in Latin America: The Whats and Wherefores* (2009), *The Strategic Dimension of Chinese Engagement with Latin America* (2013), and *China on the Ground in Latin America* (2014).

Kevin P. Gallagher is Professor of Global Development Policy at Boston University's Frederick S. Pardee School of Global Studies, where he co-directs the Global Economic Governance Initiative and the Global Development Policy Program. Co-chair of the Task Force on Regulating Capital Flows, he has served as an Advisor to the Department of State and the Environmental Protection Agency in the U.S., as well as to the United Nations Conference on Trade and Development. He has also been a Visiting or Adjunct Professor at the School for Advanced International Studies at Johns Hopkins University, the Fletcher School of Law and Diplomacy, El Colegio de Mexico in Mexico, Tsinghua University in China, and the Center for State and Society in Argentina.

Guo Jie (郭洁) is Assistant Professor and Latin American Affairs expert at Peking University and former Chinese Scholar-in-residence at the Inter-American

Dialogue. She has traveled extensively throughout Latin America and the Caribbean as a visiting scholar. Her most recent article, "Too Big to Fail? China's Economic Presence in Latin America," in *China International Strategy Review 2014* (Beijing: Foreign Languages Press, 2015), offers a comprehensive evaluation of the China–Latin America relationship from a Chinese perspective.

Amos Irwin is Chief of Staff at the Criminal Justice Policy Foundation, where he pioneers strategies to reform U.S. drug policy, and is Assistant Training Director at Law Enforcement Against Prohibition. He previously specialized the social, environmental, and economic impacts of Chinese investment in Latin America as a Research Fellow at Boston University's Global Economic Governance Initiative. Irwin earned his Master's degree in Law and Diplomacy from the Fletcher School at Tufts University and his Bachelor's degree in History and Physics from Amherst College. He speaks Mandarin Chinese, Spanish, French, German, Farsi, and Dari.

José Luis León-Manríquez is Professor of International and East Asian Studies at Universidad Autónoma Metropolitana (UAM) in Mexico City. He served as a Mexican diplomat for 14 years, and has since advised the Mexican government and international organizations such as the Inter-American Development Bank on matters of national security and external affairs. He holds a PhD in Political Science from Columbia University, a Master's degree in Latin American Studies from UNAM, and an undergraduate degree in International Relations from the Facultad de Ciencias Políticas y Sociales (FCPyS), UNAM. He co-edited *China Engages Latin America: Tracing the Trajectory*, which was published by Lynne Rienner in 2011.

Margaret Myers is Director of the China and Latin America Program at the Inter-American Dialogue, a Western Hemisphere affairs think tank in Washington, DC. She has published numerous book chapters and articles on Chinese leadership dynamics, international capital flows, Chinese agricultural policy, and Asia–Latin America relations, among other topics. She received her Bachelor's degree from the University of Virginia and conducted her graduate work at the George Washington University, Zhejiang University of Technology, and the Johns Hopkins University/Nanjing University Center for Chinese and American Studies. Myers is also an adjunct professor in the School of Foreign Service at Georgetown University.

Dawn Powell is an emerging markets private equity professional. While living in Brazil from 2010 to 2015, she researched China–Brazil trade and investment relations as a Fulbright scholar, served as a Princeton in Latin America Fellow at the China–Brazil Business Council, and worked at a boutique Brazilian investment firm. She holds a BA in International Relations with dual concentration in political economy and Latin America from the University of Southern California.

Cynthia Sanborn is Vice President for Research at the Universidad del Pacífico (CIUP) in Lima, Peru, and Professor of Political Science at the same university. She has previously been Director of the University's main research center (CIUP), and Chair of the Department of Social Sciences, and has held the Bloomberg Visiting Chair in Philanthropy at Harvard University. Currently, she is President of the Board of the Economic and Social Research Consortium of Peru (CIES), and a member of the Regional Advisory Group of the David Rockefeller Center for Lain American Studies at Harvard University. Sanborn has written and edited articles and books on issues related to Peruvian and international politics, philanthropy and corporate social responsibility, and the extractive industries. She received her PhD and MA in Government from Harvard University and a BA in Political Science for the University of Chicago.

Barbara Stallings is the William R. Rhodes Research Professor at Brown University's Watson Institute, Co-director of Brown's Graduate Program in Development, and Editor of *Studies in Comparative International Development*. She has a PhD in Economics from Cambridge University and a PhD in Political Science from Stanford University. Prior to joining the Watson Institute in 2002, she was Director of the Economic Development Division of the United Nations Economic Commission for Latin America and the Caribbean in Santiago, Chile, and Professor of Political Science at the University of Wisconsin-Madison. She has authored or edited 12 books and numerous book chapters and articles, and has served on several editorial boards.

Mariano Turzi is Senior Consultant at Berensztein as well as Professor at Torcuato Di Tella University and NYU Buenos Aires. He holds a PhD in International Studies with a focus on Latin American Studies from the Johns Hopkins School of Advanced International Studies, as well as a Master's degree in Strategic Studies. He has published a book on the BRICS and conducts research on the political economy of natural resource governance and emerging markets.

Carol Wise is Associate Professor in the School of International Relations at the University of Southern California (USC). She specializes in international political economy and development, with an emphasis on Latin America. She has written widely on trade integration, exchange rate crises, institutional reform, and the political economy of market restructuring in the region. Wise is author of the forthcoming book, *Dragonomics: The Rise of China in Latin America* (Yale University Press, 2017), which analyzes the rapid and remarkable economic ties that have developed between China and Latin America since the 1990s. Wise's recent publications include *Unexpected Outcomes: How the Emerging Economies Survived the Global Financial Crisis* (co-edited with Leslie Armijo and Saori Katada, Brookings Institution Press, 2015), and "Good-bye Financial Crash, Hello Financial Eclecticism: Latin American Responses to the 2008–09 Global Financial Crisis" (co-authored with Manuel Pastor), *Journal of International Money and Finance* (2015).

INDEX

 **Taylor & Francis eBooks**

Helping you to choose the right eBooks for your Library

Add Routledge titles to your library's digital collection today. Taylor and Francis ebooks contains over 50,000 titles in the Humanities, Social Sciences, Behavioural Sciences, Built Environment and Law.

Choose from a range of subject packages or create your own!

Benefits for you

» Free MARC records
» COUNTER-compliant usage statistics
» Flexible purchase and pricing options
» All titles DRM-free.

Benefits for your user

» Off-site, anytime access via Athens or referring URL
» Print or copy pages or chapters
» Full content search
» Bookmark, highlight and annotate text
» Access to thousands of pages of quality research at the click of a button.

REQUEST YOUR **FREE** INSTITUTIONAL TRIAL TODAY

Free Trials Available
We offer free trials to qualifying academic, corporate and government customers.

eCollections – Choose from over 30 subject eCollections, including:

Archaeology	Language Learning
Architecture	Law
Asian Studies	Literature
Business & Management	Media & Communication
Classical Studies	Middle East Studies
Construction	Music
Creative & Media Arts	Philosophy
Criminology & Criminal Justice	Planning
Economics	Politics
Education	Psychology & Mental Health
Energy	Religion
Engineering	Security
English Language & Linguistics	Social Work
Environment & Sustainability	Sociology
Geography	Sport
Health Studies	Theatre & Performance
History	Tourism, Hospitality & Events

For more information, pricing enquiries or to order a free trial, please contact your local sales team:
www.tandfebooks.com/page/sales

 Routledge
Taylor & Francis Group

The home of
Routledge books

www.tandfebooks.com